THE
FOREIGN POLICY OF
SOVIET RUSSIA
1929–1941

THE
FOREIGN POLICY OF
SOVIET RUSSIA
1929–1941

MAX BELOFF

VOLUME I
1929–1936

Issued under the auspices of the
Royal Institute of International Affairs

OXFORD UNIVERSITY PRESS
LONDON   NEW YORK   TORONTO

Oxford University Press, Amen House, London E.C.4

GLASGOW   NEW YORK   TORONTO   MELBOURNE   WELLINGTON
BOMBAY   CALCUTTA   MADRAS   KARACHI   LAHORE   DACCA
CAPE TOWN   SALISBURY   NAIROBI   IBADAN   ACCRA
KUALA LUMPUR   HONG KONG

First published 1947
Fifth impression 1963

PRINTED IN GREAT BRITAIN

TO MY FATHER

FOREWORD

I MUST thank Professor G. N. Clark for having suggested that I undertake the present work and for constant encouragement during its progress. I have tried, in difficult circumstances, to apply here the standards of objectivity and accuracy acquired as his pupil in another field of study. Professor E. H. Carr, Mr. L. G. Robinson and Mr. B. H. Sumner have given me the greatest help throughout, and their invaluable advice has saved me from very many errors and made possible many improvements in the original design. They do not, however, bear any responsibility for the final form of the book, nor for any conclusions, expressed or implied. The same is true of other authorities who have kindly allowed me to make use of their knowledge and experience; of them, I may only name here Miss Violet Conolly, who has given me the benefit of her detailed studies of the economic aspects of the subject, Sir John Pratt, K.B.E., C.M.G., who has read the sections dealing with China, Professor M. M. Postan, Mr. S. Dobrin, and Mr. A. B. Elkin.

It would not have been possible to carry out the project at all without the extreme helpfulness of many members of the Chatham House staff. I owe particular thanks to Miss Margaret Cleeve, O.B.E.; Dr. E. J. Lindgren and Mr. J. V. Wilson. Mrs. Jane Degras, another member of the Institute's staff, has been of the utmost assistance at every stage and has put me deeply in her debt by taking upon herself, in order to speed up publication, the final preparation of the MS., and by seeing it through the press. I must also thank Miss Rosalind M. Wrong for help with the index, and Mrs. Sylvia Arthur for preparing the map.

The main source of material has been the library of Chatham House itself, but I must also acknowledge the help received from the authorities and library staffs of the following: Manchester University Library; Manchester Central Reference Library; the London Library; the British Museum; the School of Oriental and African Studies; the School of Slavonic Studies, and the American Library in London. I wish to acknowledge the debt which all students of Soviet Russia owe to Philip Grierson for his bibliography, *Books on Soviet Russia, 1917–1942*.

Manchester   MAX BELOFF
November 1945

PREFACE

NO study of the political and economic prospects of the post-war world is possible without a clear understanding of the aims and policies of the Soviet Union. There does not exist, at any rate in English, a scholarly, coherent, and comprehensive account of the evolution of Soviet foreign policy between the Revolution of 1917 and the Soviet Union's entry into the war in 1941. It was therefore decided that the most useful contribution which the Institute could make to the study of this subject was the preparation of a detailed and documented narrative history of Soviet foreign policy.

The size which such a work would eventually reach suggested further limitation of its scope, if any part of it were to be ready within reasonable time. The period prior to 1929 was found to be covered to some extent by existing publications, and primary material for its study, both Soviet and non-Soviet, was also available in some quantity in English. It might indeed be said that the study of the period 1917-1929 in relation to Soviet affairs as well as to international politics generally, is passing from the domain of 'cotemporary history' to that of history proper, and it might be worth while, therefore, to wait until that process is nearer completion. The production of a history of Soviet foreign policy between the years 1917 and 1929 remains nevertheless among the tasks which the Institute has set itself for the future.

The work now being produced is therefore confined in essentials to the period 1929-1941. Originally it was planned to include an appendix of documents, but for various reasons it has proved more satisfactory to separate the two projects.

The compilation by Mrs. Jane Degras of a bibliography of documents on Soviet foreign policy covering the period 1917 to 1941 is now proceeding. It will include treaties, decrees, communiqués, the speeches of Soviet statesmen, and articles in the leading Soviet journals. The bibliography will indicate the source in the Russian language and also, where possible, in English, French or German, of the documents cited. A further volume, reproducing textually a selection of the more important documents, will be published subsequently.

The present work has been divided into two volumes in order to allow the first part to be published as soon as possible. Since the subject matter is treated for the most part chronologically, the first volume, which carries the narrative down to the spring of 1936, can be regarded as complete in itself. Certain portions of the subject have lent themselves better, however, to separate and continuous treatment under a single head. For this reason, the treatment of the attitude of the Soviet Union towards the Chinese Revolution, and of her relations with Sinkiang and Outer Mongolia, have overstepped the chronological framework of this volume, while three important questions have, on the other hand, been held over for detailed treatment in Volume II. These are: the question of the Straits, of Soviet-Turkish relations, and of Soviet policy in the Middle East. Where these questions are of immediate relevance to more general issues they are naturally referred to in the appropriate chapters of the present volume as well.

The book is based entirely upon printed sources, whose value and reliability is of course very variable. For this reason particular points have been documented in what might otherwise seem an over-scrupulous fashion. An attempt has been made to indicate those unofficial sources which appear to be the most reliable.

It was further found that by no means all printed materials known or believed to exist, were easily accessible under wartime conditions. This country was very behindhand in the systematic study of the Soviet Union and its achievements, and in the collection of documents bearing upon them. The Institute can point with pride to the fact that its own collection proved in many ways the best of those available, but a number of gaps of importance have come to light—gaps which it is hoped to fill as soon as circumstances permit. In addition, the Institute's resources in books, pamphlets, press-cuttings, etc., like those of other bodies, were less easy to use than in normal times, owing to the calls upon them by H.M. Government.

The fact that little systematic study of Soviet policy has been made in the past has meant that important classes of material in the Russian language—particularly periodicals of a specialized kind—have not been adequately explored or analysed, but it was clearly impossible for this lost ground to be made up by a single investigator in the time available. It is hoped that the present study may stimulate the further investigation of special aspects of the subject, and may give some indication of directions in which further research might prove rewarding.

The Institute is fully conscious that a study of a country's policy written outside that country, and largely from foreign sources, is bound to be defective in many respects and cannot claim to be a definitive work. But the importance of the subject and the lack of serious works on it in English may be felt to give an exceptional value even to the incomplete and partial history presented in these pages.

Chatham House　　　　　　　　　　ASTOR
　10 St. James's Square　　　　　　　*Chairman of the Council*
　　London, S.W.1
　　November 1945

CONTENTS

xi

APPENDICES

NOTE: *A bibliography for the whole work will be given in Volume Two. In the footnotes to this volume, the place of publication of works in English should be taken as being London unless otherwise indicated. In general the system of transliteration followed is that recommended by the Permanent Committee on Geographical Names for British Official Use in the Russian Glossary published by the Royal Geographical Society.*

I. THE INTERNATIONAL POSITION OF SOVIET RUSSIA IN THE AUTUMN OF 1929

Chapter One

THE INTERNATIONAL POSITION OF SOVIET RUSSIA IN THE AUTUMN OF 1929

THE autumn of 1929 saw no great turning-point in the fortunes of Soviet Russia. But for the rest of the world it marked the conclusion of a period of relative pacification and prosperity which was to prove the prelude to new upheavals of an even more far-reaching character than those of the first World War. Since these upheavals were destined profoundly to affect and eventually to engulf the Soviet Union itself—by the German attack of 22 June 1941—Soviet history cannot be treated except by reference to these external developments. A moment of relative stabilisation thus provides a suitable occasion for taking stock of the international position of the Soviet Government, and a starting-point from which to plot the by no means uniform curve which the policy of that Government was to follow in the succeeding twelve years.[1]

In spite of her increasing diplomatic activity in the past two years it was still possible to talk of the 'temporary eclipse of Russia as a dominant factor in international affairs',[2] and it was still substantially true that 'the whole trend of Soviet foreign policy' was 'first of all determined by the political isolation of the Soviet Union'.[3] The 'eclipse of Russia', although often interpreted as wholly due to the nature of the new régime inaugurated by the Revolution of November 1917, could be explained easily enough by the material weakening which the country had undergone as a direct result of the World War and its aftermath. The terrible losses of the years

---

[1] It may be pointed out that Louis Fischer's *The Soviets in World Affairs* (Cape, 1930, 2 vols.) ends with the Anglo-Russian agreement of October 1929. This work, published in 1930, remains the most comprehensive account of Soviet foreign policy in its first decade. For the unique facilities enjoyed by the author, see his *Men and Politics* (Cape, 1941), part i, chap. 7. The former book bears the impress of the sympathies which the author (at that time) cherished for the régime. This is not one of the characteristics of the important study, *La Politique Extérieure des Soviets* (2nd ed., Paris, 1936), by P. N. Milioukov, Foreign Minister in the first Provisional Government.

[2] Fischer, op. cit., p. 834.

[3] W. H. Chamberlin, *Soviet Russia* (Duckworth, 1930), p. 331.

1914–1917 were followed by the cumulative destruction of four more years of revolution, civil and foreign war, and famine. In addition to the internal havoc, Russia had lost very considerable territories, which included cities of great industrial importance, as well as all but a fraction of her Baltic coastline—territories containing some twenty-eight millions of people, now distributed between a newly enfranchised Finland, Esthonia and Latvia, a resurrected Poland and Lithuania and an aggrandised Roumania. But her isolation was more than a consequence of her weakness. It was the revolutionary origins and claims of the Soviet Government which were admitted by friend and foe alike to put her into a special category among the Powers.

The Soviet Constitution of 6 July 1923, included by way of preamble the Declaration regarding the formation of the Soviet Union adopted by the first Congress of Soviets of the U.S.S.R., on 30 December 1922. Its first paragraphs state clearly enough the fundamental preconceptions of the régime in the field of international affairs:

'Since the time of the formation of the soviet republics, the states of the world have divided into two camps: the camp of capitalism and the camp of socialism.

'There—in the camp of capitalism—national enmity and inequality, colonial slavery and chauvinism, national oppression and pogroms, imperialist brutalities and wars.

'Here—in the camp of socialism—mutual confidence and peace and the brotherly collaboration of peoples.'[1]

Between these two camps the official Marxist-Leninist philosophy of the Soviet rulers offered no prospect of permanent peace.[2] Indeed the first seizure of power by the Bolsheviks had been predicated upon a rapid spread of the revolutionary movement at least to the remainder of Europe, and although these

[1] The Constitution with subsequent amendments is printed in W. R. Batsell, *Soviet Rule in Russia* (New York, Macmillan, 1929), pp. 304–320. In spite of the author's unconcealed dislike of the régime, this is the best and most fully documented work available in English on the political and constitutional development of the Soviet State.

[2] Soviet foreign policy in its relation to Marxist-Leninist theory is analysed exhaustively if somewhat abstractly in T. A. Taracouzio, *War and Peace in Soviet Diplomacy* (New York, Macmillan, 1940). Cf. the same author's *The Soviet Union and International Law* (New York, Macmillan, 1935). Taracouzio's method is criticised in W. Gurian: 'The Foreign Policy of Soviet Russia', *Review of Politics* (University of Notre Dame, Indiana), April, 1943. For another critical account cf. also M. T. Florinsky, *World Revolution and the U.S.S.R.* (Macmillan, 1933), and his article 'Soviet Foreign Policy', *International Conciliation* (Carnegie Endowment for International Peace, New York), 1934.

hopes had proved delusive, it remained true that the Soviet Government was not just the government of the territorial entity known as 'Russia'; it was also a possible nucleus for a world federation of Soviet Socialist Republics. This was recognized in the preamble to the Constitution, which laid down that entry into the Union was open to all soviet socialist republics, both those then existing and those which might arise in the future, while Clause 1 of Chapter 1 listed among the powers of the central organs of the U.S.S.R. that of concluding treaties for the admission of new member republics.

As an instrument for the realisation of these hopes, there had existed in Moscow since March 1919 an organisation—the Third or Communist International—whose declared objective was to work for the spreading of Communism throughout the world; it was from the first dominated by the Russian Bolshevik Party, the key institution of the Soviet Russian State.[1] The continued ill-success of the Comintern's efforts, and its growing insignificance inside Russia, did not diminish the importance attached to it by foreign Powers, and in particular by those whose colonial possessions or Asiatic interests made them the object of its most conspicuous attentions after its final European débâcle in 1923–1924.[2] This equivocal relation between the Soviet Union and the Communist International served to complicate the task of Soviet diplomacy.[3]

This task itself was dictated by the same basic formula— namely, the ultimate incompatibility of the two worlds, the socialist and the non-socialist. The Soviets believed that, sooner or later, the capitalist Powers, or some of them, would combine in a renewed war of intervention in order to destroy the proletarian citadel. The business of Soviet diplomacy was to postpone this as long as possible in order to enable Soviet power to be consolidated and strengthened through 'socialist construction'.

The growing weight attached to the defensive aspects of Soviet foreign policy was reinforced by the final acceptance

[1] Batsell, op. cit., chap. 13. The Comintern still lacks its definitive historian. A valuable account, though by no means an impartial one, is that by F. Borkenau, *The Communist International* (Faber & Faber, 1938). This contains some account of the principal sources. His views can be found in summary form in an article written upon the dissolution of the Comintern in May, 1943: 'The Comintern in Retrospect', *The Dublin Review*, July, 1943.

[2] See e.g. J. Marquès-Rivière, *L'URSS dans le Monde* (Paris, 1935), pp. 235 ff.

[3] On the position of the Comintern in the autumn of 1929, see E. Vandervelde: 'Is Communism Spreading?', *Foreign Affairs* (New York), October, 1929.

into the canons of Soviet orthodoxy of the hotly disputed doctrine of 'socialism in one country'. Trotsky and the other up-
holders of the counter-doctrine of 'permanent revolution' had,
by the end of 1927, been driven into the political wilderness;
and henceforward there could be no doubt that it was the
Russian rather than the international Revolution which was
dominant in their indissoluble partnership.[1]

The methods by which the Soviet Union could be preserved
from attack—the 'peace policy' of the Soviet Union—were
multiple and complex. But they were all based on the utilisation, for Soviet Russia's benefit, of the internal divisions and
'contradictions' within the capitalist order, which Marxist-
Leninist theory taught them to expect, and which observation
could readily confirm. This is not to say that the Soviet analysis
of the external world was at any time free from error; the rigidi-
ties of the dialectic were not the scientific instruments they were
credited with being, and non-Russian Communists were not
always trustworthy interpreters of the capitalist world. The
main lines of division which the Soviet Government could hope
to use were plain enough—the antagonisms between the major
Powers arising out of the war and the peace settlement, the
antagonisms between the imperial Powers and the colonial and
'semi-colonial' peoples, and finally, the internal class conflicts
which persisted within each capitalist country. The work of
the Comintern among the colonial and oriental peoples, and
among the proletariat of the more advanced countries, became
itself defensive in object—the aim being to prevent or frustrate
an anti-Soviet coalition rather than to provoke immediate
revolution. But, as will be seen, this policy was by no means
without inconsistencies, and suffered indeed from obvious
logical imperfections, and even absurdities.

The Soviet Union's attempt to exploit popular opinion in its
favour was not confined to the activities of the Comintern and
its constituent parties. Efforts were made to capitalise the widespread pacifism of the post-war years by losing no opportunity
to point out that neither the 'pure' pacifism of the religious
kind, nor the international idealism of the Wilson brand, held
out any hope of genuine peace. This could only be obtained in

[1] It is necessary to remember that many other reasons besides the conflict
over foreign policy can be found for the Trotsky-Stalin feud which ended
so decisively in the latter's favour. Foreign observers probably overstressed
the importance of the foreign policy aspect. The whole question was one of
emphasis and of timing rather than of principle. For a clear statement of
the view that Stalin's victory was fundamental in the development of the
'peace policy', see the lecture 'Russia in Asia' by R. J. Kerner, printed in
The Renaissance of Asia (University of California, 1941).

a world which had got rid of the capitalist causes of war, but meanwhile the best guarantee for peace was disarmament, and the diplomats of the Soviet Union let no occasion slip which provided any opportunity for calling attention to the Soviet Union's willingness to accept complete all-round disarmament, and for contrasting this attitudè with the obstinacy of the more or less heavily armed victor Powers of the World War.

The final aspect under which Soviet foreign policy in the first decade may be considered is that of security.[1] Russia's ability to bargain with the Great Powers was severely limited by her weakness as well as by the mistrust in which she was held, although skilful political use had been made of the economic opportunities which she could still offer to harassed capitalism. Her proclaimed aloofness from any of the old-style groupings of Powers was a reflection of her isolation rather than its cause. On the other hand, she was less handicapped in her dealings with her immediate neighbours, all of whom, with the exception of Poland, were extremely weak, and some of whom, like Turkey and Persia, could hope to play Russia off against the 'imperialist' Powers. The aim was to link these to Russia by treaties embodying the three major principles of 'non-intervention', 'non-aggression' and 'neutrality'. In the case of the middle-eastern States, the glacis was further fortified by treaties between the States themselves, though the grouping later tended to escape to some extent from its earlier wholly Soviet inspiration. In the case of the Baltic Succession States, Russia's purpose was to prevent their accepting the leadership of the deeply mistrusted Poland. The old French project of a 'cordon sanitaire', towards which such plans seemed to tend, remained very present to the Soviet mind.[2]

It remains to be seen how far these objects had been attained by the autumn of 1929, and what new elements had been introduced into the Soviet scene by the Sixth Congress of the Comintern which met from July to September in 1928, and by the adoption of the Five-Year Plan at the Sixteenth Conference of the Communist Party of the Soviet Union in April 1929.

The first essential of Soviet foreign policy once the wars were over had been to get the new régime accepted into the comity of civilised governments. This had been a slow process and was

---

[1] See the important and documented account by M. W. Graham, Jr.: 'The Soviet Security System', *Int. Conc.*, 1929. Cf. W. W. Hartlieb, *Das Politische Vertragssystem der Sowjet-union, 1920–1935* (Leipzig, 1936).

[2] Latvia and Esthonia concluded a Defensive Alliance on 1 November 1923. On relations between Russia and the Baltic States, see *The Baltic States* (R.I.I.A., 1938), part v.

by no means complete in the autumn of 1929.[1] In Europe *de jure* recognition was still withheld by Spain and Portugal, by Holland, Belgium, Switzerland and Luxemburg, by the countries of the Little Entente and by Bulgaria and Hungary.[2] In Asia, the relations established by the treaty with China in 1924 had been broken off in 1927, when the Kuomintang had purged itself of its Communist wing,[3] though virtual protectorates had been established over Tannu Tuva and Outer Mongolia. Saudi Arabia granted recognition in 1927, and the Yemen in 1928.[4] Of the republics of the New World, Mexico and Uruguay alone had recognised the Soviet Government. Finally, relations with Great Britain, established in 1924, had been severed in 1927, on the ground that the premises of the Soviet Trade Delegation and the Soviet commercial organisation *Arcos*, were being used for illegal activities, including espionage.[5]

Although Russia had taken part in the World Economic Conference called by the League of Nations in 1927, and had participated since that year in the sessions of the Preparatory Commission on Disarmament, the Soviet attitude towards the League was still one of contempt not unmixed with the suspicion that its underlying purpose was the organisation of collective action against the Soviet Union.[6]

In dealing with the Great Powers, Russia had found it easier to go along with the defeated or the disgruntled than with the

---

[1] See H. D. Houghton, 'Policy of the United States and other Nations with Respect to the Recognition of the Russian Soviet Government, 1917–1929', *Int. Conc.*, 1929.

[2] Czechoslovakia had had economic and political contacts with Russia ever since 1922 when it had extended what amounted to *de facto* recognition. F. J. Vondracek, *The Foreign Policy of Czechoslovakia, 1918–1935* (Columbia University Press, 1937). Albania had established relations with the U.S.S.R. in 1924 but they had been broken off again in the same year after the *coup d'état* of Ahmed Zogu (King Zog).

[3] Peking broke off relations in April 1927, after the raid on the Soviet Embassy; Hankow expelled the Soviet mission in July, and Nanking withdrew recognition from the consulates and trading organisations in December. The Soviet Union was represented in Manchuria until July 1929, after the outbreak of the dispute over the Chinese Eastern Railway.

[4] Exchange of Notes with Saudi Arabia, 16 February 1926, 17 April 1927. T. A. Taracouzio, *War and Peace in Soviet Diplomacy*, p. 317. Text of Treaty of Friendship between the U.S.S.R. and the Yemen, July 1928, in V. Conolly, *Soviet Trade from the Pacific to the Levant* (Oxford University Press, 1935), App. XII.

[5] Cmd. 2895, Russia, No. 3, 1927.

[6] See K. W. Davis, *The Soviets at Geneva, 1919–1933* (Geneva, 1934) and W. L. Mahaney, Jr., *The Soviet Union, the League of Nations and Disarmament, 1917–1935* (University of Pennsylvania Press, 1940).

victorious Powers. In Europe, since the Treaty of Rapallo of April 1922, Russia had aligned herself with the revisionism of Germany. Russia's principal anxiety was lest the economic pull of the West should lead to Germany's following a path of reconciliation which could only be at Russia's expense. The Locarno treaties and Stresemann's policy of 'fulfilment' seemed to justify these fears, and Russia seized with alacrity the chance of a temporary impasse over Germany's admission to the League to conclude a treaty of friendship with Germany, the Treaty of Berlin of 24 April 1926. On 24 January 1929, a treaty of conciliation was signed between the two Powers.[1] While relations with Italy were, if not cordial, at least not unfriendly, both Great Britain and France continued to be regarded as the most implacable of the Soviet's enemies.

If it was the narrower issue of the pre-war Russian debt which loomed largest in French minds, and the strong French ties with Poland which seemed the most suspicious from the Russian point of view, the Soviet conflict with Britain had been concerned with a wider field. The rivalry between Imperial Russia and Britain in Asia, somewhat stilled by the pre-war entente, seemed to have broken out again in a new form. In the Middle East, on the frontiers of India, and above all in China, the revolutionary propaganda of the Communist International was always a possible factor of disturbance, even if its potency outside China tended to be overestimated. It was perhaps of some importance that Chicherin, the Commissar for Foreign Affairs since March 1918, brought to his office the traditions of his long apprenticeship in the Asiatic department of the Foreign Office of Imperial Russia, where anti-British sentiments had long outweighed all others.[2] In China, the most important scene of conflict, the Russians' early success in guiding and fortifying the nationalist movement had been followed, as we have noted, by a resounding check in 1927. Relations with Japan had improved after the Japanese evacuation of Siberian territory in 1922. The Russo-Japanese convention of January 1925 secured the Japanese evacuation of Northern Sakhalin, but enabled Japan to continue to make use of the important oil resources of Sakhalin for her fleet, and paved the way for a renewal of Japanese fishing rights in Soviet

---

[1] Texts in *Speeches and Documents on International Affairs*, ed. A. B. Keith (2 vols., Oxford University Press, 1938), vol. i, pp. 127–31 and 174–7.

[2] There is an interesting series of discussions of Soviet foreign policy in the 1920's, particularly in the Far East, in a series of articles with varying titles by B. Nikolaevsky, which appeared in the New York Russian quarterly *Novy Zhurnal* (The New Review), 1942–1945.

waters.[1] The decline of Russian influence in China removed
a further impediment to better relations. Japanese Communism remained indeed a disturbing factor, but Japan's policy
was ultimately determined by her Pacific ambitions.[2]

The progress made in reaching security agreements with
Russia's immediate neighbours can be chronicled briefly. In
the Middle East, Russia's position in 1929 was buttressed by
three treaties: that with Turkey of 17 December 1925, that with
Afghanistan of 31 August 1926, and that with Persia of October
1927.[3]

On Russia's western borders the position was more compli-
cated. Of the larger States in this area, Roumania was still
alienated by Russia's persistent refusal to recognise the
Roumanian annexation of Bessarabia. In Poland, the Pilsudski
coup in 1926 had brought into power elements unlikely to
modify the strongly anti-Russian tendency in Polish policy.
This, coupled with an unwillingness to get out of step with
Roumania, made Poland very reluctant to treat with the
Soviet Union except as the recognised leader of a Baltic bloc.
The murder of the Soviet ambassador to Poland in the spring
of 1927 had further embittered the relations of the two Powers.[4]
Finland was strongly prejudiced against Russia on both
national and ideological grounds, and desirous of strengthening
her ties with the Scandinavian countries.[5]

Latvia and Esthonia were both deeply suspicious of Russian
aims and of Communist propaganda—the latter had faced a
Communist rising as recently as 1924—and had little desire for
more intimate ties with the U.S.S.R., although there were signs
of a less unfriendly attitude on the part of Latvia.[6] Lithuania,

---

[1] The text of the Convention will be found in V. A. Yakhontoff, *Russia
and the Soviet Union in the Far East* (Allen & Unwin, 1932), pp. 404–10.

[2] It will be remembered that certain reactionary circles at the Court of
Nicholas II had opposed the formation of the Entente with the Western
Powers, and had advocated instead the (then) ideologically more suitable
alliance with Germany and Japan. This, by freeing Russia of European
anxieties, would, they argued, enable her once more to take up her civilising
mission in central Asia and Persia. See the memoirs of Baron (R. R.)
Rosen, *Forty Years of Diplomacy* (Allen & Unwin, 1922).

[3] Texts in *Int. Conc.*, 1929, pp. 400–1, 408–11, 416–20.

[4] Relations were governed by the Peace Treaty of Riga of 18 March 1921,
L.N.T.S., VI, pp. 151–70.

[5] The Finnish-Russian Peace Treaty had been signed at Dorpat on
14 October 1920. It contained an undertaking to support in principle the
neutralization of the Baltic, the Gulf of Finland and Lake Ladoga, L.N.T.S.,
III, pp. 69 ff.

[6] Relations with the Baltic successor-states had been established by the
Treaty of Tartu of 2 February 1920 with Esthonia, the Treaty of Moscow of
12 July 1920 with Lithuania, and the Treaty of Moscow of 11 August 1920,

with its strained relations with both Germany and Poland, and with no common frontier with the Soviet Union, had signed a pact of non-aggression on 22 December 1926.[1]

The Kellogg-Briand Pact for the renunciation of war, to which Russia was invited to adhere, gave the Soviet Government a new possibility of forwarding its security policy, and began a new era of activity in Soviet diplomacy. This first took the form of inviting its neighbours to sign a protocol bringing the Pact into force between themselves without waiting for the process of ratification of the parent instrument to be complete. The Litvinov Protocol, signed at Moscow on 9 February 1929, was a conspicuous success for Soviet diplomacy. Its original signatories, besides the U.S.S.R., were Poland, Roumania, Latvia and Esthonia. By July it had received the adhesion of Lithuania, Turkey, Persia, and of the Free City of Danzig. Thus Finland remained the only one of Russia's neighbours outside the Soviet security system.[2]

The international scene had been subjected to a new analysis by the Sixth Congress of the Comintern in the late summer of 1928; its decisions are recorded in three documents, the 'Statutes', the 'Programme' and a 'Manifesto'.[3]

The Manifesto contained the customary denunciations of the imperialist Powers with Great Britain and France at their head, of the hollowness of their pacifist pretensions, of the 'League of Nations', the product of Versailles, 'the most shameless robber treaty of the last decade', and of the 'treacherous rôle of the second international'. The attack on the Second International heralded a new leftward swing of Comintern policy, replacing the United Front tactics of the previous period. The main emphasis of the struggle of the international proletariat was to be the fight against war; and particularly against war on the Soviet Union.

'Despite all the contradictions and antagonisms which exist between the capitalist powers, and despite their deep and growing

---

with Latvia, L.N.T.S., vols. xi, iii, and ii. The U.S.S.R. and Latvia had actually initialled a Pact of Non-Aggression on 9 March 1927 (text *Int. Conc.*, 1929, pp. 415–16), and had reached a trade agreement in June 1929.

[1] Text *Int. Conc.*, 1929, pp. 412–15.

[2] *Survey for 1928*, I (i); *Survey for 1929*, I (iv). Fischer, op. cit., chap. 28. The text of the Protocol is in *Documents for 1929*.

[3] The Manifesto is printed in Batsell, op. cit., pp. 798 ff., and the Programme is analysed and important passages from it quoted in pp. 77ᶜ ff. The English text of the latter has been published as a pamphlet: *Programme of the Communist International*, 1929. The Statutes are in *Documents for 1928*. Russian documentation of Comintern history is collected in *Kommunisticheski Internatsional v Dokumentakh, 1919–1932*, ed. Bela Kun.

mutual hatred, they are preparing, with Great Britain at their head, a war against the Soviet Union. They are systematically preparing for war.'[1]

The same theme was to be found in the Programme of the Communist International:

'In view of the fact that the U.S.S.R. is the only fatherland of the international proletariat, the principal bulwark of its achievements and the most important factor for its international emancipation, the international proletariat must on its part facilitate the work of socialist construction in the U.S.S.R. and defend her against the attacks of the capitalist powers by all the means in its power.'

At the same time the international obligations of the C.P.S.U. (Communist Party of the Soviet Union)—a section of the Communist International and the leader of the proletarian dictatorship in the U.S.S.R.—were defined as being to render support 'to all the oppressed, to the labour movements in capitalist countries, to colonial movements against imperialism and to the struggle against national oppression in every form'.[2]

Hostility towards the capitalist countries did not however rule out a certain measure of co-operation with them. For the process of industrialisation which was to receive an impetus with the adoption of the Five-Year Plan in the following spring had actually been founded on the decisions of the Fourteenth Party Congress of December 1925, when Stalin had made clear the objective: 'The conversion of our country from an agrarian to an industrial country able to produce the machinery it needs by its own efforts—that is in essence the basis of our general line.'[3] The Fifteenth Congress in December 1927 had further developed this theme and had added to it what was to be the other main feature of the internal policy of the Five-Year Plan period, the collectivisation of agriculture.[4]

Industrialisation involved a definite measure of economic co-operation with the outside world. The position was clearly expounded in the Comintern Programme:

'The simultaneous existence of two economic systems: the socialist system in the U.S.S.R. and the capitalist system in other countries, imposes on the proletarian state the task of warding off the blows showered upon it by the capitalist world (boycott, blockade, etc.), and also compels it to resort to economic manœuvring with and utilising economic contacts with capitalist countries (with the aid

[1] Quoted from Batsell, op. cit., p. 799.
[2] ibid., p. 784.
[3] *History of the C.P.S.U.* (*Short Course*) (Moscow, 1939), p. 276.
[4] ibid., pp. 288–9.

of the monopoly of foreign trade—which is one of the fundamental conditions for the successful building up of socialism, and also with the aid of credits, loans, concessions, etc.). The principal and fundamental line to be followed in this connection must be the line of establishing the widest possible contact with foreign countries —within limits determined by their usefulness to the U.S.S.R., i.e. primarily for strengthening industry in the U.S.S.R., for laying the base for her own heavy industry and electrification, and finally for the development of her own socialist engineering industry. Only to the extent that the economic independence of the U.S.S.R. in the capitalist environment is secured, can solid guarantees be obtained against the danger that socialist construction in the U.S.S.R. may be destroyed and the U.S.S.R. may be transformed into an appendage of the world capitalist system.'[1]

Both the objectives of an economic foreign policy and the lengths to which the Soviet Union was prepared to go were thus defined. Particularly significant was the determination to maintain intact the foreign trade monopoly. Indeed, its operation was fortified by the withdrawal in the next couple of years of the exemptions which, largely for political reasons, had hitherto been enjoyed by Russia's Asiatic neighbours.[2]

With regard to the Western Powers, the principle of seeking such contacts as were likely to serve Russia's industrial requirements was followed without regard for political or ideological conformity. The main feature of the period since 1927 had been a marked rise in trade with the United States. The United States, as already noted, did not officially recognise the Soviet régime; but the question of the old debts was a slightly less burning one than in Great Britain or France, and her technical equipment was obviously suited to fill some of Russia's outstanding needs.

It is worth noting in conclusion that the ill-health of Chicherin was placing more and more of the work of the Foreign Affairs Commissariat (Narkomindel) in the hands of Litvinov, although the latter did not actually replace his former chief until July 1930.

[1] Quoted from Batsell, op. cit., pp. 783–4.
[2] See on this point, V. Conolly, *Soviet Economic Policy in the East* (Oxford University Press, 1933). Cf. J. D. Yanson: *Foreign Trade in the U.S.S.R.* (Gollancz, 1934), chaps. 1, 2, 3 and 5, for a Soviet account of the matter. For the organization and character of Soviet foreign trade before 1930, see C. B. Hoover, *The Economic Life of Soviet Russia* (Macmillan, 1931), chap. 6.

II. WORLD DEPRESSION AND THE RISE OF THE AGGRESSORS

Chapter Two

INTRODUCTION

THE objectives which the Soviet leaders pursued in the new period remained basically unaltered: to seek friendly contacts with Powers who could assist in the economic upbuilding of the Soviet Union; to prevent the creation of a great anti-Soviet bloc of the imperialist-capitalist Powers, and to extend the security system entered into with the Soviet Union's neighbours as an added obstacle to a new war of intervention.

As we have noted, the principles of such a system had already emerged. Its outlines were indeed visible in the first treaties which in 1920 and 1921 had stabilised conditions upon the Soviet Union's western frontiers. An analysis of these agreements shows the Soviet Government 'building upon the stipulations of conventional neutrality the broad outlines of a non-aggression system. In addition to converting the conception of a neutral obligation from a passive one such as marked nineteenth-century neutrality to one of an active and positive character, the Soviet Government insisted on giving and receiving specific guarantees of non-aggression and non-interference. Thus there was constructed for Russia and her immediate neighbours a legal bulwark of treaty stipulations yielding at least the minimum basis of safety from unanticipated attacks of a military or political nature against their territorial integrity or the security of their institutions.'[1]

The purpose of these treaties from the Soviet point of view was of course to prevent the neighbouring states from becoming the base for a renewed interventionist struggle, and to provide legal grounds for objecting to any activities thought to be preparatory for such an effort. Although the reciprocity of such arrangements had been stressed, it must be pointed out that since the Soviet Government never regarded the Communist International as an organisation of the kind barred by the treaty provisions, the value of the treaties accrued mainly to Soviet Russia.

[1] M. W. Graham, Jr., 'The Soviet Security System', *Int. Conc.*, 1929, p. 349.

An attempt was made to carry the policy a step further at the unsuccessful Moscow Disarmament Conference in December 1922.[1] This Conference drew up a multi-lateral non-aggression convention, infractions of which were to be countered by a 'policy of differential neutrality' on the part of the other signatories. This implied a modification of the laws of neutrality in order to permit a measure of discrimination against an aggressor. The Soviets at this stage could not envisage more positive sanctions, because they still believed in the hostility of the entire 'capitalist' world to the Soviet Union, and hence in the impossibility of active political co-operation with it.

Article V of the Convention also provided for the settlement of disputes by arbitration, where diplomatic means had failed.[2] The details of the machinery were held over for a supplementary convention. The arbitration provision thereafter disappeared from the Soviet Union's pacts. This Convention failed to get adopted because of the Soviet Government's refusal to dissociate it from their disarmament proposals.[3] Its text also included provisions which could be interpreted as ruling out the application of League sanctions against the Soviet Union by the other signatories. This fear of League action as an instrument for overthrowing the Soviet régime made the Geneva Protocol and the Locarno treaties objects of considerable suspicion in Moscow.

The second tier of treaties making up the Soviet security edifice was thus drawn up largely as a reply to Geneva. The new Soviet project was based on the idea of 'the precovenanting of the permanent attitude of two states towards each other in terms of explicit and indefeasible neutrality . . . it formed the complete counterpart to a system of non-aggression pure and simple by furnishing guarantees of inaction in the event of aggression or hostility in some other quarter. This policy was the only one which could work, granted the absence of an impartial tribunal for the settlement of disputes.'[4]

The first treaty to embody the neutrality provision was that with Turkey of 17 December 1925. This also added to the provisions embodied in earlier treaties a specific undertaking by both parties to seek a pacific settlement of all disputes arising between them. Similar obligations were embodied in the

---

[1] See the documents printed on *Conférence de Moscou pour la Limitation des Armements* (Moscow, 1923).
[2] ibid., p. 153.
[3] L. Fischer, *The Soviets in World Affairs*, pp. 374–81; T. A. Taracouzio, *War and Peace in Soviet Diplomacy*, pp. 115–23.
[4] Graham, op. cit., p. 361.

treaties with Germany, Afghanistan, and Lithuania in 1926.
The fullest expression of the new security policy is to be found
in the Soviet-Persian treaty of 1 October 1927. This embodied
a mutual pledge of non-aggression; a pledge of neutrality in
the event of an attack upon one of the parties by a third Power;
a pledge that neither Power would join in agreements, alliances,
boycotts or blockades directed against the other; an undertaking not to permit the formation on the soil of either party of
groups hostile to the Government of the other, or the raising or
supply of armed forces to be directed against it; and, finally, a
pledge to the settlement of all disputes by pacific means.[1]

The Litvinov Protocol of 1929 thus contained nothing which
was not in the tradition of Soviet security policy, although it
provided the first link between the Soviet system and the
wider system in which the Soviet Union now participated as a
signatory of the Pact of Paris (Briand-Kellogg Pact). The
Non-Aggression Pacts whose conclusion with various countries
in the years 1931–1933 will be chronicled in due course, add
only two new elements to their predecessors: 'provision for the
immediate liberation of the signatories from their obligations if
the other contracting party commits an act of aggression, and
the preservation of their legal rights under agreements concluded "before the coming into force of the present Pact, so
far as the said agreements contain no aggressive elements".'[2]

In contrast to the pacific direction in which Soviet diplomacy
proper appeared to be moving in 1929, the Comintern was still
steering a sharply leftward and revolutionary course, as prescribed in the directives of the Sixth Congress in 1928. Social
democracy still loomed large as the immediate enemy to be
overthrown.[3] 'Developing an irreconcilable struggle against
Social Democracy, which represents the agency of capitalism
within the working class, and smashing to atoms each and every
deviation from Leninism, which brings grist to the mill of Social
Democracy, the Communist Parties have shown they are on
the right track.'[4]

Nevertheless, it was events outside the Soviet Union, for
which Soviet policy was not directly responsible, which were
the most significant in this period for Russia's rôle among the

[1] The full texts of these treaties are given in the Appendix to Graham,
op. cit.
    [2] Taracouzio, op. cit., pp. 122–26.
    [3] This aspect will be treated in more detail in Chapter 15. The effect of
the policy in the most important field of its application. Germany, is dealt
with in Chapter 5.
    [4] J. Stalin, *Political Report to the Sixteenth Party Congress* (26 June 1930),
(Martin Lawrence, 1930), p. 23.

Powers. In the autumn of 1929 relations with Great Britain were restored. The year 1930 saw the culmination of Russo-German collaboration in Europe and a continuation of the détente with Japan in the Far East. The year 1931 saw changes in both these fields, and the tentative efforts of the Soviet Union to put relations with the other major Powers on a more friendly footing received a sudden and profound stimulus. The policy of friendship with Turkey, a feature of the early post-revolution period, was maintained and strengthened.

The limitations on Soviet action in its *rapprochement* with the West, and the depth of the divisions which still existed between Russia and her late allies of the first World War, will be illustrated to some extent in the present chapter, and will concern us again when we come to deal with Russia's rôle in connexion with the League of Nations and the Disarmament Conference. The economic aspects of foreign policy in this period are also sufficiently important to justify separate treatment, which must also be accorded to Far Eastern problems. As far as Russia was concerned, these problems were to remain subordinate to European questions. Only from Europe could a fatal blow be struck against the Soviet Union. At worst it would be easier to buy time in Asia than in Europe. For this reason, finally, relations with Germany—the core of the whole matter—must also be examined at some length.

The link between the aspects of foreign policy already mentioned, and those which will be dealt with more briefly in the present chapter, is to be found beyond doubt in the all-absorbing task set by the First Five-Year Plan. The unprecedented scale of the Plan, as accepted by the Sixteenth Party Conference in April 1929, and by the All-Union Congress of Soviets in May,[1] its repercussions on the fortunes of important social groups and on millions of individual lives, the unresolved tensions within the ruling stratum of the régime, which were not ended by the expulsion of Trotsky from the country or by the defeat of the 'right' opposition in November 1929—all these were sufficient to absorb the energies of a people and of a leadership which had already endured fifteen years of war, revolution, and civil strife.

Even if some of the repeated warnings that the Soviet Union was on the brink of war may be ascribed to the needs of internal

---

[1] The genesis and purpose of the Plan is usefully summarised in the translation of an article from *Sotsialisticheski Khozaistvo* (Socialist Economy), No. 3, 1929, by its editor M. Bronsky, in *Annals of Collective Economy* (Geneva, 1930), IV, pp. 3–27. Cf. S. and B. Webb, *Soviet Communism* (Longmans, 1935), chap. 8.

propaganda, there can be no doubt that the military needs of the Soviet Union were influential. From one point of view the most notable effect of these years was to cut short the perceptible drift towards 'normalcy' in daily life and to increase the tension under which all Soviet citizens lived—a tension which communicated itself to the Comintern and its constituent parties. Not for nothing have these years been called 'Russia's Iron Age'.

In other countries, attention was at first directed to the rigours of collectivisation and to the spectacular trials and 'purges' of the time, rather than to the material results of the plan, which could not immediately be judged.[1] In March and April 1930, there were trials at Kharkov directed against alleged Ukrainian separatism, the first of a series of its kind, connected with the ruthless collectivisation of the peasantry in that area.[2] In November 1930 came the trial of the 'Industrial Party', the charge being economic sabotage, the formation of a secret political party, and conspiracy with France to invade Russia and overthrow the régime. In March 1931, further Gosplan officials and other members of the Soviet intelligentsia were accused of counter-revolutionary activities in conspiracy with Mensheviks in Russia and with the Second International;[3] the latter charge was clearly intended to be of assistance to the Comintern in its struggle against the socialist parties of Europe.[4]

The first objective of Soviet diplomacy was naturally to seek, as a preliminary to further contacts, to establish normal diplomatic relations with countries which had not recognised the

---

[1] *Summary of the Fulfilment of the First Five-Year Plan* (Gosplan, Moscow, 1933). Cf. also 'The Balance Sheet of the Five-Year Plan', by W. H. Chamberlin, *Foreign Affairs*, XII. Much of the literature on the subject has been produced by visitors who have been enraptured by technical or social achievements although totally ignorant of industrial technique and conditions and of social services in other countries including their own. For a balanced account by a foreign expert employed in these years, see A. Monkhouse, *Moscow, 1911–1933* (Gollancz, 1933), chaps. 13 and 14. The progress of the Plan month by month can be followed in *Osteuropa* (Berlin). It is significant that it is to Germany that one must look for any systematic foreign survey of Soviet progress. See also *Ostwirtschaft*, the organ of German business men trading with Russia.

[2] W. E. D. Allen, *The Ukraine* (Cambridge University Press, 1940), pp. 324–33.

[3] Webb, op. cit., pp. 550–7; Sir John Maynard, *The Russian Peasant and other Studies* (Gollancz, 1942), p. 259; B. Souvarine, *Stalin* (Secker & Warburg, 1939), chap. 10.

[4] The Soviet case is given in the pamphlet, *The Menshevik Trial* (1931). The reply of the Second International is contained in *The Moscow Trial* (published by the Labour Party).

régime, and to restore them where they had been broken off, as in the case of Great Britain.[1]

Britain's resumption of relations with the U.S.S.R. after the Labour victory in the general election of 1929 was not as speedy as the Russians had expected, in spite of the hopes of increased trade held out to the British delegation which had visited Russia in the spring. The main reason was the Russian insistence that the resumption of relations should precede negotiations over questions dividing the two countries.[2] The protocol of 3 October 1929 (ratified by the Soviet Government on 11 November) could therefore be regarded as a victory for the Russian standpoint. The only concession to the British view was the provision that the exchange of Ambassadors should be accompanied by reciprocal confirmation of the article on propaganda (Article 16) of the treaty of 1924.[3] In spite of Conservative attacks on the agreement and on the British Government's surrender, the agreement was approved by the House of Commons on 5 November. Ambassadors were appointed during the next fortnight; on 20 December M. G. Sokolnikov presented his credentials in London and Sir Esmond Ovey followed suit in Moscow two days later.[4] In a statement to the press M. Sokolnikov emphasised the economic advantages to be obtained from the agreement and pointed to the improved figures of Anglo-Soviet trade in the previous two months.[5] M. Litvinov had discussed Anglo-Soviet relations at greater length in a report on 4 December, expressing the hope that with goodwill the outstanding questions might be settled. But the tone of his remarks was not very cordial and he noted the clouding of relations owing to 'Great Britain's association with America's appearance in the Manchurian conflict'.[6]

Further discord was injected into Anglo-Soviet relations by the controversy over the treatment of religion in Russia after the Soviet Decree of 8 April 1929.[7] The Pope's protest, made

---

[1] The fullest account of Anglo-Soviet relations is contained in W. P. and Z. K. Coates, *A History of Anglo-Soviet Relations* (Lawrence & Wishart: Pilot Press, 1943). Its theme is the political and economic loss inflicted upon Britain by the failure of British Governments to respond to the Soviet desire for friendly relations.

[2] Fischer, *The Soviets in World Affairs*, pp. 816–9.

[3] This was a peculiar procedure, as, owing to the fall of the MacDonald Government, the treaty of 1924 had not been ratified or come into force.

[4] *Documents for 1929*, pp. 116–18. The statement there that the agreement was 'ratified' by the House of Commons is of course incorrect; there was nothing in the agreement to require such unusual procedure.

[5] ibid., pp. 128–30.   [6] ibid., pp. 198–210.

[7] The text of the decree is in *Int. Conc.*, 1930, pp. 303–17. It governed the formation and compulsory registration of religious societies and groups

on 2 February 1930,[1] was followed on 2 April 1930 by a Debate in the House of Lords, during which one speaker dissented from the Government spokesman's reference to Russia as a friendly Power and declared amid cheers that it was on the contrary a distinctly hostile Power. These expressions of political animosity did not affect the trade negotiations however, and on 16 April, a trade agreement was signed by M. Sokolnikov and Mr. Arthur Henderson.[2]

The question of debts remained, and conversations on the subject were begun in October without appreciable progress being made. The economic agreement produced little real improvement in the political relations of the two countries. M. Stalin's speech to the Sixteenth Party Congress on 26 June cast doubts on the British Socialists' desire for peace, and the speeches of Molotov and Manuilsky on 5 July, with their insulting references to the British Government's policy of repression at home and in India, appeared to indicate that the anti-propaganda pledge had not finally settled that question.[3] The trial of Professor Ramzin and other Soviet technicians, which took place at Moscow from 25 November to 7 December 1930, was marked by accusations that the military authorities of England and France had been accomplices in a plot against the Soviet regime. This provoked official protests from the British Government on 1 and 15 December.[4] The year thus ended on an ominous note.

Just as relations with Britain retained their old atmosphere of coldness and suspicion, so those with Germany remained fairly

---

of believers, and excluded from the scope of their activities all functions other than that of providing for the conduct of acts of worship. While local authorities could allot buildings for religious purposes to religious groups, their upkeep and the other expenses connected with the provision of religious services had to be met entirely by voluntary subscription. Religious ceremonies could not be held except in the premises thus assigned, with the exception of the last rites for the dying, and burial ceremonies. No organisation larger than a single congregation was given corporate recognition. Speaking in February, 1930, Molotov said: 'Recently the anti-Soviet campaign abroad has developed most extensively in connexion with religion . . . the exceptionally violent anti-Soviet campaign is intended to serve as a preliminary on the part of the imperialists to the attack on the Soviet Union.' *The New Phase in the Soviet Union* (Modern Books, 1930), pp. 1-2.

[1] *Int. Conc.*, 1930, pp. 318-21.

[2] Cmd. 3552, 1930. Britain gave the required six months' notice that she was denouncing the agreement on 17 October 1932, in pursuance of undertakings entered into at the Ottawa Conference, *Survey for 1932*, p. 29.

[3] Stalin, *Political Report to the Sixteenth Party Congress*. All three speeches will be found in the Russian stenographic record of the Congress: *Shestnatsty S'ezd Vsesoyuznoy Kommunisticheskoy Partii*.

[4] W. H. Chamberlin, *Russia's Iron Age* (Duckworth, 1935), pp. 162-3.

cordial, in spite of certain difficulties in the early part of 1930 over questions of trade and propaganda.[1] The political collaboration of these two Powers was reinforced by a Soviet *rapprochement* with Italy, with whom a trade agreement was concluded on 2 August.[2] The three Powers frequently found themselves in agreement with regard to the Briand Pan-Europa scheme and at the Disarmament Conference. On 24 November 1930, Signor Grandi met M. Litvinov at Milan. On 28 April 1931, a new commercial agreement was signed, and the years 1930–1931 saw important developments in trade between the two countries.

With France itself, the heart of the European system against which Germany and Italy were rebelling, Russian relations were if anything worse than ever. In spite of the work of official and unofficial bodies, the old problems of debts and propaganda were still unsolved.[3] To them was now added the new question of 'dumping'.[4] The French took certain measures against Soviet imports in October, and Soviet reprisals followed at once. Nevertheless, the following year, 1931, saw the first important step forward in the relationships of the two countries since the recognition of the Soviet Government in 1924.[5]

[1] *Survey for 1930*, pp. 125–30: 'Note on the Rapprochement between Germany, the U.S.S.R., and Italy.'

[2] The alignment was explained by Litvinov in a press interview on 25 July 1930. He said that the Powers which had imposed the Peace Treaties were the more aggressive towards the Soviet Union and that there 'had come about a certain community of interests between the Soviet Union and the States which had suffered through the war'. *The Times*, 26 July 1930.

[3] For Franco-Soviet relations see A. Wolfers, *Britain and France between two Wars* (New York, Harcourt Brace, 1940), pp. 132–41. A resolution of the Eleventh Plenum of the Comintern Executive, which met in March-April 1931, declared that the trials of the 'Industrial' Party and the 'Mensheviks' had shown preparations in the spring of 1930 and again in 1931 for an attack on Soviet Russia to be conducted by French (and British) imperialism through their vassal states, Poland, Roumania, and Finland, with the co-operation of the Second International. Kun, op. cit., p. 956. The 'Comité Consultatif de la Dette Russe' and de Monzie's official 'Comité Consultatif des Affaires Russes' were both at work on the debts question from 1925 till 1932. H. Slovès, *La France et l'Union Soviétique* (Paris, Rieder, 1935), pp. 307–11. Milioukov, op. cit., pp. 377–9.

[4] *infra*, chap. 3. For the opposition to a French *rapprochement* with the U.S.S.R., see 'Dumping et Crise Financière des Soviets' by F. Eccard, and 'L'URSS et la crise mondiale' by T. Aubert, *Revue des Deux Mondes* (Paris), 1 November 1931 and 15 February 1932.

[5] See *Survey for 1931*, pp. 105, 117–18, 155 and 284 n.; Hartlieb, op. cit., p. 258; Slovès, op. cit., pp. 313–19; O. Hoetzsch, *Le Caractère et la Situation Internationale de l'Union des Soviets* (Geneva, 1932), pp. 55–6; *Osteuropa*, VII, pp. 7–11.

The initiation and early course of these Franco-Russian discussions were not revealed at the time and are still partially obscure. A possible indication of Russia's desire for improved relations with France can perhaps be detected in Molotov's speech to the Sixth Congress of Soviets in March 1931.[1] The first recorded conversations were those in May 1931 between the Soviet Ambassador to Paris, Dovgalevsky, and Philippe Berthelot, the powerful Secrétaire Général of the French Foreign Office. In the same month M. Berthelot's chief, M. Briand, conferred with Litvinov at Geneva. At some date soon afterwards, the German Government was duly informed that negotiations were in progress for the conclusion of a pact on the model of the Treaty of Berlin of April 1926. On 1 June it was announced in Paris that conversations had been resumed on the subject of trade relations and as a result the measures and counter-measures of the previous October were lifted. A report that the negotiations were in progress came from Paris on 19 August, and in spite of conflicting rumours the pact seems actually to have been initialled at about that time. The first official mention of it was in Molotov's speech in Moscow on 7 November.[2]

The news of these transactions was not received altogether favourably in France, and the Quai d'Orsay found it advisable to state on 21 December that reports of the Pact's conclusion were premature. On 4 January 1932, however, it was made known that agreement had been reached as to the procedure of conciliation which was to be a condition of the entry into force of the agreement, and it was reported that signature was to be subject to the conclusion of pacts between the U.S.S.R. on the one hand and Poland and Roumania on the other.[3]

With regard to Poland, conditions for an agreement looked more favourable than they had been since the negotiations for

---

[1] Molotov: 'The present relations between France and the Soviet Union are a threat to peace. The Soviet's proposal for the conclusion of a guarantee-pact was rejected by France. Nevertheless the Soviet Union is prepared to continue its efforts to improve relations, in case a sincere response from France can be obtained.' See the report of the speech in *Osteuropa*, VI, pp. 415–17. Kamenev stressed at the same Congress the responsibility of the French General Staff for current plans of intervention against the Soviets. Ibid., p. 418.

[2] *Osteuropa*, VII, pp. 154–5.

[3] The Russians kept Berlin informed of these negotiations and on 28 August 1931 Litvinov went to Berlin to discuss them with Dr. Curtius, the Foreign Minister in the Brüning Government. On 24 June, protocols had been signed prolonging the Russo-German treaties of 24 April 1926 and 24 January 1929 until June 1933. They were to be terminable subsequently at one year's notice.

a pact of this kind had been suspended after the murder of the Soviet Ambassador to Warsaw in June 1927. In addition to the Polish fears of Germany, economic circumstances were propitious, since the years 1928–1931 witnessed a marked rise in the volume of trade between the two countries.[1] As early as July 1931, the Warsaw Press was observed to have modulated its habitual antagonistic tone towards Russia.[2] A draft of the proposed Pact was handed to Litvinov by the Polish Minister on 23 August, and the exchange of information on armaments in September was a further encouraging sign.

In the course of the negotiations both sides made concessions. Poland agreed (since the Litvinov Protocol already included them), to waive her demand that the Pact be framed so as to include the other western neighbours of the Soviet Union, while the Soviet Union for its part agreed to negotiate separate pacts with the Baltic States, as a preliminary to the signature of the Pact with Poland. Poland likewise abandoned her demand for a convention on arbitration which the Soviet Union had always proclaimed inadmissible in political questions, on the ground that there could be no impartiality between the Soviet Union and a capitalist State.[3] On the other hand it was agreed that Poland's obligations towards her Allies and towards the League of Nations should be expressly mentioned in the Pact.[4] The Pact was accordingly initialled on 25 January 1932, final signature being delayed apparently in the hope that a Russo-Roumanian agreement would be reached.

The Baltic States provided little trouble. The non-aggression pacts with Finland, Latvia, and Esthonia were signed on 21 January, 5 February, and 4 May 1932 respectively.[5] Lithuania was covered by the Pact of 22 December 1926, which was prolonged on 6 May 1931.[6] Supplementary Conventions of Conciliation were signed with Esthonia on 16 June and Latvia on 18 June 1932.[7]

[1] See the note: 'Poland and the U.S.S.R., 1928–1935', *Survey for 1935*, I, pp. 277–9.
[2] *Osteuropa*, VI, pp. 667–8.
[3] Taracouzio, *The Soviet Union and International Law*, pp. 295–7.
[4] Poland was allied with France and Roumania by treaties of 18 February and 3 March 1921, respectively.
[5] Texts in M. Litvinov, *Against Aggression* (Lawrence & Wishart, 1939), pp. 148–51, 152–5, 160–3.
[6] *Survey for 1934*, pp. 412–13.
[7] 'The Latvian and Esthonian Treaties, the terms of which were practically identical' represented a compromise with the Soviet Government's principles. Each contained a clause to the effect that the obligations under the present Treaty should not affect the international obligations devolving on the contracting parties from treaties concluded or obligations assumed

c

The question of Roumania was less easy to settle. The decision of the Allies in 1920 (the Treaty of 28 October) recognising the Roumanian possession of Bessarabia had never been accepted by the Soviet Union, and this had caused a breakdown in the negotiations for the resumption of diplomatic and commercial relations in 1924.[1] Although Communist agitation and frontier incidents had died down, the Russians had continued to make it clear that the question was not regarded as closed, and the small autonomous Moldavian Republic, created on the left bank of the Dniester by the Russians in October 1924, provided a nucleus of which Bessarabia could be regarded as an irredenta. This territorial question, as well as fear of Communism, was a major preoccupation of Roumanian diplomacy. Her allies of the Little Entente were not directly interested, but Roumania's treaty with Poland of 3 March 1921, renewed on 26 March 1926 and 15 January 1931 strengthened her position. France was not committed to defend the Roumanian frontier with Russia by her own treaty with Roumania of 10 June 1926, but was indirectly bound by her alliance with Poland.[2]

Although the Bessarabian question had not prevented the signature of the Litvinov Protocol by Roumania (in 1931 its Roumanian signatory had made it known that he understood at the time that the Soviet Union did not intend to resort to force in the matter),[3] the dispute still existed. Negotiations,

prior to the entry into force of the present Treaty in so far as the latter contained no "elements of aggression within the meaning of the present Treaty". On the other hand, the Baltic States gave way over the question of the appointment of a neutral chairman on the Conciliation Commissions provided for by the supplementary Conventions of Conciliation. Both the Esthonian and Latvian Treaties, as well as the Soviet-Lithuanian Non-Aggression Pact of 1926, were renewed until 31 December 1945 by Protocols signed in Moscow on 4 April 1934, while the Soviet-Finnish Treaty was also renewed for the same period on 7 April of that year.' *The Baltic States*, p. 76. For the Soviet attitude to conciliation procedure, see Taracouzio, op. cit., pp. 293–5, and for the earlier history of 'non-aggression pacts', ibid., pp. 308–10. The Soviet Convention defining Aggression, of July 1933, to which the Baltic States adhered, is dealt with *infra*, chap. 4.

[1] *Survey for 1920–3*, pp. 273–8; *Survey for 1924*, pp. 263–6; Taracouzio, op. cit., p. 187. The Roumanians had annexed Bessarabia in the spring of 1919, in spite of having in March 1918 concluded a treaty with the R.F.S.F.R. promising to evacuate it. (The text is in Taracouzio, op. cit., App. XIV.) The Treaty of 1920 was ratified by Great Britain in 1922, by France in 1924 and by Italy in 1927. Japan, the remaining signatory, did not ratify.

[2] J. S. Roucek, *Contemporary Roumania* (Stanford University Press, 1932), pp. 173–5.

[3] Letter from O. A. Davila to *New York Times*, 23 February 1931, cited by Roucek, op. cit., p. 176.

opened at Riga on 6 January 1932, speedily reached a dead-lock.

With the assistance of the Polish Government a formula to cover the Bessarabian question was found, and at the end of September the Roumanians announced that the talks would continue. At this point, however, a new Roumanian Government presented an alternative formula, which was in turn rejected by the Russians; at the end of November, the Russians having refused to submit the dispute to arbitration, the talks again came to a standstill.[1]

By then, however, the Poles had agreed to wait no longer. The non-aggression pact had been signed on 25 July,[2] and on 23 November a Conciliation Convention was added.[3]

For the French, too, the rising temper of German nationalism made the case for proceeding with the Russian *rapprochement* more than ever urgent. The Roumanian difficulty was got over, first, by Titulescu informing the French Government that the Roumanians did not wish any longer to stand in France's way, and second, by direct assurances from Russia that the undertakings given in the Kellogg Pact and the Litvinov Protocol effectively precluded a resort to force over the Bessarabian issue.

The signature of the Franco-Soviet Non-Aggression Pact on 29 November 1932 had been preceded by much public discussion of its purport.[4] It proved to follow the general line of Soviet non-aggression pacts in its principal clauses, with safeguards for the prior engagements of both sides and a declaration that such engagements could oblige neither to participate in the aggression of a third State against the other party. Two additional provisions set it apart, however, from the other pacts of the series. Article 4 prohibited the participation of either of the two States in any international combination directed against the foreign trade of the other. Article 5 tackled the old question of propaganda:

'Each of the High Contracting Parties undertakes to respect in every connection the sovereignty or authority of the other Party over the whole of that Party's territories as defined in Article 1 of the present Treaty (i.e. including territories which it represents in external relations and the administration of which it controls), not to interfere in any way in its internal affairs, and to abstain more

---

[1] *Survey for 1932*, p. 608; *Survey for 1934*, pp. 382–3.
[2] Text in *Against Aggression*, pp. 156–60. On 5 May 1934 it was prolonged until 31 December 1945.
[3] Taracouzio, op. cit., pp. 268–9.
[4] The text of the Pact is in *Against Aggression*, pp. 164–7.

particularly from action of any kind calculated to promote· or encourage agitation, propaganda or attempted intervention designed
to prejudice its territorial integrity or to transform by force the
political or social régime of all or part of its territories.

'Each of the High Contracting Parties undertakes in particular
not to create, protect, equip, subsidise or permit on its territory
either military organisations which have as their aim armed combat
with the other Party or organisations which assume the rôle of
government or representative of all or part of its territories.'[1]

On the other hand, there was no clause to foreshadow any
such close relationship as was envisaged in the Treaty with
Germany of 24 April 1926, where paragraph 2 of Article 1 ran:

'The German Government and the Government of the Union of
Socialist Soviet Republics shall remain in friendly touch in order to
promote an understanding with regard to all political and economic
questions jointly affecting their two countries.'[2]

On the day of the Pact's signature, *Izvestia* pointed out that
the European Press would be mistaken if it saw in the conclusion of the pacts (with Poland and France) a proof of an
alteration in Moscow's foreign policy. 'Even the ratification of
the pact,' added *Pravda* on the same day, would not 'remove
the danger of war menacing the U.S.S.R.' And Molotov,
speaking on 23 January 1933, a week before Hitler came into
power, emphasised the special relationship between Russia
and Germany.

The advent of Hitler did it is true produce some evidence of
a growing suspicion of Germany which made the U.S.S.R.
more eager to settle relations with other countries. Importance
was attached in Moscow to Litvinov's speech at Geneva on
6 February 1933, introducing the Soviet draft convention for
the definition of aggression.[3]

The attack on the German Communist Party in February,
and the raids in April on branches of one of the Soviet commercial agencies, were minor causes of disturbance compared

---

[1] Reciprocal engagements of this kind were not new in Soviet diplomacy.
They were included in the Economic Agreement with Great Britain of
16 March 1921. Taracouzio, *The Soviet Union and International Law*, p. 258.
Parallels to Articles 4 and 5 of the French pact were Articles 2 and 3 of
the Treaty of Neutrality and Non-Aggression with Afghanistan signed on
24 June 1931, and prolonged for ten years on 29 March 1936. Text in
Against Aggression, pp. 144–7.

[2] L.N.T.S., LIII. 1269, pp. 392–6.

[3] Minutes of the General Commission of the Disarmament Conference,
vol. II, p. 234. Cf. Florinsky, *World Revolution and the U.S.S.R.*, pp. 237–8.

with the fact that the author of *Mein Kampf* was now the ruler of Germany, with Herr Alfred Rosenberg, the latter-day Teutonic knight, as a trusted adviser. Nevertheless German *Realpolitik* was as capable of preventing the Nazi ideology from getting in the way of German foreign policy as was Russian realism of keeping apart the respective fields of Soviet diplomacy and Comintern agitation. Hitler's speech on 23 March 1933 showed this quite clearly:

'The Government of the Reich are ready to cultivate with the Soviet Union friendly relations profitable to both parties. It is above all the government of the National Revolution who feel themselves in a position to adopt such a positive policy with regard to Soviet Russia. The fight against Communism in Germany is our internal affair in which we will never permit interference from outside. Our political relations with other Powers to whom we are bound by common interests will not be affected thereby.'[1]

Russia may have proved the more receptive to these overtures in view of the circulation at that time of the first reports of the proposed Four-Power Pact, which could only be regarded as a new move to isolate the Soviet Union and to settle Europe's affairs without Soviet participation.[2]

Hitler received the Soviet Ambassador for the first time on 28 April 1933, and on 5 May ratifications were exchanged of the protocols of June 1931, thus bringing into force again the Non-aggression Treaty of 1926 and the Conciliation Convention of 1929. *Izvestia's* comment on the following day accepted the German thesis: 'The people of the Soviet Union will undoubtedly endorse the re-entry into force of the Berlin treaty . . . in spite of their attitude to Fascism the people of (the) U.S.S.R. wish to live in peace with Germany . . . and have no desire to make any change or revisions in Soviet policy with regard to Germany.'[3]

Nevertheless a revision had taken place, as was clearly revealed in a series of articles contributed by Radek to *Izvestia* between 12 and 24 May. In these he placed the Soviet Union for the first time among the States opposed to the revision of the Peace Treaties, and declared that revisionism could lead only to war.[4]

[1] *Hitler's Speeches*, ed. N. H. Baynes (2 vols., Oxford University Press; R.I.I.A., 1942), p. 1019.
[2] *Survey for 1932*, II (ii); F. L. Schuman, *Europe on the Eve* (Hale, 1939), pp. 38–40. These events will be dealt with at greater length, *infra*, III, 2.
[3] Quoted by E. Fraenkel in *Review of Politics*, II, p. 56.
[4] Radek's articles on foreign policy in 1933 are reprinted in his book, significantly entitled, *Podgotovka Borby za novy Peredel Mira* (*The Preparation of the Struggle for a New Partition of the World*), (Moscow, 1934).

This attitude was not altered by Hitler's speech of 17 May 1933. In it Hitler expounded the peaceful intentions of the new Germany but did not specifically mention Russia, although the danger that Communism might spread as the result of war was given as the reason for his pacific policy.[1] The repercussions of this speech were of a nature to disturb the Russians, since it put an end to the first wave of anti-Hitler feeling in Britain— a feeling which had so recently turned Herr Rosenberg's visit to London into a fiasco. But if the Russians shared the dismay which the French felt at the gullibility of the British public, they gave no sign. They did not even react to the speech on 16 June at the World Economic Conference of the German Minister of Economics, Herr Hugenberg, in which he demanded that Germany be granted a mandate to use its 'constructive and creative genius' to 'reorganise' Russia. Litvinov seemed to treat the affair as a joke; ten days later Hugenberg left office.

Indeed, with Germany only beginning full-scale rearmament, there was no immediate danger unless she should become part of an anti-Soviet coalition, which seemed for a time less likely with Hitler at the helm than during the chancellorship of the 'respectable' von Papen. Additional motives for remaining on good terms could still be found in the economic field, and it is possible that the contacts of the two armies had not yet ceased to have their effect.[2]

Something of the Soviet leaders' complacency could be gauged from the apparent apathy of the press and people. As a foreign worker at Chelyabinsk in the Urals noted in the middle of the summer of 1933, the only people afraid of the results of the Nazi revolution were the German workers there. 'Hitler was consolidating his position. The Soviet Press in general was somewhat indifferent and most of the Russians had no particular antipathies for the Nazi.'[3] Before dealing with the transformation of the next three years it is necessary to fill in the outline which has thus hastily been sketched, and to try to delve a little further towards the roots of Soviet policy in this and the succeeding periods.

[1] *Hitler's Speeches*, pp. 1041–58.
[2] It has been suggested that contacts between the two armies continued until the spring of 1935 and were then terminated by Hitler. H. Rosinski, *The German Army* (Hogarth Press, 1939), p. 195; E. Wollenberg, *The Red Army* (Secker & Warburg, 1940), p. 237.
[3] John Scott, *Behind the Urals* (Secker & Warburg, 1943), p. 92.

Chapter Three

INTERNATIONAL ASPECTS OF THE FIRST FIVE-YEAR PLAN

AS has already been noted, the great internal readjustment known as the First Five-Year Plan provides the master-key to every aspect of Russian policy in the years immediately following 1929.

In the first place, the fulfilment of the Plan itself demanded certain specific conditions whose attainment was the primary objective of these years of Russian diplomacy. In the second place, the prospects of the Plan itself, visions of its success or failure, the economic effects of Russia's position as a buyer and seller on world markets, the possible influence of the Plan on the military potential of the Red Army—all these were bound to exert a considerable influence on public opinion in the outside world and hence on the policy of the 'capitalist' States towards the U.S.S.R. The crushing blows dealt to the public confidence in the ability of the capitalist order to 'deliver the goods' helped to give an added and partly fortuitous interest to all news about the 'socialist sixth of the world'. But in the general upheaval a really rational analysis of the world situation and of Russia's position in particular was the last thing demanded by the angry and confused peoples of the West—and the last thing that most of their leaders were apparently qualified to give.

Economic questions overshadowed all others in the international relationships of the rest of the world at the time. The predominance of political preoccupations in the later nineteen-thirties and in the war years makes it difficult to recall the picture of a world genuinely petrified by such events as the closure of banks, the decline in share values and stagnation in trade and industry.[1]

One curious feature of this concentration upon economic issues was that opinion about the 'Plan' and about the Soviet system in general was largely conditioned by the prospect of the markets that might be opened to foreign producers.

Upon one point nearly all observers were agreed. Whatever the military aspects of industrialisation, the immediate effect of the Plan was to intensify Russia's need for peace. When Litvinov said 'the larger the scale of our constructive work, the

[1] The opening chapter of the *Survey for 1931* is entitled 'Annus Terribilis, 1931' as though human fortunes had reached rock bottom.

27

more rapid its tempo, the greater our interest in the preservation of peace', he was obviously speaking the truth.[1] Stalin
put it simply and bluntly: 'Our policy is a policy of peace and
strengthening of trading relations with all countries.'[2] A couple
of years later a well-qualified foreign student of Russian affairs
put it more baldly still, though with a nuance which would
scarcely have been acceptable to the Soviet leaders:

'Anyone who, like myself, was in Russia in 1929, and saw the
extent to which the mobilization of Bluecher's army in the conflict
with China over the Manchurian frontier disturbed the "Plan" and
everything which depends on it, knows as well as the rulers in the
Kremlin, that the U.S.S.R. could not bear the extraordinarily
intensive effort demanded by a war, in what is called the decisive
year of the Five-Year Plan.'[3]

Stalin's coupling of trade with peace is a pointer to the fact
that a mere absence of war was not sufficient for the Soviet
Union in the new stage of its development. The Plan no doubt
tended towards a form of economic autarky. This was no new
thing in Russian history, and was favoured by the diversity of
the country's resources and the wide range of climatic conditions within the frontiers of the Union. But the immediate
result was to strengthen and not to weaken economic ties with
the capitalist world.[4]

For the execution of the Plan, Russia required various forms
of outside assistance. The old style 'concession' played an unimportant rôle in this period. Machinery and other capital
goods were directly imported and foreign specialists and
technicians were employed, often under the 'licence' or
'technical aid contract' systems, which involved both the
purchase of foreign goods and the employment of foreigners.[5]
It was thus necessary at the same time to engage an abnormal
proportion of the country's internal resources on long-term

[1] Speech on 25 July 1930. *Vneshnaya Politika SSSR (The Foreign Policy of
the U.S.S.R.)*, p. 59.
[2] *Political Report to the Sixteenth Party Congress* (London, 1930), p. 32.
[3] O. Hoetzch, *Le Caractère et la Situation Internationale de l'Union des Soviets*,
p. 84.
[4] W. Winkler, 'Autarchy in the Soviet Union', *Annals of Collective
Economy*, VII (1931), pp. 41–80. For the actual figures, see App. I to this
chapter.
[5] C. B. Hoover, *The Economic Life of Soviet Russia* (Macmillan, 1931),
pp. 37–9, 166. The exports of Russia in the years immediately before 1914
had consisted largely of foodstuffs. Exports during the period of the Plan
and immediately before it consisted mainly of oil, timber and other industrial products. These categories accounted for 60·5 per cent of the whole in
1928–1929 compared with 19·2 per cent in 1913. Ibid., p. 161. Cf. S. P.
Turin: 'Foreign Trade of the U.S.S.R.', *Slavonic Review*, X.

schemes for the production of capital equipment and to pay off the external obligations created by the country's mounting imports.

The whole process was summed up in an official League of Nations survey as follows:

'Monetary expansion has been accompanied by Government monopoly of foreign trade and the foreign exchanges, the external value of the rouble being maintained at gold parity, while its domestic value has depreciated. Despite rapidly increasing production of industrial raw materials, and to a less extent of heavy manufactures, standards of living have remained low and have even decreased, the extra resources made available being used for capital construction. In fact, also, the equipment programme has been facilitated by long credit on the part of exporters in foreign countries, and by the shipment abroad, particularly in 1930-31, of large quantities of foodstuffs and raw materials, for example wheat, wood and petrol.'[1]

(Of the last three commodities mentioned, wheat, of which the amount exported was the same in 1934-1935 after the Plan as in 1927-1928 before it, was negligible in quantity by the standards of the great world exporters.)[2] Another source of gold and foreign exchange was provided by the 'Torgsin' shops, where from 1931 a variety of otherwise unobtainable goods could be bought with foreign currencies, and by those who still owned any of the precious metals or who had relatives abroad who could be encouraged to send them presents in the form of *valuta* credits.[3]

There were in this period some instances of direct barter, as for instance when Russian oil was exchanged for Canadian aluminium,[4] but for the most part the Soviet purchasers had

[1] League of Nations, *World Economic Survey, 1932-1933*, p. 72. A statistical account of Soviet foreign trade during the First Five-Year Plan is given in chap. 4 of Yanson, op. cit. For details on the position in 1930, see H. Lorenz, *Handbuch des Aussenhandels und des Verkehrs mit der UdSSR*. See also H. R. Knickerbocker, *The Soviet Five-Year Plan and its Effect on World Trade* (Lane, 1931), and *Soviet Trade and World Depression* (Lane, 1931), for foreign estimates of the position in 1931. A brief account of Russia's foreign trade for the whole period 1929-1941 is given in Yugow, *Russia's Economic Front for War and Peace* (Watts, 1943), chap. 5.
[2] H. V. Hodson, *Slump and Recovery* (Oxford University Press, 1938), pp. 234-5.
[3] W. Höffding: 'German Trade with the Soviet Union', *Slavonic Review*, XIV, pp. 482-5. This was published also as Monograph No. 10 of The School of Slavonic Studies (January 1936). Cf. Monographs 7 and 8 published together (July 1935): *The Prospects of British and American Trade with the Soviet Union*.
[4] Hodson, op. cit., pp. 108-9.

to pay cash or rely on such credits as they could obtain. Long-term funded loans such as had helped to develop industrialisation elsewhere were not forthcoming, and the greater portion of the credits obtained were short-term commercial credits. Soviet foreign indebtedness rose from 415 million roubles in October 1929 to 625 million and 855 million in successive years, standing finally at 975 million in June 1932.[1] (From 1933 the return to an active trade balance, coupled with increasing gold production, rapidly diminished the outstanding indebtedness.)[2]

The big American firms were in the best position to give what long-term credits there were, in spite of the unfriendly attitude towards Russia of the American Government and of some American financial circles.[3] Sometimes, as for instance in the case of the General Electric Company, a technical aid contract might include credit facilities;[4] but generally speaking Germany remained the main source of credits.

For the greater part, however, imports had to be paid for by immediate exports, and this altered to some extent the previous relationship between economic and political considerations in the sphere of foreign policy. Russian trade had been regarded at times very largely as a weapon in the service of the Soviet Foreign Office; prospects of orders from Russia were held out as a bait to secure recognition, while their curtailment could be used as a reprisal for hostile acts in the political sphere, as had been the case in Anglo-Russian relations after 1927. Nevertheless the case of America, which had been able to trade with Russia without conferring recognition upon the régime, showed that the policy was a purely opportunist one. Russia needed American trade and saw no prospect of browbeating the United States into political concessions by the threat of stopping it. Political as well as economic considerations were also believed to have dictated the exceptionally favourable trade terms granted to Russia's Asiatic neighbours. It was hoped to detach these peoples from their ties with Britain and to injure Britain economically by excluding it from important markets.[5]

The time for these political and ideological luxuries was now over. Foreign machines and foreign technical experts were

[1] League of Nations, *World Economic Survey*, 1932–1933, p. 72 n.

[2] Höffding, loc. cit.

[3] For American credits during the Five-Year Plan period, see *Prospects of British and American Trade with the Soviet Union*, pp. 30–1.

[4] Hoover, op. cit., pp. 37–9.

[5] Hoover, op. cit., pp. 165–7; Conolly, *Soviet Economic Policy in the East*, pp. 1–5.

indispensable, and the range of choice as to their country of origin was not very wide.[1]

Goods had to be sold and again the choice of outlets was not wholly a matter for the Soviet trading authorities. They had with regard to most of their exportable products to face opposition from the producers of other countries, who had, in the case of oil, already shown their ability to make use of the political dislike felt for the Soviet system, in their propaganda against Soviet exports. The classing of the Soviet trading methods under the familiar category of 'dumping' was of course an error. Dumping, as the capitalist world knew, was a method of getting rid of surpluses for which the internal market had no room, at prices below those on the home market. The Russians, on the other hand, were not concerned with internal market or with the situation of a particular industry. Their sole concern at this period was to secure a given amount of foreign currency to pay for indispensable imports. They were ready to sell any goods that could find a market without regard to whether an internal demand for the same goods existed. The prices asked were those which could tempt the foreign buyer and did not bear any particular relation to costs of production. Russian exports tended to disturb international markets because their nature and quantity were not predictable by ordinary commercial standards. The likelihood of Russian

[1] The number of foreign specialists actually employed in Russia during the execution of the First Five-Year Plan has been variously estimated. In his report to the enlarged Presidium of the Executive Committee of the Communist International, on 25 February 1930, Molotov stated that Soviet factories then employed 850 foreign 'experts' and 550 foreign skilled workers. 'Most of these came from Germany. The recruiting of new workers from Germany and also from America will be increased in the future.' *The New Phase in the Soviet Union*, p. 39. In March 1931, a director of the Supreme Council of National Economy declared that 'about 5,000 foreign specialists and workmen were then employed in Soviet industry'. M. Gurevich, *The Five-Year Plan* (Society for Cultural Relations with the U.S.S.R., 1931), p. 12. The American gold-mining expert John Littlepage was engaged in 1928 and helped to recruit more mining engineers in 1929. For a couple of years about 175 American mining engineers were employed in Russia: then the numbers fell off. J. Littlepage and D. Bess: *In Search of Soviet Gold* (Harrap, 1939), p. 64. For some of the books giving accounts of Russia as seen by foreigners employed there, see P. Grierson, *Books on Soviet Russia* (Methuen, 1943), pp. 233-6. To these should be added the important book by John Scott, *Behind the Urals*. The ability to command foreign technical assistance was of real importance for the success of the Plan. For instance, the first plant for the large-scale production of ammonia for fertilisers was a foreign-made plant, erected in the Donetz by German and Italian engineers in 1932. The first Soviet-made plant of this kind was put up in 1936 and only started production in 1937. *Science in Soviet Russia*, ed. J. Needham and J. S. Davies (Watts, 1942), p. 21.

competition proving permanent was overestimated by people who could not rid themselves of the idea that exports (of oil for instance) must denote a 'surplus'.[1]

This helps to explain the importance which was generally attached to Russia's reappearance on the world markets at a time when its share of world trade was well below that of pre-Revolutionary Russia, and when the Soviet Union stood only eleventh in order of importance among the trading nations of the world.[2] It helps also to explain the various measures of discrimination taken against Soviet trade.[3]

The increase in Russia's exports which set in with the inception of the Five-Year Plan was very marked. The year 1930 was the peak year, exports reaching a total of 533 million dollars (compared with 775 million in 1913). From 1931 a decline set in. Imports also increased in value until 1931 and then dropped sharply.

This decline reflected the depressed state of the world market. As prices fell, it was necessary for the Russians to force up the volume of goods sold (at the expense of their own consumers) in order to secure the requisite amount of foreign currency. Taking Russia's trade as a percentage of world trade, one can observe a fairly sharp upward movement from the 1·34 per cent of 1929 to the 2·44 per cent of 1932, the peak year, although, as already observed, this was well below the 3·8 per cent of 1913.

Any notion that Russia was insulated from the effects of world economic tendencies was thus clearly erroneous. According to one estimate, Russia's exports fell by rather less than 40 per cent between 1929 and 1932, compared with a drop of 70 per cent in American exports, 64 per cent in those of Great Britain and 58 per cent in those of Germany.[4] But we have

---

[1] Hoover, op. cit., pp. 153–69; *Survey for 1930*, pp. 449–50.

[2] Appendix to this chapter, *infra*. Cf. W. O. Scroggs, 'Russia and World Trade', *Foreign Affairs*, XII. Russia in 1932 was responsible for 2·44 per cent of the world's trade as compared with the United States' 10·92 per cent and Britain's 13·38 per cent.

[3] The following countries took special measures of various degrees of severity: France, 3 October 1930; Roumania, 15 December 1930; Belgium, 24 October 1930; United States, 24 November 1930; Yugoslavia 9 March 1931; Canada, 27 February 1931. *Documents relating to the Foreign Economic Relations of the U.S.S.R.* (Prepared for the World Economic Conference at London, 1933), pp. 17–18. Other American measures are listed in *Prospects of British and American Trade*, p. 29. The decree of the Soviet Government of 20 October 1930, empowering the Commissar for Foreign Trade to take reprisals against countries discriminating against Russian exports, is printed in App. XXI of Taracouzio, *The Soviet Union and International Law*; see also pp. 297–9 ibid.

[4] Scroggs, loc. cit.

already pointed out the price paid for this very relative advantage. According to another authority 'the contraction of Soviet imports during these years was probably greater than in any capitalist country.'[1]

From the point of view of foreign policy, it is however the direction as much as the volume of trade which is of importance.[2] As already made clear, the Germans had considerable advantages over all their competitors. This was partly the outcome of technical and geographical factors. In 1913, Germany had supplied 47·5 per cent of Russia's imports and taken 29·8 per cent of her exports. After the war, the political connexions between the two countries were an additional favourable influence. Germany was 'the first to come into direct touch commercially with the Soviet economy' and had remained Russia's most important purchaser and purveyor and had thus helped to build up its neighbour's economy.[3] For so important a trading country as Germany, Russian markets could not be of overwhelming importance. In 1928, Russia took 3·3 per cent of German exports and supplied 2·7 per cent of her imports. On the other hand Russia's demands were largely for the products of those German heavy industries which suffered most severely of all from lack of markets. Russia took 8·1 per cent of Germany's exports of machinery in 1930, 18·2 per cent in 1931 and 30·5 per cent in 1932.[4]

For Russia, Germany was still more important, taking, in 1928, 28·9 per cent of Russia's exports (more than Great Britain) and supplying 28 per cent of her imports (more than the United States). Germany was an important purchaser of Russian maganese ore, timber, oil and furs. Other exports to Germany included platinum, apatite, flax, hemp, bristles and asbestos. One reason for Germany's large share in Russia's imports, to which we have already referred, was the ability of her industrialists to give credit. This was due to the assistance given by the Reich and State Governments in the form of guaranteed credits or cheap credit-insurance facilities. The German lead over the United States was temporarily lost in 1929, when the latter supplied a quarter of Russia's total imports. On 14 April 1931, however, the Russians were granted by the 'Pyatakov' agreement further credits of 300,000,000 Rm., and German exports to Russia shot up even above the estimated

---

[1] Höffding, loc. cit., p. 481.
[2] Appendices 3 and 4, *infra*.
[3] E. Kretschmer: 'Germano-Russian Trade Relations and the Five-Year Plan', *Annals of Collective Economy*, 1930, vol. vi, p. 112.
[4] Höffding, loc. cit.

totals.[1] In 1931 Germany supplied 37 per cent and in 1932
46 per cent of Russia's imports. In the latter year the share of
the United States had sunk to 5 per cent. On the other hand,
German industrialists were confronted no less than Russia's
other suppliers by the problems arising from the sharp curtailment of Russia's export trade and by the repercussions of
Germany's own import restrictions.[2]

Britain, which had in 1913 supplied 12·6 per cent of Russia's
imports, suffered throughout the period of the Plan from the
after-effects of the 1927–1929 breach in diplomatic relations
between the two countries, although some firms did maintain
business activity in Russia even during the period of the breach.
Russian technicians, however, were sent to Germany and the
United States to study, rather than to Great Britain, and they
were naturally uninterested in the possibilities of purchasing
equipment from a country of whose industrial capacity they
were ignorant.[3]

After the resumption of relations and the commercial agreement of 16 April 1930 trade with Great Britain improved, and
British manufacturers supplied altogether some £15,000,000
worth of machinery throughout the whole period of the Plan.[4]
It is not unreasonable, perhaps, to assume that a more liberal
credit policy would have enabled trade between the two
countries to be increased still further. As it was, the absence of
State backing forced suppliers to Russia to sell Soviet obligations on the open market at a discouragingly high discount, and
at a time when their German competitors were receiving every
assistance.[5]

Russian trade with Britain (apart from the complex question
of freights which, so the Russians claimed, reversed the position

[1] The agreement and its successor of 15 June 1932, are summarized in
Foreign Economic Relations of the U.S.S.R., pp. 31–6.

[2] Höffding, loc. cit., pp. 476–7. H. Kraemer: 'Neue Grundlagen der
deutsch-russischen Wirtschaftsbeziehungen', *Osteuropa*, VII, pp. 627–31
(August 1932); Yanson, op. cit., pp. 125–7.

[3] The question of whether to purchase in one country or in another had in
the case of certain specialised goods to be determined by technical rather
than political or even financial considerations, and this must have played
some part in determining policy.

[4] Monkhouse, op. cit., chap. xvii. 'British Firms and the Five-Year
Plan'; P. Winterton, 'Soviet Economic Development since 1928', *Economic
Journal* (London, 1933), XLIII, pp. 449–52.

[5] In 1931, Great Britain guaranteed export credits for twenty-four months
up to the value of £6,000,000; this was to guarantee 75 per cent of Russia's
sterling orders. Other countries whose governments provided credit assistance for Soviet purchases in this period were Japan, Poland, Czechoslovakia, Austria, Finland, Norway, Denmark. *Foreign Economic Relations
of the U.S.S.R.*, pp. 36–7.

in Britain's favour)[1] retained a remarkably unbalanced character. Britain, which had taken 17·6 per cent of Russia's exports in 1913, took 22 per cent in 1929, 27 per cent in 1930 and 32 per cent in 1931 (compared with the 16 per cent taken by Germany and the 3 per cent taken by the United States). But from 1931, with the increasing development of exchange controls, etc., the Soviet Union suffered in the case of Britain as elsewhere by her inability freely to make use of balances in one country to pay for imports from another.[2] (This disability was of course not Russia's alone.) In 1932 the Soviet Union sold to Britain goods to the value of £19,697,013 and bought goods (including re-exports) to the value of £10,619,687. The trade agreement was denounced by Great Britain on 17 October 1932, after the Imperial Conference at Ottawa. A further set-back was caused by the arrest in March 1933 of certain British subjects employed by Metropolitan-Vickers Ltd. in Moscow. On 20 March, commercial negotiations in progress between the two countries were suspended by the British, and on 5–6 April a statute empowering the Government to prohibit the import of Russian goods was passed. This was put into effect with regard to goods accounting for some two-thirds of Britain's normal imports from Russia, on 19 April, two days after the expiry of the existing trade agreement and one day after the end of the trial and the sentencing to imprisonment of two British subjects. The Soviet Government proclaimed an embargo on British goods and recalled the chiefs of its trade delegation in London. On 26 June, conversations were begun between Sir John Simon and M. Litvinov, then in London for the World Economic Conference, and on 1 July, the two British prisoners were released and the embargoes withdrawn.[3]

With regard to the other major Powers, France, looked on as the hard core of political and economic anti-Sovietism, the country in which the question of the Tsarist debts still rankled most, was obviously poorly placed for taking advantage of the economic opportunities of the Russian market. (There were indeed legal as well as financial difficulties in the way of its extension.)[4]

As a matter of fact, France's share in Russia's imports in 1928, 4·3 per cent, was slightly higher than her share in 1913, but after 1929 there came a sharp recession, her share in 1932

[1] On this, see Yanson, op. cit., chap. 6: 'The Chartering of Foreign Ships for Soviet Trade'.
[2] W. H. Chamberlin, *Russia's Iron Age*, pp. 211 ff.
[3] Cmd. 4286 and 4290, 1933
[4] Russia had hoped to buy aluminium as well as the products of the French automobile, aviation, and cinematograph industries. A. Barmine, *Memoirs of a Soviet Diplomat* (Lovat Dickson, 1937), pp. 239–41, 249.

falling to the negligible figure of 0·5 per cent. The position with regard to imports from Russia was rather different, as Russian oil had certain attractions for a consuming country feeling the pressure of the great international oil trusts. Her share of Russian exports in 1932 was 4·9 per cent compared with 6·6 per cent in 1913. (Two-thirds of the total were represented by oil products which amounted to about a fifth of France's total imports under this head.) Manganese imports became very important in 1931–1932.

Soviet reprisals following on the French 'anti-dumping' decree of 3 October 1930 and the ill-success of the quota scheme of the summer of 1931, served to show that Russia had the upper hand in so far as there was any question of economic warfare between the two countries. For whereas, in 1928, France's trade with Russia had been on a fairly equal basis, in 1932 France was actually buying from the Soviet Union about ten times as much as she exported to that country. There were thus certain economic as well as political reasons for France to seek less strained relations between the two former allies.[1]

Italy's commerce with Russia was never of first importance to either side. A sharp rise in Italian exports to Russia in 1931 brought them to about the 1913 level, but this was insufficient to alter the balance, which remained unfavourable to Italy, in spite of the fact that her imports from Russia were well below the pre-war figure.[2]

The Low Countries were not important in Soviet trade in this period. In 1929–1930, Belgium supplied 0·5 per cent of the Soviet Union's imports, and Holland 0·2 per cent. In 1932 the figures were 0·1 per cent and 0·5 per cent respectively. Thereafter the trade with both showed some improvement, largely no doubt owing to purchases of colonial products made through the Belgian and Dutch markets. The peak year for Belgium was 1937, when it supplied 5 per cent of the Soviet Union's imports. Holland supplied 8·1 per cent in 1935 and 7·9 per cent in 1937. In neither case does political recognition or the lack of it seem to have played any part. The imports

---

[1] H. Slovès, *La France et l'Union Soviétique*, chap. 6; 'Le Commerce'. M. Slovès' figures are taken from French official statistics and differ slightly from the League of Nations statistics which have been used here. Cf. Yanson, op. cit., pp. 127–33. A new trade agreement was in fact signed on 11 January 1934.

[2] G. Dobbert, 'UdSSR und Italien', *Osteuropa*, VIII, 1932–1933. Italy was third among Russia's customers in 1930 and 1931, and in 1931 went up from seventeenth to sixth place among Russia's suppliers. Fiat cars, aero-engines, dockyard plant and ships were bought from Italy. Barmine, op. cit., pp. 251–3.

of both countries from the Soviet Union showed a fairly steady rise. Belgium took 0·7 per cent of the Soviet Union's exports in 1929–1930, and 7·5 per cent in 1937; Holland took 1·5 per cent in 1929–1930 and 6·5 per cent in 1937.[1]

It is however not merely to the commercial contacts with the Western countries that one should look in order to appreciate the influence of the Five-Year Plan upon Russia's foreign policy. Although it has been pointed out that the planned redistribution of industry away from the 'old' areas—the Moscow region and the Ukraine—was a feature of the Plan's two successors rather than of the First Five-Year Plan itself, these years undoubtedly saw a slight eastwards shift in the economic centre of gravity of the Soviet Union. The opening in 1930 of the Turksib Railway was perhaps its most striking feature. As in the exploitation of the peasant to pay for industrial advance, this trend was in line with pre-Revolutionary development.[2] The potential importance of this shift and of the projected new metallurgical base in the Urals was stressed by Stalin in his speech of 26 June 1930.[3]

The development of these new resources gained an added importance from the fact that they enabled vital industries to be built up in areas less vulnerable to attack than the old industrialised regions of Western Russia. It is possible that political importance was attached to the transfers of population involved in so far as they might counteract any dangerously centrifugal tendencies on the part of the national minorities. It is certainly significant that the years of the Plan and of the forcible collectivisation of agriculture saw a series of trials (from 1930 to 1933) directed against Ukrainian 'nationalism'. In addition to the movement of Ukrainians to other parts of Russia, which had been going on already before the Revolution, there is evidence of a renewal of the pre-1917 migration of Great Russians into the Ukraine in connexion with the expansion of industry there.[4]

[1] League of Nations, *International Trade Statistics*. In the period of the First Five-Year Plan, the Soviet Union imported some oil direct from the Netherlands East Indies. Conolly, *Soviet Trade from the Pacific to the Levant*, pp. 95–7. Belgium recognized the U.S.S.R. on 12 June 1935.

[2] An official estimate of the eastward movement is to be found in *Summary of the Fulfilment of the Five-Year Plan*, 1933, pp. 239–66. Cf. Yugow, op. cit., chap. 7, and G. Vernadsky: 'The Expansion of Russia', *Transactions of the Connecticut Academy of Arts and Sciences*, XXXI, 1933.

[3] *Report to Sixteenth Party Congress*, pp. 113–14.

[4] W. E. D. Allen, *The Ukraine* (Cambridge University Press, 1940), pp. 324–30 and 362–70. His views on the political motivation of changes in the Ukrainian economic structure seem more sweeping than his materials warrant

D

The further opening up of Siberia and of Soviet Central Asia to railway development was of course outstandingly significant in the development of Russia's Asiatic trade, which remained of relatively greater importance than in pre-Revolutionary years. In this sphere the new predominance of economic over political and propagandist considerations was particularly marked. In fact the practices resorted to in the Russian export drive and the cancellation of the exemptions from the trade monopoly previously granted to Russia's Asiatic neighbours caused a certain amount of friction, which will be treated when relations with these countries individually come to be considered.[1]

The development of the Soviet Far East will also be examined independently later. But it may be noted that the idea of a plan of development for the Far Eastern region itself went back at least to 1926, and the 'First Five-Year Plan of 1928 therefore, in so far as the Far East was concerned, gave official sanction to ideas which had long been in the air.'[2]

Very extensive plans were laid down for colonisation and industrialisation but execution fell far short of the sanguine hopes of the planners, and the changed political situation after 1931 made a reconsideration of the whole position inevitable.

There was no improvement during the period of the First Five-Year Plan, in the somewhat stagnant trading relations between Russia and Japan. Russia's important timber exports to Japan actually declined, as did her imports of apparatus for the fishing industry and the employment of Japanese in the fishing and canning industry.

Altogether Japan accounted for 1·5 per cent of Russia's exports in 1930 and 1·7 per cent in 1932, and she figured among Russia's suppliers to the extent of 1·6 per cent in 1930 and 0·7 per cent in 1932. In spite of repeated negotiations, the necessary credit arrangements to provide for the large-scale import of Japanese-made capital goods were not carried through. There does not seem to have been any considerable employment of Japanese technicians, although Molotov stated in February 1930 that a group of engineers was being brought from Japan

---

[1] Conolly, op. cit., *passim*. Yanson, op. cit., pp. 133–7. During the First Five-Year Plan, Russian trade increased with Afghanistan, Sinkiang and Outer Mongolia, but decreased with Turkey, Persia, China, and Japan. The nature of the trade remained of course wholly unlike that with Europe or the United States. Russia exported very largely manufactured goods and imported raw materials, in particular wool, cotton and hides. Russia's total imports of cotton declined from 154 million roubles (16·3 per cent of her total imports) in 1927–1928, to 6½ million roubles (2·8 per cent of total imports) in 1934.

[2] V. Conolly, *Soviet Trade from the Pacific to the Levant*, p. 11.

'to work on the rationalisation of the railway transport system'. Contact was thus of local rather than general significance.[1]

As one thus surveys the various aspects of the Five-Year Plan, it does indeed become evident that foreign policy could not but be determined by the tasks which the Plan imposed and by questions of internal politics arising out of it. The genuineness in these years of the Russians' often proclaimed desire for peace is unquestionable. And it was not merely the absence of warfare but genuine good relations in the economic field which the Soviet authorities required. Russian non-aggression proposals envisaged above all economic non-aggression. The preponderant share of Germany in supplying the equipment required under the Plan made good relations with that country in particular of the highest importance. The governments of the three countries which might most easily have competed with Germany in this sphere—Great Britain, the United States, and France, were none of them predisposed to make particular efforts to assist their nationals in building up trade with the outcast Bolsheviks. Even had there been no political reasons for the continuance of the Russo-German alignment, their mutual economic dependence would have exercised an almost over-whelming influence in that direction, certainly in so far as the Russians themselves were concerned.

There is considerable evidence, indeed, that in the years 1932–1934, when from the political aspect Russo-German co-operation seemed to be becoming more and more impos-isble, the industrial and commercial links between the two countries prevented their mutual hostility becoming more than verbal.

[1] Conolly, op. cit., chap. 2; H. Rosinski: 'UdSSR und Japan', *Osteuropa*, VIII.

Appendix 1

RUSSIA'S FOREIGN TRADE

(In millions of dollars)

Year				Exports	Imports	Balance
1913	.	.	.	775	700	+ 75
1925	.	.	.	326	424	− 98
1926	.	.	.	364	346	+ 18
1927	.	.	.	411	367	+ 44
1928	.	.	.	404	490	− 86
1929	.	.	.	482	453	+ 29
1930	.	.	.	533	545	− 12
1931	.	.	.	417	569	−152
1932	.	.	.	295	362	− 67
1933	.	.	.	254	179	+ 75
1934	.	.	.	215	119	+ 96
1935	.	.	.	189	124	+ 65
1936	.	.	.	159	158	+ 1
1937	.	.	.	193	151	+ 42
1938	.	.	.	148	158	− 10

Appendix 2

RUSSIA'S FOREIGN TRADE AS PERCENTAGE OF WORLD TRADE

1913 . 3·8	1925 . 1·2	1930 . 1·36	1935 . 1·27
1921 . 0·3	1926 . 1·18	1931 . 1·95	1936 . 1·2
1922 . 0·4	1927 . 1·2	1932 . 1·44	1937 . 1·09
1923 . 0·4	1928 . 1·36	1933 . 1·79	1938 . 1·11
1924 . 0·5	1929 . 1·34	1934 . 1·39	

Appendix 3

SOURCE OF RUSSIAN IMPORTS
DURING FIRST FIVE-YEAR PLAN (PERCENTAGES)

				U.S.A.	U.K.	Germany	France
1913	.	.	.	5·8	12·6	47·5	4·1
1929	.	.	.	20·1	6·2	22·1	4·3
1930	.	.	.	25·0	8·0	24·0	2·8
1931	.	.	.	21·0	6·0	37·0	1·3
1932	.	.	.	5·0	5·0	46·0	0·5

Appendix 4

DESTINATION OF RUSSIAN EXPORTS
DURING FIRST FIVE-YEAR PLAN (PERCENTAGES)

	U.S.A.	U.K.	Germany	France
1913	0·9	17·6	29·8	6·6
1929	4·6	22·0	23·3	4·5
1930	4·0	27·0	19·0	4·2
1931	3·0	32·0	16·0	3·5
1932	3·0	24·0	17·0	4·9

Chapter Four

THE U.S.S.R. AND THE ORGANS OF INTERNATIONAL
CO-OPERATION

HITHERTO the history of Russia's relations with the international organisations of the inter-war period had reflected the vicissitudes in her relations with individual Powers and groups of Powers. From its foundation, the League of Nations had been regarded with suspicion by the Soviet Union. It was denounced at the First Congress of the Communist International as 'the Holy Alliance of the bourgeoisie for the suppression of the proletarian revolution'. As late as 1928, the Manifesto of the Sixth Congress declared: 'The League of Nations, the product of Versailles, the most shameless robber treaty of the last decade, cloaks the war-like work of its members by working out projects for disarmament.' In the period with which we are now concerned the development of Russia's policy must also be illustrated by her activities in the broader field of international co-operation and organisation. Russia's eventual approach to the League was indirect. Her first important contacts had been established through her membership of the Preparatory Commission on Disarmament. In the new period she proved willing to co-operate in other schemes for international action, both political and economic.

The project for closer European union, the so-called Pan-Europa scheme, was launched by Briand in a speech before the League of Nations Assembly on 5 September 1929. In this speech the French statesman suggested that 'among peoples constituting geographical groups like the peoples of Europe, there should be some kind of federal bond'. Following private discussions with the representatives of other States-members of the League, a memorandum 'sur l'organisation fédérale européenne' was circulated by Briand in May 1930 to the Governments concerned.[1] In their replies both Germany and Italy urged the necessity for the inclusion of the Soviet Union (as well as Turkey) in any such scheme. But a plan sponsored by France could hardly at that date be expected to commend itself to the Russians. Stalin's report to the C.P.S.U. of 26 June 1930, makes the Soviet attitude clear:

[1] Printed with a summary of the replies received in *Documents for 1930*, pp. 61–79. The replies are printed in full in *Int. Conc.*, 1930, pp. 653–748.

'The most striking representative,' we read there, 'of the bourgeois movement towards intervention against the Soviet Union is
the bourgeois France of to-day, the fatherland of Pan-Europe, the
cradle of the Kellogg Pact, the most aggressive and militaristic
country, among all aggressive and militaristic countries of the
world.'[1]

In spite of the criticisms which the plan received both from
those who thought it might weaken the more universal machinery of the League and from those who feared that it would
strengthen the political hegemony of France, a commission of
enquiry into the plan, composed of the European States-
members of the League, was set up on 17 September 1930.
When the second session of the Commission began on
16 January 1931, the inclusion of Russia, a non-member of
the League, was strongly pressed by Germany and Italy with
rather lukewarm support from Great Britain, against the opposition of France and her associates. The opposition stressed not
only the political aspects of the question but also the view that
the economic aims of the proposed Union could not be attained
if European markets were thrown open to Russian 'dumping'.
The outcry against the Soviet export drive was at its height in
France at the time.[2] On 20 January it was decided by the
Commission to invite Russia and two other non-Member States
in question, Turkey and Iceland, to participate in the study of
the world economic crisis in so far as it affected Europe as a
whole.[3]

Litvinov's reply to the invitation dealt sharply with the
hesitancies in the Commission's attitude and did not conceal
the profound misgivings of his Government as to the real objects
of the scheme. Nevertheless the invitation was accepted. The
Soviet position was summed-up by *Pravda*:

'The Genevan Pan-Europeans will have to reveal to the great
masses of the people, with what methods and by what means, at
what price and at whose expense, they propose to restore the health
of European capitalism which is suffering from the results of the
world crisis. The Soviet Union does not fear such a discussion and
will not flinch from it. It has in any case plenty of things in general
to discuss with the Genevan "doctors". By taking part in the work
of the European Commission, the Soviet Union will wreck the plans

---

[1] *Documents for 1930*, pp. 122–3. This equivocal reference to the Kellogg
Pact did not prevent Stalin from referring to the Soviet Union's adhesion
to that instrument as one of the results of the Soviet peace policy.

[2] H. Slovès, *La France et l'Union Soviétique*, pp. 307–11; Milioukov, op. cit.,
pp. 377–9.

[3] *Survey for 1930*, pp. 140–1; Davis, op. cit., pp. 223–7.

of the leaders of the Commission, plans for the secret elaboration of
anti-Soviet projects. Let the game be played with the cards on the
table.'[1]

On 16 May, M. Briand welcomed the Russian delegation to
the Commission. M. Litvinov's speech on this occasion had a
new note of seriousness. It was an attempt to refute charges of
particular Russian guilt in the matter of 'dumping', and to
emphasise the importance of the Russian market for the industries of certain countries at a time of increasing economic
depression. Furthermore he put forward a positive proposal in
the shape of an 'economic non-aggression pact'. Each signatory
would reaffirm the declaration of the World Economic Conference of 1927 concerning the possibility of the peaceful co-
existence of two different economic systems and make a pledge
of non-discrimination in future economic relations with the
other participating powers.[2] Neither of the two positive proposals before the Conference could be expected to appeal to
Litvinov. The establishment of an international agricultural
mortgage credit company had been given wide publicity as a
'cure' for Bolshevism in eastern and central Europe. The
proposal for a preferential tariff grouping of these countries was
even more strongly opposed by Litvinov, who was supported by
the German delegate, both of them fearing the exclusion of
their own trade in favour of France and her eastern allies.

When the session ended the tariff proposals as well as the
suggested pact were left for further discussion but the atmosphere was comparatively optimistic. The real difficulties of
co-operation were illustrated at the London conference of
wheat-exporting countries on 18–23 May 1931. Russia's
refusal to consider the restriction of production showed how
far her different economic system prevented her from adopting
methods possible in other countries, and was to some degree
responsible for the conference's failure to come to an agreement.[3]
The deadlock in London proved a better index to Russia's
relationship to the capitalist world at this time than did the
comparative cordiality of Geneva. The fourth session of the
European Union Commission at the beginning of September
1931 produced a serious clash over the proposal that the suggested economic non-aggression pact should be submitted to

[1] Cited in *Osteuropa*, VI, pp. 354–5.
[2] *Report and Proceedings of the International Economic Conference* (League of
Nations Document C. 356, M. 129, 1927). Cf. Florinsky, *World Revolution
and the U.S.S.R.*, pp. 228–9. For the Litvinov proposals, see League Documents, 1931, VII, C. 395, M. 158, pp. 30, 39.
[3] *Survey for 1931*, p. 67; H. V. Hodson, *Slump and Recovery*, p. 231.

the League Assembly. The Russians were still determined not to let their increasingly frequent sojourns in the League's out-works be made an excuse for hauling them in under the leaky roof of the main edifice.

By the end of 1931 the question of dumping had largely fallen into the background owing to a slackening in Russian exports. The Sixth Session of the Commission on European Union, meeting in October 1932, devoted itself to considering schemes for bolstering up the price of cereals--schemes which Litvinov strongly opposed.[1] After this—and with nothing done —the Commission quietly expired.

The other major international activity in which the Soviet Union participated at this time was the discussion of disarmament.[2] As a weak power in the military sense, the Soviet Union had everything to gain from disarmament proposals, however radical.[3] At the same time, the U.S.S.R. could usefully and safely proclaim its adherence to the doctrine of disarmament, even when there was no hope of achieving anything, in order to embarrass the capitalist states by showing up the hypocrisy of their 'pacifism'. After the Preparatory Commission for Disarmament, appointed by the League in 1925, and attended by Soviet representatives from November 1927, had rejected

---

[1] This meeting followed the Stresa Conference in which the Soviet Union had not participated. *Survey for 1932*, I (ii). (The sixth session is there wrongly described as the fifth session.) League of Nations, Document C. 724. M. 342. 1932 VII.

[2] The full proceedings of the Preparatory Commission for Disarmament can be found in the following League documents, Section IX: C. 9. M. 5., C. 425. M. 158., C. 739. M. 278., C. 738. M. 277., 1926; C. 740. M. 279., C. 310. M. 109., C. 667. M. 225. 1927; C. 165. M. 150., C. 358. M. 112., C. 46. M. 23. 1928; C. 195. M. 74. 1929; C. 357. M. 149., C. 687. M. 288. 1930; C. 4. M. 4. 1931. See also Davis, op. cit., chap. 6; Mahaney, op. cit., chaps. 1 and 2. The principal documents on the Soviet side are listed in Taracouzio, *The Soviet Union and International Law*, pp. 305 ff., and many of them are printed in *The Soviet Union and Peace* (Martin Lawrence, 1929), and *L'URSS à la Conférence du Désarmement* (1932). For an authoritative Soviet view see E. A. Korovin 'The U.S.S.R. and Disarmament', *Int. Conc.*, 1933.

[3] The size of the Red Army following the fundamental reorganization of 1925 was 562,000 men. Of the annual contingent of about 1,200,000, 800,000 were reckoned as liable to serve. 260,000 served two years with the Army, 200,000 in the territorial militia, and 340,000 received short-term training outside the regular army. In 1930 the Soviet Union possessed 750 military aircraft. The Navy, mostly concentrated in the Baltic, was not formidable. League of Nations, *Armaments Year Book*, 1926–1927, pp. 845–69; 1930–1931, pp. 872–97; 1939–1940, pp. 345–7. See also A. A. Zaitsov, 'The Armed Forces', in P. Malevsky-Malevitch (ed.), *Russia: U.S.S.R.* (N.Y., Payson, 1933), where figures for the pre-Revolutionary army are also given.

the alternative schemes for total and partial disarmament put
forward by the Soviet Government in 1927 and 1928, the Soviet
members of the Commission continued to use the platform
which the Commission provided in order to demonstrate the
superior humanity and greater consistency of the Soviet viewpoint compared with that of all other countries. In the April-
May 1929 session of the Preparatory Commission, this had led
M. Litvinov to give Russian support to the German thesis that
the 'victor' Powers should reduce their armaments to the
German level, prohibit air bombardment and include trained
reserves in the calculation of effectives. On the other hand, all
Soviet pleas for general disarmament had been met with
scepticism in most foreign quarters, if only because of the contradiction between this policy, and the unrepudiated Soviet
doctrine of the necessary armament of the Proletarian Dictatorship—the Soviet State itself. According to the 1928 programme
of the Communist International, real peace would only be
obtained by the armed peoples of belligerent states turning
their arms against their own ruling classes, turning imperialist
war into civil war.

No considerable change in the Russian attitude was to be
noted when the second meeting of the Sixth (and final) session
of the Preparatory Commission was held at Geneva from
6 November to 9 December 1930. This meeting had been preceded by two important events. At the London Naval Conference (January-April 1930), Great Britain, the United States
and Japan had succeeded in reaching an agreement, although
the differences between France and Italy had proved unbridge-
able.[1] Of equal or greater significance in the sphere of disarmament was the result of the German elections of September
1930. The striking success of the Nazis had not unnaturally
stiffened French insistence that 'security' should have priority
over measures of actual disarmament.

When the Preparatory Commission met, the Russians once
again supported the Germans in their opposition to the majority

[1] For the London Conference, see *Survey for 1930*, I, 11. Cf. C. G. Dawes,
Journal as Ambassador to Great Britain (New York, Macmillan, 1939). Soviet
opinion was that the over-riding antagonism between capitalist states was
that between the British Empire and the United States, and that it was
bound to lead to armed conflict. Molotov in his speech on 5 July, treated
American expressions of sympathy for the Indian nationalist movement as
part of a deliberate campaign to weaken the British Empire for the benefit
of the United States. He bolstered the thesis of the inevitable conflict by a
quotation from Ludwell Denny, the author of *America Conquers Britain* (New
York, Knopf, 1930). *Shestnatsty S'ezd Vsezoyuznoy Kommunisticheskoy Partii (b)*,
(*Sixteenth Congress of the C.P.S.U.*), pp. 413–14. Cf. the remarks of Rykov on
22 May 1929, *Documents for 1929*, pp. 178–9.

proposals and in attempts to go back to questions which had already been settled. The two delegations, together with the Italians, normally formed a solid bloc in voting on controversial issues and were joined from time to time by Turkey and Bulgaria, the United States, and by some of the small ex-neutrals, in opposition to France and her associates and usually to Great Britain as well. On two points, budgetary limitation (Article 10 of the draft convention) and derogations (Article 50), the Soviet Government voted alone in opposition.[1] Similarly, whereas Germany was prepared to allow the final report to go forward with many express reservations, the Russians refused to be associated with it in any way, partly because the report would go to the League Council, a body unrecognised by the U.S.S.R. Their distaste for the League did not however prevent them from demanding that a Memorandum setting out their own views on the subject should be appended to the report; this privilege was refused, but the Memorandum was included in the Minutes and thus circulated to all the Governments concerned.

These were not the only ways in which the Soviet Government emphasised its aloofness. M. Litvinov persisted in his attempts to score off the Powers which were considered to be in the front line of the Soviet Union's enemies. On the question of naval disarmament, for instance, he brought up the question of Tsarist ships seized by the French during and after the Civil War. Nevertheless he continued to be the only member of the Commission who could command a full house of both delegates and journalists, and he enjoyed a considerable measure of sympathy.[2]

Before the Sixth Session concluded its deliberations, M. Litvinov himself went off to meet Signor Grandi at Milan—and significantly enough, travelled by way of Berlin. There on 27 November, he gave a press interview in which he denounced the preponderant Powers in Europe for refusing to reduce their own armaments and the Preparatory Commission for throwing a veil over these tendencies instead of revealing them.[3]

[1] *Survey for 1930*, I (iv); Davis, op. cit., pp. 156–62. For the Draft Convention see *Documents for 1931*, pp. 18–38. By 'derogation' was meant the possibility of a temporary increase in armaments in special circumstances. The Report of the Sixth Session is in League Documents, 1931, IX. C. 4. M. 4.

[2] He was less popular with diplomats and soldiers of the old school. See H. Wilson, *A Diplomat between Wars* (New York, Longmans, 1941), pp. 254–5. For a sympathetic summary of Litvinov's work and attitude to Soviet Foreign Policy, see Louis Fischer, *Men and Politics*, pp. 124–7.

[3] *Survey for 1930*, p. 120 n.; Mahaney, op. cit., p. 104.

Russia's dissatisfaction with the Draft Convention did not of course diminish M. Litvinov's determination that the Soviet Government should be represented on the even bigger stage of the World Disarmament Conference itself. The preparations for the Conference were in the hands of the League Council. Russia called attention to the unfairness of this procedure to those Powers who were included in the disarmament negotiations but not in the League itself. This was done in a remarkable note addressed on 12 January 1931 to those Governments on the League Council with whom Russia had diplomatic relations. In this communication, the President of the Preparatory Commission, M. Loudon, was accused of anti-Soviet bias. This was to be explained by the fact that his own country, Holland, had no relations with the Soviet Union and was thus misinformed about conditions there. The President of the Conference should not come from a State of this kind, nor from one which had

'taken up a distinctly negative position towards disarmament at the Preparatory Commission, nor from a State whose developed armament industry made her economically interested in the growth of armaments on an international scale.'

The final provision was clearly directed against Dr. Benes, whom the Russians (and the Germans) considered altogether too pro-French. The disquisition on a choice of President for the Conference concluded by objecting to anyone who had shown hostile feelings towards 'one or another of the countries represented'. In addition the Soviet Government objected to the Conference being held in Switzerland, where the atmosphere, poisoned by the Geneva press and local anti-Soviet groups, was not a congenial one for the Soviet delegation to work in.[1] On 22 May, Mr. Arthur Henderson, the British Foreign Minister, was appointed President of the Conference, but Geneva was chosen as the meeting place. The Swiss Government had never recognised the Soviet Government, and relations had been very strained since the murder in 1923 of Vorovsky, a Soviet delegate to the Lausanne Conference. An invitation despatched to the U.S.S.R. in September, to be represented on the Third Committee of the League Assembly to discuss Italian proposals for an armaments truce, was rejected on account of the shortness of the notice, but the truce was agreed to by the Soviet Government.[2]

When the Disarmament Conference opened on 2 February

[1] *Documents for 1931*, pp. 68–70.
[2] ibid., pp. 39 and 97–104.

1932, the U.S.S.R. supplied the eleventh of the fourteen vice-presidents elected, receiving fewer votes than Japan, one of the two States which, as M. Litvinov put it in his speech on the 11th, though 'mutually bound by the Covenant and the Paris Pact of 1928' had been 'in a state of war, *de facto*, if not *de jure*, for five months'.[1] Such symptoms of the international mistrust of the Soviet Union did not prevent Litvinov from stating the customary Soviet thesis with his usual intransigence, if in a slightly more conciliatory manner than usual. The Soviet Government still stood by their view that security against war could only result from 'total disarmament'. The French proposals of 5 February—the Tardieu plan—came in for severe criticism.[2] An international army under the control of the League would be an insufficient deterrent for a stronger State wishing to attack a weaker; and although the 'unsophisticated man-in-the-street' could probably correctly name the aggressor in any particular incident, the competence of governments and international organizations in this respect was more doubtful.

'I pass over,' said Litvinov, 'the question of the extent to which the Soviet Union could be expected to confide its security and a part of its own armies to an international organisation of states openly hostile to it even to the extent of refusing to maintain normal relations with it.'

Events in the Far East, and in particular the activities of Russian emigrés, were declared to be a cause of special anxiety to the Soviet Union, which would however not prevent the Soviet Union from agreeing to disarm 'to the same extent and at the same rate' as other Powers.

After the conclusion of the general debates of the Conference, the scene shifted on 24–25 February to the General Commission, at which there was another discussion of the Soviet thesis put forward in a written communication of 18 February. This took the form of an amended version of the Draft Convention presented to the Preparatory Commission by the Russians on 23 March 1928.[3] The Soviet objective remained total disarmament, but they claimed that the principle of the proportionate reduction of armaments could be reconciled with this objective by setting the goal of reduction at 'parity at zero'. The Soviet proposals found support only from Germany,

---

[1] *Records of the Disarmament Conference, Series A*, vol. I. p. 81. For this and the following paragraphs, see Mahaney, op. cit., chap. 4; Davis, op. cit., pp. 166–93.

[2] The Tardieu plan is summarised in *Documents for 1931*, p. 160–1.

[3] *Documents for 1932*, p. 168; League Documents 1932, IX. Conf. D. 82.

Turkey and Persia; nor would M. Litvinov agree to an attempt
by the Spanish delegate to bridge the differences by a formula.
The Soviet delegation, in order to avoid a charge of obstruction,
ultimately agreed to the British proposal to proceed on the
basis of the draft convention of the Preparatory Commission.

In the discussion of Article 1 of this Draft Convention on
12 April, Litvinov put forward concrete suggestions for the
proportionate reduction of existing armed forces. These were
based on an amended version of the Soviet Draft Convention
of 23 March 1928.[1] M. Litvinov declared that the Soviet
Government were not committed to the figures in their draft
and would be satisfied with the acceptance of its principles:
compulsory and substantial reduction of all armaments on the
progressive-proportional principle, and the abolition of all
'aggressive' armaments. The ensuing discussion saw an important cleavage between the Russian and the German viewpoints.
The Germans declined to accept 'the principle of purely
mechanical reduction' and urged the necessity of recognising
'the special circumstances of each State' as provided for in
Article 8 of the League Covenant. This principle was adopted
by the General Commission on 20 April, Litvinov's being the
only negative vote.

The Soviet delegation also participated in the work of the
technical commissions set up to classify naval, land, and air
armaments according to their 'aggressive' qualities. In the
Naval Commission, which failed to reach any agreement, the
Soviet representatives tended to find themselves at one with the
majority of the Commission in opposition to the representatives
of the great naval Powers. The report of the Land Commission
was accompanied by a Soviet reservation to the effect that the
long recital of the difficulties of classification which the report
contained was 'preparing the ground for bringing the whole
principle of qualitative disarmament into question'. The
majority report of the Air Commission was also rejected on the
ground that all air armaments were aggressive. In the Committee on Effectives, which also found agreement impossible,
the U.S.S.R. again linked up with Germany to oppose a French
proposal to limit the definition of 'pre-military training' to that
undergone by youths under eighteen.

The Soviet Government took no part in the series of private
discussions held in June between some of the Great Powers to
find some way forward from the existing deadlock. When the
General Commission was reconvened, an effort to chart progress was made in a resolution presented by Dr. Benes on

[1] *Minutes of the General Commission*, vol. I, p. 46.

20 July.[1] To this extremely cautious document, M. Litvinov proposed a number of amendments. The first of these would have replaced the last paragraph of the preamble with the following unequivocal text:

'[The Conference] decides that a reduction of existing armaments by not less than 33⅓ per cent shall be effected in all categories of land, naval and other armaments, with exemption for small countries respectively possessing armies of not above 30,000 men and a total naval tonnage of not above 100,000 tons, and also for countries which have been subjected to disarmament in virtue of other international agreements.'

Albania, Lithuania, Colombia and Turkey were the only States to join the U.S.S.R. in voting for the amendment. Thirty States voted against and sixteen, including Germany and Italy, abstained. The remaining amendments, all on familiar lines, were also rejected.

The Benes resolution was put to the vote on 23 July and adopted by 41 votes to 2—the U.S.S.R. and Germany. (Italy, China and Turkey were among the eight abstainers.) The nature of the Russian stand was made plain in M. Litvinov's closing remark: 'I vote for disarmament but against the resolution.' The Germans on the other hand were now openly concerned about 'equality' for themselves rather than disarmament, and declared their unwillingness to participate further in the work of the Conference until equality was conceded. They were thus not present when the Bureau met in September. This did not prevent Litvinov from urging (unsuccessfully) that the Bureau should proceed forthwith to an examination of the various plans for disamament already before the Conference. Instead, informal five-Power talks at Geneva in December (in which the Russians took no part) produced a formula sufficiently acceptable to the Germans for them to take their places again when the Conference reassembled.

The General Commission, meeting again on 14 December 1932, took note of this result and of a new French plan for disarmament and security which had been made public in November, and then once more adjourned, leaving the work to be carried on in informal private discussions—a procedure against which M. Litvinov protested. It met again on 2 February 1933 (three days after Hitler had become German Chancellor) to consider the French plan, which received critical handling from the Germans and Italians. M. Litvinov, who spoke on the 6th, confined his remarks almost entirely to

[1] *Documents for 1932*, pp. 232-4.

Chapter I of the French plan.[1] This amounted to an extension of the principles of the Kellogg Pact to include the taking of measures against the aggressor. To these proposals the Soviet Government were prepared to agree. M. Litvinov however insisted that the reservations which various Powers had made to the Kellogg Pact itself should be repudiated or cancelled by international agreement. Since the French plan involved the naming of an aggressor before action could be taken, M. Litvinov further proposed a draft convention for the definition of aggression of an all-embracing kind. This document included not only lists of acts which would be held to constitute aggression, but also a list of circumstances whose existence was not to be alleged as excuse for military measures or for a blockade. These reflected very clearly the various reasons which had been put forward for foreign intervention in Russia during the Civil War.

These suggestions of M. Litvinov mark a fundamental transition from the previous emphasis on 'disarmament' to an alternative conception of 'security'.[2] As such they were welcomed by France, the Little Entente and most of the smaller States, including Russia's neighbours. On the other hand there was no official indication of any weakening in Russia's distrust of existing international institutions.

The Soviet definition of aggression was referred to a Sub-Committee on Security Questions, where its rigidity was criticized by several delegates, including those of Great Britain, Germany and Italy. Meanwhile the main deliberations of the Conference turned upon a British proposal that the European States should make a solemn affirmation of their determination not to resort to force. Faithful to the Soviet doctrine of universalism, M. Litvinov in vain urged the extension of the declaration to cover the whole world and this was supported by Turkey, Persia, and Afghanistan, and not unnaturally by China.[3]

The next stage was the discussion of the British Draft Convention, the 'MacDonald Plan' of 16 March.[4] M. Dovgalevsky, the Soviet representative, criticised the plan for giving figures of effectives for European countries only (and not for all of these) and pointed out that the table for aircraft was likewise incomplete. The Soviet delegation was 'more partiularly conc-

[1] *Documents for 1932*, pp. 217–34. *General Commission Minutes*, vol. II, p. 234.
[2] For the importance attached to these proposals and especially to the non-intervention aspect, see Florinsky, op. cit., pp. 237–8.
[3] The Declaration was accepted by twenty-six votes to none with many abstentions.
[4] *Documents for 1933*, pp. 151–93.

cerned with the air forces of certain of its neighbours, among them first and foremost those of Japan,' account being had of the fact that the latter country had 'recently made it possible for itself to form a supplementary air fleet outside its own frontiers'. The British retention of air-bombing for police purposes in certain outlying areas also came in for criticism, while the naval clauses were criticised as being biased in favour of the signatories of the Washington and London Treaties.

In further discussions of the British Draft (April–May 1933), the Polish delegates proposed the amendment of Part 1 so as to ensure the continued collaboration of non-League States and particularly of the United States and the U.S.S.R. in the question of disarmament. The Soviet amendments were designed to strengthen the security provisions, and to dissociate these as far as possible from the machinery of the League. The Soviet delegates proposed that the suggested limitation on the numbers of effectives be extended to non-European Powers.

The principle of a Permanent Disarmament Commission with supervisory functions, provided for in Part V, was accepted by the Soviet delegation, but it was declared that the Soviets would have proposals to make with regard to the composition of the Commission.[1]

Meanwhile on 24 May, the Sub-Committee on Security Questions had presented a resolution on the definition of an aggressor which embodied most of the Soviet proposals.[2] In the General Commission, the main objector was Mr. Eden, on the usual British ground that rigid commitments were to be avoided. Like Sir Austen Chamberlain before him, he thought that 'such a definition would be liable to be a trap for the innocent and a protection for the guilty'.[3]

No more was heard of the subject at the Conference itself, but M. Litvinov revived the idea during his visit to London for the World Economic Conference.[4] He proposed that the parties to the Litvinov Protocol of 1929 should sign a multi-lateral treaty of non-aggression based on the Sub-Committee's resolution of 24 May. On 3 July, a treaty of this kind was accordingly signed by representatives of the U.S.S.R., Afghanistan, Esthonia,

[1] Cf. Arts. 47–54 of the Soviet Draft Convention of 15 February 1928. Professional soldiers and officials in war ministries, together with those financially or professionally interested in the manufacture of arms, would be excluded. *Int. Conc.*, 1933, pp. 327–9.
[2] *Documents of the Conference for the Reduction and Limitation of Armaments.* vol. ii, pp. 679–90.
[3] *House of Commons Debates*, 24 November 1927.
[4] The Disarmament Conference adjourned on 8 June 1933; the World Economic Conference met on 12 June and adjourned on 27 July 1933.

E

Latvia, Persia, Poland, Roumania and Turkey. On 5 July, an identical agreement was signed between the U.S.S.R. and Lithuania. On the previous day a similar convention had been concluded by the U.S.S.R., Turkey, Roumania, Czecho-slovakia, and Yugoslavia, but on this occasion the agreement was specifically left open for the adherence of all other countries.[1] Finland adhered to it on 23 July.[2] Thus Soviet activities at Geneva had culminated in a further strengthening on familiar lines of their old security policy.

On the other hand, the schemes put forward at the World Economic Conference by the Soviet representatives were once again without effect. On 14 June, the Soviet delegation proposed a mutual withdrawal of all discriminations against the trade of particular countries (the dispute with Britain had not yet been ended) and M. Litvinov again elaborated his idea of an economic non-aggression pact.[3] Another project was to arrange some scheme of credits which would enable Russia (and other needy countries) to increase their purchases on the over-stocked markets of the world. Nothing came of either of these proposals. The Soviet delegation, however, unruffled by the bitter attacks made upon their competition in the field of timber by the Canadians,[4] or even by the extraordinary outburst on 16 June by Herr Hugenberg on the subject of Germany's needs for eastern expansion, remained in a remarkably conciliatory mood throughout, even agreeing to consider in common with other affected States a future limitation of their wheat exports.[5] The Soviet delegation also agreed to a tariff truce resolution, in contrast to their attitude in 1927, when they

[1] *Documents for 1933*, pp. 230–3; cf. *The Baltic States* (R.I.I.A.), pp. 76–8.

[2] *Survey for 1933*, p. 183.

[3] The only supporters of the proposal for an economic non-aggression pact were Turkey, Poland, and the Irish Free State. Litvinov's speech of 14 June is printed in *Soviet Union Review*, July-August 1933.

[4] The Russian view was that Canadian and Russian exports, being of different kinds of timber, could not compete and that the attacks on the exports of Russian timber were political. Yanson, op. cit., pp. 111 ff. The Canadians finally succeeded in getting Britain to reduce her proposed imports from Russia for 1934. Britain had agreed to such action at the Ottawa Conference. W. K. Hancock, *Survey of British Commonwealth Affairs* (Oxford University Press for R.I.I.A., 3 vols., 1937–1942), II, i, 226. The controversy was already a long-standing one. See the pamphlet *Forced Labour in Russia*, published by the *British Russian Gazette* in March 1931; and the *Statement on Russian Timber* by a committee of the Timber Trade Federation of the United Kingdom (April 1931).

[5] A Wheat Conference met on 20 August and an agreement was signed on the 25th (text in *Documents for 1933*, pp. 111–15). The Soviet export quota for 1933–1934 was left over for negotiation. In actual fact Soviet wheat exports were henceforward negligible in quantity.

argued that such proposals took no account of the Soviet trade monopoly system.

The only reflection of the old intransigence was to be found in the final speech of M. Maisky, who had been left to deal with the latter part of the Conference, after the departure first of M. Litvinov and then of M. Mezhlauk. He foresaw in the unrestricted economic nationalism which the Conference had revealed the forerunner of possible armed conflicts. 'The whole work of the Conference,' he observed, 'has been deeply penetrated by one fundamental mood, one aspiration: adjournment —to adjourn the adoption of any serious or binding decisions on those problems.'

Chapter Five

RUSSIA AND THE WEIMAR REPUBLIC

THE fundamental change in Soviet foreign policy between 1929 and 1936 was in the relationships between Russia and Germany. The dynamic element in this change was clearly the German one—the transition from the Weimar Republic to the Third Reich. It was the aggressive potentialities of the latter which drove the Soviet Union to seek new guarantees for its security and at the same time made other countries less unwilling to enter into agreements with this hitherto outcast régime. In no sphere was the basic dualism between national and revolutionary policies revealed more clearly than in the contacts between Russia and Germany, and in none were its repercussions more lasting.

The primary rôle played by Germany in Soviet foreign policy during the first twelve years after the Revolution requires little explanation. Geographical propinquity had of necessity made her the principal agent of 'westernisation' in Russia since the eighteenth century, and the latest phase of Russian history could from one angle be regarded as merely a continuation of this process. The mutual sympathies of the two Empires before 1914 had made it difficult to break the links forged by Bismarckian diplomacy even in face of the implications for Russia of the *Drang nach Osten*.[1] And the breach when it did come was regretted by a not inconsiderable section of Russian right-wing opinion.

Russia's massive contribution to the Allied victory in the Great War, although obscured in Western minds by the events of 1917, was never overlooked by the vanquished. The post-war diplomacy of Germany under all its leaders was dominated by a fixed determination to avoid the errors of over-confidence attributed to William II and to assure Germany's recovery by neutralising either Russia or the West. But the policy of friendship with Russia, renewed by the Treaty of Rapallo in April 1922, was not without its problems, even if there was a new binding link in the temporary isolation and weakness of both Powers.[2] For the war, the Russian Revolution and the German

---

[1] In spite of the penetration of French capital into pre-Revolutionary Russia, Germany, whose capital was required at home, remained by far Russia's most important commercial partner.

[2] On this, see *Survey for 1920–1923*, pp. 30–1; *Survey for 1925*, II, pp. 63–6; *Survey for 1927*, II, E, (v).

quasi-Revolution (or *révolution manquée*) altered and complicated the material, ideological and even psychological relationships between the two countries.[1] Until the débâcle of the extreme left in Germany in 1923, the dominant factor in many Russian minds was the possibility of a Communist revolution in Germany. After 1923 this became less plausible as an immediate possibility.[2] At the same time, Stresemann's policy of 'fulfilment' led to a reorientation of German policy along lines to which the Locarno treaties and her entry into the League of Nations were the most conspicuous signposts. Nevertheless, although, as already noted, the efforts of Soviet diplomacy to prevent this development were on the whole without effect, the Russian link, in spite of the internal difficulties which it created, was too valuable a weapon in the still lean arsenal of German diplomacy for it to be lightly abandoned, and the Treaty of 1926, and the convention regarding conciliation procedure of 25 January 1929, marked a substantial confirmation of the earlier intimacy.[3] Russia's slower approach to some sort of accommodation with the Western Powers met with a less cordial response, but even so, her hitherto almost total dependence on Germany was appreciably mitigated. The new freedom of manœuvre possessed by both sides enabled them to indulge in occasional disharmonies without disturbing the basis of their co-operation, which was discontent with the existing state of affairs in Europe, even though the nature of the changes hoped for was scarcely identical in the two cases. This co-operation, as has been noted, reached its peak in 1930.

[1] There is a useful and documented survey of Russo-German relations, 1918–1933, in Taracouzio, *War and Peace in Soviet Diplomacy*, pp. 177–86; cf. Ernst Fraenkel: 'German-Russian Relations since 1918', *Review of Politics*, January 1940; J. H. Morgan, *Assize of Arms*, vol. I (Methuen, 1945), pp. 145–73.

[2] For the rôle of the Comintern in the revolutionary movement in 1923 and the abortive Hamburg Communist rising, see A. Rosenberg, *History of Bolshevism* (Oxford University Press, 1939), chap. 9. Cf. D. Dallin, *Russia and Post-War Europe* (Yale University Press, 1943), pp. 56–7. Radek, the Comintern's agent in Germany, seems to have acted as a drag rather than as a spur. *Survey for 1924*, pp. 212–17.

[3] The Treaty of Berlin was accompanied by assurances designed to dispel Russian fears that Art. XVI of the League Covenant could be used by the League Powers to bring Germany into an attack upon the régime. Exchange of letters between Stresemann and Krestinsky, *Int. Conc.*, 1929, pp. 406–8. It has been suggested that the German orientation of Soviet foreign policy after 1924 was largely attributable to the influence of Stalin, and explained by him on the ground that Germany was an 'oppressed' nation and support of Germany therefore justifiable on Marxist lines. B. I. Nikolaevsky: 'Vneshnaya Politika Moskvi' (The Foreign Policy of Moscow), *Novy Zhurnal*, No. 3. The same article gives some interesting data on the pro-Russian elements in German politics (apart from the Communists).

A further link between the two countries was the existence between them of a resurrected Poland, functioning as a pivot of the French alliance system in Eastern Europe. Russia had threatened to intervene in the first half of 1923, in case Poland took advantage of the Ruhr crisis to attack East Prussia.[1] The limitations in the outlook of the Western Powers revealed by Locarno suggested that German expansion in the East might not meet with their whole-hearted opposition. But the increasing friction between Poland and Germany did not lead to any substantial *rapprochement* between the two Slav Powers.[2] Indeed, in spite of the anti-Polish orientation of Stresemann's policy, Germany remained on a better footing with both Russia and Poland than the two could attain with respect to each other.[3]

The fairly consistent support which Germany received from Russia both on reparations, to which Russia renounced all rights by the Rapallo Treaty, and on disarmament, is thus not hard to explain. In addition, there was as already noted a very considerable degree of economic co-operation, which brought to the support of Russo-German collaboration precisely those social groups among whom the greatest dislike of the Russian régime might normally be expected to exist.

In spite of their horror of Bolshevism, some German military leaders were apparently prepared in the immediate post-war years for a full alliance with Russia. It is possible that the first attempt of this kind was only frustrated by the collapse of the Russian offensive against Warsaw in 1920.[4] In 1921, while Lenin was busy securing the full obedience of the German Communists to the Communist International, Radek would seem to have been in contact with such prominent personalities of the German military machine as General Hoffmann and Colonel Bauer.[5] In 1923 German Communists and German Nationalists were to be found fighting Rhenish separatism under the same slogans, and a so-called nationalist-bolshevist move-

---

[1] Fischer, op. cit., chap. 15. Later in the year the evolution of Germany towards a revolutionary crisis temporarily altered the emphasis in Soviet policy.

[2] Relations between Poland and Germany, 1926–1932, are dealt with in *Survey for 1932*, IV (ii).

[3] At the time of the Russo-Polish tension in the summer of 1927, we find Austen Chamberlain appealing to Stresemann that 'having regard to the relations between the two countries' he should 'take the initiative in using his influence on Russia' so as to find a settlement. G. Stresemann, *Diaries, Letters and Papers* (3 vols., Macmillan, 1935–1940), vol. iii, pp. 161–5.

[4] E. Wollenberg, *The Red Army*, pp. 235–7.

[5] These transactions were revealed by Radek in 1926 during a period of temporary estrangement between the two Powers. See the first of Nikolaevsky's articles in *Novy Zhurnal*, No. 1.

ment was started to link the two struggles.[1] Whatever be the truth about the political aspects of these contacts, there is no doubt that some kind of agreement between the two armies followed Rapallo. In May 1922 a liaison bureau of the German Army is said to have been set up in Moscow. Factories were set up in Russia by Junkers and other German firms; forbidden armaments were manufactured and experiments in aeronautics and chemical warfare carried out. In addition, German specialist troops and airmen were trained, while the Russians on their side received valuable assistance in converting the Red Army into a modern fighting force. The period of active co-operation did not last very long. The Junkers factory seems to have closed down in 1925.[2]

The German Social-Democrats were the first to draw public attention to these contacts. This aggravated the Comintern's hostility towards them.

The Russian Government's pre-occupation with Germany was paralleled by that of the Comintern with the German Communist Party. The respect which Russian revolutionaries had acquired in exile for the solidly organised phalanx of German Social Democracy had been genuine enough, even if tinged with a humorous contempt for the 'respectability' and 'legalism' of the German Left.[3] The conduct of the German Social-Democrats during the war and the German 'revolution' had changed this respect to unmitigated hostility, but something of the old aura remained attached to the German Communist Party,[4] in spite of its sad history of defeats, schisms, and purges. The hope thus placed in the revolutionary abilities of the German Communist Party did not imply of course any

---

[1] G. Reimann, *Germany, World Empire or World Revolution* (Secker & Warburg, 1938), p. 29. National-bolshevism is dealt with by Fraenkel, loc. cit., pp. 43–7. Its adherents were later absorbed by the Communists and the Nazis.

[2] G. R. Treviranus, *Revolution in Russia* (New York, Harper, 1944), pp. 221–2. Treviranus was a member of Brüning's Government, 1930–1932. H. Rosinski, *The German Army*, pp. 192–5; Fraenkel, loc. cit., p. 52; E. Schmidt-Pauli, *General von Seeckt*, pp. 107–12; L. Fischer, *The Soviets in World Affairs*, p. 601. Fischer writes that 'responsible Bolshevik statesmen have denied to the writer the existence of any such arrangement or co-operation', but see note 1 on p. 69 *infra*.

[3] See Stalin's remarks to Emil Ludwig on 31 December 1931; *Bolshevik* (Moscow, C.P.S.U.), 30 April 1932.

[4] See the remarks on this point of E. Wollenberg, op. cit., pp. 266–71. In 1928, the German Communist Party was second in size only to that of Czechoslovakia among the non-Russian parties. W. H. Chamberlin, *Soviet Russia*, p. 280. In July 1930 Molotov called it 'the best party of the Communist International' next to the C.P.S.U. *Report to Sixteenth Congress of the C.P.S.U.*, p. 39.

variation from the normal Comintern practice of dictating the policy of its constituent members from Moscow. No doubt, however, the German scene was to some extent interpreted through the eyes of the German Communists and the errors made by the Russians can to some extent presumably be explained by this.[1]

The first major contribution of the Communists towards the débâcle of the German Republic was their decision to run a Presidential candidate in 1925—a decision which made possible the victory of Hindenburg. Between that date and 1933, their rôle continued to be a dual one. By word and deed they made fatal inroads into what elements of resistance to Fascism existed in the German working-class and trade-union movement. In the second place, they helped the extreme nationalists to make physical terror and violence the normal agents of Germany's internal political life. From this too, Hitler alone profited.

The intensification of the drive against Social Democracy (Social-Fascism in the Comintern jargon of the time) whether by direct assault or by the indirect approach of the 'united front from below', was the major if not the only achievement of the Sixth Comintern Congress in 1928, and of the Fifth Congress of the Profintern (the Red International of Labour Unions) in 1930. As far as Germany is concerned, the policy must be pronounced a success, for in the later stages of the Republic's agony there is no doubt that the Comintern, if not all German Communists, viewed the possibility of a period of Nazi rule with something like equanimity.

The miscalculation, whose depths were only revealed in 1941–1942, is even now difficult to explain.

It is possible that the Russians were prepared to accept a period of Fascism in Germany, with its inevitable exacerbation of class-conflict, as a necessary prelude to an ultimate Communist victory. It is also possible that the Russian leaders may

---

[1] The fundamental books for understanding this aspect of Russo-German relations are: F. Borkenau, *The Communist International*, and A. Rosenberg, *History of the German Republic* (Methuen, 1936), and *History of Bolshevism*. 'Revelations' like those of W. G. Krivitsky, *I was Stalin's Agent* (Hamish Hamilton, 1939), must of course be treated with caution. Impressive among them is *Out of the Night* (Heinemann, 1941), by 'Jan Valtin', valuable for its picture of the total moral disarray of large sections of German youth—a moral disarray which, like the economic and social maladies of German society, was used to much greater effect by the Nazis than by the Communists. The best account of the later years of Weimar is that of R. T. Clark, *The Fall of the German Republic* (Allen & Unwin, 1935). Also useful is J. Wheeler-Bennett, *Hindenburg: The Wooden Titan* (Macmillan, 1936). Every aspect of German politics is covered in the copious annotated bibliography to *Hitler's Speeches*, ed. N. H. Baynes.

have been aware all along that the Communists had no immediate chance of triumphing in Germany and would not indeed have welcomed a full-scale Communist upheaval which would interfere with the delicate and important commercial relationships between the two countries.

The alternative policy of co-operation with the Social Democrats might have strengthened this party, and therewith the forces in Germany favourable to a *rapprochement* with the West.

These interpretations still leave unexplained the total misapprehension, on the Communist side, of the nature and purposes of the Nazi movement, which the Comintern Plenum described in April 1931 as a petty-bourgeois movement at the service of the German bourgeoisie.[1] Communist theory made no allowance for a movement which was at once revolutionary and non-proletarian.

The Comintern Congress of 1928 was followed at once by an important intervention on the part of Moscow in the affairs of the German Communist Party, which had gained a considerable success in the May elections, having secured 54 seats in the Reichstag.[2] The vote of the Social-Democrats and Communists taken together had reached 40 per cent of the whole, and some of the leaders of the Communist Party were in favour of a measure of co-operation with the other working-class party. These leaders were however removed in favour of the more pliant Thaelmann, and the way was clear for carrying out the

---

[1] Bela Kun, *Kommunisticheski Internatsional v Dokumentakh* (*The Communist International in Documents*), pp. 958–9. The share of the Comintern in bringing about the rise of Hitler must be accounted a very considerable one. It is perhaps interesting to note that this responsibility is one of the chief accusations made by Trotsky and his followers against the Comintern. Trotsky himself writes: 'the defeat of the Chinese revolution in 1925–1927, which untied the hands of Japanese militarism in the East, and the shattering of the German proletariat which led to Hitler and the mad growth of German militarism, are alike the fruits of the policy of the Communist International', *The Revolution Betrayed* (Faber & Faber, 1937), p. 183. B. Souvarine writes: 'Just as the Polish Communists supported the military *coup d'état* of Pilsudski before burning their fingers with it, so those of Germany had several times made common cause with Hitler, only to expiate soon after in concentration camps and on the scaffold the insane policy of their leaders'. *Stalin*, p. 586. Victor Serge writes of Comintern policy in Germany 'cette tactique criminelle aura pour résultat l'écrasement sans combat du prolétariat allemand'. *Destin d'une Révolution* (Paris, 1937), p. 292. Cf. C. L. R. James, *World Revolution* (Secker & Warburg, 1937), chap. 12, 'After Hitler, Our Turn'; R. T. Clark, op. cit., pp. 199–208; A. J. P. Taylor, *The Course of German History* (Hamish Hamilton, 1945), pp. 193–4. See note 2 on p. 69 *infra*.

[2] Appendix to this chapter.

fight against Social Democracy with the full vigour prescribed by the central authority.[1]

In foreign politics the Communists joined with the Nationalist parties in violent propaganda against any *rapprochement* with the Western Powers and against the acceptance of the Young Plan for the settlement of the Reparations question. This agitation marked the autumn of 1929 and the succeeding winter months, earning praise for the Party's greater 'discipline' from the meeting of the enlarged Plenum of the Comintern in February.[2]

The elections of September 1930 had been preceded by Communist gains in local elections, and, with the wave of extremism sweeping the country, the Party may well have anticipated a considerable measure of success. Their propaganda was primarily directed against the Social-Democrats, whose solid phalanxes they had so far failed to weaken in either the political or industrial field, but their real appeal was evidently to the desperate sections of the middle-classes, to the unemployed and to new voters particularly among the young. The Nazis, concerned at this stage with garnering all the middle-class and Nationalist vote, made no attempt to compete for the votes of the proletariat. In the upshot (in a larger Reichstag) there were sixteen more Communists and two fewer Socialists. The Nazis had however increased their vote by over $4\frac{1}{2}$ million and their membership in the Reichstag from 13 to 105, making them the second largest party.

The Social-Democrats could in the circumstances adopt no other policy than that of support for Brüning. The Communists, unremittingly pursuing their vendetta against them, now adopted the deliberate wrecking tactics of the 'united front from below'. Meanwhile they assisted the Nazis in making constitutional government as difficult as possible by rowdyism in the Reichstag.[3] There is some evidence that early in 1931 a deliberate decision was taken to co-operate in the country with the Nazis in order to accelerate the destruction of the Social-Democratic Party and its organisations.[4] This was strictly in accordance with the declared view of the Eleventh

[1] Borkenau, op. cit., p. 337.
[2] Clark, op. cit., p. 269. Kun, op. cit., pp. 944 ff.
[3] Clark, op. cit., pp. 307–11; Borkenau, op. cit., p. 342.
[4] Clark, op. cit., p. 311. The actual growth of the Nazis at this time was almost entirely at the expense of the non-Catholic bourgeois parties. The 'Works Councils' elections in 1930 and 1931, while registering a slight advance for the Communists, showed that the organised workers were still overwhelmingly Social-Democrat. M. S. Wertheimer, 'The Political Outlook in Germany', *Foreign Policy Reports* (Foreign Policy Association, New York), 27 April 1932.

Plenum of the Comintern (March–April 1931) that the German Social-Democratic Party, the strongest party in the Second International, was the most active party in Germany in preparing for an attack on the Soviet Union.[1]

When, in April 1931 (the month in which the 'Piatakov' trade agreement was signed), the Nazis and Nationalists succeeded in their demand for a referendum aiming at the overthrow of the Socialist-led Government of Prussia, the Communists took part in the campaign on their side. On this occasion a large number of Communists clearly refused to follow their leaders into the Nazi-Nationalist camp. It has nevertheless been estimated that the referendum received from $2\frac{1}{2}$ to 3 million Communist votes.[2] Meanwhile Russo-German links remained firm. The 1926 Treaty and 1929 Conciliation Convention were prolonged by a protocol signed at Moscow on 24 June 1931.[3]

The Communists again played a lone hand in the Presidential election of March–April 1932. Besides their growing strength among the normally Nationalist elements of the population, the Nazis polled strongly in some working-class districts and demonstrated their strength again in various State elections.[4]

The Communist tactics in the July Reichstag elections were substantially unaltered. Having finally rejected the idea of a genuine united front,[5] they appear to have lost all sight of a definite objective, at times co-operating with the Nazis against the Social-Democratic 'Iron Front', and at other times engaging in sanguinary street fighting with the Nazis themselves. (The main result of the disorders was to provide von Papen later in the year with an excuse for dismissing the Prussian Government as unable to keep order.)

The result of the July elections showed that the solid voting-strength of the Centre and Social-Democrat Parties was un-

---

[1] Kun, op. cit., p. 969.   [2] Borkenau, op. cit., pp. 323–4 and 343–4.

[3] The German ratification of the protocol only took place on 5 May 1933. *Survey for 1933*, p. 588. Fraenkel argues that this did not happen before because Brüning and his successor Papen both feared that its ratification would be attacked by the parties opposed to a Russian orientation and in particular by the Nazis, loc. cit., p. 40.

[4] On the final stages of the Nazi rise to power, see *Survey for 1933*, II (i), (b) and (c). Rosenberg points out that the peak of the Communist electoral success was to obtain 5,000,000 or so votes, whereas at one time the unemployed with their dependants had alone a voting strength of 9,000,000. *History of Bolshevism*, p. 234.

[5] Heinrich Mann in *Der Hass* (Amsterdam, 1933), refers to unsuccessful efforts made in 1932 to bring about co-operation between Communists and Social-Democrats (p. 121).

diminished. In a slightly enlarged Reichstag, in which the Nazi
strength rose from 105 to 230 seats, the Communists had gained
a mere dozen seats. Hitler's unequivocal triumph was acclaimed
by the Communists as a success for themselves.

The replacing of Brüning by Papen was by no means welcomed in Moscow, where the latter was regarded as 'the
advocate of a conservative entente between France and
Germany, the spearhead of which was to be directed against
the Soviet Union'.[1] Nevertheless, on 23 July 1932, Russian
and German policies at the Disarmament Conference, which
had shown signs of diverging from each other, again became
identical and their delegations formed a minority of two
against the 'Benes resolution'.

With regard to Germany's internal politics, Moscow still
denounced the Social-Democrats for having supported von
Papen as the 'lesser evil' (i.e. as preferable to Hitler). They
had, it was alleged, carried their support into the realm of
foreign policy.[2] Dubious arithmetical calculations were made
to show that the Communists had made important strides in
proletarian areas, and in a Soviet periodical the situation was
discussed under the heading: 'The German Communist Party
on the Eve of Winning a Majority.'[3]

In the circumstances it is hardly surprising that the Communists, in spite of much revolutionary talk, were unable to
turn to account the situation in the autumn of 1932, which one
competent observer (R. T. Clark) described as genuinely revolutionary. The Communists were apparently bewildered, and
failed to receive a clear lead which would enable them to make
use of the left-ward trend noticeable even among the Storm-
troopers themselves at a time when their wages, like the Nazi
Party's funds generally, were running low. There was no
attempt to reconsider their policy in the light of the changing
circumstances in Germany. Slogans such as 'Defend the Soviet
Union' and 'Defend China' could hardly compete with Herr
Hitler's nationalist demagogy.

The Twelfth Plenum of the Executive Committee of the
Comintern in September 1932 gave an opportunity for such a

---

[1] See Litvinov's remarks on 29 December 1933, *Documents for 1933*, p. 434.

[2] The powerful Comintern leader, Piatnitsky, had recently denounced
the policy of the 'lesser evil' in a speech to foreign Party workers. *Bolshevik*,
15 May 1932. For the importance of Piatnitsky, see Borkenau, op. cit.,
pp. 359–60.

[3] V. Florin: 'Itogi Vyborov v Germanii' (The Results of the Elections in
Germany), *Bolshevik*, 31 July 1932. It should be noted that Communist as
well as Nazi propaganda contributed to the legend that Hitler 'saved
Germany from Bolshevism'.

reconsideration, but it was not taken. Self-congratulation on the rightness of the Communist 'line' was combined with exhortations to more determined leadership, and over the whole scene was spread a thick layer of determinist optimism.

'It would be a mistake to think that the fundamental process going on at present in Germany is Fascism. That is a mistake. The fundamental process in Germany is the collapse of German economy, the sharpening of its contradictions, the growing strength of Communism, parallelled by the growth of Fascism as the concentration of the strength of the bourgeoisie for the struggle with the revolution. The growth of the party of revolution is answered by the organisation and mobilisation of the forces of the counter-revolution. The German Communist Party has become stronger and has grown, its mass-basis has broadened, and it has acquired a strong political armour.'

This optimism led to the advocacy of tactics which could admittedly not bring victory and which demanded the sacrifice of members of the German Party to no very clear purpose.

'The workers are still disarmed, the bourgeoisie are armed and are provoking the proletariat into a premature rising. The proletariat cannot yet take up the struggle but it must not surrender the streets to Fascism, otherwise it would be acting in the same way as the Social-Democrats. It must deal it a partial rebuff. This rebuff has a great importance in principle. The successes still further awaken the working masses, unite these masses, strengthen their confidence, produce heroes, mobilise the masses for struggles on a larger scale, raise the struggle to a higher level, and open new roads to the unification of the masses. There is a great difference between what happened on the 1st of May, 1929, and what recently happened at Altona.[1] Then a few acted without the support of the masses. On the latter occasion we had considerable mass support. These events aroused and encouraged the masses. A small civil war leads to a greater one.'[2]

In the upshot a disingenuous attempt was made to outbid the Nazis by combining the revolutionary and national appeal. The German section of the 'Theses' declared the task of the German Communist Party to be:

[1] For the abortive and bloody Communist Party putsch at Altona on 12 July 1932, see Valtin, *Out of the Night*, chap. 24.
[2] Speech by V. Knorin to the Twelfth Plenum on 4 September 1932, *Bolshevik*, 30 November 1932. Cf. Kuusinen's article on the task of the German C.P., ibid., 31 December 1932. 'It is impossible,' writes R. T. Clark, 'to read the Communist literature and letters of the period without a shudder at the depths to which a refusal to use their intelligence independently can conduct intelligent men.' op. cit., p. 475.

'to mobilise the vast masses of toilers in defence of their vital interests against the bandit policy of monopolist capital, against Fascism, against emergency decrees, against nationalism and chauvinism, and, by developing economic and political strikes, by struggling for proletarian internationalism, by means of demonstrations, to lead the masses to the point of the *general political strike*; to win over the bulk of the social democratic masses, and definitely overcome the weaknesses in trade union work. The chief slogan which the German Communist Party must put forward to offset the slogan of the Fascist Dictatorship (the "Third Reich") and the slogan of the Social-Democrat Party (the Second Republic) is the slogan of the *workers and peasants republic*, i.e. Soviet Socialist Germany, which will guarantee the possibility of the voluntary affiliation of the Austrian and other German territories.'[1]

The most dramatic action of the German Communists in this period was their collaboration with the Nazis in the Berlin transport strike on the eve of the November elections.[2]

Meanwhile there were renewed signs of the Soviet and German Governments drifting apart in their international policies. For, as we have seen, the unwillingness of Germany to attend further meetings of the Disarmament Conference until her claim for 'equality' was met, had not prevented M. Litvinov from urging at the September meeting of the Conference Bureau, that the plans before the Conference be examined forthwith.

The November elections themselves showed a fall in both the Social-Democrat and the Nazi voting-strength and further Communist gains brought their Reichstag membership up to the hundred mark for the first time. But this did little but encourage them to pursue their foredoomed tactics to the grim end.[3] Encouraged by the election figures to believe that the major danger from Hitler was over, they concentrated on renewed attacks upon the Social-Democrats. A hopelessly divided German working-class could provide no real obstacle

---

[1] *Twelfth Plenum of the Executive Committee of the Communist International; Theses and Resolutions* (Modern Books, 1932).

[2] Clark, op. cit., pp. 417–21

[3] There seems to have been another attempt to bring about common action between the Socialist and Communist Parties. According to one version, the Social-Democrats took the initiative, and in the autumn of 1932 Friedrich Stampfer, editor of the Social-Democratic *Vorwaerts*, is said to have seen the Soviet Ambassador, Leo Khinchuk. Subsequent discussions are said to have taken place with another member of the Embassy, Vinogradov. The latter is said to have broken off the talks in January 1933, on the ground that Moscow was convinced that the road to Soviet Germany lay 'through Hitler'. D. Dallin, *Russia and Post-War Europe*, p. 61 n.

to the plots and counter-plots of the Hindenburg–von Papen–Schleicher–Hitler quartet.[1]

Even the assumption of power by Herr Hitler did not, as we have seen, serve to awake the dreamers of Moscow.[2] For immediate inaction it was necessary to find some excuse.

'The German Communist Party,' Radek wrote, 'has not yet managed to win over a majority of the Proletariat. Without a majority of the Proletariat, to go into the struggle for power in a country with a high degree of organisation of the masses of the people means to go in for an adventure, the more so since the crisis has aroused from their slumber and political indifference the great masses of the petty bourgeoisie and driven them into the camp of Fascism.'

This doubt about immediate possibilities was compensated for by the usual rosy hopes of the future.

'Hitler may be able to destroy the legal organisation of the Communist Party. But every blow against it will help to rally the working masses to its support. A Party that receives six million votes, deeply linked with the entire history of the German working class, cannot be dismissed from the balance sheet of history. This cannot be done by administrative decrees declaring it illegal; it cannot be done by a bloody terror, or else this terror will have to be directed against the whole working class.'[3]

The answer to this piece of logic was the Reichstag fire and the aftermath in the concentration camps.

No doubt the optimism was genuine in the sense that, in spite of declarations that Fascism would bring Germany nearer war, the rulers of the Soviet Union did not yet feel themselves directly menaced. In the same article, Radek pointed out that three ways lay open before Hitler. He could attempt to revive the von Papen offer of an alliance to France against Russia, or offer Poland the bait of the Soviet Ukraine in return for the cession of the Pomorze (the so-called Corridor), or finally adopt the Rosenberg plan of an alliance with Great Britain and Italy against France and Russia. Wisely he pointed out the obstacles

---

[1] 'It was not until February, 1933, when Hitler was already Chancellor, that the Communists accepted, though in a non-committal way, a Socialist invitation to discuss joint resistance to the Nazis. The first meeting was arranged for the very same evening that the Reichstag went up in flames.' A. Sturmthal, *The Tragedy of European Labour* (Gollancz, 1944), p. 170.

[2] For the slowness of the Comintern reaction to the advent of Hitler, see Borkenau, op. cit., chap. 22, and his references there to the position taken up by the Basle *Rundschau*, successor to the defunct Comintern organ *Imprecorr*. Cf. Wollenberg, op. cit., pp. 278–80.

[3] K. Radek, 'Novye Etapi Fashizatsii Germanii' (New Stages in the Fascist development of Germany), *Bolshevik*, 15 February 1933, pp. 56–7.

to each of these. But a spectacular resurgence of German military might to the extent that Germany alone could threaten the very existence of the Soviet Union—that possibility was naturally not discussed.

In April 1933 it was still possible for the Comintern to regard the Hitler triumph as a hopeful sign and as due only to the terror of the bourgeoisie at the rise of the German Communists.[1] The Social-Democrats were now blamed for having rejected an insurrection as premature.[2] The implications for German foreign policy of the Nazi triumph were not mentioned, perhaps in an access of discretion, as there was already some tension between the Governments in spite of Goering's reassuring remarks.[3] Restraint was, as we have seen, justified, as on 5 May 1933 the Protocol signed in 1931, prolonging the 1926 Treaty, was at last ratified in Berlin.

Appendix

RISE AND FALL OF THE GERMAN COMMUNIST PARTY, 1928–1933
REICHSTAG ELECTIONS (SEATS)

	1928 (May)	1930 (September)	1932 (July)	1932 (November)	1933 (March)
Centre . . .	61	68	75	70	73
Social-Democrats .	153	143	143	121	120
Communists . .	54	77	89	100	81
Nazis . . .	13	105	230	196	288
Others . . .	210	183	161	97	85

ELECTIONS 1928–1933 (VOTES)

1928	*Reichstag*	1930	*Reichstag*
Communists .	3,263,000	Communists .	4,587,000
Nazis . . .	809,000	Nazis .	6,401,000

[1] E. Varga: 'Germanski Fashizm u Vlasti' (German Fascism in Power), *Mirovoe Khozaistvo i Mirovaya Politika* (World Economy and World Politics), April 1933. Cf. 'The Collapse of Weimar Germany and the Preparation for Weimar October', *Communist International* (Moscow), 15 April 1933.

[2] The Presidium of the Comintern Executive passed the following resolution on 1 April: 'The Presidium of the Executive Committee of the Communist International, having heard the report of Comrade Heckert on the situation in Germany, declares that the policy carried out by the Executive Committee of the Communist Party of Germany with Comrade Thaelmann at its head up to and during the time of the Hitlerite *coup* (*perevorot*) was absolutely correct.' Versailles, the German capitalist oppression and the Social-Democrats are held responsible for the Nazi victory.

[3] 'Our campaign for the extirpation of Communism in Germany has nothing to do with German-Russian relations. I am fully convinced they will remain as friendly as in former years.' Interview with *Amsterdaamer Telegraaf*, 21 March 1933, quoted in *Osteuropa*, VIII, p. 410.

1932	*Presidential* (*March*)	*Presidential* (*April*)	*Reichstag* (*July*)	*Reichstag* (*November*)
Communists	. 4,982,000	3,706,000	5,277,000	5,980,000
Nazis .	. 11,339,000	13,417,000	13,732,000	11,737,000

1933	*Reichstag*	
Communists	. 4,848,000	Nearly 4 million additional voters
Nazis .	. 17,277,000	went to the polls in March 1933, and
		the new Reichstag had therefore 646
		instead of 586 members.

NOTE 1.—For further information on Soviet assistance towards Germany's illegal rearmament (pp. 58–9 *supra*), see W. M. Knight-Patterson, *Germany from Defeat to Conquest, 1913–1933* (Allen & Unwin, 1946), pp. 397–403, 408–9.

NOTE 2.—The account given in the above chapter of the conduct of the German Communist Party during the period of Hitler's rise to power is fully borne out by Konrad Heiden in his book *Der Fuehrer* (Gollancz, 1944). This book also contains further details on the abortive last-minute attempt of the Social Democrats to reach an agreement with the Communists through the medium of the Soviet Ambassador. See in particular pp. 332, 363–72, 412–14, 431–2.

Chapter Six

RUSSIA AND THE FAR EAST, 1929-1933

FROM the second half of the nineteenth century, the Far East has loomed large in Russian foreign policy, and at no time would it have been correct either to underrate this fact or to overlook the close and constant interaction between Far Eastern and European policy. This was true both when Russia's problem was one of expansion and when, as in the period with which we are to deal, it was primarily one of defence. It must be accounted a major aim of Russian diplomacy in that period to avoid simultaneous wars in the Far East and in Europe by preventing the coalescence of her potential enemies in the two spheres.

Russia's Far Eastern policy underwent in this period changes almost as striking as those we have noted and shall still have to note in her European outlook. It is a triple theme which will have to be developed: the emergence of an aggressive Japan as the primary danger in the Far East and a consequent recasting of the Russian attitude to the other major Powers in that area and notably to the United States; the renewal of contact between the Russian and Kuomintang Governments and the effect of this upon the Communist movement in China; and, finally, the reinforcement of Russia's own position by the economic and military development of the Soviet Far East, and by the strengthening of the virtual Russian protectorate over Outer Mongolia and of the rather more ambiguous relationship with Sinkiang (Chinese Turkestan).

In dealing with the diplomatic events of the period, it will be necessary to bear in mind that Russia's position in the Far East was affected by the contemporary history of the Chinese Communist movement.[1]

[1] Although a good deal of attention has been paid to Communist activities in China between 1923 and 1927, the subsequent years have not received the study they deserve. The great mass of writing on Far Eastern affairs which is available is American, and in as far as the Soviet Union and Chinese Communism are concerned, suffers either from a marked distaste for this aspect of affairs or from an equally marked and equally misleading enthusiasm. A good deal might perhaps be added by the systematic study of Soviet publications, particularly of specialist periodicals dealing with Far Eastern matters. The handbook *Strany Tikhovo Okeana* (*Countries of the Pacific*), published in 1942, which has much useful information, singles out Japan as the main enemy of Chinese nationalism throughout, and tends to play down the part of the Communists in the Chinese Revolution, and of the

The severance of diplomatic relations between the Chinese National Government and the U.S.S.R. in 1927 had put an end to direct contact between Russia and the greater part of China. The renewal of Russian concentration upon the Far Eastern scene which marked the summer and autumn of 1929 came about, however, through circumstances in a part of China which had not in 1927 accepted the authority of the National Government and was not therefore affected by its rupture with the Soviet Union. Even after the death of the Manchurian war-lord Chang Tso-lin, and the decision of his son and successor Chang Hsueh-liang to make terms with the Nanking Government in December 1928, in return for the confirmation of his authority in North China (i.e. Manchuria and Jehol), the Russian position remained unimpaired.[1] The Chinese Government had, in its own words,

'manifested a tolerant attitude towards the staff members of the Soviet Embassy and Consulates, commercial agents and Soviet national commercial organizations in North China, and permitted them to maintain the *status quo*, and this in the hope that Soviet Russia would repent her misdeeds so that Sino-Russian relations might be restored to a normal basis.'[2]

On the other hand the position of Russia in Manchuria had presented difficulties of its own ever since the Soviet Government had come into the inheritance of Tsarist imperialism in this area by the recognition of its title to the Chinese Eastern Railway in the treaties made with the Peking Government on 31 May 1924, and with the Mukden authorities on 20 September 1924. In 1929, 75 per cent of the Railway's employees were Russians and they held all the controlling posts. This survival of Russian domination in Manchuria was as unwelcome to the new nationalist China as were all other evidences of its unequal status, and the recovery in full sovereignty of Manchuria,

---

Chinese Soviets and Chinese Red Army after 1927. The formation of the Chinese Soviet 'Government' in 1931 and its declaration of war against Japan in February 1932, are not mentioned. The most famous event in the history of the Chinese Communists, the Long March of the Red Army to the North-West in 1934-1935, is mentioned in the chronology of events but not in the 'historical sketch' of China in the body of the book.

[1] On the situation in Manchuria to the time of the Japanese attack in the autumn of 1931, see Appeal by the Chinese Government: *Report of the Commission of Enquiry* (League of Nations Document, C. 663. M. 320. 1932, VII 12), hereafter referred to as the *Lytton Report*, chaps. 1 and 2. Extracts are printed in *Documents for 1932*, pp. 320-38.

[2] Statement of Chinese Government issued at Nanking, 20 July 1929, and quoted from the *China Year Book, 1929-1930*, p. 1223. Chap. 27 of this issue gives the main documents in the conflict up to 25 October 1929.

irrespective of Russian (or Japanese) pretensions (and the diversion of trade from the foreign to the new Chinese lines and from Vladivostok to Chinese ports), was an integral part of the nationalist programme.[1] China seemed determined to deal with Russia first, as the weaker of the two intruders, even at the price of removing one counter-weight to a potentially stronger antagonist.

The recognition by the Chinese that ownership of the Railway was vested in the Soviet Government had not put an end to friction arising out of the Railway question. In January 1926, for instance, Chang Tso-lin had arrested the Russian manager of the line, and other Russian officials, but had later been forced to abandon this attempt to squeeze out the Russians. There had been indeed a long series of encroachments on Russian treaty rights, and Russia's attitude had lately encouraged the Chinese to believe that no serious resistance would be forthcoming.[2] The defeat of the Communist wing of the Kuomintang and the agreement with Nanking had, by the summer of 1929, convinced the Manchurian authorities that a radical solution in their favour of the question of control was now possible. No doubt, too, the Chinese believed that recent events in Russia had seriously weakened the Stalin régime and that the Russians would be in no position to resist a well-timed *coup*.[3]

Finally, Chinese nationalism had been vastly encouraged by the conciliatory attitude of the other foreign Powers to the demands of Nanking.

Raids on Soviet Consulates at various points on the Railway on 27 May 1929 were accompanied by the seizure of documents and by the arrest of some eighty Soviet citizens, officials of the Consular Service and of the Railway. A Soviet protest to

[1] *China and Japan* (R.I.I.A., 3rd ed., 1941), pp. 40–5. China's main advantage from a long-term point of view was demographic rather than political. Even before 1914, the immigration of Chinese peasants into Manchuria was proceeding rapidly and at a pace well in excess of that of the parallel Russian movement into the Far Eastern Province of Siberia. The further influx from 1923 to 1930 was enormously greater than either the Russian eastward movement or than Japanese and Korean immigration into Manchuria itself. B. H. Sumner, *Tsardom and Imperialism in the Far East and the Middle East, 1880–1914* (Raleigh Lecture of the British Academy, 1940), p. 18; H. S. Quigley and G. H. Blakeslee, *The Far East* (Boston, World Peace Foundation, 1938), pp. 16–17. For some general remarks on the nature of Russian expansion in this area before and after the Revolution, and on the Chinese reaction, see Owen Lattimore, *Manchuria, Cradle of Conflict* (2nd ed., New York, Macmillan, 1935), pp. 294–7

[2] *Survey for 1929*, pp. 344–69; K. K. Kakawami: 'The Russo-Chinese Conflict in Manchuria', *Foreign Affairs*, October 1929; V. Conolly, *Soviet Trade from the Pacific to the Levant*, chap. 4.

[3] Milioukov, op. cit., pp. 273–6.

Nanking on 29 May was followed three days later by more arrests. Finally, on 10 and 11 July, a further widespread series of arrests and other actions effectively gave the Chinese control of the Railway and its subsidiary services, while all other Soviet organisations in Manchuria were shut down. As in 1926, Communist activity was the pretext—this may be asserted without going into the question of how far the charges that Soviet Consulates and other institutions were being used for propaganda may have been justified in this particular case.

A Russian ultimatum to the Nanking Government on 13 July 1929, was countered on the 17th by a note which defended the Chinese action on the grounds that the Treaty of 1924 had been violated by the Soviet Government, in particular with regard to propaganda. The U.S.S.R. thereupon broke off the remaining consular relations with China, and the Chinese Government followed suit on 20 July. (The various declarations of Chinese intentions and attitudes which accompanied these transactions were primarily intended to still the suspicions of other Powers which had 'unequal treaties' with China, and are of no immediate relevance to Sino-Russian relations.) Meanwhile the Mukden authorities, no doubt alarmed by clear evidence of military preparations on the part of the Russians, made an effort to settle the dispute directly with Moscow, but this was no more successful than were various attempts by Nanking to make use of the good offices of Japan, Great Britain and Germany, in order to find a way out. The Russians would be content with nothing less than a preliminary return to the *status quo*.

These long-range diplomatic exchanges were contemporaneous with the first military operations which began in mid-August.[1] In mid-November, a sudden intensification of Russian military pressure brought about the collapse of the Manchurian forces. Mukden promptly resumed direct overtures. A provisional agreement was reached at Nikolsk on 3 December, and this was succeeded by the definitive Protocol concluded at Khabarovsk on the 22nd.[2] The Protocol provided for a restoration of the *status quo* both with reference to the Railway and in the matter of the commercial and consular relations between Manchuria and the Soviet Far East. The further provision that outstanding questions, including a resumption of full diplomatic relations by the Nanking Government, should be the subject of a conference was harder to put into practice, since it was not a matter with which the Mukden

---

[1] For this campaign, see Eugene Lyons, *Assignment in Utopia* (Harrap, 1938), chap. 14, 'The War Nobody Knew'.

[2] The texts of both agreements are printed in *Documents for 1929*, pp. 280–4.

negotiators had been competent to deal. The demonstration of Russia's considerable strength in the Far Eastern theatre did not diminish the Chinese Government's suspicions of Soviet intentions. The Chinese delegation reached Moscow on 8 May 1930, instead of 25 January, as had been arranged, and even then it was discovered that their instructions forbade them to deal with the question of the resumption of diplomatic relations. In consequence, the conference was opened in October after an interchange of letters between Moscow and Mukden, in which, following Soviet complaints, the latter promised to prevent 'White' Russian activities in the Provinces under its control.[1] (On 30 December, Moscow complained in a further note that the undertaking had not been carried out.) The first session of the conference soon adjourned, as did the second session in December. The Chinese appeared to consider the position satisfactory, to judge from a speech by Dr. C. T. Wang on 29 December, in which he stated that the Russians had failed in their intention of sowing discord between Nanking and Manchuria and that in consequence good progress was now possible.[2] From the Russian point of view, all that could be said at the end of 1930 was that the position in Manchuria had been restored but that where China proper was concerned, there had been no perceptible advance.

The Chinese Eastern Railway crisis was given more than local significance by the invocation of the Kellogg Pact. The Pact was brought to the attention of the disputing Powers as early as 19 July 1929, on American initiative, and the peaceful intentions of the Soviet Government were immediately asserted by the Soviet Ambassadors at Paris and Tokio to the Foreign Ministers of the respective Powers.[3] The renewal of the American suggestion led on 2 December to simultaneous memoranda from the United States, Great Britain, anxious to keep in step with any American initiative in the international field, France and Italy, and this was followed by notes from some of the smaller Powers. (Germany, as the Power in charge of the interests of both parties, and Japan, the Power best in a position to appreciate the realities of the situation, held aloof.[4]) The

---

[1] The Soviet Government claimed that the considerable Russian emigré colony centred in Harbin was a mainspring of anti-Soviet activity in the Far East. Cf. *infra*, chap. 13.

[2] *Documents for 1930*, pp. 178–9.

[3] *Papers Relating to the Foreign Relations of the United States*, 1929, II (United States Dept. of State, 1943, pp. 186–435). G. C. Dawes, *Diary as Ambassador to Great Britain*, p. 108.

[4] For Japan's attitude, see the speech of Baron Shidehara, 21 January 1930, *Documents for 1930*, pp. 185–6.

Russians' reaction—with their position now assured—was prompt and disconcerting. The Soviet Government blankly refused to receive a communication from the Roumanian Government with which it was not in diplomatic relations. The affront to the United States was less spectacular, but M. Litvinov's reply left no doubt of his Government's attitude. Declaring that Russia was acting purely in self-defence, and suggesting that the only purpose of the intervention of the Powers was to influence the negotiations which they knew to be in progress, he denied the notion that the Pact provided that any one of its signatories should assume the function of its guardian.

'The Government of the Soviet Union,' he concluded (in his note of 4 December), 'cannot abstain from expressing its astonishment that the Government of the U.S.A. which, at its own wish, maintains no official relations with the Government of the Soviet Union, finds it possible to address advice and directions to the latter.'[1]

In a speech made on the same date, M. Litvinov gave a general review of the conflict and went even further in calculated rudeness by affirming that even if one dismissed the 'highly probable supposition' that China had been forced into the struggle by some imperialist Power or group of Powers, it still remained true that her whole attitude was determined by her knowledge that she could count on the general hostility to the Soviet Union prevailing in the capitalist world.[2]

The whole incident, and the Russian note in particular, served to revive American memories of Russian imperialist aggressiveness, with the result, according to one British observer, that for the moment at least, American opinion, not uninfluenced perhaps by a strong Japanese lobby at Washington, was as hostile to Russia and as friendly to Japan as in 1899.[3] Japan, on the other hand, had remained markedly neutral, and had refused to transport Chinese troops over the South Manchurian Railway.

The next major event in Far Eastern affairs, the Japanese invasion of Manchuria, did not concern Russia as directly as the events of 1929, but its effects were more far-reaching. Russia's policy towards Japan had passed through a number of distinct phases since the emergence of the latter as an active political force. From the middle of the nineteenth century

---

[1] *Survey for 1929*, pp. 353-4 and pp. 364-7. *Documents for 1929*, pp. 274-80.

[2] *Documents for 1929*, pp. 192-8.

[3] D. Smith, *America and the Axis War* (Cape, 1942), p. 38. Note too the strong pro-Japanese and anti-Russian bias of those chapters of Hugh Wilson's, *A Diplomat between Wars*, which deal with the Far East.

until the outbreak of the Russo-Japanese war, the story is one
of Russian expansion in north-eastern Asia and of increasing
fear on the part of Japan as to Russia's intentions regarding
Manchuria, Korea, and North China, where the consolidation
of Russian power might menace her independence.

Taken together, the two Far Eastern wars of 1894–1895 and
1904–1905 marked a definite check to Russia and a consolidation of Japan's position. The Treaty of Portsmouth (August
1905) inaugurated a new era. Another treaty between Russia
and Japan, that of 1907, began a period of improved relations,
which were confirmed by further treaties in 1910, 1912, and
1916.[1] These agreements were to some extent intended to
counter the Chinese efforts to win American and British support
against Russian and Japanese encroachments in Manchuria by
granting the Anglo-Saxon Powers large-scale railway concessions in China itself.

This second period was in turn ended by the Russian Revolution. The collapse of Russian military power, the elimination
of Germany, the increasing paralysis of China, the preoccupation of the Anglo-Saxon Powers and of France with European
affairs and their overriding hostility to Bolshevism—all these
combined for a while to give Japanese imperialism an almost
free run on the Asiatic mainland.[2] Large Japanese forces were
in control of Russian Far Eastern territory. After the Washington Conference, Japan's position could no longer be usefully
maintained and a less intransigent attitude was forced upon
her rulers. The mainland, including Vladivostok, was evacuated in 1922, but relations with the Soviet Government were
only re-established by the Convention of 20 January 1925,
which liquidated the last vestiges of Japanese 'intervention' by
the withdrawal of Japanese troops from North Sakhalin.[3]

Up to 1922, Russian policy in the Far East had on the whole
been favourable to the United States, as the Power most likely
to insist on Japan's withdrawal from Siberia. But the failure
to develop a more permanent and durable relationship with the
United States, and the fact of the Japanese withdrawal meant
that, by 1925, the Russians were in a mood to go further on the
path of co-operation with Japan, particularly as at the time this

[1] E. B. Price, *The Russo-Japanese Treaties of 1907–1916 concerning Manchuria and Mongolia* (Baltimore, Johns Hopkins University Press, 1933).

[2] See V. A. Yakhontoff, *Russia and the Soviet Union in the Far East*; R. J. Kerner, 'Soviet Russia in Asia', in *The Renaissance of Asia* (Berkeley, University of California, 1941); G. Bienstock, *The Struggle for the Pacific* (Allen & Unwin, 1937)

[3] For the text, see Yakhontoff, op. cit., pp. 404–10.

seemed compatible with a close association with the Chinese nationalist movement. This friendship was also in line with the anti-British and pro-German direction of Russian foreign policy at the time. It could be reconciled with the still dominant revolutionary *motif* in the Soviet's Asiatic policy by choosing to regard Japan's 'Asia for the Asiatics' as a revolutionary rather than a racial slogan.[1] Such at least seemed to be the import of Stalin's published interview with a Japanese journalist, given on 4 July 1925.[2]

This Soviet-Japanese *rapprochement* reached its height during the year 1925, and thereafter declined somewhat, although, as one authority remarks:

'despite occasional friction, Soviet-Japanese relations were marked by comparative stability during the period 1925–31, and were not strained even by the clash which occurred in 1929 between the Soviet Union and China concerning the Chinese Eastern Railway.'[3]

There was friction over the perennial rivalry in Manchuria between the two railway systems and over the question of Japanese fishing rights in Russian north Pacific waters early in 1931, and an attempt on the life of the Soviet trade representative in Tokyo was ascribed to a bitter Press campaign inspired by Japanese fishery interests. The fisheries dispute was, however, settled in June, and in September the Japanese Government arranged to guarantee the credits on certain exports to the U.S.S.R.

A violent reaction might nevertheless have been expected after the full-scale military occupation of Manchuria in 1931–1932, and the establishment there of a puppet-state.

[1] It should be noted that there is some evidence for the belief that Sun Yat-sen himself had hopes at one time of receiving assistance from pan-Asiatic circles in Japan, particularly the Black Dragon Society. See, e.g. Hugh Byas, *Government by Assassination* (Allen & Unwin, 1943), pp. 190–1. Later Sun became disillusioned.

[2] Quoted by Nikolaevsky in *Novy Zhurnal*. Although on the face of it the 1925 treaty does no more than renew the Treaty of Portsmouth, Nikolaevsky accepts the statement of the Soviet ex-diplomat Bessedovsky that a secret clause guaranteed the Japanese rear in the event of a war between Japan and the United States. It is possible that the account given in these articles of Russo-Japanese co-operation in Asia is exaggerated; its plausibility depends upon accepting the evidence of the German geopolitician Haushofer who then advocated a line-up of Japan, China, Russia, and Germany.

[3] V. M. Dean: 'The Soviet Union and Japan in the Far East', *Foreign Policy Reports*, 17 August 1932.

For the threat to Russia's Far Eastern Territory could scarcely be overlooked, since Manchuria is the strategic key to North-Eastern Asia.[1] Nevertheless, Russia's policy still proved to be one of 'invincible restraint and impenetrable reserve'. The rights of Russia in the Chinese Eastern Railway, vindicated in 1929 as against China, were now trampled on by the Japanese with equal roughness, but the Russians 'kept their heads and held their hands'.[2]

The period between the opening of hostilities in Manchuria on 19 September 1931, and the publication of the Lytton Report on 2 October 1932, can be divided, from the Russian point of view, into two phases. The first was marked by increasing tension as the wide scope of Japanese ambitions became more and more apparent. During the second, which began in the late spring of 1932, this tension was appreciably diminished.

The first Russian reactions in September were temperate: 'the burden of Soviet criticism was directed less against Japan than against the existing peace machinery'.[3] But the occupation of Changchun, the junction between the C.E.R. and the Japanese-owned South Manchurian Railway, evoked a Soviet protest and despite Japanese reassurances there were signs of increasing nervousness on the part of Moscow. By the middle of October, the Soviet Government seemed however to have accepted the change in the local situation as a *fait accompli*, and Russian comment was directed to the wider aspects of the matter. Later in October the situation worsened again, with reports that the Soviet Government had given help to the Chinese general, Ma Chan-shan, and that Russian troops were being concentrated on the frontier. To a Japanese warning against sending Soviet troops to strengthen the guard on the C.E.R. and to other protests, Karakhan replied on 14 November by denying that any breach of neutrality had been or was contemplated. Soviet comment became more hostile, their reports dwelling on the old theme of 'White Guard' activities. They took note of reported dealings between the Japanese and Ataman Semenov, whom the Japanese were believed to be

---

[1] For a treatment of the historical rôle of Manchuria, see Owen Lattimore, *Inner Asian Frontiers of China* (Oxford University Press, 1940), chap. v. Cf. his *Manchuria, Cradle of Conflict*.

[2] *Survey for 1932*, pp. 533 and 535. The Japanese did not on the whole dispute the fact of Russia's self-effacement. 'During the Sino-Japanese crisis 1931–1932, the Soviet Union on the whole maintained strict neutrality.' R. Hidemichi Asaki, *Japan's Foreign Relations* (Tokio, 1936), p. 540. Cf. N. Peffer: *Prerequisites to Peace in the Far East* (I.P.R., 1940), p. 279.

[3] Dean, loc. cit., p. 141.

desirous of using to create trouble in Mongolia.[1] Diplomatic exchanges on the future of the C.E.R. were however proceeding when the Japanese advance to Tsitsihar took place. M. Litvinov, in accepting Japanese assurances that the new advance was a temporary measure, took occasion on 21 November to reject any parallel between Japanese activities and those of the Soviet troops in 1929. The first Russian proposal of a non-aggression pact with Japan was made to Kenichi Yoshizawa when the newly appointed Foreign Minister stopped in Moscow on his way to Tokyo. The overture was renewed by M. Alexander Troyanovsky, the Soviet Ambassador at Tokyo, on 12 January 1932, but was almost at once rejected by the Japanese Cabinet.[2] This was scarcely surprising, since Japan at this time 'was at pains to represent herself in Western eyes as a bulwark against the penetration of Communists into the Far East by way of Manchuria'.[3] Between 1929 and 1931, a Soviet régime had been set up with its centre in Kiangsi, but at times exercising influence further afield. In contrast to the earlier Communist movement, which had been crushed in 1927-1928, the present one was almost exclusively peasant in its composition, though it had inherited a nucleus of party workers from Communist deserters from the Kuomintang armies and other survivors of

[1] The Japanese were disappointed in any hopes they may have had of widespread support from among the White Russian colony in Manchuria— nor did those among them who did make some attempt at collaboration get anything out of it. Semenov was in any event quite unacceptable as a leader. Between 1918 and 1921 Semenov, with some Japanese assistance, had worked for an independent Cossack state in eastern Siberia. See Fischer, op. cit., and G. R. Stewart, *The White Armies of Russia* (Macmillan, 1933). In 1941, he was apparently still being maintained by the Japanese at Dairen. Cf. S. Postnikov, 'Separatist Tendencies among the Russian Emigrés', *Slavonic Review*, January 1939; C. A. Buss, *War and Diplomacy in Eastern Asia* (New York, Macmillan, 1941), p. 474.

[2] In February 1932, however, Tass found it necessary to deny foreign rumours that the U.S.S.R. and Japan had reached an agreement with regard to Manchuria.

[3] *Survey for 1932*, p. 535. It is possible that Japan hoped for even greater results from the play of this factor. An American authority (quoted in *Survey for 1931*, pp. 479 ff), wrote: 'I think Japan hoped that United States opinion would view her action sympathetically as a necessary police operation on the Far Eastern "Caribbean" and as a defence of Western capitalism against Russian and Chinese Bolshevism, and she also hoped to play the League, the United States, and the U.S.S.R. against each other.' If Japan's success in spreading an anti-Communist version of her motives was not very marked it was not for want of considerable support on this point from the Soviet Press itself. British interests in China, as represented by the *North China Herald*, were both sympathetic to the Japanese position and markedly anti-Soviet. I. Friedman, *British Relations with China, 1931-1939* (I.P.R., 1940), p. 26.

Chiang Kai-shek's massacres. From December 1930 Chiang Kai-shek fought a series of campaigns against the Communists in Kiangsi. The hostile reaction of Moscow to the news of the rejection of the proferred pact was intensified by the disputes over the carriage of Japanese troops on the C.E.R. which was the occasion rather than the reason for the occupation of Harbin on 5 February and the remainder of Manchuria.

In spite of Russian concessions in the matter of the use of the Railway, reports came from both sides of the massing of troops in the Russo-Manchurian frontier zones. The fighting at Shanghai between Japanese and Chinese, which lasted from 28 January to 3 March, seemed to confirm the Russian view that Manchuria was only a beginning, so that the position looked ugly enough when it was further complicated by the proclamation on 1 March of the independent State of 'Manchukuo'.[1]

So far the Manchurian crisis had been treated in the Soviet Press to a large extent merely as one example of the current exacerbation of imperialist rivalries as a result of the world depression, and as a preparation for an ultimate attack upon the Soviet Union.

'The war in Manchuria and Shanghai represents for the imperialists a prelude to a war of intervention against the Soviet Union and to a new imperialist war for the hegemony of the world. The preparation for a war of intervention against the Soviet Union is a direct continuation of the struggle of the bourgeoisie for a capitalist way out of the crisis inside their own countries. . . . But in the East we have only the beginning of the war. The strategic plan of Japanese imperialism leads through Manchuria and Shanghai to war against the Chinese Soviets, to a war of intervention against the Soviet Union, and to a decisive struggle with American imperialism for hegemony in the Pacific.'

Efforts among the imperialists to come to an agreement regarding an attack on the Chinese Soviets and on the U.S.S.R. would continue, but their forces were divided, since behind the Japanese-American conflict loomed the still greater conflict between the rival imperialisms of Great Britain and the United States. Whatever their immediate gains, the plans of the imperialists would ultimately be frustrated by the rising revolu-

[1] 'This Government (the Pu Yi Government of Manchukuo) has in some measure to conceal the undeniably clear fact, that Manchuria with its reserves of coal, oil and iron and its timber wealth—all this is becoming the object of the practically uncontrolled naked exploitation of Japanese imperialism.' N. Mossin, reviewing *Imperialism i Mandzuria* (*Imperialism and Manchuria*), by V. Avarin, *Bolshevik*, 29 February 1932, p. 82.

tionary temper of the masses in China and in the imperialist countries themselves.[1] After 1 March these long-range speculations were somewhat obscured by the apparent development of an immediate threat to Soviet territory. To this, by now, the Soviet Government felt in a position to give an unequivocal answer:

'The peaceful policy of the U.S.S.R. is not a policy of ignoring facts. The Soviet Government has pursued, is pursuing and will continue to pursue a policy of peace and non-interference in the events taking place in China. But this by no means signifies that the Soviet Union will permit anyone to violate the security of Soviet frontiers, to invade Soviet territory, or to seize even the smallest portion of Soviet land.'[2]

Soviet scepticism as to the sincerity of the League Powers was further manifested in their contemptuous attitude towards the activities of the Lytton Commission and their refusal of a League request, made on 20 April, that Soviet officials in Manchuria should be permitted to give evidence before it. This did not prevent the Soviet Press from charging the Japanese with inventing 'Red plots' for the benefit of the Commission.

Various elements in the situation combined to keep the issues at stake very much alive. Anti-Communist agitation in Manchuria was accompanied by the arrest of a large number of Soviet citizens; the Soviet's commercial interests had in consequence to be progressively liquidated. Each Power was blamed by the other for various bandit outrages on the Chinese Eastern Railway. Reports of the reinforcement of the Soviet Far Eastern army and of the hasty reconditioning of the Trans-Siberian Railway began to receive ample confirmation. The May Day 1932 speech of General Bluecher to his troops at Khabarovsk was defiant in the extreme. 'The Red Army will prevent any alien foot from trampling on the soil of the collective farms.'[3]

Nevertheless, the new phase in Russo-Japanese relations which began in May was considerably less disturbed. 'The concentration of Soviet troops, far from precipitating a border clash, apparently served to clear the atmosphere.'[4] The first indication of an improvement was the fact that difficulties which had arisen over the fisheries were overcome and the existing agreement revised, the final settlement being reached

---

[1] Leading article: 'Krisis Kapitalisma i Opastnost Voiny' (The Crisis of Capitalism and the Danger of War), *Bolshevik*, 29 February 1932.
[2] *Izvestia*, 4 March 1932, cited by Dean, loc. cit., p. 144.
[3] *Survey for 1932*, p. 437.　　　　[4] Dean, loc. cit., p. 145.

on 13 August.[1] The press of the two countries became less hostile and on 2 June Admiral Saito, the new Japanese Premier, made a statement obviously designed to calm Russian suspicions. Furthermore, the operations carried out by the Japanese Army in the summer months did not increase the threat to Russian interests. Notwithstanding, therefore, on the one hand, the losses to the Soviet Government arising from the disorganisation of traffic on the C.E.R.,[2] and, on the other hand, the Japanese 'recognition' of Manchukuo on 15 September 1932, the relations between the two Powers at that date were less strained perhaps than at any time during the previous twelve months.[3]

There can be little doubt that the Russians realised from the first that they were in no position to intervene successfully in Manchuria and that the best they could hope for was that Japan would have its hands too full actually to encroach upon Soviet territory—an encroachment which they could not have avoided resisting. In all probability their passivity at this time was due not to any underestimate of the importance of Manchuria, but to the Soviet régime's still more urgent preoccupations at home and in Europe.[4] Moreover, the prospect of a direct Japanese attack seemed on the whole unlikely, although it would be difficult to come to this conclusion on the basis of Soviet sources alone.[5] These writings played up the Japanese war threat, and

[1] Conolly, *Soviet Trade from the Pacific to the Levant*, pp. 39–40. The original agreement, concluded on 28 January 1928, is given as Appendix VI.

[2] For the decline of traffic on the C.E.R. and the consequent falling-off in the trade of Vladivostok, see the statistical data in Conolly, op. cit., pp. 30 and 85–6.

[3] The protocol set no limits upon the number of Japanese troops to be stationed in Manchukuo and no time-limit upon their retention there. It is printed in *Documents for 1932*, pp. 312–13.

[4] It must not be assumed that the Soviet leaders were unanimous in this passive policy. There was a party in favour of more determined resistance to Japan. According to Milioukov, op. cit., pp. 382–9, its leader was Voroshilov; according to E. Wollenberg, *The Red Army* (1940 ed.), pp. 247–8, its leaders were Tukhachevsky and Gamarnik. Bluecher was also thought to be among them. 'The main front of Russian advance', remarked an American authority, 'is not Manchuria but Mongolia and Central Asia. Nevertheless Manchuria is the pivot on which turns the main advance because it commands the Pacific outlet which is imperative if the main advance is to be turned into a permanent occupation and given facilities of continued growth.' O. Lattimore, *Manchuria: Cradle of Conflict*, p. 295.

[5] It was possible indeed for a Russian emigré writer to take an entirely cynical view of the whole series of threats and provocations on both sides which marked Russo-Japanese (and Sino-Russian) relations in this period. 'All that happened later [i.e. after 1929] up to the end of 1934 between Moscow and Nanking and Moscow and Tokyo fundamentally was nothing more than sham fighting and camouflage.' Bienstock, op. cit., pp. 171–2.

the resistance to it of the Japanese proletariat. The class war, we read, 'is developing with massive strength inside Japan where the slogans: "Defend the Soviet Union", "Banzai our fatherland the U.S.S.R.", are becoming the most popular slogans of every strike and every workers' demonstration'.[1]

Japan's position could not of course be estimated without taking into account the whole complex of power relationships in the Far East. But Russia's diplomatic isolation was far more complete than Japan's, in spite of the sympathy which had been mobilised for China through the League of Nations. Although it might suit Soviet spokesmen to blame American influence for the fact that diplomatic relations with China had not been restored,[2] there were a number of genuine antagonisms strong enough to weigh in the balance against their common fear of Japan. To begin with there was the virtual Soviet protectorate in Outer Mongolia, which had already made Chinese 'sovereignty' there a mere fiction. The destiny of Sinkiang was also a possible source of dispute. Most important of all was the question of the Chinese Soviets, which the Kuomintang had not succeeded in crushing. There was constant Comintern propaganda against Chiang Kai-shek and Communist spokesmen declared that his Government had no serious intention of resisting Japanese aggression.[3] Chinese resistance at Shanghai at the beginning of 1932 was attributed mainly to the influence exercised upon the Cantonese Nineteenth Army by the working masses of the city (for Communist hostility was no less profound against the 'Left-wing' Kuomintang group at Canton).[4] From the spring of 1932 an increasingly national and anti-Japanese trend was perceptible among the Chinese Communists themselves

The Russian appraisal of the attitudes of the various Great Powers to what was going on in China was not unrealistic, although as usual it over-accentuated the divergences between Great Britain and America. The Soviet angle can conveniently be studied in the article by Karl Radek already referred to,

[1] Mossin, loc. cit., p. 90.
[2] K. Radek, 'The War in the Far East: A Soviet View', *Foreign Affairs*, July 1932.
[3] Wang-Ming, 'Uglublenie Revolutsionovo Krisisa v Kitai i Zadachi Kitaiskoy Kompartii' (The Deepening of the Revolutionary Crisis in China and the Problems of the Chinese Communist Party), *Bolshevik*, 31 March 1932. See, for a 'Trotskyist' account of the situation, H. Isaacs, *The Tragedy of the Chinese Revolution* (Secker & Warburg, 1938), pp. 438 ff.
[4] G. Voytinsky, E. Iolk, and N. Nasonov, 'Sobitie na Dalnem Vostoke i Opasnost Voiny' (Events in the Far East and the Danger of War), *Bolshevik*, 31 March 1932.

though the fact that the article was intended for an American audience should of course be borne in mind.[1]

Radek declared that there were three tendencies against which Japan was fighting: 'first, the inevitable unification of China; second, the desire of the United States to conquer China economically; and third, the socialistic industrialisation of Soviet Russia not only in Europe but also in Siberia.' Japan was in a hurry. The League was not recognised as an independent entity. 'The League is a thorn in the relations of the Great Powers. In practice it can do nothing that England and France do not want it to do.'

Germany's sympathy for Japan was not brought out, but France was declared to be favourable to Japan because the rise of oriental nationalism made it fearful for its own colonies, and because of its hostility to the Soviet Union. This tendency was 'emphasised by the relationship held by France towards the European neighbours of the Soviet Union'. By this was implied the Poles, who, the Russians believed, were trying to provoke further trouble between Japan and the Soviet Union which might lead to actual war.[2]

The decisive position was, however, held by England. Playing on American anti-British prejudice, Radek insinuated that imperialist Britain was in fact in favour of the Japanese venture as both anti-Chinese and anti-American. Towards America itself, Radek took up a different position and assumed that American interests were actually opposed to those of Japan but that the Americans were hopelessly handicapped by their refusal to act in concert with the Soviet Union, with whom they still had no official relations.

'The attitude of the United States towards the Soviet Union, which entails sacrificing the advantages of an economic and political *rapprochement* to the consideration of parochial politicians in search of thrillers for home consumption, is an example of the complete lack of vision and determination in the foreign policy of the United States.'

Soviet courtship of the United States was beginning. 'In the effort to maintain peace the Soviet Union will collaborate with

---

[1] It is interesting to compare this analysis of the attitudes of the Powers with that in the *Survey for 1932*, pp. 518–33. On German aims in the Far East, see K. Bloch, *German Interests and Policies in the Far East* (I.P.R., 1940).

[2] Voytinsky, Iolk, and Nasonov, loc. cit., p. 54. It is certainly true that some anti-Russian extremists in Poland were prepared to contemplate co-operation with the Japanese for the 'liberation' of Siberia. R. L. Buell, *Poland: Key to Europe* (3rd ed., New York, Knopf, 1939), p. 329.

any Power which desires the peaceful development of the Far East.' The implication was meant to be unmistakable.

The tension between Russia and Japan was, as we have noted, at its height in the spring of 1932; it diminished somewhat later in the year, as the probability of an immediate attack on Russian territory seemed to recede. This was perhaps due in part to the much-advertised strengthening of Russian defences in the Far Eastern Territory.

From a long-term point of view, however, these Far Eastern events produced a realignment of Russian relations in the Far East which was at the same time related to the changed position in Europe. The first question on the diplomatic agenda was that of China itself. From the Soviet point of view, the fierce attacks made upon Chiang Kai-shek in every Russian comment on Chinese internal affairs were no bar to a correct relationship with the Government at Nanking in which he was the leading figure. A resumption of relations with that Government had in fact been hoped for in Moscow ever since the breach. Negotiations for the purpose had begun in the spring of 1932 at Geneva between the respective delegates of the two countries to the Disarmament Conference. On that occasion, China had offered to conclude a Pact of non-aggression with the U.S.S.R. This offer had however been declined, partly, no doubt, on the usual principle that the maintenance of normal diplomatic relations with the U.S.S.R. should be the condition of any common action, and that the establishment or re-establishment of such relations should be unconditional.

Soviet eagerness to come to terms with China was no doubt increased by the events of 1932, by the Japanese threat to the Soviet Far East, and perhaps by the fear that as the inability of the League Powers to take any practical steps to halt Japan became more evident, the Chinese leader might be driven to an understanding with Japan which could hardly fail to be at the expense of the Soviet Union.[1] In addition there was the hope that an improvement of relations with China might lead at last to the attainment of a still more important objective of Soviet diplomacy, namely recognition by the United States.

China was also anxious to come to terms, because of her sense of isolation, and the hope that the U.S.S.R. might be ready to

[1] Although it was rarely recognised at the time, Japan's position had been rendered impregnable for the time being by the Washington Conference of 1921-1922. For the view that Chiang Kai-shek 'belongs to that type of Chinese statesman whom one may call "Little Chinese"' and as such was always capable of finding a basis of *de facto* agreement with Japan of the kind that more or less came about in the latter half of 1933, see Bienstock, op. cit., pp. 182-4.

give her material support. The two Governments had in common a desire to restore peace in the Far East with the minimum of sacrifice to Japanese appetites.

The attitude of the Soviet press to the Lytton Report was so hostile as to discourage any hopes of Soviet participation in further League measures. This was partly due to the Report's acceptance of the Japanese thesis on the 'Communist menace', which Chinese evidence to the Commission had also stressed.[1]

One further incident threw more light upon the tense relations between Russia and Japan at this time, and also upon the growing confidence of the Soviet Government. This was the rebellion, in September 1932, of General Su Ping-wen against the Manchurian authorities. The area which he controlled, the north-west corner of Manchuria, bordering upon the U.S.S.R. and Outer Mongolia, had so far escaped occupation by Japanese troops, and was clearly of cardinal importance from the point of view of Soviet strategy. It is therefore not surprising to find the Russians attempting to act as mediators between the General and the Japanese. They succeeded in arranging for the evacuation of Japanese citizens from Manchouli, but were unsuccessful in wider issues. At the beginning of December the Japanese crossed the Kingham Range, hitherto the limit of their advance, and established themselves in the area in question. General Su and his forces crossed over into Soviet territory and were interned.[2]

On 8 December the Japanese demanded through M. Amo, their Chargé d'Affaires at Moscow, that the General and his troops be handed over to them, for fear they should be allowed to go to China. M. Karakhan refused even to discuss the matter, as being the domestic affair of the U.S.S.R., a neutral country. Amo denied that neutrality applied, since Su was not a belligerent but a rebel and common criminal. Karakhan pointed out that the Japanese Government had repeatedly expressed their appreciation of Russia's neutrality and had agreed to negotiate with the General on Soviet (i.e. neutral) territory, thus clearly recognising his belligerent status. The Japanese demands were now moderated. It was now asked that the General himself be interned and the Japanese Government consulted as to the future of his troops. This new suggestion was no more successful. Karakhan's refusal took the form of a counter-attack:

[1] V. K. Wellington Koo, *Memoranda Presented to the Lytton Commission* (New York, 1932).

[2] *Survey for 1932*, pp. 438–9.

'White Guard generals and thousands of White Guard military were inhabiting the territory of Japan, principally Manchukuo territory, and enjoying complete freedom in the activities they conducted that were inimical to the U.S.S.R. On Manchukuo territory the White Guards had their organisations, military and otherwise, which enjoyed the patronage of official personages, and they occupied various official posts in the police and other public bodies.'

They persecuted Soviet citizens and attempted to worsen Russo-Japanese and Russo-Manchurian relations. Amo repeated his *démarche* on the 10th and received another rebuff. On the 11th, the whole story featured prominently in the Moscow Press.[1]

Meanwhile, in response to a Japanese request for information, M. Litvinov had admitted as early as 4 November that a proposal to resume relations with China had been made, but said that no steps had been taken. In fact, negotiations were completed on 12 December, when the two Governments agreed to resume relations.[2] The news produced an expression of extreme hostility from the Japanese. Their official spokesman was quoted as saying:

'The elements most disturbing to the peace of the world have now joined hands and Japan stands squarely against these forces. The question for the Powers is whether to allow the forces of destruction to rule in the Orient or the forces of consolidation. The restoration of Sino-Soviet relations poses this issue squarely: beside it the future of Manchuria is comparatively insignificant.'

On 13 December 1932, Japan replied in the negative to the year-old proposal for a non-aggression pact with the Soviet Union, saying that it would be necessary first of all to settle a number of outstanding points of conflict.[3] The Soviet Government's reply, on 4 January 1933, underlined its dissatisfaction:

'We regret that Japan refuses to make a step forward along the lines of the Kellogg Pact. Japan regards it as openly accepted that non-aggression pacts should only be made with those States with whom no points of conflict exist, which, taking into account current economic and political relations between neighbouring States, is a

---

[1] *China Year Book*, 1933, p. 550.
[2] *Soviet Union Review*, January 1933, p. 2.
[3] The matter had been discussed with M. Matsuoka when he passed through Moscow on his way to Geneva in November. *Survey for 1932*, p. 535. According to one account, the Japanese were very much fêted in the Russian capital. F. W. Moore, *With Japan's Leaders* (New York, Scribner, 1942), p. 132.

state of affairs which hardly exists and would hardly be possible. It is therefore doubtful whether the refusal of a State to conclude a non-aggression pact is calculated to solve points of conflict or to clear up misunderstandings as Japan wishes.'[1]

[1] Quoted from *Osteuropa*, VIII, p. 306.

III. THE SEARCH FOR COLLECTIVE SECURITY

Chapter Seven

INTRODUCTION

IN as far as it is reasonable at all to impose artificial divisions upon an essentially continuous theme, the period from the spring of 1933 to the spring of 1936 forms a fairly obvious one in the history of Soviet foreign policy. Its unifying factor, in the case of Russia, as in the case of every other European Power, was provided by the rebirth of German military might under the aegis of the Hitler régime. The repercussions of this were the more marked in that after a quiet start, the tone adopted by the new German Government towards the Soviet Union grew steadily more strident, reaching in 1936 a pitch of vituperativeness hitherto unknown in the intercourse of civilised nations. Whereas in the rest of Europe the growth of the German menace was met by an irregular but marked readiness to make concessions, and to abandon in everything but name the international machinery for keeping the peace, the Soviet attitude during these years, at least in so far as it could be ascertained from public speech and action, was precisely the reverse. For one thing, the Soviet Union was unaffected by the two major influences responsible for the disastrous ineffectiveness of the Western democracies: the ingrained pacifism of the left with its readiness to excuse German excesses as a retribution for the alleged iniquities of Versailles, and the readiness of large sections of the right to take at their face value the protestations of the Nazi régime that its maintenance was essential as a bulwark against the Bolshevist menace. In addition, the Soviet Union's own pet illusion had received a shattering blow by the complete failure of the German working-class to prevent the rise of Hitler or to hamper the remilitarisation of Germany. The limelight shed upon the German Communist Party by the Reichstag trial, and the martyrdom in less dramatic circumstances of other opponents of the new order of things, could not hide the fact that resistance would henceforward be the affair of a comparatively negligible minority and that the Germany that would have to be reckoned with would be the Germany of Hitler and his associates.

While the ultimate objectives of the German Government

would prove to be a matter concerning which the writings and speeches of Hitler gave little room for doubt,[1] the tactics which Germany might follow in the achievement of her strategy of conquest could not of course be foreseen, nor could, in their entirety, the reactions of the other major Powers.

The most obvious and comparatively direct tasks of M. Litvinov, who seems in these years to have had a fairly free hand in the day-to-day conduct of Soviet foreign policy, were three in number. The first was to prevent the new threat in the West from combining its pressure with the old threat in the East.[2] That meant making concessions to Japan, of which by far the most important was the sale of the Chinese Eastern Railway and with it the liquidation of the Russian stake in Manchuria. As a further line of defence there was the attempt to come to some arrangement with the United States. The Chinese, also, were to be encouraged to keep Japan busy without however forcing Russia to appear as a principal on the Chinese scene.

The second task was to avert the old bugbear of a general capitalist coalition against the Soviet Union. This became equivalent to unshakable and not unnatural hostility to the idea of the so-called Four-Power Pact, the notion that the outstanding political and armament problems of Europe should be settled by direct conversations between Great Britain, France, Germany, and Italy. Launched by Mussolini in March 1933, this method of settling European problems never completely vanished from view until the outbreak of war.[3] Soviet hostility to the idea, made clear from the beginning, was shared by Poland and the Little Entente; and France, fearing to lose her influence over her Eastern European allies, secured the elimination from the text of the Pact of all references to the possibility of treaty revision (apart from a mention of Article 19 of the Covenant), and to equality of status for Germany, the two features which had been the heart of the original Anglo-Italian plan.[4] This did not suffice to allay suspicions in the

---

[1] According to his not altogether reliable American biographer, Litvinov had read *Mein Kampf* as early as 1928. An enquiry at Geneva in 1936 revealed that he was the only statesman of those regularly attending conferences there who had read it in full. A. U. Pope, *Maxim Litvinoff* (New York, Fischer, 1943), pp. 317–18.

[2] Nervousness about a German-Japanese understanding was expressed in Litvinov's speech of 29 December 1933, *Documents for 1933*, pp. 425–42.

[3] The origins of the Four-Power Pact are discussed in *Survey for 1933*, II (ii).

[4] The Pact was initialed on 7 June and signed on 15 July 1933, *Documents for 1933*, pp. 236–7.

Soviet Union, where the pact was regarded as primarily a bid for British leadership in European affairs, with the object of averting an Italian-German alignment which would come into head-on conflict with France. British policy was considered to be contemplating the revival in a new form of the Pan-Europa scheme of Briand with a general anti-Soviet coalition as its fundamental *raison d'être*.[1] M. Litvinov, in his Moscow speech on 29 December 1933 pointed out that proposals for treaty revision involved the satisfaction of territorial claims at the expense of the U.S.S.R. and the Baltic States, which had not themselves been beneficiaries of Versailles, and that projects of this kind were the determining factor in the Soviet attitude to the Four-Power Pact as well as to other international problems.[2]

The aim of preventing an anti-Soviet coalition was pursued by the obvious method of cultivating friendly relations with as many States as possible and in particular with those bordering upon the Soviet Union. Friendship with Turkey was maintained, and in May 1935 the Turks received Soviet support at the League Council on the question of their grievances under the Straits Convention.[3] The non-aggression pact signed with Italy on 2 September 1933, proved to be the last of the series.[4] Henceforth more positive guarantees were sought.

As it was clear that German power would continue to grow unchecked, it was reasonable to anticipate that Germany would one day embark single-handed or with only secondary allies upon its planned career of eastward expansion. The danger appeared greater in that there were elements in the Western democracies who might not be unwilling to direct the Nazi flood into eastward channels, thus freeing the west, at least for a time, from both the Nazi and the Bolshevik peril. The danger of a German attack of this kind, even if Japan held aloof, was obviously considerable at a time when the reconstruction of the defence industries under the Second Five-Year Plan was only just getting into its stride, and when the internal troubles of the period of agricultural collectivisation were still an important factor in precisely those regions which Hitler most openly coveted and in which Russia's productive capacity was still so largely concentrated. To avoid or at least delay the struggle with Germany was thus the third major imperative of Soviet policy in the years under discussion.

Faced with a somewhat similar and in a sense more immediate version of the same problem, the Polish Government had

[1] See Radek's article 'The Pact of Four', *Izvestia*, 2 June 1933.
[2] *Documents for 1933*, pp. 425-42.   [3] *Survey for 1936*, IV (i).
[4] *Documents for 1933*, pp. 233-6.

finally attempted a radical solution. In January 1934, Poland
concluded a ten-year pact of non-aggression with her formidable
neighbour.[1] A similar course of action was for obvious reasons
not open to Soviet Russia. The only deterrent which it seemed
reasonable to hope for was the re-awakening of the old German
fear of a war on two fronts. To do this it was necessary to make
it self-evident that any German aggression in the east would
be the signal for a general war. Two alternative paths towards
this goal seemed to be open. The first was to revivify the existing international organs and to turn them into weapons for the
mobilisation of armed resistance to Germany and her associates.
It was this policy which culminated in Russia's entry into the
League of Nations and the emergence of M. Litvinov as the
most determined and most vocal adherent of a 'strong' League.[2]
The second path—and one simultaneously pursued—was to
complete the Locarno system of guarantees by parallel arrangements in the East and to bridge the two systems of security by
giving a positive content to the recent *rapprochement* with France.
The negotiations for an Eastern Security Pact in the years
1934–1935 broke against the resistance of Germany to any
multilateral arrangement which might act as a curb on her
eastern ambitions, and the refusal of Poland to enter into an
arrangement in which Germany had no place prevented even
a more modest measure being adopted.[3] The only tangible
results were the pacts of 1935 with France and Czechoslovakia.

Considerations of defence thus dominated Soviet policy in
the years 1933–1936 to a greater extent than in the preceding

[1] Text of the Polish-German Declaration of 26 January 1934, *Documents
for 1933*, pp. 424–5. Cf. *Survey for 1933*, pp. 183–8. German-Polish relations
from January 1934 to May 1936 are discussed in *Survey for 1935*, vol. i, I (vii).
After the pact with Germany was signed, a report was circulated that
Poland had acted thus because of the refusal by France to agree to a proposal made by Pilsudski that France should join Poland in a preventive
war against Germany. This report was given wide currency by 'Pertinax',
who used it in his attacks upon French statesmen whom he accused of
weakness towards Germany. It has also been reaffirmed from time to time
in Polish circles, but no strictly contemporary evidence for it has as yet
come to light. Later, 'Pertinax' seems to have come round to the view
that the Poles made this offer, knowing it would be refused, so as to be able
to point to the refusal as an excuse for the *rapprochement* with Germany
which they had already decided upon. 'Pertinax', *Les Fossoyeurs* (New
York, Maison Française, 1943), vol. ii, p. 83. Cf. the article by 'Augure',
'The Foreign Policy of Poland', *Slavonic Review*, January 1937, where, however, the German-Polish crisis of 1933 is misdated 1934.

[2] This is the principal theme of the study of Russian foreign policy in the
Survey for 1934, III, B, (1).

[3] The Eastern Pact negotiations are recorded in *Survey for 1935*, vol. i, I.
They are discussed *infra*, chap. 12.

period. Questions of trade, though not overlooked, were less decisive than purely political issues, since the Second Five-Year Plan made smaller demands for imports and credits than its predecessor, while the recovery from the depression in the outside world made Soviet markets and the competition for them of comparatively minor interest to foreign statesmen. From 1933 to 1937 Russia had a favourable balance of trade and with the expansion of her gold production towards the end of the period, basic imports could be obtained without undue difficulty.[1]

The position of the Soviet Union as an avowed centre of world revolutionary activity became less and less compatible with a diplomatic course which was directed towards ever closer relations with individual capitalist countries. The old dichotomy between the two worlds had to be discarded in favour of a differentiation between the actively aggressive, the passively indifferent and the actively co-operative States.[2] In only the first of these could the Communist parties be encouraged to engage in revolutionary activity—and it was in these States that the Communists were anyhow weakest. In the others— and in particular in the 'peace-loving' States such as France and China—it became the business of the Communist parties to prevent the emergence of governments ready to compromise with the aggressor. This involved the end of the 'leftward' turn of 1928 in favour of a new era of 'popular fronts'. This policy, accepted and acclaimed by the Seventh (and last) Comintern Congress in July-August 1935, proved as unfruitful as its predecessors, and the mere existence of the Comintern continued to complicate the tasks of Litvinov's diplomacy.

[1] See the Appendix to chap. 3, *supra* and cf. Yugow, op. cit., p. 99.

[2] The tripartite differentiation was made by Litvinov in the speech of 29 December 1933, already referred to and of which extracts are in *Documents for 1933*. See on this point especially pp. 425–6. In addition, of course, the comparative recovery in the world economic situation gave less scope for revolutionary activity.

Chapter Eight

RUSSIA AND THE NAZI REICH

THE development of Russo-German relations between the summer of 1933 and the spring of 1936 could only be dealt with fully against the general background of events both in Europe and Asia and with an eye to the closely guarded secrets of both countries, rearmament. The reliability of some of the evidence which is public—for instance the reports of the Russian State trials of 1936 and 1937—has been the subject of much discussion.[1] The relations between the two Governments (with which alone this chapter is concerned) were largely carried on in the form of a long-range oratorical bombardment. In these exchanges Germany was clearly the aggressor and the rarer speeches of the Soviet leaders invariably emphasised their desire to remain on amicable terms.[2] It is probable that these anti-Soviet outbursts of the Nazi leaders can to some extent be discounted. The group round Alfred Rosenberg were of course implacably anti-Soviet.[3] But the parade of anti-Bolshevik sentiments proved the most potent instrument in sterilising anti-Nazi reactions in the democratic countries of Europe and America.

There were genuine reasons for doubting whether the public exchanges between the two countries really expressed their policies towards each other. It was obvious from fairly early on that no real resistance to the Nazi régime was likely from the democratic or socialist elements in the Reich. And the Communists, whatever their intentions, had suffered such an extreme of physical suppression that the Russians could not

[1] E Fraenkel: 'German-Russian relations since 1918', *Review of Politics* (University of Notre Dame), January 1940.

[2] The evidence provided by the Nuremburg trial of German 'war criminals' which began in November 1945 did not appear in time for consideration here. Its tendency is to show that the major question for Germany's rulers after 1933 was not *whether* to attack other European countries, including Russia, but *when* and in *what order* to attack them. The scope of the plans grew with Germany's increasing strength. See the *Indictment* presented on 18 October 1945. Cmd. 6696 (1945).

[3] The Rosenberg group looked forward to territorial expansion at the Soviet Union's expense. As early as the autumn of 1932 a conspicuous figure in Rosenberg's entourage was Skoropadsky, who had headed the German puppet government in the Ukraine in 1918. B. Fromm, *Blood and Banquets* (Bles, 1944), pp. 57–8. For Skoropadsky's régime in 1918, see Chamberlin, *The Russian Revolution* (Macmillan, 1935), vol. ii, pp. 125–30.

have much hope of useful activity on their part.[1] On the other hand a complete accord on questions of foreign policy could hardly be expected from the amalgam of Conservative and parvenu elements which now ruled Germany. It was clear that there still remained important factions favourable to the pro-Russian orientation already noted among a section of the German right.[2] It was however economic interests which

[1] It took some time for the new situation to be appreciated in Moscow. As late as 31 December 1933, *Bolshevik* printed the following: 'In Germany the proletarian revolution is nearer to realisation than in any other country; and the victory of the proletarian revolution in Germany means victory of proletarian revolution throughout Europe, since capitalist Europe cannot exist if it loses its heart. . . . He who does not understand the German question does not understand the development of proletarian revolution in Europe.' Quoted in D. Dallin, *Russia and Post-war Europe* (Yale University Press, 1943), p. 62.

[2] On the German side a persistent thread of military-political thinking favourable to a pro-Russian alignment was provided by the teachings of the Munich school of geopolitics under General Haushofer. His chief personal link with the Hitler circle, Rudolf Hess, abandoned Haushofer's ideas in favour of making an anti-Communist ideology the basis of the country's foreign policy. The Anti-Comintern Pact of 1936 ran against all the ideas of the Haushofer school, which had since 1924 striven uninterruptedly for an alliance which should ultimately embrace not only Russia and Japan but also China and a 'liberated' India. Haushofer's apparent defeat at the hands of Rosenberg was of course reversed, though only partially and temporarily, by the Russo-German pact of August 1939. A second negative influence was that of Oswald Spengler, whose specious, though modish, philosophy regarded Russia as a country of the future. Russia, whose destiny was now Asiatic, could not, he argued, be conquered from Europe, of whose Marches Germany was the defender. 'To make even the attempt impossible', he wrote in 1933, 'the Bolsheviks have transferred the centre of gravity of their system farther and farther eastward. The great industrial areas which are important to power-politics have one and all been built up east of Moscow, for the greater part east of the Urals as far as the Altai, and on the south down to the Caucasus. The whole area west of Moscow, White Russia, the Ukraine, once from Riga to Odessa the most vital portion of the Tsar's empire—forms to-day a fantastic glacis against "Europe". It could be sacrificed without a crash of the whole system. But by the same token any idea of an offensive from the West has become senseless. It would be a thrust into empty space.' O. Spengler, *The Hour of Decision* (Allen & Unwin, 1934), p. 61. Cf. H. Weigert: *Generals and Geographers* (New York, Oxford University Press, 1942). The whole of this study of the geopoliticians is very suggestive for a student of Russo-German relations, though there is no evidence that geopolitics was seriously studied on the Soviet side. General Niedermayer, one of Haushofer's associates, was a military attaché in Moscow from 1933 to 1939. The possibility of a German reaction towards friendship with Russia at the expense of Poland and the Western Powers was not overlooked by some observers. See the anonymous article 'Russo-German relations since the War', *Slavonic Review*, July 1936. 'The continuation of a Russian policy was by no means unpopular among the National Socialist leaders. Apart from Rosenberg, there were few prominent members of the Party who would not have preferred a Russian to the

seemed to provide the best guarantee against a total cessation
of relations between the two countries. The heavy imports of
goods from Germany dropped off sharply after 1932, although
Russian exports to Germany showed no corresponding decline
until 1936. (These exports were of course largely made in
order to enable Russia to repay the credits previously received.)
From having supplied 46·5 per cent of Russia's imports in 1932,
the German share declined to 9 per cent in 1935.[1] Germany's
primacy among Russia's suppliers had been lost to Great
Britain in the previous year. In 1932, Russia had taken
30·5 per cent of Germany's exports of machinery; in 1934 she
took only 5 per cent. In 1935, Great Britain replaced Germany
as Russia's principal foreign market. Russian purchases from
America also took a sharp upward turn from 1934.[2] Germany
made strong and persistent efforts to remedy this situation, as
the loss of the Russian market could ill be afforded. Negotiations for the prolongation of German credits in return for new
Russian orders were taken up without success no fewer than
four times in 1934.[3] On 9 April 1935, an agreement was
reached extending to the Soviet Union a new credit of 200
million marks in return for the promise of new purchases.[4]

Polish pact.' H. Rauschning, *Germany's Revolution of Destruction* (Heinemann,
1939), pp. 272–3.

[1] SOVIET-GERMAN TRADE

	Exports to Germany		Imports from Germany	
	In R.M. millions	Percentage of total Soviet Exports	In R.M. millions	Percentage of total Soviet Imports
1931 . . .	304	15·9	763	37·1
1932 . . .	271	17·9	626	46·5
1933 . . .	194	17·3	282	42·5
1934 . . .	210	23·4	63	12·4
1935 . . .	215	18·0	39	9·0
1936 . . .	93	8·6	126	22·8
1937 . . .	65	6·2	117	15·0
1938 . . .	47	6·6	32	4·7

League of Nations Economic Intelligence Service: *International Trade
Statistics.* Yugow, op. cit., p. 108 (1938 figures only).

[2] An understanding that Russian purchases from America would be
increased appears to have been part of the bargain made by Litvinov in
November 1933. W. E. Dodd, *Ambassador Dodd's Diary* (Gollancz, 1941),
p. 75. There was no trade agreement until July 1935. The point is further
discussed *infra*, chap. 10.

[3] *Survey for 1936*, p. 390.

[4] The agreement is analysed by Höffding, *Slavonic Review*, 1935–1936. The
same authority points out that in the second half of 1934 and in the early
part of 1935, Soviet trade in Germany was in a more favourable position

These were slow to come in but their volume rose towards the end of the year.[1] On 29 April 1936, a new credit agreement was signed and the year was to see a marked growth of trade between the two countries. Germany in this year supplied no less than 22·8 per cent of Russia's imports, half as much again as Great Britain and only slightly less than the United States.[2]

The advent of the Nazis had at first led to a slight *détente* on the diplomatic side of Russo-German relations. On 5 May 1933, the German-Soviet conciliation agreement of 25 January 1931, and the protocol of 24 June 1931, prolonging the neutrality treaty of 24 April 1926, had at last been ratified.[3] On the following day, *Izvestia* made this comment: 'in spite of their attitude towards Fascism, the people of the U.S.S.R. wish to live in peace with Germany and consider that the development of German-Soviet relations is in the interests of both countries.'[4] Events in the summer and autumn did not give much encouragement to such hopes, and Russia's movement towards the *status quo* camp in Europe became more and more marked. Hitler's speeches in the electoral campaign which followed Germany's withdrawal from the Disarmament Conference and the League were charged with anti-Communist venom.[5] The

---

than that of any other country, since it was not subjected to the exchange control. The Soviet Trade Delegation were accused of using this position to force up the prices of their goods, and even of importing into Germany non-Soviet goods as Soviet products, and of reaping large profits from this procedure. Whatever the truth of this, subsequent regulations made such combinations impracticable.

[1] In his speech on 11 January 1936, M. Molotov referred to the offer of a new and larger credit, this time for a period of ten years: 'Although we are not chasing after foreign credit and, in contradistinction to past days, are now to a large extent purchasing abroad for cash and not on credit, we have not refused and are not now refusing, to consider also this business proposal of the German Government.' *Documents for 1935*, I, p. 226.

[2] In 1937, despite the further renewal of the credit for one year, Russian imports from Germany fell off again, though not back to the low level of 1935. Exports from Russia to Germany continued to decline and reached a new low level in 1937. As has been noted, Russia had a considerable favourable balance in her foreign trade in the years 1933–1935; in 1936 this almost vanished owing to a sharp fall in Russian exports. The position was largely restored in 1937. In 1938, Russia had the first unfavourable balance since 1932. (Appendix to chap. 3, *supra*.) In 1935, the Soviet Union also claimed to be the second largest producer of gold in the world. See the article by Rosengoltz, Commissar for Foreign Trade, in *Pravda* (7 November 1935), quoted by Coates, *Anglo-Soviet Relations*, pp. 545–6.

[3] Text of protocols of ratification, L.N.T.S., vol. 157, p. 383.

[4] *Izvestia*, 6 May 1933, cited by V. M. Dean, 'The Soviet Union as a European Power', *Foreign Policy Reports*, 2 August 1933.

[5] *Hitler's Speeches*, pp. 1059, 1115–16, 1127.

moderate and conciliatory nature of the Russian reaction was apparent in the speeches delivered at the end of September before the Central Executive Committee of the U.S.S.R.:

'Remaining true to our principles,' observed M. Molotov on the 28th, 'the principles of defending world peace and the independence of our country, the U.S.S.R. has no reason to alter her policy towards Germany. However, on the part of the ruling group in Germany, many attempts have been made in the past year to revise relations with the Soviet Union.'

After mentioning Rosenberg and Hugenberg, he emphasised that the best interests of both countries would be served by their mutual endeavour to maintain peace and develop economic relations.[1] On the following day, the 29th, M. Litvinov took up the same theme at greater length. He referred somewhat sarcastically to the evidence of a German-Japanese *rapprochement*, and pointed out as significant the continued circulation in Germany of unexpurgated versions of *Mein Kampf*. He denied that Russia was itself turning against Germany because of its internal policy and in particular because of its persecution of Communists:

'We of course sympathise with the sufferings of our German comrades, but we Marxists are the last who can be reproached with allowing our feelings to dictate our policy.
'The whole world knows that we can and do maintain good relations with capitalist States of any régime including the Fascist. We do not interfere in the internal affairs of Germany, as we do not interfere in that of other countries, and our relations with her are conditioned not by her internal but by her external policy.'

It was impossible, he declared, not to take into account speeches and facts in direct contradiction to the official declarations of the German Government about their desire for good relations with the Soviet Union. Let Germany look to the actions of her emissaries and agents if she wish to prove her sincerity. 'But,' he continued, 'we also declare the following: We desire to have with Germany, as with other States, the best of relations. Nothing but good can result from such relations, both for the Soviet Union and Germany.' The Soviet Union had no expansionist designs and would never attack the territory or rights of the German people or encourage other States to make attacks upon them. In his speech before the Seventeenth Congress of the C.P.S.U. on 26 January 1934, Stalin made the same points with even greater vehemence,

[1] *Soviet Foreign Policy* (Pamphlet of the Anglo-Russian Parliamentary Committee, January 1934), p. 17.

denying that the Soviet Union had entered upon a new anti-German orientation, but saying that it could not remain indifferent to the fact that the new policy of expansion at Russia's expense was clearly gaining ground in German opinion.[1]

Hitler in his speech to the Reichstag on 30 January took an optimistic view of the implications of Stalin's speech. He declared that the German people desired to live at peace with all nations whatever their dominant philosophy:

'This is the only explanation of why, in spite of the great difference of the two prevailing forms of philosophy, the German Reich continued to endeavour in this year to cultivate friendly relations with Russia. As M. Stalin in his last great speech expressed the fear that forces hostile to the Soviet might be active in Germany, I must correct this opinion in so far by stating here that Communistic tendencies or even propaganda would be no more tolerated in Germany than German National Socialistic tendencies would be tolerated in Russia. The more clearly and unambiguously this fact becomes evident and is respected by both parties, the easier will be the cultivation of interests common to both countries. Hence we greet the effort to stabilise relations in the East of Europe by a system of pacts, if the leading idea of this activity is the strengthening of peace rather than tactical and political aims.'[2]

Relations between the two countries for the remainder of the year scarcely lived up to these expectations. For one thing, there was the increasing evidence of a *rapprochement* between Germany and Japan.[3] Hitler's greeting on 7 February 1935, to the new Japanese Ambassador was distinctly cordial.[4] Equally important was Germany's opposition to the Eastern Pact. The nature of this was made quite clear when M. Litvinov spoke to Neurath in Berlin on 13 June 1934.[5] Finally, there were indications that Russia's admittance to the League might be an additional obstacle to Germany's return.[6]

---

[1] *Socialism Victorious* (Martin Lawrence, 1934), pp. 20–1.

[2] *Hitler's Speeches*, p. 1161.

[3] On 17 May 1934, the United States Military Attaché in Berlin reported that evidence was accumulating which tended 'to show the existence of unusually close and friendly relations between Germany and Japan even to the extent of a possible secret alliance'. *Peace and War* (U.S. State Department, 1943), pp. 222–3. Cf. the note by the Minister to Austria (Messersmith) of his conversation with Ambassador Dodd on 22 March 1935, ibid., p. 255.

[4] *Hitler's Speeches*, p. 1204.   [5] *Survey for 1935*, vol. i, p. 64.

[6] On 13 September, Hitler told the correspondent of the Paris paper, *L'Intransigeant*, that 'it would be necessary to follow the development of the situation created by the admission (to the League) of new members, who pursue the realisation of a particular programme, as for example, the

Nevertheless there were those who considered that the possibility of a *rapprochement* was not excluded and rumours to this effect were in circulation during the commercial talks in November.[1] Nothing occurred to justify these suspicions; the commercial negotiations were not completed and Hitler, in a conversation with the Polish Ambassador on 22 January 1935, again referred to the dangers confronting Germany and Poland from Russia's growing military strength.

M. Molotov again took up the theme of Russo-German relations in his speech of 28 January 1935, before the All-Union Congress of Soviets:

'It is impossible to close our eyes to the changes that have taken place in Soviet-German relations with the coming to power of National Socialism. As for ourselves, we can say that we have not had and do not have any other wish than to continue further good relations with Germany. . . .'

He went on to draw attention once more to the familiar passages from *Mein Kampf*, repeated in new editions of the book, and asked whether they still continued in force. Clearly, he argued, this was so 'as only on this surmise does a great deal become clear in the present relations of the German Government to the Soviet Union and also to the project of an Eastern Pact'.[2]

---

diffusion of the Communist ideal throughout the world'. *Hitler's Speeches*, p. 1189. The interview was printed on the 21st. Cf. the more guarded remarks of Neurath in his speech of the 19th, *Documents for 1934*, p. 334.

[1] Commenting on the commercial negotiations in his diary on 9 November, Ambassador Dodd wrote: 'The fact that a great number of high German officials and generals of the Reichswehr were most conspicuous at the Russian reception two days ago, indicated something, though Hitler, Goering, and Goebbels were not present. In my judgment the Reichswehr, the Foreign Office and the royalists are all pressing Hitler for a Russian pact like that with Poland, which was a surprise to all the world in 1933 [*sic*.] The idea is to isolate France and to find a market for German goods as the former régime found. The Russian idea is to let the United States know that they are not so important. It all points to peace for a few years, that is, until Germany can be entirely ready to command Europe.' Dodd, op. cit., p. 197. The next evening he was told by the Polish Ambassador that 'he thought a German-Russian pact was in progress, perhaps already signed''. ibid. On the 17th Dodd had a further discussion with Lipski who was frank: 'The pact of last winter is only a temporary affair. Germany intends to re-annex part of our country, the maps posted all over Germany show this clearly. I protested against this a few days ago but received no satisfactory answer from the Foreign Office. The Russians and the Germans are negotiating a commercial treaty which I think has a political and military pact attached, but it is secret and these negotiations are going on largely to isolate France.' ibid., pp. 201–2. In October 1934, a new Soviet Ambassador, Jacob Suritz, was appointed to Berlin.

[2] *Documents for 1934*, pp. 412–14.

The open increase in German military strength and the re-introduction of conscription were the main factors in Soviet-German relations in 1935.[1] M. Litvinov's fear that the latter measure was a preparation for aggression was voiced in his speech to the League Council on 17 April.[2]

In explaining, in a speech on 21 May 1935, the German objections to the Eastern Pact, Herr Hitler emphasised that apart from the question of principle, this was a special case because of the diametrical opposition between National-Socialism and the international ideas of Soviet Russia. He reproached France for having brought an 'element of legal insecurity' into the Locarno Pact by signing the Franco-Russian Pact (on 2 May).[3]

It is fairly clear that the Russians' fears were not wholly without foundation. In January 1935, General Goering visited Warsaw and in a conversation with the Under-Secretary for Foreign Affairs expounded his views on the necessity of Polish-German friendship: 'further discussing Polish-German relations, Goering pointed out that Poland formed a link between the Baltic and the Black Sea and that great opportunities were open to her on the Ukrainian side'. According to M. Lipski, Goering went even further in his talks with Polish generals, 'almost suggesting an anti-Russian alliance and a joint attack on Russia. He gave it to be understood that the Ukraine would become a Polish sphere of influence and North-Western Russia would be Germany's.' Similar hints were apparently made by Goering to Pilsudski himself but without much response.[4] In a conversation between Goering and Lipski (in Germany) at the end of April 1935, Goering again expounded his anti-Soviet views.[5] He had a further opportunity of talking to Polish statesmen when visiting Cracow for Pilsudski's funeral on 18 May. On the 22nd, Herr Hitler himself had a long colloquy with M. Lipski: 'In his Eastern policy the Chancellor took up the position that a *rapprochement* with Poland was more advantageous

[1] *Survey for 1935*, vol. i, I, (vi). Russians noted the large rôle assigned to cavalry in plans for the new German army in view of the possible use of this arm for a campaign in the steppes of Southern Russia. Milioukov, op. cit., p. 489.

[2] L.N.O.J., 1935, pp. 556 ff. Note that the new commercial agreement had nevertheless been signed on the 9th.

[3] *Hitler's Speeches*, pp. 1234–7.

[4] *Polish White Book* (London, n.d. [1939]), pp. 25–6. 'The Marshal in reply *tat gestutzt* (stiffened), as M. Goering later put it, and gave it to be understood that despite all this it was impossible to stand continually at the ready on such a long line as the Polish-Soviet frontier.'

[5] *Polish White Book*, pp. 26–7. On 7 April, Poland had (though unenthusiastically) cast her vote at Geneva for the Anglo-French-Italian resolution condemning Germany's violation of the Versailles Treaty.

H

to Germany than uneasy relations with Russia. Russia is Asia he said.'[1] M. Beck's visit to Berlin at the beginning of July 1935, and the announcement that 'the conversations revealed a far-reaching agreement of views', were also calculated to alarm Moscow.[2]

Fear of a German-Japanese agreement would also seem to have been a constant preoccupation of the Russian leaders.[3] The Comintern Congress in July–August gave Hitler a further opportunity of denouncing Bolshevism.[4] Everything indeed seemed to point to an increase in the tension between Russia and Germany. M. Litvinov, speaking at Geneva on 14 September, denounced the 'political conception that is fighting the idea of collective security and advocating bilateral pacts'. Some States, secured by a pact of non-aggression on their rear or flank, obtained by this means 'the facility of attacking with impunity third States. . . . He who says localisation of war, means freedom of war, its legalisation. . . .' There were two theories, security of peaceable nations and security of aggression. 'Fortunately the latter theory is common to a very few countries and stigmatises them before the whole world as probable disturbers of the peace.'[5] A protest from Beck, who took these remarks as addressed at least in part to Poland, was answered by Litvinov with the assurance that Germany alone was envisaged.[6]

On 13 December 1935, in a conversation with Sir Eric Phipps,

---

[1] *Survey for 1935*, vol. i, p. 206. *Polish White Book*, pp. 29–30.

[2] Official communiqué of 4 July, ibid., pp. 30–1. Speaking of this meeting in a talk with Dodd on the 6th, Neurath said: 'We are on the best of terms. Our object was to defeat the French-Russian pact and prevent the Danube agreement proposed at Stresa . . . (there was no) agreement with Poland about our control of the Baltic Sea. We must control that area to keep Russia off the ocean.' Dodd, op. cit., p. 264. The Stresa Conference is dealt with in *Survey for 1935*, vol. i, I (vi) (3). Russo-Polish relations now took a turn for the worse. The Soviet Press was sharply critical of Polish policy. In August the Polish Press representative in Moscow was expelled and the Tass Agency correspondent in Warsaw had his permit cancelled in retaliation. ibid., p. 279.

[3] On 29 May, the Soviet Ambassador to Berlin mentioned to Dodd his suspicion that an agreement of this kind existed. Dodd, op. cit., p. 258. The American Ambassador in Tokyo had noted on 2 April 1935 that they had indications of 'an intimate exchange of views and information' between Germany and Japan. J. C. Grew, *Ten Years in Japan* (New York, Simon and Schuster, 1944), p. 155.

[4] Proclamation of 11 September 1935 in *Hitler's Speeches*, p. 1252. Cf. Neurath's remarks to Sir Eric Phipps on 16 September. Cmd. 5143 (1936), p. 57.

[5] *Documents for 1935*, vol. i, p. 250.

[6] *Survey for 1935*, vol. i, p. 279; R. Machray, *The Poland of Pilsudski* (Allen & Unwin, 1936), pp. 414–15.

Herr Hitler not only refused to participate in any general European settlement to which Russia should be a party, but for the first time declared that the Franco-Russian pact made any 'Western air-pact' out of the question.[1] This declaration was apparently accompanied by one of his most furious outbursts against communism.[2] On 18 December, Hitler treated Lipski to another of these tirades.[3]

The German Chancellor's New Year proclamation, with its anti-Bolshevist theme, provided an inauspicious beginning to the year 1936.[4]

Molotov's speech of 11 January before the Central Executive Committee did not conceal the tense state of affairs.[5]

'I must say quite frankly', he declared, 'that the Soviet Government would have desired the establishment of better relations with Germany than exist at present. . . . But the realisation of such a policy depends not only on us but also on the German Government.'

He again reverted to the offending passages from *Mein Kampf* which had not been repudiated:

'Carrying their plans to extremes, Messieurs the National Socialists, as we all know, are driving their preparations precisely in the direction of such aggrandisement, although not in this direction alone.'

He went on to denounce the elements in Finland and Poland which were echoing propaganda of this kind and expatiated on the danger threatening Czechoslovakia. After referring at some length to the evidence of friction with Japan, he went on:

'Reports recently appeared of the conclusion of a military agreement between Japan and Germany and of Poland's complicity in this matter. There is nothing unexpected in this for us. It is not for nothing that both Germany and Japan left the League of Nations in good time, in order to have their hands free, and, with good reason, are regarded by the whole world as the Powers with the most aggressive foreign policy.

'The Fascist rulers of Germany sometimes endeavour to divert

---

[1] Cmd. 5143, pp. 61–2.   [2] Dodd, op. cit., pp. 294, 318–19.

[3] 'He was resolutely opposed to drawing Russia into the West. . . . Germany had had to pay for her *rapprochement* with Soviet Russia by a social revolution. He was afraid that other countries also would have to atone for it. He was in favour of European solidarity, but in his opinion this solidarity ended at the Polish-Soviet frontier. The most general of air pacts could embrace only those States which recognised the same ethical principles in international policy. How could there be any association with Soviet Russia, which proclaimed world revolution?' *Polish White Book*, p. 31.

[4] *Hitler's Speeches*, p. 1257.

[5] See the extracts in *Documents for 1935*, vol. i, pp. 222–30.

the attention of naïve people from their plans of conquest with regard to the Soviet Union by referring to the absence of common frontiers between Germany and the U.S.S.R. But we know, on the other hand, that Germany, encouraged by certain foreign Powers, is feverishly preparing to occupy a dominant position in the Baltic and has established special relations with Poland, which has fairly extensive common frontiers with the Soviet Union.'[1]

Marshal Tukhachevsky, in a speech devoted to the need for strengthening the country's defences, said:

'You know well that Schlieffen, in preparing an offensive march against France, aimed his main blow, not where Germany had contiguous borders with France, but exactly where Germany had no contiguous borders with France whatsoever. . . . It goes without saying that in present circumstances, when between Germany and ourselves there are certain States with whom the Germans are maintaining special relations, the German Army, should the desire be very great, will find ways of invading our territory.'[2]

Although there is no evidence of Polish willingness to listen to German solicitations, there is ample proof of the German persistence in them. On 12 February, Frank, the German Minister for Justice, visited Warsaw and put forward the idea of Polish-French-German collaboration as 'the only way to an effective struggle against the barbarism which would come from the East'.[3] Between the 19th and 23rd February, Goering also visited Poland, allegedly on a hunting trip. Herr Hitler was also doing his best to present Nazi Germany as the Western World's surest bulwark against Communism.[4]

[1] Dodd wrote in his diary on 29 February 1936 that Neurath had told him that Germany would not be drawn into a war with Russia even if Japan did attack the Soviet Union, but commented: 'there is much evidence here that Germany and Japan are in some way tied up'. Op. cit., p. 322. Hitler endeavoured on 4 February, in his interview with Lord Londonderry, to convince the latter that a defeat of Japan would be no advantage to Great Britain. Marquess of Londonderry, *Ourselves and Germany* (Hale, 1938), p. 105.
[2] Speech of 15 January 1936; translation in *Slavonic Review*, XIV.
[3] *Polish White Book*, p. 31. The reference to collaboration with France as well probably represents part of the 'war of nerves' being carried on in order to prevent France ratifying the pact with the U.S.S.R.
[4] In an interview with Lord Londonderry on 4 February Hitler elaborated his anti-Communist theme. Lord Londonderry made these views public in a speech in England on 23 February. Marquess of Londonderry, *Ourselves and Germany*, pp. 94–107; *Wings of Destiny* (Macmillan, 1943), pp. 158–64. In an interview with a French journalist on 21 February, Hitler declared that it was necessary 'not to overlook the fact that Soviet Russia was a political element having at its disposal an explosive revolutionary idea and gigantic armaments'. *Hitler's Speeches*, pp. 1266–71. The interview was not published until 28 February, the Franco-Soviet Pact having been

The way was thus clear for the speech of 7 March 1936, in which Chancellor Hitler brought his anti-Soviet campaign to a verbal climax by using the Franco-Soviet pact as an excuse for the repudiation of Locarno.[1]

'Comparing the German nation with the Russian in regard to territory, the Russians have eighteen times more land for each member of the population than the Germans have. . . .

'If my international opponents reproach me to-day that I have refused this co-operation with Russia, I make them the following declaration: I do not and did not reject co-operation with Russia but with Bolshevism, which lays claim to a world rulership. . . .

'With this Bolshevik section of Europe we desire no closer contact than the ordinary political and economic relations. . . .

'This new Franco-Soviet agreement introduces the threatening military power of a mighty Empire into the centre of Europe by the roundabout way of Czechoslovakia, the latter country having also signed an agreement with Russia. . . .

'Soviet Russia is the exponent of a revolutionary political and philosophical system organized in the form of a State. Its political creed is the confession of faith in the world revolution. . . .'

He went on to argue that if this philosophy were to triumph in France, then this 'new Bolshevik State would be a section of the Bolshevik International'. This meant that 'the decision as to aggression or non-aggression' would not be made by two different States but according to orders from a single head-quarters—Moscow.

'For purely territorial reasons alone, Germany is not in a position to attack Russia; but Russia could at any time bring about a conflict with Germany by the indirect way of her own advanced positions.'

---

ratified by the Chamber on the previous day. The Germans alleged, probably correctly, that the publication of the interview was held up by the French Government in order that it should not influence the vote.

[1] The speech is printed in *Hitler's Speeches*, pp. 1271–93. According to Mr. Wickham Steed, Hitler was told in February 1936 by his Moscow Embassy that conditions in the Ukraine had so improved that he could expect no internal rising in his favour; the time may therefore have been thought unpropitious for a direct challenge to Russia. *International Affairs*, 1937, p. 193.

Chapter Nine

RUSSIA AND GREAT BRITAIN

THE improvement in Anglo-Soviet relations which followed the settlement of the Metro-Vickers dispute was a strictly limited one and never reached even that degree of intimacy which was achieved in Franco-Soviet relations before the assassination of Barthou on 9 October 1934.

In seeking for the explanation of this failure, it must be admitted that there were minor irritations for which the Russians must take their share of blame, but there was little to give Great Britain cause for a revival of the suspicions of the nineteen-twenties. The British Communist Party was not large enough for their propaganda at home to be a serious cause for worry,[1] nor does it seem that Communist agitation in colonial territories and in Asiatic countries was taken as seriously as it had been in the past, though Comintern policy remained unchanged. The Comintern Congress of July-August 1935 could not but revive suspicions of this kind, and a protest against some of the speeches was duly registered by the British Ambassador on 19 August.[2] In China, once the focal point of Anglo-Soviet friction, it might indeed have seemed that the dangers of a clash were over, since Japanese militarism had replaced the Chinese nationalist movement as the main threat to European interests. At the same time, Russian influence, once exerted to turn the nationalist movement into specifically anti-British channels, was increasingly being directed towards fortifying and galvanising resistance to Japan. Sinkiang, the one area where Soviet penetration was unmistakably on the increase, was too remote to be a major consideration in the general relations of the two countries. Nevertheless, the Far East remained a disturbing factor, if only because Russian opinion persisted in attributing the 'weakness' of Britain's reactions to Japanese

[1] On the other hand, the policy of 'infiltration' which the Communists practised during the period of 'popular fronts' was regarded as dangerous by the organisations upon whom these tactics were practised. It was preferable, as more than one Socialist body discovered, to have the Communists against one rather than as one's allies, and some of the irritation they caused was no doubt vented upon the Soviet Union.

[2] The Ambassador was Lord Chilston, who had replaced Sir Esmond Ovey (October 1933). The latter had made himself unpopular in Moscow by his handling of the Metro-Vickers affair. See Molotov's remarks on 28 January 1935, *Documents for 1934*, p. 412.

aggression to concealed anti-Soviet motives.[1] But the test of goodwill towards the U.S.S.R. was the attitude which other countries took towards the rise of Hitler in Europe. It is necessary therefore to consider the general British position regarding the problems of this time as it appeared in the light of Moscow's all-absorbing craving for security, and of the demands by Soviet statesmen that this should be met by the multiplication and strengthening of provisions for immediate and automatic assistance to a Power which was the victim of aggression.

It is not necessary—though it has been done—to treat British policy as fundamentally anti-Russian in order to see to what an extent M. Litvinov's conceptions of the indivisibility of peace and of collective security ran counter to the predominant British approach to these matters.[2]

Britain's fundamental object was to use international organs such as the League for promoting conciliation and economic recovery: for these purposes universality of membership rather than automatism of obligations was what counted. She wished, too, to confine her own liabilities strictly to the immediate geographical sphere where her vital interests were at stake. Hence the popularity of Locarno, in all except extreme 'isolationist' circles, and Britain's readiness to seek settlements of single issues, such as Germany's demand for equality in armaments, with a view to diminishing tension at the vital point. Thus while Great Britain was prepared to sponsor the entry of the Soviet Union into the League, she did not regard this as any reason for ceasing her endeavours to bring Germany back to Geneva, whereas, for Russia, it was precisely the fact that 'the most belligerent aggressive elements' had begun to leave which was the signal for her own entry.[3] Similarly, British diplomacy did not feel itself inhibited, by consideration of their effect upon Eastern Europe, from such local and partial efforts to sterilise potential conflicts as were embodied in the proposed Western Air Pact or in the bilateral Anglo-German naval

---

[1] They were given every encouragement by the British Government's critics at home (see, e.g. 'Vigilantes', *Inquest on Peace* (Gollancz, 1935), chap. 1), and by a school of American writers who were always willing to find a bogy in British 'imperialism'. Neither group appreciated the fact that there was 'as cover for the Manchurian adventure, a definite Japanese naval superiority in Asiatic waters from Kamchatka to Luzon'. G. F. Hudson, *The Far East in World Politics* (Clarendon Press, 1937), p. 254. Cf. Sir J. Pratt, *War and Politics in China* (Cape, 1943), *passim*.

[2] F. L. Schuman argues for instance that the U.S.S.R. was the greatest menace to the British 'oligarchy' and hence that British policy was throughout fundamentally anti-Soviet. *Europe on the Eve* (Hale, 1939), chap. 6 (v) and chap. 11 (i).

[3] See the remarks of Molotov, 28 January 1935, *Documents for 1934*, p. 407.

agreement. For this reason British support for the Eastern Pact was readily forthcoming so long as it was subordinate to a general scheme of pacification and so long as it did not increase Britain's own commitments.[1] It became less pronounced when what finally emerged was an obligation upon France to intervene in case of an attack upon Russia, and on Russia to intervene in the less likely event of a direct assault upon France. In Eastern Europe (it seems to have been felt) the maintenance of the peace could be left to an 'isolated balance of power' between Germany and Russia.[2]

Contemporary opinion varied in its interpretation of British policy. For the Russians it was most natural to seek an explanation in the pressures exerted upon the Government by various sections of public opinion. On the one hand there were those, particularly in industrial and commercial circles, who genuinely welcomed Hitler as a bulwark against Communism, in spite of the popular outcry against the savageries of the new régime. Among politicians of the first rank, Lloyd George, in spite of his earlier (and later) championship of the U.S.S.R., was the most notable advocate of the theory that Hitler should be supported lest he be overthrown in favour of a Communist régime.[3] Even more outspoken were such Conservative politicians as Lord Londonderry, who later frankly declared: 'I was at a loss to understand why we could not make common ground in some form or other in opposition to Communism.'[4] Others went as far as openly to encourage Hitler's presumed designs on Russian territory.[5] Most influential, perhaps, was Lloyd

[1] For a good expression of the traditional view, see the chapter on 'Great Britain' by Sir Austen Chamberlain in *The Foreign Policy of the Powers* (ed. Armstrong, New York, Harper, 1935). Sir Austen, once 'public enemy No. 1' of the U.S.S.R., became a strong advocate of *rapprochement* with Russia after the rise of Hitler. Cf. the interview with him published by *Pravda* on 26 March 1935, and cited by Coates, *Anglo-Soviet Relations*, p. 538.

[2] The phrase is that of Arnold Wolfers, op. cit., p. 308.

[3] See the speech reported in *The Times*, 23 September 1933, and his speech in Parliament on 28 November 1934, cited in *Inquest on Peace*, pp. 356–7. See also his letter to Lord Londonderry after his visit to Hitler in September 1936, cited by Lord Londonderry, *Wings of Destiny*, p. 176.

[4] Londonderry, *Ourselves and Germany*, p. 129. Cf. *Wings of Destiny*. Lord Londonderry was Secretary of State for Air, November 1931—June 1935, and Lord Privy Seal, June—November 1935.

[5] See Lord Rothermere's article in the *Daily Mail*, 28 November 1933. 'Once Germany had acquired the additional territory she needs in Western Russia, the problem of the Polish Corridor could be settled without difficulty. In exchange for the recovery of the northern part of the Corridor restoring her old connexion with East Prussia, Germany would be able to offer Poland not only an alternative outlet to the sea, through Memel, but to restore to her the immense advantage she enjoyed in the sixteenth century of access to the Black Sea, by opening to her the great port of Odessa . . .', see G. Bilainkin, *Diary of a Diplomatic Correspondent* (Allen & Unwin, 1942) p. 110.

George's old associate, Lord Lothian, and the Russians can scarcely have been unaware of his opinions and activities.[1]

It would however be a mistake to identify opposition to the Russian security programme wholly with the right wing in British politics. It was the left which had always been the most ready to absorb German propaganda about the alleged iniquities of Versailles, and which continued for some time to reiterate its belief that the best method of dealing with Hitler was to remedy German grievances and assent to her demands for equality. A contented Germany would have no further use for the Nazis.[2] The Socialists were thus by no means enthusiastic for the Franco-Soviet Pact, with its implication of strengthened armaments.

As already pointed out, the crux of the whole matter was the attitude to be adopted towards the violation of the Locarno Treaty by the re-occupation of the Rhineland, under the pretext that it had been rendered invalid by the Franco-Soviet Pact. Without anticipating the later narrative of its political consequences, one can call attention to the remarkable volume of 'sentimental pro-Germanism', which it called forth in England and which cannot fail to have been taken into account by the framers of Soviet policy.[3]

[1] He was confident of peace after his visit to Hitler in February 1934. See the letter cited by Lord Londonderry, *Wings of Destiny*, p. 111. See also his article in *The Times*, 1 February 1935, and his letter, ibid., 11 March. See also the abstract of a letter by him noted by Ambassador Dodd in his diary on 6 May: 'He indicated clearly that he favoured a coalition of the democracies to block any German move in their direction and to turn Germany's course eastwards. That this might lead to a war between Russia and Germany does not seem to disturb him seriously. In fact he seems to feel that this would be a good solution of the difficulties imposed on Germany by the Versailles Treaty.' Op. cit., p. 249. Sir Eric Phipps appealed to Dodd to write to Lothian frankly about the real situation in Germany: 'it would do more good than one of my letters', ibid., pp. 260–1.

[2] A brief but pungent analysis of the effect of German propaganda, including its use of the Russian bogy, will be found in Sir G. Knox, *The Last Peace and the Next* (Hutchinson, 1942). For the English Left, see D. W. Brogan, *Is Innocence Enough?* (Hamilton, 1941), especially chap. 2.

[3] The phrase was used by Miss Eleanor Rathbone in the course of a series of discussions on the question at Chatham House in March and April 1936, discussions which provide invaluable evidence of the current British attitude, and in which more than one speaker supported Miss Rathbone's description of the reaction of the general public. Lord Lothian, who gave one of the three principal addresses, completely accepted the German case. While expressing alarm at certain latent tendencies of the Nazi régime, he declared: 'I confess I have no confidence in Russia either. I think Russia wants peace. But if my reading both of the essence of the Communist dialect and of Mr. Litvinov's policy is correct, Russia is confident that the way to security and peace for herself is to maintain discord in Europe. As long as Europe is discordant there is no chance of there being an attack by capitalist Powers on Russia. And if the discord does precipitate itself in

Negotiations for a new trade agreement between Great Britain and the Soviet Union began on 10 July 1933. Grave difficulties arose out of Britain's attempt to insert an 'unprecedented' clause enabling the Government to place an embargo on the import of goods, if a charge of 'dumping' was made in respect of them—an obligation imposed by Article 21 of the Ottawa Agreement with Canada.[1] The Soviet negotiators not unnaturally refused to accept this and a compromise was eventually found enabling such questions to be dealt with by negotiation. Other obstacles also cropped up and at the end of the year the discussions were still going on.

Bolshevik in an editorial (in November 1933) attributed to Radek had declared: 'Our principal enemy in Europe during the intervention and ever since has been England.' Speaking on 28 December 1933, M. Molotov regretted that Russian efforts to improve relations with all the big Powers had not been wholly successful in the case of England.[2] On the following day, M. Litvinov added his comments:

'Our relations with (Great Britain) cannot boast of stability or continuity. There are no objective reasons for this, and I am certain that the British people as a whole desire to live in peace and friendship with us. But there are elements there who are still rapt in the sweet dream of a general capitalist struggle against the Socialist country.'[3]

On 17 January 1934, M. Kaganovich declared: 'Our relations with England continue to be constantly strained. The diehards are striving to become the principal organisers of all intrigues down to war against us.'[4] Finally, Stalin himself, speaking on 26 January, recalled 'the pressure that was brought to bear upon us by England, the embargo on our exports, the

---

war, Communism itself may well be the beneficiary. I thought the most sinister speech ever made at the Council of the League since its inception was that of Mr. Litvinov a few weeks ago—a speech which was a bid not for peace but for sowing discord in Europe.' *Germany and the Rhineland* (R.I.A.), p. 55. The reference is presumably to the speech made by Litvinov on 17 March at the special meeting of the Council held in London to deal with the Rhineland crisis. L.N.O.J., April 1936, part 1, p. 319. Lord Lloyd, another speaker in the Chatham House discussion 'said that he found himself in cordial agreement with Lord Lothian in his estimate of the present dangerous activities of Russia. The Franco-Soviet Pact was indeed one of the most difficult features of the situation for those who, like himself, believed that we were bound both by interest and in honour to stand by France.' (p. 63.)

[1] Coates, op. cit., pp. 513–8.
[2] Quoted by Dallin, *Russia and Post-war Europe*, p. 104.
[3] *Documents for 1933*, p. 431.   [4] Cited by Dallin, op. cit., p. 105.

attempt to interfere in our internal affairs and to put out feelers
to test our powers of resistance', and refused to regard these
events as accidental.[1]

Negotiations, however, now proceeded more rapidly, and in
spite of a British attempt at the last minute to introduce reservations about claims for the pre-Soviet debts and under other
heads, the agreement was signed on 16 February 1934.[2] It was
welcomed in the Soviet Press both for its economic significance
and as providing a basis for an improvement in political relations.[3] The agreement was approved by the House of Commons on 1 March without a division.[4] Henceforth Great
Britain remained in the forefront of the Soviet Union's trading
partners, taking 16·6 per cent of her exports in 1934 (compared
with 17·5 per cent in 1933), 23·5 per cent in 1935, 26·6 per cent
in 1936, 32·7 per cent in 1937 and 28·2 per cent in 1938. Of
the Soviet Union's requirements, Britain supplied 19·9 per cent
in 1934 (compared with 8·8 per cent in 1933), 18·0 per cent in
1935, 15·1 per cent in 1936, 14·3 per cent in 1937 and 16·9 per
cent in 1938.[5]

[1] *Socialism Victorious*, p. 22.
[2] Maisky countered the British last-minute move by suggesting the old
counter-reservations in respect of Soviet claims for damage done during the
'intervention'. Of the lesser disputes left untouched, the one which bulked
largest was the claim of the Lena Goldfields shareholders. Their concession
had been cancelled in 1929, and the Soviet Government had refused to
recognise the competence of the arbitration court which had heard their
claim for compensation in 1930, or to accept its award of £13 million. A
direct agreement for £3 million, to be paid in instalments, was arrived at
in November 1934, and confirmed in the following March. Coates, op. cit.,
pp. 467, 514–17, 523.
[3] See the citations from *Izvestia* and *Pravda* of 17 February in Coates,
op. cit., pp. 518–19.
[4] Cmd. 4567, 1934.
[5] League of Nations, *International Trade Statistics*. Yugow, op. cit., p. 108.
Although the growth of Anglo-Soviet trade under the agreement was
marked, the ratio of British exports to imports did not correspond to that
set out in the schedule to the treaty. It could be argued that Britain's
unfavourable balance was largely wiped out by her invisible exports to the
Soviet Union. The figures were as follows:

	Soviet Exports to Great Britain	Soviet Imports from Great Britain (including British re-Exports) (As Percentage of British Exports)	
	£	£	%
1933	17,391,099	4,298,770	0·9
1934	17,326,619	7,545,900	0·9
1935	21,763,984	9,726,057	0·8
1936	18,903,385	13,345,741	2·6
1937	29,124,460	19,504,856	3·3
1938	19,543,030	17,419,518	3·3

The British Government took an active part in paving the way for Russia's entry into the League of Nations, and in the early discussions on the proposed Eastern Pact. On 23 June it was agreed for the first time that military attachés should be exchanged between London and Moscow, and on 18 July a cordial conversation took place between M. Maisky and Sir R. Vansittart.[1] Apart from the irreconcilables, the evolution of British opinion seemed favourable, although a shock was felt at the reports of the summary executions which followed the murder on 1 December 1934 of the Leningrad Party leader, S. Kirov—executions followed by the arrest and banishment of Zinoviev, Kamenev, and other members of the 'old guard' of the Party.

'Our relations' with Great Britain, declared M. Molotov on 28 January 1935, 'have entered a normal phase, the trade agreement concluded a year ago opening favourable opportunities for the development of Anglo-Soviet trade.'[2] Nevertheless a certain amount of uneasiness was caused by the diplomatic developments of the new year. The Anglo-French declaration of 4 February, with its offer of a Western air-pact as well as an Eastern Locarno, when read in conjunction with Hitler's reply, and with some of the contemporary British comments, was almost certain to revive the old nightmare of an agreement excluding the Soviet Union, and hence at the latter's expense[3]. On 13 February, M. Maisky saw Vansittart, who is reported to have 'made it clear that the German danger was a common danger to all Europe and that for this reason it would be impossible to think that Great Britain could remain disinterested in the event of a conflict between Germany and Russia'.[4] The Russian note of 20 February 1935 firmly emphasised the absolute indivisibility of any real security plan.[5] As a further measure of reassurance to the Russians, their invitation to send a British Minister to Moscow as a counterpart to Sir John Simon's projected visit to Berlin, was taken into consideration.[6] The

---

[1] Bilainkin, *Maisky*, pp. 123–4.   [2] *Documents for 1935*, vol. i, p. 223.

[3] *Survey for 1935*, vol. i, I (vi), (a).

[4] The quotation is from a despatch of the French Ambassador Corbin. It was published by the Germans in July 1942, when it was stated that it had been found in the archives of the Quai d'Orsay, after the French defeat. It is probable that the Germans had in fact acquired it and other documents of a like nature at a much earlier date.

[5] *Documents for 1935*, vol. i, pp. 36–8.

[6] The Russians had shown considerable disquiet at the news of the proposed visit to Berlin. 'We wish to believe,' wrote *Izvestia* on the 3rd, 'that the trip . . . has the aim to strengthen the cause of peace. Tactics which consist in hanging on Germany's lips and even reading in her eyes what she really desires can only increase tension in Eastern Europe. The first such

publication on 4 March of the British Government's White Paper on defence led on the following day to the announcement from Berlin that Herr Hitler had a 'cold' and that Sir John's visit would have to be postponed. On 7 March it was announced that Mr. Eden would visit Moscow and Warsaw, and this may have been responsible for the notification from Berlin two days later that the British visit would be welcome later in the month.[1] The British protest of 18 March 1935 against the new German conscription law was accompanied by an enquiry as to whether the Germans were still prepared to hold security talks on the lines originally proposed. On the following day the British made it known that the arrangements for the Berlin visit would stand. This was regarded by the Russians as culpably weak. *Pravda* went so far on 20 March as to write 'the line of British imperialism in the defence of the interests of Fascist Germany to the detriment of the cause of peace is being followed with unparalleled zeal.'[2]

Russia's anxiety might perhaps have been regarded as somewhat overdone. It is true that at this stage German rearmament was probably not a direct menace to the Soviet Union. It was generally assumed that the conscription law would give Germany an army of from 550,000 to 600,000.[3] Tukhachevsky had declared on 20 January 1935 that the Red Army had grown during the past year from 600,000 to 940,000. On the other hand it should not be overlooked that, as the Assistant Commissar for Defence pointed out, Russia, unlike Germany, required what were substantially separate armies for her Eastern

result might be to place the Baltic States at the mercy of German Fascism, deprived of all effective defence and assistance, and this is precisely the objective significance of the compromises suggested by Sir John Simon. In general, British tactics provide an evil lesson to Europe because everybody is going to ask: "Whence comes this extreme kindness?" The answer is clear. This kindness is the result of German rearmament. No sooner had Germany provided herself with a few hundred bombers than certain people no longer dared to say to her firmly and openly: "Hands off the frontiers of other countries." ' Coates, op. cit., p. 536.

[1] Some comment was caused by the fact that it was Eden, a junior minister, who was to undertake the Moscow visit. A diffusion of the responsibilities of the Foreign Office had been a feature of the British political scene for some time. When Hitler came into power, Sir John Simon was Foreign Secretary under Ramsay MacDonald, himself not without a taste for personal diplomacy. In addition, Eden as Lord Privy Seal, after 1934, became virtually an additional Foreign Secretary. On 7 June 1935, MacDonald and Simon were replaced respectively by Baldwin and Sir Samuel Hoare. Eden now became Minister for League of Nations Affairs— a most suggestive dichotomy.

[2] Cited Dallin, op. cit., p. 111. Cf. Milioukov, p. 490.

[3] *Survey for 1935*, vol. i, p. 144.

and Western frontiers.[1] Furthermore the recent revelations about the construction of a German air force had shown to what an extent concealed rearmament was possible under totalitarian conditions.

The omens for the success of Eden's Moscow visit improved when it became known that the British Ministers had been far from favourably impressed by their conversations in Berlin on 25 and 26 March 1935. The visit which took place on 27–31 March seems to have passed off cordially, MM. Stalin and Molotov as well as Litvinov taking part in the conversations. M. Litvinov in a speech of welcome on 28 March delivered a sidelong caution against British tenderness towards German rearmament. No weapon, he pointed out, had yet been invented which could shoot only in one direction and which, turned in the other direction, would unavoidably misfire.[2]

In spite of the statement in the communiqué issued at the close of Mr. Eden's visit, that there existed 'no conflict of interest between the two Governments on any of the main issues of international policy', the talks of March 1935 seem to have marked what was to prove for a long time the high-water mark of Anglo-Soviet friendship. The different points of view of the two countries on the all-important issue of security were not slow in revealing themselves. At the special session of the League Council called to deal with German rearmament which began on 15 April 1935, M. Litvinov expressed concern lest the draft resolution put forward by the three Powers—Great Britain, France, and Italy—whose representatives had just met at Stresa should be construed as suggesting that violations of treaties outside the European continent were less important than those affecting Europe directly. He signified his intention of making a reservation upon this point—an intention which Sir John Simon vigorously denounced as departing from the sphere of the immediate and practical. Eventually the Russian reservation was not pressed.[3]

This clash on 17 April 1935 was to be the last in which Sir John Simon was M. Litvinov's antagonist, as on 7 June the British Foreign Secretary was succeeded in his office by Sir Samuel Hoare. The passing over of Mr. Eden, who was in some sense specially identified with a Russian orientation, was a dis-

[1] *Documents for 1934*, pp. 416–17. At that date, of course, Russia, unlike Germany, had a large number of trained reserves.
[2] *Survey for 1935*, vol. i, pp. 147–51. The official communiqué of 31 March is printed in *Documents for 1935*, vol. i, p. 147.
[3] *Survey for 1935*, vol. i, I (vi), (e) and (f).

turbing sign, nor was the new Foreign Secretary likely on his personal record to find favour in Moscow.[1] The first major diplomatic achievement which followed the change—the Anglo-German naval agreement—seemed to confirm Moscow's suspicions and substantially worsened the relations between Great Britain and Russia. Older sources of friction were called into life by the Comintern Congress in July-August, and by the British protest of 19 August. To these unfavourable influences, the improved economic relations could only supply a comparatively minor counter-weight.

The major diplomatic events of the second half of 1935 and the first two months of the new year, revolving as they did around the Italo-Abyssinian dispute, did not bring the two Governments into opposition. One indirect outcome of the conflict—the supersession of Hoare by Eden on 21 December—can only have been regarded as auspicious. Molotov, in his speech of 11 January 1936, referred with satisfaction to Mr. Eden's visit and declared that conditions favoured 'a further development of Anglo-Soviet relations'.[2] At the end of the month M. Litvinov, accompanied by Marshal Tukhachevsky, represented the Soviet Government at the funeral of King George V.

[1] The *Observer* noted that in Germany 'much satisfaction' was felt that Sir Samuel Hoare could not be styled pro-French and that it was thought a good sign that he was 'reported to be slightly anti-Soviet'. French circles were quoted for the view that his personal tendencies were 'anti-French, anti-Russian and pro-German'. Bilainkin, op. cit., p. 142.

[2] *Documents for 1935*, vol. i, p. 235. Later in the month the Russians appointed a Naval Attaché to the London Embassy for the first time.

Chapter Ten

RUSSIA AND AMERICA

AT the beginning of 1933, only one of the Great Powers of
the world still stood out against maintaining diplomatic
contact with the Soviet Union. The hostility of the United
States, shown in its policy of non-recognition, was apparently
shared throughout the New World.[1] For after the severing of
relations between the Soviet Union and Mexico in 1930,
Uruguay was the only State in the Western Hemisphere with
which the U.S.S.R. was even nominally on speaking terms.
Elsewhere in Latin America, the fear of Communism was sufficient to compel continued adhesion to the principles of the joint
non-recognition agreement of 1920. In the case of the United
States, however, two main currents in world affairs were to
combine in the course of the coming year to force upon the
Administration a reversal of policy and to lead in November to
the long-deferred step of full recognition.

American reluctance cannot be attributed to any particular
anti-American feeling on the part of the U.S.S.R. If America
was the stronghold of world capitalism, it was at the same time
the home of a technique which it was the ambition of the
Russians to imitate and improve upon, and Russian technicians
who went there for the purposes of study were impressed by the
absence of those obstacles to efficiency and marks of social
inequality which were still apparent in the bourgeois society of
Western Europe. In the political sphere the Soviet Union had
no fears of hostile American designs such as it attributed to the
imperialists of France and Great Britain. In the Far East, the
United States had proved its value as a check upon Japanese
ambition in 1922, although Russia's support of the Chinese
Revolution and *rapprochement* with Japan caused considerable
friction between 1924 and 1929.[2]

Thus, whereas Soviet Russia tried to use her trade as a
political lever in her dealings with Europe, she was prepared
to trade with the United States without political concessions
or recognition of the special nature of her trading institutions.

[1] See, on American recognition policies, N. D. Houghton: 'The Policy of
the United States and other Governments with respect to the recognition
of Soviet Russia', *Int. Conc.*, 1929.

[2] The Russo-Japanese Treaty of 20 January 1925, giving Japan the oil
from Sakhalin which it required for its fleet, was symptomatic of the Russo-
American estrangement.

The fundamental reason for the American policy of non-recognition was, it has been said, 'the irreconcilability of the revolutionary Communistic theory and practice of government with the theory and practice of American democracy and capitalism'.[1] It is true that the emotional attachment of the United States to the economic and institutional arrangements of capitalist democracy was more deep-seated than that of most of the countries of the old world, but it should not be overlooked that the United States were freer than were most of these to render this attachment effective in the sphere of foreign policy:

'the non-recognition of the Soviet Government had been one of the political luxuries in which the United States had felt itself free to indulge during the period of peculiar local prosperity in North America which may be said to have begun on the morrow of the Armistice of 11 November 1918, and to have ended with the break on Wall Street in the autumn of 1929 on the economic plane, and on the political plane with the Japanese outbreak in Manchuria in the autumn of 1931. During those years of prosperity the Americans had felt no need of Russia's good will, either in politics or in trade, while they had resented the existence of the Communist régime, in the former domain of the Russian Czardom, as an incarnate criticism—outrageously insolent and insufferably inept—of an established system of society whose virtue was demonstrated, in the American opinion of the day, by the dazzling success of its local incarnation in the United States. This passionate and almost personal antagonism to the Soviet Government was prevalent during the years of prosperity in the United States, in the American-born upper stratum of the American working-class as well as among the bourgeois business men, small and great; and any sympathy towards Soviet Russia which was manifested by the American proletariat or intelligentsia was branded as "un-American" and subversive by the makers of orthodox American public opinion.'[2]

This antagonism was in no way due to any striking successes by

[1] S. F. Bemis, *A Diplomatic History of the United States* (Cape, 1937), pp. 728–9. See on this, F. L. Schuman: *American Policy toward Russia since 1917* (New York, International Publishers, 1928); M. W. Graham, 'Russian-American Relations, 1917–1933: an Interpretation', *American Political Science Review*, XXVIII, 1934, pp. 387 ff.; *The United States in World Affairs, 1933* (New York, Council on Foreign Relations), App. 8; Fischer, *The Soviets in World Affairs*, especially chaps. 8, 7, 31; Sumner Welles, *The Time for Decision* (New York, Harper, 1944), pp. 306–35. Some documents on the subject were published in *Sovetsko-Amerikanskie Otnoshenia (Soviet-American Relations)*, 1919–1933 (Moscow, Narkomindel, 1934). Various American publications have since thrown more light on relations during Wilson's Presidency. See the excellent bibliographies in L. Strakhovsky, *The Origins of American Intervention in N. Russia, 1918* (Princeton University Press, 1937); *Intervention at Archangel* (Princeton University Press, 1944).

[2] *Survey for 1933*, p. 532.

I

Communist propaganda in the United States. The American Communist Party, founded in 1919, was from the beginning subject to the same weaknesses, the same schisms and purges, as its European counterparts, and unlike some of these it never at any time attained a mass following. From the beginning Communism in America was a creed primarily of a section of the intelligentsia.[1] A House of Representatives Committee in 1930, while claiming that there were five or six hundred thousand Communists and Communist sympathisers working in the country under the orders of Moscow, did not put the dues-paying membership of the Party above 12,000, and could point to no section of the community where communism could be said to have a considerable influence.[2] Electorally speaking, their most successful year was 1932, when their candidate for the Presidency polled 102,000 votes, or about one vote in four hundred. (In the first election after recognition, that of 1936, their vote dropped by one-fifth.) Before dismissing American Communism as a negligible factor, it is perhaps fair to say that, according to one intensive student of American politics, 'the Communists, realising the barrenness of pure politics, have devoted their energies not to getting a few more or a few less impressive—and futile—votes, but to influencing more important bodies.'[3]

The absence of any powerful Communist movement did not of course make anti-communism a less effective slogan for those who opposed recognition before 1933 and closer relations thereafter. 'Russia is the arch symbol of ways that are different, economic change, dictatorship, radicalism, immorality, and an all-round threat to Middletown's own cultural security.'

---

[1] For the beginnings of the American Communist Party, see Granville Hicks, *John Reed* (Macmillan, 1936); for the Communist intelligentsia see Joseph Freeman, *An American Testament* (Gollancz, 1938).

[2] See V. M. Dean in 'The Outlook for Soviet-American Relations', *Foreign Policy Reports*, March 1933.

[3] D. W. Brogan, *U.S.A.* (Oxford University Press, 1941), p. 49.

[4] R. S. and H. M. Lynd, *Middletown In Transition* (New York, Harcourt Brace, 1937), p. 430. In America to a greater extent than in other democratic countries, the charge of 'Communism' was an ever-ready bludgeon with which to strike at any manifestation of radical or progressive thought. The Lynds quote the President of Middletown's Rotary as saying in 1933, 'We are getting pretty close to Communism right now in Washington. We have known out-and-out Liberals in the Government.' Further quotations of the same kind from Middletown's press are given, ibid., pp. 430 ff. It must be remembered that a strong ethical aversion to Communist doctrine in all its aspects was felt by many Americans who were neither narrow-minded nor provincial.

With this background, successive American administrations could pursue their policy with little fear of criticism except from occasional intellectuals or interested businessmen. They managed also to evade the accusation of overtly disregarding their normal policy of recognising every Government which exercised stable authority without enquiring into the legitimacy of its origins. The spokesmen for the American Government repeatedly declared that recognition was not withheld on account of their disapproval of the Soviet régime as such, but because of Soviet acts definitely inimical to American interests. As Secretary of State Hughes put it on 18 December 1923:

". . . there would seem to be at this time no reason for negotiations. . . . If the Soviet authorities are ready to restore the confiscated property of American citizens or make effective compensation they can do so. If the Soviet authorities are ready to repeal their decree repudiating Russia's obligations to this country and appropriately recognize them, they can do so. It requires no conference or negotiations to accomplish these results, which can and should be achieved at Moscow as evidence of good faith. The American Government has not incurred liabilities to Russia or repudiated obligations. Most serious is the continued propaganda to overthrow the institutions of this country. This Government can enter into no negotiations until these efforts directed from Moscow are abandoned.'[1]

This position was maintained unaltered by Mr. Hughes's successors, Messrs. Kellogg and Stimson. Nor did the former of these two admit the contention of a distinguished American jurist that the Soviet régime had received implicit recognition by being allowed to adhere to the Kellogg Peace Pact.[2] It was indeed Mr. Stimson's temerity in calling the attention of the Soviet Government to its obligations under the Pact, in connexion with the Chinese Eastern Railway dispute, which drew forth the sharpest of Soviet comments upon American non-recognition.

The only exception to the uniformly unhappy relations between the two countries had been in the sphere of trade. A Soviet trading organisation, *Amtorg*, had been incorporated in the United States in February 1924, and trade between the two countries had risen fairly steadily until 1930.[3]

Despite the absence of diplomatic relations, American citizens had been able to travel to Russia on business, live there as press

[1] *U.S. Foreign Relations, 1923*, vol. ii, p. 788.
[2] See Dean, loc. cit., pp. 3–7.
[3] The following official United States statistics are quoted from Dean, loc. cit., p. 8.

correspondents, and accept employment as specialists and skilled workers—in the latter case without figuring in any of the sabotage and industrial espionage incidents. But the favourable state of Soviet-American economic relations suddenly deteriorated, and that at a time when American industry could least afford to lose its markets. Exports to the Soviet Union dropped only slightly in 1931 as compared with the peak year, 1930, but America's imports were only just over half those of 1930. In 1932, however, while the drop in imports was less spectacular, exports to the Soviet Union fell off catastrophically. In 1930 the United States had supplied a quarter of Russia's imports—more than any other country; in 1932 this decreased to one-twentieth. The drop in imports had been due partly to action and agitation in America against 'dumping' and the import of the 'products of forced labour'. Simultaneously, American exporters, lacking Government support and guarantees, and with the big banks hostile, continued to find themselves unable to compete in the matter of offering credits with the Germans, who had replaced them as Russia's chief suppliers. Advocates of recognition now urged with more vehemence and greater plausibility that the establishment of normal relations between the two Governments (and the cessation of discriminatory action) would produce an increase of orders for American industry. And there was evidence that this argument was finding support in influential political as well as in business circles at the end of 1932. Many business men however appear still to have hoped that some agreement in regard to the 'Kerensky debt' and confiscated property could be obtained as the price of recognition.[1]

Year		American Exports to Russia (million dollars)	American Imports from Russia (million dollars)
1924	. .	42·1	8·2
1925	. .	68·9	13·2
1926	. .	49·9	14·1
1927	. .	64·9	12·9
1928	. .	74·1	14·0
1929	. .	85·0	22·6
1930	. .	114·4	24·4
1931	. .	103·7	13·2
1932	. .	12·5	9·1

See the analysis in W. Chapin Huntingdon, 'The Prospects of American Trade with the Soviet Union', *Slavonic Review*, July 1935. Cf. *The United States in World Affairs*, 1933, App. 8.

[1] See e.g. E. M. Friedmann, *Russia in Transition: a Business Man's Appraisal*, (New York, Viking Press, 1932). The United States Government had lent no money to the Tsarist Government, but had made a substantial loan to Kerensky's Provisional Government in 1917.

In the arguments in the press, economic advantage was balanced against the presumed dictates of public morality.

'In all this public discussion,' it was noted, 'the question of redressing the rudely disturbed balance of power in the Pacific was hardly mentioned and was perhaps hardly in the minds of the majority of American citizens who were taking an interest in the debate. On the other hand, the Soviet Government, from the first moment when they had an opportunity of making their voice heard, made no secret of the fact that, in their mind, the political consideration was uppermost; and there can be little doubt that this consideration also played an important part in the private councils of the Administration at Washington.'[1]

The Soviet Government had in fact, in the latter half of 1932, unmistakably hinted that they were more anxious than ever to come to some arrangement with the United States. Nevertheless, they clearly had no intention of abandoning their claim to absolute equality of treatment by agreeing to anything short of unconditional recognition. This principle had been established as early as 1922. In August of that year, when proposals for re-opening Russo-American trade were being discussed, the Soviet Government had been sounded regarding the possibility of sending an American technical commission to study economic conditions in the U.S.S.R., and to report thereon to the United States Government. The Soviet reply had been that permission would be granted provided a Soviet commission were allowed to investigate economic conditions in the United States![2] The Russians were still as sensitive as ever with regard to their country being treated as an international curiosity. Speaking before the Central Executive Committee of the Union on 23 January 1933, Molotov said:

'The question of resuming diplomatic relations with the Soviet Union is now again under discussion in various countries. News has reached us that there are still some knowing persons who think that a special "study" of the Soviet Union is necessary. . . . The Soviet Power has already been in existence for fifteen years. . . . Nevertheless Ministers of countries like the United States follow in the footsteps of Czechoslovakia. It is high time that what the Soviet Union stands for should be understood, in particular since the fulfilment of the first Five-Year Plan. I think it is not easy to overlook how much the strength of the Soviet Union has grown, how great is this growth and how much the international significance of the Soviet Union has increased.'[3]

An additional cause of disquiet in the United States was found in the course taken by Soviet relations with Latin

---

[1] *Survey for 1933*, p. 533. Cf. *Osteuropa*, VIII, pp. 225–6.
[2] Dean, loc. cit., p. 6.   [3] Quoted from *Osteuropa*, VIII, p. 356.

America. Mexico, which had recognised the Soviet Union in 1924, severed relations on 23 January 1930. With Uruguay, which had granted recognition in 1926, missions were not exchanged until 1934. In 1931, the Soviet trading organisation in Buenos Aires was raided and closed as a result of alleged propagandist activities. (It was set up again in Montevideo.)

The growing menace to the American position in the Far East owing to the expansion of Japanese imperialism must have overshadowed all such minor considerations, and have been the determining factor in persuading the United States to bring to an end the breach with Russia. But public opinion at home, as well as an unwillingness to provoke Japan, caused this motive to be played down in American utterances on the subject.

It was not until the assumption of office by President Roosevelt in March 1933, that the favourable current of opinion in the United States itself could be translated into action.[1]

The first informal contacts were made during the World Economic Conference. On 22 June 1933, Mr. William C. Bullitt (head of President Wilson's abortive mission to Russia in 1919), called on M. Litvinov at the Soviet Embassy in London. On 2 July, M. Litvinov had a talk with Mr. Raymond Moley, the Assistant Secretary of State, ostensibly on the subject of purchasing American cotton. Mr. Bullitt and Col. Raymond Robins, another advocate of Soviet-American friendship since the earliest days of the régime, visited Russia during the summer and were well received.[2] In the early autumn, Bullitt was again the intermediary in negotiations whose successful conclusion was marked by the Roosevelt-Kalinin exchange of letters in October, which itself paved the way for M. Litvinov's visit to Washington.[3] While American comments on the

[1] This and the following paragraphs are based on *Survey for 1933*, IV (vi); *The United States in World Affairs, 1933*, chap. 14; Pope, *Maxim Litvinoff*, pp. 286–312. It was noted that the Soviet Government had been included among the addressees of Roosevelt's disarmament message of 16 May. (The message was not sent to Manchukuo and Salvador, whose Governments were also not recognised.) *The United States in World Affairs, 1933*, p. 242; text in *Documents for 1933*, pp. 194–6.

[2] See the article 'Amerika "otkrivaet" SSSR' (America 'discovers' the U.S.S.R.) by Radek, printed in *Izvestia* after recognition had been announced, and reprinted, op. cit., pp. 149–55. He gives credit to five non-communist Americans for their persistent efforts towards this end—the other three were Senator Borah, Louis Fischer, and Walter Duranty.

[3] Roosevelt to Kalinin, 10 October; Kalinin to Roosevelt, 17 October. The latter made direct reference to the fact that the continuance of the Russian-American breach had had the effect of 'complicating the process of consolidating world peace and encouraging forces tending to upset that peace'. *Documents for 1933*, pp. 460–1.

approaching negotiations continued to stress the economic aspect of recognition, the Russians openly indicated that for them the primary concern was the question of security in the Pacific. M. Litvinov arrived in the United States on 7 November 1933. Negotiations at Washington lasted from the following day until 16 November, when the points on which agreement had been reached were set out in a number of communications between the President and M. Litvinov.[1] Apart from immediate recognition of the Soviet Government, these were as follows: a mutual pledge to abstain from hostile propaganda; freedom of worship for American nationals in Russia; legal protection, on most-favoured-nation terms, for American nationals, to be included in a consular convention (an assurance to which M. Litvinov added an explanatory note on the Soviet definition of economic espionage);[2] the waiving by the Soviet Government of certain Russian claims against the American Government and American nationals, and finally, the waiving by the Soviet Government of all claims arising out of the American intervention in Siberia from 1918 to 1921. The implication here was that the intervention had been anti-Japanese in purpose.

A joint statement indicated that matters dealing with outstanding indebtedness and claims were under discussion. Further talks were held before M. Litvinov left the United States on 25 November, after a cordial exchange of letters with the President,[3] who in a speech on 18 November emphasised the two countries' desire for peace as the main motive for the steps taken.[4] Meanwhile the Soviet Press had given great prominence to the new diplomatic success, although the official instructions had been not to overdo the celebrations lest the dignity of the Soviet Union be compromised.[5]

[1] ibid., pp. 462–71.

[2] No such consular convention appears to have been concluded. The status of diplomatic agents and foreign consuls in Soviet Russia was regulated in laws of 30 June 1921, and 14 January 1927. The English text of the latter is given in A. H. Feller and M. O. Hudson, *Diplomatic and Consular Laws and Regulations* (Washington, Carnegie Endowment, 1933), pp. 1212 ff. See on this, Taracouzio, *The Soviet Union and International Law*, pp. 207–9.

[3] Pope (op. cit., pp. 309–10) gives the texts. Bullitt was appointed American Ambassador to the Soviet Union on 17 November; Alexander Troyanovsky, a former Soviet Ambassador to Japan, was appointed to the Washington Embassy on 19 November, and presented his credentials on 8 January. F. D. Roosevelt, *Public Papers and Addresses* (New York, Macmillan, 1934), vol. 3, pp. 24–5. The choice of Russia's leading expert on Japan for the post was regarded as very significant, particularly in Tokio. Grew, *Ten Years in Japan*, p. 107.

[4] Roosevelt, op. cit., vol. 2, p. 492.

[5] Lyons, *Assignment in Utopia*, p. 592; Fischer, *Men and Politics*, p. 284.

The new era in Soviet-American relations which seemed to be opening at the end of 1933 was not in fact destined to live up to its original promise, in spite of the fact that both Governments were showing increasing awareness of the danger from Germany and Japan.[1] Differences soon arose over financial questions and over propaganda. This was primarily due to the ambiguity of the agreements reached at Washington.[2]

The debt negotiations began in Moscow early in 1934. The Kerensky debt was reckoned at 188 million dollars and private claims at 400 million dollars.[3] The Soviet Government demanded a loan as a condition of any debt agreement. Matters were complicated by the decision of the legal advisers of the American Government that the 'Johnson Act' applied to the Soviet Government, which meant both that it was held fully liable for its predecessor's obligations and that, pending a full settlement, it could hope for no private credits in the United States.[4] Late in May the negotiations reached a deadlock. They opened again in July—this time in Washington—and continued through August and September, again without result. In an interview on 1 February 1935, Secretary Hull told Troyanovsky that there was no purpose in going on.[5] This failure meant that government credits were also barred to the Soviet Union, since hostile Congressmen had forced the Export-Import Bank, set up for this purpose in February 1934, to promise that no credits would be given until a settlement was reached.[6] It may well be doubted whether anything but the

[1] For growing awareness in American official circles of German and Japanese war preparations, see J. C. Grew, *Ten Years in Japan* (Hammond & Hammond, 1944), *passim*; *Papers Relating to the Foreign Relations of the United States: Japan, 1931–1941* (U.S. State Department, 1943); *Peace and War* (U.S. State Department, 1943), pp. 13–28; ibid., pp. 191–5 (letters from G. S. Messersmith, Consul-General at Berlin, of 26 June and 23 November 1933); pp. 211–14 (memorandum of Douglas Miller, commercial attaché at Berlin, 17 April 1934); pp. 233–4 (letter from Consul at Berlin, 15 September 1934)

[2] Dodd was told by Bullitt on 9 December 1933, that 'Litvinov had agreed to pay the debt of $100,000,000 [*sic*] and to open Russian markets to American industrial goods and leave the Germans in the lurch since they were indignant about Hitler's attacks upon all Communists'. Dodd, op. cit. p. 75.

[3] *The United States in World Affairs, 1934–1935*, pp. 82–4.

[4] The Act of 13 April 1934, is printed in *Documents for 1934*, p. 194.

[5] *Slavonic Review*, XIII, p. 699. F. R. Dulles, *The Road to Teheran* (Princeton University Press, 1944), pp. 200–1. It was decided to withdraw from Moscow the American Consul-General and various officials, including the Air and Naval Attachés.

[6] *The United States in World Affairs, 1934–1935*, pp. 104–6; Huntingdon, loc. cit., pp. 235–8; Roosevelt, *Public Papers and Addresses*, vol. 3, pp. 76–8.

prospect of a substantial credit could have persuaded the U.S.S.R. even to discuss the debt question; the United States held only 7 per cent of Russia's war debt compared with Great Britain's 70 per cent and France's 19 per cent, and any settlement would have had repercussions in those countries.[1] Trade between the United States and the U.S.S.R. was, however, encouraged by the revocation on 24 January 1934 of the American measures of discrimination.[2]

Negotiations for a trade agreement under the American Trade Agreements Act of 12 June 1934, were conducted in 1935 and culminated in the exchange of Notes of 13 July 1935. In return for the grant to Soviet goods of minimum tariff rates, the Soviet Government agreed substantially to increase its purchases of American goods.[3]

This single and unspectacular success was too little to satisfy Bullitt, who had hoped that the Moscow Embassy would provide him with the opportunity of a great personal triumph. His early enthusiasm for Soviet Russia faded, and M. Litvinov, who regarded him as 'ambitious and impatient', found him difficult to get on with.[4]

These difficult personal questions aggravated the differences which arose over the speeches made by American delegates at

[1] *The United States in World Affairs, 1934–1935*, p. 84.

[2] Huntingdon, loc. cit., p. 234.

[3] *The United States in World Affairs, 1934–1935*, pp. 118–19. Bullitt issued a statement saying that Soviet purchases during the ensuing year would amount to 30 million dollars, two and a half times the average amount for the preceding three years. On 11 July 1936, this agreement was renewed for a further year on the same terms. *The United States in World Affairs, 1936*, p. 265. The trade agreement was thereafter renewed annually. In 1938, the minimum amount to be purchased by the Soviet Union was increased to 40 million dollars' worth of goods. E. C. Roper, 'American-Soviet Trade Relations', *The Russian Review*, Autumn, 1943. The actual figures of Soviet-American Trade from 1933 to 1938 were as follows (in dollars):

Year	American Exports to Russia	(Percentage of Russia's total Imports)	American Imports from Russia
1933	. . 9,000,000	4·8	12,000,000
1934	. . 15,000,000	7·7	12,000,000
1935	. . 25,000,000	12·2	18,000,000
1936	. . 33,000,000	15·5	21,000,000
1937	. . 43,000,000	18·2	31,000,000
1938	. . 70,000,000	28·5	24,000,000

[4] Fischer, *Men and Politics*, pp. 284–8; Pope, op. cit., pp. 401–3; E. Lyons, *Assignment in Utopia*, pp. 563–4. Bullitt's strongly anti-Soviet views, however acquired, must be regarded as important because of his later position as Ambassador to France. Dodd, op. cit., pp. 396–7.

the Seventh Congress of the Comintern which was held from 25 July to 21 August. On 25 July, Bullitt delivered a Note of protest which asserted that this was a flagrant breach of the no-propaganda clause in the Washington agreements. The Soviet Government, replying on the 27th July, asserted that the pledge could not be taken as referring to the Comintern, an organisation for which the Soviet Government could not accept responsibility. A statement by the American Secretary of State on 1 September showed that the American Government was not satisfied with this customary answer.[1]

Mr. Bullitt was not apparently content to be just the formal representative of the State Department's wrath. He is said to have tried to influence other diplomats in Moscow to protest, and to have carried on an active anti-Soviet propaganda campaign through American and other foreign journalists in the Russian capital.[2] When Bullitt passed through Berlin on his way to America in November, Ambassador Dodd noted the complete change in his sentiments since the previous year. Mr. Bullitt even asserted that the Japanese would soon—and quite justifiably—annex the Maritime Territory.[3]

The Soviet Government did not refrain from showing its

---

[1] *The United States in World Affairs, 1934–1935*, pp. 119–20; *Survey for 1935*, vol. i, p. 430. Litvinov claimed that the Soviet position had been clarified at Washington. Fischer, op. cit., p. 290. The text of the clause ran: 'Not to permit the formation or residence on its (Soviet) territory of any organisation or group—and to prevent the activity on its (Soviet) territory of any organisation or group or of the representatives of any organisation or group —which has as an aim the overthrow or the preparation for the overthrow of, or the bringing about by force of a change in, the political or social order of the whole or any part of the United States, its territories or possessions.' *Documents for 1933*, p. 463.

[2] Fischer, op. cit., p. 292.

[3] Dodd, op. cit., p. 285. He saw Bullitt again on 12 February 1936, when the latter was on his way back to Moscow. Bullitt now declared himself in full agreement with the Lloyd George–Lothian opposition to the policy of bringing Russia into a combination to check German aggression, and indifferent to that aggression's possible results on the world balance of power. Dodd also noted a rumour that Bullitt had been instrumental in persuading France to reject a Soviet request for a loan, p. 316. For the friction between Bullitt and Litvinov during the latter part of Bullitt's period as Ambassador, see J. E. Davies, *Mission to Moscow* (Gollancz, 1942), pp. 19–20. Sumner Welles, the former American Under-Secretary of State, makes the following comment on American-Soviet relations after 1933: 'Unfortunately, the supervision of Soviet-American relations in Washington and Moscow was largely entrusted by this Government to men who proved incapable and unsympathetic to the task of bettering the ties between the two countries. Nor, it must be frankly stated, were friendly relations encouraged by the continued subversive activities of Communist International agents in other parts of the Western Hemisphere, notably in Mexico, Uruguay, and Brazil.' *The Time for Decision*, p. 246.

annoyance at the way events were going. Speaking on 11 January 1936, Molotov declared that while relations with the United States 'had on the whole developed normally, chiefly in the commercial and economic field', it was impossible to ignore the anti-Soviet campaign artificially worked up in a section of the American Press by pro-Fascist circles.[1]

In Latin America, only one Republic had followed the United States' example in recognising the Soviet Government, Colombia doing so on 26 June 1935.[2] This was more than counter-balanced by the action of Uruguay, which severed relations on 27 December 1935, on the ground that the Legation at Montevideo had been engaged in spreading Communist propaganda, more particularly in Brazil. On 28 December, Uruguay refused to accept a Russian reply. In a second Note, on 30 December, the Soviet Minister, M. Mitkin, denied the charges.[3] On 23 January 1936, the Soviet Government brought the matter to the notice of the League under Article XI of the Covenant, and it was considered by the Council on 23 and 24 January. M. Litvinov managed to put the action of the Uruguayan Government in a rather unfavourable light, while the latter produced no evidence in support of its charges.[4] The Council was content to take note of this fact and to express the hope—destined to remain unfulfilled—that the interruption in relations would only be of short duration.

[1] *Documents for 1935*, I, p. 224.
[2] Hartlieb, op. cit., p. 265.
[3] L.N.O.J., 1936, p. 236.
[4] ibid., 1936, p. 90.

Chapter Eleven

THE U.S.S.R. AND THE LEAGUE OF NATIONS

SOVIET policy in the last stages of the Disarmament Conference and in regard to the League of Nations reflected primarily Russia's new adherence to the anti-revisionist grouping in Europe. The Russian quest for security found further expression in the negotiations for an Eastern Pact, while Russia's entry into the League involved a new departure from the absolute negative which the Soviets had originally returned to any 'bourgeois' or 'imperialist' attempts to organise peace. By virtue of its entry into the League and its pacts with France and Czechoslovakia, the Soviet Union definitely took sides in the political struggles dividing the non-Soviet world, and became less and less a unique and unprecedented apparition in the world and more like a Great Power among Great Powers—a process which had important effects on its internal life as well as in its international relations. The whole process, welcome as it was to friends of peace outside the Soviet Union, was decidedly unwelcome to the devotees of social upheaval, for whom the changes were summed up in the title of Trotsky's book, *The Revolution Betrayed*.[1]

The summer and early autumn of 1933 were passed in discussions between the President of the Disarmament Conference and other European statesmen on the possibility of finding some agreement which would enable the work of the Conference to be taken up again.[2] Mr. Henderson's pilgrimage took him to Berlin, London, Paris, and Rome, but not to Moscow. When the Bureau of the Conference met on 14 October 1933, Sir John Simon put forward a revised version of the British draft Convention, under which, during the first of two four-year periods devoted to the attainment of the principle of 'equality', continental armies would gradually be transformed into short-term armies and a permanent system of supervision set up. On the same afternoon the German Government announced its withdrawal from the Conference on the ground that the new draft did not grant Germany the promised equality.[3] The General Commission met on 16 October to approve a reply to Berlin,

[1] (Faber, 1937.)
[2] This and the following paragraphs are based on the *Survey for 1933*, II (iii).
[3] *Documents for 1933*, pp. 281–98.

which regretted the German decision and denied the validity of the arguments adduced in its support. Four States abstained from registering their approval of this document: Hungary and Poland, the U.S.S.R. and Turkey. The reason in the case of the last three Powers was their objection to the secrecy of the preceding negotiations, and to their own exclusion from them. In Russian and Polish eyes the technique which had been adopted was too much like that of the odious Four-Power Pact.

The fact that the concessions made by France, in accepting the British plan of 14 October, had proved insufficient, and that she was now to undergo still further pressure, provided an admirable opportunity for those Radicals, like M. Herriot and Pierre Cot, whose solution for France's difficulties was an agreement with Russia.[1]

The further postponement in November of the meeting of the General Commission of the Conference, appears to have been partly due to Japan's refusing to consider supervision of its armaments. This had been made known in reply to a Russian proposal for universal supervision. Japan's refusal would clearly involve that of the U.S.S.R., and so render hopeless any plan of which supervision was an integral part.

The confident survey of Russia's international position given by M. Litvinov before the Central Executive Committee on 29 December 1933, in which satisfaction was expressed with regard to recent developments in relations with Italy and France, contained a significant passage on the Disarmament issue: the corpse of the Disarmament Conference could be galvanised into life, but it would be a conference not for disarmament but for additional armaments;

'We went to the Conference to take part in the framing of guarantees of peace, of common safety, but the rearmament of any State whatever can in no sense be considered such a guarantee. When they tell us additional armaments for some and disarmament for others, we fear that only the first part of this formula will be carried out, without the second; for it is quite clear that they will not succeed in disarming to any extent precisely those nations which are already

---

[1] A. Géraud, 'France, Russia, and the Pact of Mutual Assistance', *Foreign Affairs*, January 1935. Cf. E. R. Cameron, *Prologue to Appeasement* (University of Pennsylvania Press, 1942), chap. 2. The internal situation in France is discussed, ibid., chap. 3, and in A. Werth, *France in Ferment* (Jarrolds, 1934), and in 'Pertinax' (A. Géraud), *Les Fossoyeurs*. Herriot spent the first fortnight of September 1933, in Russia; Pierre Cot, the Air Minister, paid an official visit to Moscow in the same month. The first Soviet overtures for a closer Franco-Soviet alignment were apparently made in November 1933. A. Wolfers, *Britain and France between Two Wars*, pp. 136–8.

making practical use of their arms and openly threatening to employ them on a still larger scale in the near future. It will be impossible to demand that only those Governments shall disarm against which such threats are directed.'[1]

Further negotiations on disarmament were again conducted between Germany and the Western Powers in the spring of 1934, and once again there seems to have been no direct approach to the Soviet Union.[2] Meanwhile, in the Soviet Union the note of military preparedness for all eventualities became increasingly dominant.

'We stand for peace and champion the cause of peace,' declared Stalin. 'But we are not afraid of threats and are prepared to answer blow for blow against the instigators of war . . . those who try to attack our country will receive a stunning rebuff to teach them not to poke their pig's snout into our Soviet garden again.'

Stalin's report to the Seventeenth Party Congress (26 January to 10 February 1934), from which this is taken, was complemented by Marshal Voroshilov's account of the defence situation, and both revealed the confidence born of growing strength.[3]

Meanwhile a feature of the disarmament talks was the unconcealed determination of the new French Foreign Minister Louis Barthou to see that no Disarmament Convention materialised whose execution depended upon the good faith of the Germans. It was this fact, together with the quickening *rapprochement* between France and the U.S.S.R., which brought to an end the period of informal consultations. Before the reassembly of the Conference on 29 May 1934, there had taken place on 18 May (also at Geneva) the crucial meeting between M. Barthou and M. Litvinov after which it became known that Litvinov would propose that the Conference should henceforth concentrate on the organisation of security.[4] M. Litvinov's speech on the opening day dealt in a spirit of outspoken realism with the real obstacles to any genuine plan of disarmament.

'What was to be done,' he asked, 'with States whose rulers had quite openly sketched out a programme of conquest of foreign territories (of course by means of war, since no-one gave up his territory voluntarily), and when the abstract principle of equality came face to face with the very real perils involved in its application.' The only safe course was to postpone disarmament discussions to a more

---

[1] *Documents for 1933*, pp. 425–42.
[2] *Survey for 1935*, vol. i, I, (ii); *Documents for 1933*, pp. 298–384.
[3] *Socialism Victorious*, pp. 1–93.
[4] For the final phases of the Conference, see *Survey for 1935*, 1, I, (iii); *Documents for 1934*, pp. 123–73.

propitious moment and to concentrate on security by 'the transformation of the Conference into a permanent body, concerned to
preserve by every possible means the security of all nations and
safeguard universal peace . . . a permanent and regularly assembling
Conference of Peace.'[1]

Sir John Simon's speech on the following day showed that
the British opinion was that disarmament negotiations properly
so-called were still possible. This view was subsequently shown
to be shared by the United States and by the small European
ex-neutrals. Barthou however made it clear that France had
not retreated from its position and praised M. Litvinov as a
man who accepted realities.

'While there were parts of his speech which he would find it
difficult to endorse, he had to recognise that in M. Litvinov's speech
also there was one idea which predominated and which he was ready
to believe had inspired his whole speech—the idea of security.'

At a later stage of these proceedings M. Litvinov proposed
that pending consideration of his larger scheme the Political
Commission, in abeyance since May 1933, should be revived
in order to study the French proposals for pacts of mutual
assistance. The Franco-Russian standpoint on security found
support from the Little Entente and the newly-formed Balkan
Entente.[2] A compromise between this point of view and that
of the British-American bloc was reached in the resolution of

[1] Minutes of the General Commission, vol. iii, p. 658.

[2] On 9 June 1934, Czechoslovakia and Roumania, after a meeting of the
Council of the Little Entente, extended *de jure* recognition to the Soviet
Union, normal diplomatic relations being thus restored. Soviet Russia had
been represented at Prague since 1922, when *de facto* recognition had been
granted. Discussions on *de jure* recognition had been postponed pending a
Russian decision to enter the League. It was also announced now that the
Yugoslav Government would take the matter into active consideration, but
the antipathy of the Royal Family to the Russian regicides was strong
enough to prevent action. In addition the Yugoslavs feared the Italians
and not the Germans, and did not wish to do anything to antagonise the
latter. F. J. Vondracek, *The Foreign Policy of Czechoslovakia*, pp. 372–89.
Documents for 1934, pp. 402–5. Diplomatic relations between the U.S.S.R.
and Hungary had been established on 6 February 1934 and were entered
into with Bulgaria on 23 July and with Albania on 17 September, ibid.,
pp. 401–5. The Balkan Entente had been formed on 9 February 1934. After
June, Yugoslavia was the only one of its members not in diplomatic relations
with the U.S.S.R., ibid., pp. 298–304. 'The Balkan Entente,' wrote a
French commentator, 'derives its most practical value from the fact that it
heralded Turkey's falling into line in defence of the *status quo*: and Mustapha
Kemal engaged himself on the point only under direct and sustained pressure
from Moscow.' A. Géraud ('Pertinax'), *Foreign Affairs*, XIII, p. 228. The
other European countries which recognized the U.S.S.R. in this period
were Spain (19 July 1933), Belgium (12 July 1935), and Luxemburg
(26 August 1935).

8 June, by which two new committees were set up, one to deal with security proposals and the other with 'guarantees of execution' and with 'supervision', while the Litvinov scheme was referred to the Governments for consideration.

These decisions were clearly only useful in so far as the Conference was continued in being while talks of greater moment proceeded outside its machinery. The work of the Committees was in fact half-hearted and intermittent. At a meeting of the League Assembly in September 1934, the first at which Russia was represented, M. Litvinov made an attempt, which was not pressed, to get the disarmament question taken up with the purpose of furthering the Russian proposals. In November a meeting of the Bureau of the Conference referred the Litvinov scheme to the Committee on Miscellaneous Provisions. But the Committee, meeting in February 1935, decided to postpone its consideration.

Meanwhile the question of disarmament had once more become an object of informal discussion between the other Great Powers. The Franco-Italian agreement of 7 January 1935, while no doubt a possible barrier to revisionism in South-Eastern Europe, came under some suspicion in Moscow. The Pact seemed to herald a new Four-Power grouping, and to weaken Franco-Soviet ties by providing France with a partner of less ominous associations among the *bienpensants*.

The scene then moved to London, where British and French statesmen were in conference between 1 and 3 February 1935. Their joint communique of the latter date denounced the uni-lateral repudiation of existing disarmament obligations but expressed the hope of German participation in a new general settlement, as part of which Part V of the Treaty of Versailles should be replaced by a new agreement embodying 'equality of rights in a system of security'. The most novel proposal was however that for a Western Air Pact. The reactions of the German Government were so markedly favourable to this idea and so markedly cold towards the other elements of the proposed general settlement, that it was not surprising that Russia and the Little Entente regarded the suggested Air Pact as a reversion to Locarno and as implying the offer of a free hand for German expansion in the East. The Russians made their attitude clear in a note of 20 February, which emphasised that their own interpretation of the Anglo-French declaration was that the two Western Powers now accepted what had long been the Soviet view, namely that

'the impossibility of realising complete disarmament and the diffi-culty of controlling and limiting armaments having been manifested, the only means of counteracting the approaching real danger of a fresh armed conflict of the nations is a system of regional pacts providing for mutual assistance on the part of those States which are sincerely striving to ward off that danger.'

The chances of any agreement on disarmament were still further reduced by the British Government's statement on defence of 4 March 1935, the French Government's announcement on the 5th of its decision to prolong the period of military service, and the German law of 16 March 1935 re-establishing conscription.[1]

The French Government's action in appealing to the League over this violation of the Versailles Treaty by the reintroduction of conscription, was something of a difficulty to the representative of a Government whose spokesmen had habitually denounced the Versailles Treaty as an example of predatory imperialism. M. Litvinov proved equal to the occasion and, without justifying the violated treaty, once more presented his thesis that the principle of equality in armaments could not be applied to a State ruled by people 'who have announced to the whole world a foreign policy consisting not only of a policy of *revanche* but also of unlimited conquests of foreign territory, and the destruction of the independence of entire States.'[2]

The Anglo-German naval agreement of 18 June 1935 was far from welcome in Rome, Moscow and Paris. But British efforts to allay their mistrust were mainly confined to talks with the French, although Lord Chilston discussed it with M. Litvinov on 21 June. In Russia, the pact was interpreted as a sign of Britain's weakness and of her desire to divert Germany from air preparations to naval building, where she felt stronger. It might also serve to divert Germany's attention eastward and to allow Britain to disengage herself from Europe, so as to salvage her menaced position in the Far East. A new field of activity would be open for British advocates of an entente with Germany. The Germans would not, the Russians argued, observe the agreement, and only welcomed it as a breach in the treaties.[3] It was clear that the German command of the Baltic would henceforth be unassailable. Nor does there seem any reason to doubt that it was the Baltic situation which Herr

---

[1] *Survey for 1935*, vol. I, pp. 113–27, 132–55, 194–203; *Documents for 1935* vol. I, pp. 15–25, 36–76.

[2] *Documents for 1935*, vol. I, pp. 80–116. The Stresa Conference which preceded the meeting of the League Council and which had assembled under the impact of the announcement on 9 April of the decision to conclude a pact between France and the U.S.S.R. will be discussed in another context.

[3] *Le Temps*, 21, 22 and 26 June; *Manchester Guardian*, 24 June 1935; cf. Coates, *Anglo-Soviet Relations*, pp. 544–5; Milioukov, op. cit., pp. 504–5.

K

Hitler had chiefly in mind.[1] In the midst of these forebodings
and with the Mediterranean crisis looming ahead, the Disarmament Conference quietly expired.

Meanwhile, however, the Soviet Union had taken a further
important step towards co-operation with the 'peace-loving'
States. A significant passage from M. Litvinov's speech of
29 May 1934, had been his reference to the relationship which
his proposed Permanent Peace Conference should bear to the
League of Nations. The League of Nations was bound by its
Covenant to pursue ends similar to those of the proposed new
organisation, but it was hampered by the multiplicity of its
tasks and by the rigidity of its procedure;

'it had been created at a time when the peril of war seemed to many
to be eliminated for years to come. To-day when the peril of war
stood before men's very eyes, it was feasible to consider the creation
of a special body with all its activity concentrated upon one objective—the preventing or lessening the danger of war. . . . Let the
Conference continue to be considered an organ of the League, using
the services of the League; let it be far from replacing the League
which would maintain its prerogatives in their entirety.'[2]

This was far removed in tone from earlier Soviet references
to the League;[3] but statements betraying a revised Soviet attitude on this point could be traced in Russian pronouncements
from the end of the previous year, even though as recently as
5 December 1933, M. Litvinov himself had denied that Russia
was likely to join the League in any foreseeable future.

[1] *The Times*, 6 July 1935; cf. *The Baltic States* (R.I.I.A.), p. 85. See also
Survey for 1934, III, B, (ii); *Survey for 1935*, vol. 1, I, (vii). *Survey for 1936*,
III, (v). The implications for Poland of the Anglo-German naval agreement were discussed when Beck visited Berlin in July 1935. *Survey for 1935*,
vol. i, pp. 206–7. There are some revealing entries on the subject in Dodd,
op. cit., pp. 260–5. The naval tension in the Baltic was formally ended
by the successful outcome of the negotiations for the adherence of Germany
and the U.S.S.R. to the provisions of the London Naval Treaty of 25 March
1936, relating to the qualitative limitation of naval armaments and to the
exchange of information as regards naval building programmes. Negotiations for Russia's adherence started on 20 May 1936, and on 30 July it
was announced that agreement had been reached. The bilateral treaties,
Great Britain—Germany and Great Britain—U.S.S.R. were finally signed
on 17 July 1937, special allowance being made for Russia's position *vis-à-vis*
Japan, which was not a signatory of the London Treaty. *Survey for 1936*,
pp. 49–116, especially pp. 113–16; *Documents for 1936*, pp. 598–642. Cmd.
5518 (1937).
[2] *Minutes of the General Commission*, vol. iii, pp. 657 ff.
[3] *The Soviet Encyclopaedia of State and Law* (1925–1926, p. 749, I) described
the League as 'a political combination or a group of nations interested in
the preservation and utilisation of the post-war international status'.
Quoted in *Int. Conc.*, January 1943, pp. 21–4.

In March 1934 it was reported that Moscow was taking sound-ings on the subject in London and Paris.[1] The negotiations for a mutual assistance pact with France made it clear that such a pact could only be reconciled with the Locarno Treaty in the event of France's partner being a member of the League. A formal suggestion that the U.S.S.R. should become a member of the League was therefore made by M. Barthou to M. Litvinov at their meeting on 18 May 1934. Although the response was favourable, Soviet opinion inclined to the view that the mutual assistance pact should be concluded before Russia joined the League, whereas the French regarded the latter step as a desirable preliminary to the former. This argu-ment was settled in July in favour of the French thesis.[2]

Meanwhile it was necessary first of all to discover what repercussions such a step would have in other countries. Spain and the Little Entente were the first to signify their approval, and on 13 July 1934 an official British pronouncement wel-comed the proposal as an essential part of the scheme for Euro-pean security. Steps to ascertain the views of other States-members were taken in August by the British, French, and Italian Governments, and by the beginning of September it was known that the Assembly would be asked to invite the Soviet Union to join the League. This avoided the necessity for an application by the Soviet Government, which would necessarily lead to a formal scrutiny of that Government's qualifications for League membership. The procedure of invitation had previously been used only in 1931 and 1932, for Mexico and Turkey, for whose admission universal agreement was obtainable. To the admis-sion of the Soviet Union there were, on the other hand, a number of objectors, especially since it was known that the Soviet Union was to be granted a permanent seat on the Council. The skill of the experts on procedure was severely tested, but as usual emerged triumphant.

Certain of the dissenting States were moved by ideological and religious considerations, but these were not Powers of great political importance.[3] The only serious objection came from

---

[1] Vondracek, op. cit., p. 386. The events leading up to Russia's entry into the League are given in detail in *Survey for 1934*, III, B, (i), (c). Cf. *Documents for 1934*, pp. 98–109.

[2] A. Géraud, 'France, Russia and the Pact of Mutual Assistance', *Foreign Affairs*, January 1935.

[3] The self-styled 'exiled Ukrainian Government' in Lvov submitted a protest on 18 September, along with representatives of Ukrainians in Europe and America, the Ukrainian members of the Polish Parliament and 'representatives' of Caucasia and Turkestan. A. Shulgin, 'The Ukraine and its Political Aspirations', *Slavonic Review*, January 1935.

the side of Poland. Poland objected to the award to Russia of a permanent seat on the Council, which had been denied to Poland herself. In addition the Poles feared that the presence of the Soviet Union in the League would enable her to create internal embarrassments for Poland by raising the question of Poland's treatment of her national minorities. The Poles wished the Russians to bind themselves by a minorities treaty before entering the League; but the Russians preferred to give the Poles an assurance (on 10 September) that they would deal with all questions arising between them on the basis of the Riga Treaty, the Polish-Soviet non-aggression pact and the 1933 convention for the Definition of Aggression. This assurance was not thought sufficient by the Polish Government, and on 13 September, M. Beck, speaking at Geneva, announced their intention of repudiating the minorities treaty of 28 June 1919. In spite of the objections raised to this precedent for unilateral repudiation, M. Barthou preferred not to press his opposition, in order not to jeopardise the Polish vote for Russia's admission to the League.[1]

On 10 September 1934, the Council, meeting in secret session, decided *nemine contradicente* with two abstentions (Portugal and Argentine) in favour of the Soviet Government being awarded a permanent seat.

The Soviet delegation appeared in the League Assembly for the first time on 17 September 1934.[2] In July 1935 the Soviet Union for the first time participated in an annual Conference

---

[1] R. Machray, *The Poland of Pilsudski*, p. 364. The relevant clauses of the Riga Treaty ran as follows:

'Art. 5. Each of the contracting parties mutually undertakes to respect in every way the political sovereignty of the other party, to refrain from interfering in its internal affairs and to refrain from all agitation, propaganda or interference of any kind and not to encourage any such movement. . . .

'Art. 7 (1). Russia and the Ukraine undertake that persons of Polish nationality in Russia, the Ukraine and White Ruthenia, shall in conformity with the principle of the equality of peoples enjoy full guarantees of free intellectual development, the use of their national language and the exercise of their religion. Poland undertakes to recognise the same rights in the case of persons of the Russian, Ukrainian or White Ruthenian nationalities in Poland.

'(2). The two parties mutually undertake not to interfere directly or indirectly in questions concerning the work of the Church and of the religious organisations within the territory of the other party.'

Int. Conc., 1943, pp. 53–4. The notes exchanged on 10 September 1934 are in the *Polish White Book*, pp. 180–1.

[2] This paragraph summarizes material which is dealt with at greater length in Appendix A to this volume, 'The U.S.S.R. and International Organisation'.

of the I.L.O. Once inside the League, the Soviet Union acted as a loyal and even enthusiastic member,[1] but it was obviously no more willing than any other power to risk vital national interests for the sake of demonstrating its devotion to League principles. Thus, in the matter of sanctions against Italy, it was prepared to go at least as far as any other power, but not to bear more than its fair share of the burden.[2] On the other hand, it refused to help create a dangerous precedent by 'recognising' the conquest of Abyssinia.

[1] The Soviet Union's submission to the League of its dispute with Uruguay has been dealt with *supra*, chap. 10.

[2] Manuilsky said in a speech on 14 September 1935, that only the U.S.S.R. would lose if it applied sanctions against Italy with the other powers abstaining. D. Z. Manuilsky, *The Work of the Seventh Congress of the Communist International* (Moscow, 1935), pp. 30–1.

Chapter Twelve

THE RUSSIAN SECURITY PACTS

EVEN before the Soviet Union entered the League of Nations, its Government was seeking more definite and reliable assurances of assistance in the event of an attack on her by Nazi Germany, than the Covenant of the League appeared to afford. A similar desire to strengthen the eastern bulwarks against German expansion was shown by the French, and for a time the two countries seemed to be working in fairly close harmony with each other.[1] The early history of what came to be known as the Eastern Pact is obscure: the Russians later described the initiative as having come from France, while French spokesmen gave the impression that it had come from the Soviet side.[2] These proposals were put forward at a time when other States and groups of States were seeking to reinforce their own security, and the Franco-Russian initiative received considerable support from Benes in Czechoslovakia and from Titulescu in Roumania.[3] On the other hand, efforts were being made at the same time to secure a general agreed settlement of European problems, in which Germany should be a free participant. These efforts were mainly inspired by Great Britain, and British opinion tended to regard the Franco-Russian plans as possible obstacles to the attainment of this paramount objective.[4]

[1] The negotiations for an Eastern Pact are dealt with in *Survey for 1935*, vol. I, I, (iv). The principal official source is the report presented to the French Chamber by M. Torrès before the debate on the Franco-Soviet Pact which began on 11 February 1936: extracts are in *Documents for 1935*, vol. i, I, pp. 119–35. Bibliographical notes and a chronology of the negotiations are in Baynes, *Hitler's Speeches*, pp. 1734–41. Cf. *Correspondence showing the course of certain Diplomatic Discussions directed towards securing a European Settlement.* Cmd. 5143 (1936).

[2] Speaking on 28 January 1935, Molotov described the Soviet attitude as one of 'active support' for the 'proposals of France'.

[3] For developments in the security policies of the Little Entente, see *Survey for 1933*, II, (ii); *Survey for 1934*, III, C, (ii). For the Balkan Pact, see ibid., III, D, (i); R. J. Kerner and H. N. Howard, *The Balkan Conferences and the Balkan Entente* (University of California Press, 1936); T. I. Geshkoff, *Balkan Union* (New York, Columbia University Press, 1940). For the Baltic Pact, see *Survey for 1934*, III, B, (ii).

[4] In recording a conversation with the German Ambassador on 6 March 1936, Mr. Eden said that he had pointed out that 'in Germany much was being said and written at this time about the fear of encirclement. It had even been suggested that we were at the back of the Franco-Soviet Pact.

It is possible that the projected extension of the Soviet security system was first discussed in Paris in the summer of 1933, or during the visits that year of M. Herriot and M. Pierre Cot to the U.S.S.R. In the early autumn, the French Foreign Minister had a talk with the Soviet Ambassador Dovgalevsky, and he also spoke with M. Litvinov when the latter passed through Paris on 31 October 1933.[1] Serious negotiations did not begin, however, before the breakdown, in April 1934, of the efforts being made to bring Germany back to the Disarmament Conference.

Meanwhile the *rapprochement* between the U.S.S.R. and France proceeded.[2] In view of later controversies it is worth noting that opinion in France was, from the beginning, not altogether favourable to tightening French links with the Soviet Union, and that early support for such a move seems to have come mainly from the army. Marshal Pétain, General Weygand and General Gamelin seem to have been numbered among the early advocates of a pact of this kind, and it is said that there

---

The Ambassador would know from what I had told him in previous interviews between us that there was no truth whatever in this suggestion.' Cmd. 5143, pp. 72–3. Italian policy underwent several sharp changes in this period. In spite of the reaction in Italy to the attempted Nazi coup in Austria in 1934, Italy's differences with France prevented her adhering solidly to the *status quo* camp. The application of sanctions against her in the autumn and winter of 1935 paved the way for an Italian-German understanding, and for the first time fundamentally estranged Italy from the Soviet Union.

[1] A. Géraud ('Pertinax'), 'France, Russia and the Pact of Mutual Assistance', *Foreign Affairs*, January 1935; *Survey for 1935*, vol. 1, p. 62.

[2] A temporary commercial agreement was initialled on 11 January 1934 and prolonged on 6 January 1936. No long-term credits were granted by France and Franco-Russian trade remained relatively unimportant:

| | Imports from France | | Exports to France | |
	(Roubles)	(Percentage of Russia's Imports)	(Roubles)	(Percentage of Russia's Exports)
1931 .	. 15,000,000	1·3	28,300,000	3·4
1932 .	. 4,300,000	0·6	28,700,000	5·0
1933 .	. 5,200,000	1·5	22,900,000	4·6
1934 .	. 11,600,000	5·0	21,900,000	5·2
1935 .	. 17,600,000	7·3	18,000,000	4·9
1936 .	. 42,100,000	3·1	103,000,000	7·6
1937 .	. 28,300,000	2·1	87,000,000	5·1
1938 .	. 39,000,000	2·7	60,000,000	4·5

From 1936 the figures are in 'new' roubles and for purposes of comparison should be divided by 4·38. League of Nations, *International Trade Statistics*. Yugow, op. cit., pp. 107–8. During 1934 visits were exchanged between the two Air Forces. *Survey for 1934*, pp. 385–6. Cf. V. M. Dean: 'Towards a New Balance of Power in Europe', *Foreign Policy Reports*, 9 May 1934.

were intermittent contacts between the Soviet Military Attaché in Paris, Colonel Ventsov, and Colonel de Lattre de Tassigny, a member of Weygand's staff. It should however be noted that the French generals, and such professional diplomats as Alexis Léger, regarded a Franco-Soviet agreement as desirable mainly in order to destroy any bonds which might remain between the U.S.S.R. and Germany, and to strengthen the position of Poland and Roumania. The Red Army was not thought of as a serious supplement to the armed might of France and her allies.[1]

The Soviet Government was also busy with proposals to the Soviet Union's western neighbours. Towards the end of December 1933 the Soviet and Polish Governments were reported to have made inquiries of the governments of the Baltic Republics and of Finland, as to whether these four States would accept a joint Russian-Polish guarantee against the danger of aggression by Germany.[2] This suggestion was apparently unwelcome and can hardly have been pressed by Poland, in view of the agreement concluded on 26 January 1934, between herself and Germany. Soviet reactions to this pact were moderate in tone, but there were suggestions in the Soviet press that any renunciation by Germany of her aggressive designs on Polish territory, must imply a resolve to seek compensation elsewhere.[3]

The Poles made some attempt to allay any suspicions that they were committed to a less friendly attitude towards the Soviet Union.[4] On 5 May 1934, the Soviet-Polish non-aggression pact was renewed.[5] With regard to the other countries involved in these plans, the Soviet Union attempted to reach a direct agreement with Germany, and on 28 March 1934 pro-

---

[1] 'Pertinax', *Les Fossoyeurs*, vol. 1, pp. 15, 293–4; vol. 2, p. 43. H. Torrès, *Pierre Laval* (Gollancz, 1941), p. 139.

[2] *Survey for 1934*, pp. 410–11.

[3] *Survey for 1935*, I, p. 62. The journalist Linton Wells asserts that Litvinov told him in January 1934, that an anti-Russian alliance existed between Germany, Poland and Finland. Germany was to get the 'corridor', Memel, part of Lithuania and exclusive rights in the Donetz Basin; Poland was to get the remainder of Lithuania, White Russia and possibly Esthonia and Latvia; Finland was to get part of N-W. Russia including the Karelian Peninsula. Linton Wells, *Blood on the Moon* (Houghton Mifflin, 1937), pp. 352–3.

[4] See Beck's speech on 5 February, printed in J. H. Harley, *The Authentic Biography of Colonel Beck* (Hutchinson, 1939), pp. 127–30; also the speeches made by Beck and Litvinov on 14 February in Moscow and the joint communiqué about this meeting issued on the following day. *Polish White Book*, pp. 175–9. Afterwards the respective legations of the two countries were raised to the rank of embassies.

[5] *Documents for 1934*, pp. 392–4.

posed a joint Russo-German guarantee of Finland and the Baltic States. This proposal was rejected by Germany on 14 April.[1] On 4 April the existing pacts of non-aggression between the U.S.S.R. and the Baltic States were prolonged until 1945 by protocols signed in Moscow.[2]

'May the modest document(s) signed by us to-day', significantly remarked Litvinov, in his speech on the occasion of the ceremony, 'be a reminder to the world that there are States who perceive their international duty to lie in the consolidation of peace, or its consolidation at least; on that sector where its consolidation is to some extent dependent upon them.'[3]

The project for an Eastern Pact of mutual assistance between the U.S.S.R., France, Poland, the Little Entente, and the Baltic States was apparently discussed at the meeting between M. Litvinov and the French Foreign Minister M. Barthou on 18 May 1934.[4] M. Litvinov received no encouragement for the suggestion that Germany might adhere to it, when he met Neurath in Berlin on 13 June,[5] and Hitler and Mussolini agreed to oppose the idea when they met at Venice for their talks of 14 and 15 June 1934.

The Council of the Little Entente resolved on 20 June 'to uphold with all its strength the organisation of security and to participate in the regional conventions of mutual assistance' which 'were in course of discussion'.[6] Yugoslavia, however, was less enthusiastic than her two partners. King Alexander's dislike of the Soviet régime was undiminished and Yugoslavia did not feel in any way menaced by the growing strength of Germany.

[1] Extracts from the notes exchanged between Germany and Russia are given in W. P. and Z. K. Coates, *World Affairs and the U.S.S.R.* (Lawrence and Wishart, 1939), pp. 18–21.

[2] L.N.T.S., vol. 148, p. 119; vol. 186, p. 267; vol. 150, p. 87.

[3] *Against Aggression*, pp. 137–9. The Baltic States were also strengthening the ties which linked them to each other. The defensive alliance concluded in 1923, between Esthonia and Latvia, was replaced by a new treaty on 17 February 1934. L.N.T.S., vol. 150, pp. 104–9. On 12 September these two states joined Lithuania in a treaty which set up the 'Baltic Conference', machinery whereby they could act as a unit in their foreign relations. ibid., vol. 154, p. 93.

[4] *Survey for 1935*, vol. 1, p. 63.

[5] The American Ambassador, W. E. Dodd, noted in his diary on 18 June 1934 an explanation of the German rejection of the proposal given by the Under-Secretary Von Bülow: 'We declined the Far East [*sic*] pact with Russia and Poland which Litvinov urged because we are not armed and could not participate on equal and safe terms. It involved Germany in a guarantee of the Baltic States' safety and also Czechoslovakia against aggression of any kind.' op. cit., p. 124.

[6] *Documents for 1934*, pp. 365–7.

A memorandum communicated by the French to the British
Government on 27 June 1934 contained the first draft of the proposed pact.[1] This involved, first of all, an agreement providing
for consultation and mutual assistance in conformity with the
League Covenant. This agreement was to be entered into
between the U.S.S.R., Germany, Poland, Czechoslovakia,
Finland, and the Baltic States. The signatories were to undertake the same commitments against non-signatory as against
signatory Powers. Secondly, there was to be an agreement
between France and the U.S.S.R. The text of this is important,
as it was the germ of the Franco-Soviet pact of 1935.

'II. AGREEMENT BETWEEN FRANCE AND RUSSIA,

(1) As towards France, Russia would accept the obligations arising
from the Treaty of Locarno as though the Soviet Union were a
signatory of that Treaty on the same footing as Great Britain or
Italy.

(2) As towards Russia, France would accept the commitments which
would arise for her under Part I, paragraphs (1) and (2) [mutual
assistance and non-aggression provisions] of the Regional Treaty
as if she were a signatory in cases where it is a question of action
in fulfilment of article 16 of the Covenant, or decisive action
taken by the Assembly or the Council in fulfilment of paragraph
7 of article 15 of the Covenant.

(3) France would be invited, if the case arose, to participate in the
consultations provided for in the Treaty of Regional Assistance
under the terms of article (3) of Part II.'

The whole was made dependent upon Russia's entry into the
League of Nations.

Conversations were held in London on 9 and 10 July, between
the British and French Governments.[2] It was decided that
Germany should be brought into Part II of the proposed pact
so that she would now benefit from assistance on the Locarno
terms, from France if attacked by Russia, and from Russia if
attacked by France.[3] It was also agreed that Germany's
participation would afford the best ground for the resumption
of negotiations directed towards 'the application of the principle

[1] Cmd. 5143, pp. 7–8.
[2] Communiqués in *Documents for 1934*, pp. 313–4. (Cmd. 5143 gives the
11th and 12th as the dates of these talks; *Survey for 1935*, the 8th and 9th,
both wrongly.)
[3] Sir John Simon to Sir Eric Phipps. 12 July 1934. Cmd. 5143, p. 8.
Torrès did not mention the fact that this change was only introduced at
this stage, and Géraud denies that any change was made at London.
Foreign Affairs, loc. cit. *Documents for 1934*, pp. 175–82.

of German equality of rights in armaments within a régime of security for all nations'.

The British Government showed some enthusiasm for the revised plan and, on 12 July, their representatives in Berlin, Rome, and Warsaw were instructed to explain it to the respective Governments. Mussolini, in a note on the 13th welcomed the British initiative, and particularly the suggestion which it contained of a new approach to the problem of disarmament.[1] In Warsaw and in Berlin, the proposals met with a very cold reception. The Polish attitude was to be, in the end, responsible for the failure to achieve even a limited version of the Eastern security scheme, and demands some consideration.[2] The Polish-German declaration of 26 January 1934 signified a definite turn in Polish foreign policy. Recent events had seemed to the Poles to demonstrate an indifference on the part of France to the requirements of her eastern allies, and an attempt was consequently made to come to terms with Germany. Some Polish statesmen appear to have believed that Nazi expansionism had a genuinely 'racial' basis and was less dangerous than the old Prussian 'imperialism'. They hoped that the leaders of the Third Reich, for the most part non-Prussians, would not succumb to the traditional Prussian hostility towards Poland and would be more concerned with such 'indubitably German' territories as Austria and the Sudetenland, while being ready to reach a compromise over Danzig, by which the German character of the city should be preserved without the sacrifice of Poland's commercial interests.[3] Even after their non-aggression pact with the U.S.S.R., the Poles remained unconvinced, for the most part, as to the

[1] *Documents for 1934*, p. 182. This departure by Mussolini from his attitude at the Venice meeting a month earlier, must have been due to the events of 30 June in Germany, and to the unrest in Austria, culminating in the Nazi *putsch* of 25 July. *Survey for 1934*, III, C, (i).

[2] A decade later, a Polish publicist claiming to interpret the true legacy of Pilsudski gave that statesman the credit for having frustrated the Eastern Pact. We are told that Pilsudski regarded the idea as of Soviet rather than French origin and 'knew' that the Soviet Government really desired all along a return to Russo-German co-operation at Poland's expense. S. Mackiewicz, *Colonel Beck and his Policy* (Eyre & Spottiswoode, 1944), chap. 9.

[3] See the Introduction to the *Polish White Book* [1939]. For Polish foreign policy in this period see also C. Smogorzewski, 'Poland, Free, Peaceful and Strong', *Foreign Affairs*, July 1935; 'Poland's Foreign Relations', *Slavonic Review*, April, July 1938; J. Donnadieu, 'Les Nouvelles Tendances de la Politique Extérieure Polonaise', *Revue Politique et Parlementaire*, October 1937. An apologia for Beck's policy together with the English texts of some of his speeches is to be found in J. H. Harley, *The Authentic Biography of Colonel Beck*.

genuineness of the new orientation in Soviet foreign policy.[1] Their suspicions of militant communism, and memories of the war of 1920, were undimmed. Although there was no evidence of any desire on the part of the Soviet Union to revise existing frontiers, the debatable problem of the Eastern marchlands could never be wholly forgotten.[2] During the First World War, the Imperial Government had never gone beyond 'autonomy' for Poland. The Provisional Government had accepted independence as the Allies' aim for Poland, but without specifying frontiers. Probably no Russians—except the Bolsheviks, for transitory tactical reasons—envisaged anything like the Riga frontier.[3] The Russians had indeed numbered among their

---

[1] The treaty which was signed on 25 July 1932 and ratified in November, is printed in L.N.T.S., vol. 136, p. 41. It was followed by a temporary improvement in Russo-Polish trade and in 1933, the peak year, Poland supplied 3·7 per cent of the Soviet Union's imports and took 1 per cent of her exports:

	Imports from Poland Roubles	Exports to Poland Roubles
1931	31,200,000	7,500,000
1932	5,600,000	4,800,000
1933	13,000,000	5,100,000
1934	5,200,000	3,600,000
1935	2,600,000	3,400,000
1936	8,700,000	14,600,000
1937	4,500,000	13,000,000
1938	1,500,000	7,100,000

(From 1936 'new' roubles are used and the figures should for purposes of comparison be divided by 4·38.) League of Nations, *International Trade Statistics.* Yugow, op. cit., p. 107.

[2] An invaluable historical analysis of the Russo-Polish problem will be found in B. H. Sumner, *Survey of Russian History* (Duckworth, 1944), chap. 5. The making of Poland's Eastern frontier after the rebirth of the Polish State is described in *History of the Peace Conference*, vol. vi, chap. 2, and chap. 3, part ii. The matter is discussed at greater length but from an angle wholly favourable to the Polish point of view in *The Cambridge History of Poland* (Cambridge University Press, 1941). Cf. O. Halecki, 'Poland's Eastern Frontiers', *Journal of Central European Affairs*, July, October 1941; 'Polish-Russian Relations', *Review of Politics*, June 1943.

[3] See, e.g., chaps. 13 and 14 of *Fateful Years* (Cape, 1928), by S. Sazonov, Foreign Minister of Russia, 1910–1916. 'There is no doubt,' he writes, 'that the Russian Revolution settled the Polish question quicker and more radically than would have been done by the Imperial Government which was in the hands of men with no real power or strength of character. But has it been settled justly and permanently? The answer must be in the negative if only because Russia has had no part in the settlement of it and her national interests have been overlooked . . . the Polish patriots were overcome with megalomania, an old hereditary disease of the Poles, and began building up the Polish State without any regard to ethnographical boundaries.' p. 315.

own territorial aims, the acquisition of Galicia with its Ukrainian population.[1]

Some observers had uttered warnings against Poland's taking advantage of Russia's temporary weakness to incorporate in the Polish State regions to the east of the 'Curzon' line, largely inhabited by non-Polish populations.[2] The Ukrainian problem did not serve to unite the Polish and Soviet Governments, as the old Polish problem had united the Tsarist and German Empires. Historically it appears 'that Ukrainian popular antagonism to the Poles has been much deeper and more continuous than to the Great Russians'.[3] Polish-Ukrainian friction in the new Poland served to keep the question alive.[4] After 1929, the Soviet Union also witnessed a serious recrudescence of Ukrainian nationalism.[5] It was to be feared that in the event of a full agreement between Germany and Poland, the latter might be offered a free hand in the Ukraine in exchange for cessions to Germany in the west. This would enable those

[1] In a memorandum presented to the Tsar after the outbreak of war, Baron Taube wrote that 'since this unfortunate war had arrived, it was Galicia (this "red Russia" which had already belonged to St. Vladimir) and Constantinople with the Turkish Straits which should recompense the Russian people for their enormous sacrifices'. M. de Taube, *La Politique Russe de l'avant Guerre et la Fin de l'Empire des Tsars* (Leroux, Paris, 1928), p. 398. Vladimir, Prince of Kiev, reigned *c*. 978–1015. W. E. D. Allen, *The Ukraine*, pp. 270 ff.

[2] 'A Polish occupation of these regions means the hostility of every Russian, Bolshevik or Monarchist, Liberal or Reactionary. In the end this must involve . . . an alliance of Russia and Germany against Poland. It is almost impossible that Poland could hold her own against such an alliance. A solidly united and homogeneous country might perhaps in favourable circumstances be able to do so, but the very facts which are the source of Russian hostility are likely also to be a source of Polish weakness.' H. J. Paton, in *History of the Peace Conference* (ed. H. W. V. Temperley), vol. vi, p. 278. (R.I.I.A., 1924). The origin of the 'Curzon' line and its ethnographical validity are discussed with unusual objectivity in the article 'The Russian-Polish Frontier', *The Times*, 12 January 1944. Cf. the article, 'Russia and Poland', ibid., 14 January 1944.

[3] Sumner, *Survey of Russian History*, p. 224.

[4] Allen, op. cit., pp. 317–43.

[5] For an account of Soviet-Ukrainian relations from an Ukrainian nationalist standpoint (ferociously anti-Bolshevik and anti-Russian) see I. Mazepa: 'Ukrainia under Bolshevik rule', *Slavonic Review*, January 1934. According to another writer of similar tendencies, Ukrainian nationalism in Galicia took an anti-Soviet rather than an anti-Polish turn after 1932. After the Ukrainian famine in 1933, 'Committees of Assistance' were formed in Lwow and Ukrainian deputies in the Polish Parliament with representatives of Ukrainians in the Bukovina and elsewhere made a *démarche* to the Fourteenth Assembly of the League. A. Shulgin: 'The Ukraine and its Political Aspirations', *Slavonic Review*, January 1935. Mazepa was President and Shulgin Foreign Minister of the Ukrainian Republic of 1919.

Poles who regarded the Treaty of Riga as a 'typical peace of compromise',[1] to solve the Ukrainian question in a broader fashion. The whole of the Ukraine and the other marchlands would be incorporated with Poland in a single federal state, the Great Power Poland visualised by Pilsudski, instead of the Small Power Poland of Versailles.[2]

In fact, there is no evidence that responsible Polish circles contemplated accepting the German bait.[3] But the Poles were determined not to allow their country to become the battleground for the Soviet and German armies, and believed that this could best be achieved by refusing to take part in any pact to which Germany was not also a party. Social as well as national

[1] The phrase is used by O. Halecki, *Journal of Central European Affairs*, October 1941, p. 332.

[2] W. Rostworowski, 'La Politique Extérieure de la Pologne', *Politique Etrangère*, June 1939. 'Pilsudski,' says another Polish writer, '. . . realised the precariousness of Poland's position between Russia and Germany. He knew that their weakness would not last for ever. But his national pride rejected both the Studnicki conception of collaboration with Germany against Russia and the Dmowski plan of a Russian alliance against Germany which had become impracticable since the bolshevik revolution. He also knew perfectly well that Poland's security cannot be based exclusively on distant alliances with France, Britain, America, or Japan. There was only one way out left and it was the most difficult of all: the creation of a political system centred round Poland and held together by the common German-Russian menace. . . . He visualized a Poland, as strong as possible, associated with a Ukraine governed from Kiev and supported in turn by a free Caucasus. . . . His eyes went from the snows of Sweden and Finland to the Mosques of Turkey.' S. Mackiewicz, op. cit., pp. 76–7. The extreme of Polish expansionism was represented in the 'Promethean' movement which also supported the idea of independence of the Caucasian peoples of the U.S.S.R. R. L. Buell, *Poland, Key to Europe* (N. Y. Knopf, 1939), pp. 282–6, 328; R. Machray, *The Poland of Pilsudski*, pp. 342–6; S. Postnikov, 'Separatist Tendencies among the Russian Emigrés', *Slavonic Review*, XVII; Allen, op. cit., pp. 324 ff.

[3] For Polish-Soviet relations, 1928–1935, see *Survey for 1935*, vol. 1, pp. 277–9. The Polish Minister to Germany, reporting an interview with Hitler on 2 May 1933, wrote: 'The Chancellor recently examined statistical tables showing the number of births in Russia. The astonishing fertility of that nation caused him to reflect seriously on the dangers to Europe and therefore to Poland, which might arise from this fact. The Chancellor mentioned this to give me an example of his unprejudiced attitude towards our country.' *Polish White Book*, p. 12. In another interview on 13 July, Hitler 'extensively discussed the situation in Russia', ibid., p. 16. 'Poland', said Hitler to the Minister's successor on 15 November, 'is an outpost against Asia. The destruction of Poland would be a misfortune for the States which would consequently become neighbours of Asia. The other States should realise Poland's rôle as an outpost.' ibid., p. 17. In an interview given in 1934, Hitler, asked about rumours that a joint Polish-German attack on Russia was contemplated, laughed incredulously and replied: 'What! We take territory from Russia? Ridiculous!' Quoted from *Daily Mail*, 17 February 1934, by Baynes, *Hitler's Speeches*, p. 1173.

considerations made them unwilling to contemplate the possibility of the Red Army appearing on Polish soil even as an ally
of the Polish State.

Among secondary reasons for Polish hostility to the idea of an
Eastern Pact was the long-standing dispute with Lithuania over
Vilna. The Poles considered that it was Russian support which
prevented Lithuania from recognising the *fait accompli* and from
re-establishing normal relations with Poland.[1]

In addition, Poland's relations with Czechoslovakia had
never been cordial, whereas the defence of Czechoslovakia was
obviously integral to the whole Eastern Pact scheme. The
Polish claim on Teschen was only one of the issues dividing the
two countries.[2] Relations were still further exacerbated by the
fact that Czechoslovakia provided a haven for Ukrainian
nationalists from Poland.[3] The Poles were also aware that
many Czechs regretted that the Riga treaty had deprived them
of a common frontier with the U.S.S.R., and had thus made it

[1] The Vilna issue is summarised in *The Baltic States* (R.I.I.A.), pp. 89–93.
In 1926, on the occasion of the signing of the Russian-Lithuanian non-
aggression pact on 28 September, notes were exchanged between Chicherin
and the Lithuanian Minister, in which the Soviet Union announced that it
still did not recognize the '*de facto* violation of the Lithuanian frontiers'. A
Polish protest received an evasive reply. (*Survey for 1927*, pp. 225–6. The
Pact and the exchange of notes are printed, ibid., pp. 545–6.) The necessary protocol to prolong the Russo-Polish non-aggression pact originally
concluded for three years was postponed until Russia gave assurances on
this point. (C. Smogorzewski, in *Foreign Affairs*, XIII, p. 657.) The Protocol
of 5 May 1934, duly contained the following passage: 'The Government of
the U.S.S.R. confirms that the note from the People's Commissar, G. V.
Chicherin, of 28 September 1926, to the Lithuanian Government cannot
be interpreted to mean that the note implied any intention on the part of
the Soviet Government to interfere in the settlement of the territorial questions mentioned therein.' *Polish White Book*, pp. 179–80. Poland's objections to being associated in a pact with Lithuania were reinforced by the
latter's dispute with Germany over the Memel question. *The Baltic States*,
pp. 89–102. Cf. *Survey for 1935*, vol. 1, I, (vii), (c) and (d).
[2] Polish-Czech antagonism is discussed in Vondracek, op. cit., pp. 148–62,
178–81, 263–5, 334–6 and in *Survey for 1935*, vol. i. Cf. H. P. Perdrieux:
'Vicissitudes des rapports Polono-Tchéques', *Revue Politique et Parlementaire*,
December 1938—excellent on the different attitudes of the two countries
towards Russia.
[3] 'The most important Ukrainian party . . . U.N.D.O. was on the best of
terms with the Government of the Czechoslovak Republic. Antagonism to
Poland had become a tradition in Prague since 1920, when the passage of
arms to Poland during the war with the Soviets was refused. Ukrainian
refugees from both Soviet Ukraine and Galicia were sure of a kindly reception in the Czech capital, which between the years 1925–1935 became, if
not the Ukrainian political centre, at least the cultural and educational
focus, where the idea of a greater Ukraine, independent and sovereign,
was openly preached in the high schools (in many of which special
Ukrainian courses were available for students).' Allen, op. cit., pp. 339–40.

more difficult for them to rely on Russian backing against Germany. For their part, the Poles regretted that the elongation of the Czech State by the inclusion of sub-Carpathian Ruthenia had deprived them of a common frontier with Hungary, a country with whose social outlook they had much in common. Finally, the Poles regarded themselves as the Eastern outpost of Catholic Europe, against first Orthodox, and then atheist, but never wholly civilised Russia; the Czechs regarded themselves as the destined link between Europe and Russia, partaking in equal measure of the essential elements of both worlds.[1]

While delaying Poland's own reply, Beck apparently endeavoured, unsuccessfully, to persuade Latvia and Esthonia to range themselves among the opponents of the Anglo-French scheme of July 1934. By the first week in August, all three Baltic States had in fact issued declarations favourable to the idea of the pact. On 10 September Germany's formal rejection of the scheme was made known. Germany would not participate in any new security scheme or in the League unless equality of armaments was granted, and the German preference for bilateral over multilateral agreements was stressed. Finally, Germany refused to attach any reality to the proposed French and Soviet guarantees of her security.[2]

On 27 September, after the Soviet Union's entry into the League, the Polish reply was at last communicated to the French. Poland would not enter into any agreement to which Germany was not also a party, and would not participate in the guarantees of the Lithuanian or Czechoslovak frontiers. Prospects of an active attempt by France to overcome the difficulties were diminished by the assassination of M. Barthou on 9 October; the simultaneous assassination of King Alexander of Yugoslavia was also unpropitious to a southward extension of the proposed security sphere. Conversations were in fact held with the Polish and German Governments by M. Barthou's successor M. Laval, but without result.[3]

M. Laval seems to have decided to allay Soviet suspicions that his approaches to Germany might result in some direct arrangement from which they would be excluded. This appears to be so from the fact that on 5 December 1934, M. Laval and

[1] The growth of Russophil sentiment among the Czechs can be followed in the later chapters of R. W. Seton-Watson, *A History of the Czechs and Slovaks* (Hutchinson, 1942).
[2] Cmd. 5143, pp. 9–14.
[3] On the rôle of Laval in Franco-Soviet relations, see H. Torrès, *Pierre Laval*, chap. 11, and 'Pertinax', *Les Fossoyeurs*, *passim*.

M. Litvinov signed a protocol at Geneva which pledged the two Governments to continue their efforts towards the conclusion of an Eastern Pact, and to refrain from entering into negotiations with other Powers prejudicial to it.[1] This agreement was adhered to by Czechoslovakia in the course of the next few days. In a statement by M. Litvinov on the 9th, it was pointed out that the protocol was not a bar to the conclusion of direct arrangements between France and the Soviet Union, either immediately, or in case of the eventual breakdown of the negotiations for an Eastern Pact. This seemed to confirm the rumours that an alliance between the two Powers was imminent. In a speech on 18 December 1934, M. Laval spoke warmly of France's friendship for the Soviet Union, but still proclaimed his intention of trying to bring Germany and Poland into the proposed security organisation. The conversations which both M. Laval and Litvinov had with M. Beck at Geneva in January did not produce any sign of progress in the one direction; and the German response to a new French note of 16 January was unpromising as to the other. M. Laval now seems to have given a definite pledge to Litvinov and M. Benes, that France would proceed with the plans for mutual assistance even without Germany and Poland.

Molotov in his speech on 28 January 1935, stressed the past year's *rapprochement* with France, and his hope that France would show adequate consistency in pursuit of the new policy. This note of warning may have been due to the conclusion earlier in the month of the Franco-Italian agreement on Danubian security, which had not endeared itself to Moscow.[2] The Soviet policy with regard to the Eastern Pact was stated to be unchanged:

'The Soviet Government not only showed initiative but supported the steps of other Governments directed to the defence of peace and international security. In connection with this it is worth while noting the active support we gave to the proposal of France of the so-called Eastern Pact of mutual assistance. This pact should also embrace besides the U.S.S.R., countries such as France, Germany, Czechoslovakia, Poland, Lithuania, Esthonia, Latvia.

The signatories of this agreement should render each other every kind of support, including military, in the event of an attack by one of the countries signatory to the pact. . . . I will not dwell now on those reasons why Germany, and with her Poland, till now refuse to give consent to signing it. But the importance of the Eastern Pact for all advocates of peace in Europe is understood. . . . We will

---

[1] *Documents for 1934*, pp. 184–5.
[2] *Survey for 1935*, vol. 1, pp. 113–14; *Documents for 1935*, vol. 1, pp. 23–4.

L

regard success in this matter as a step forward in the cause of guaranteeing peace in Europe.'[1]

At this stage, however, a new attempt was made by the Western powers to come to an agreement with Germany directly.[2] On the Polish side, the obstacles to an agreement on the lines desired by the Soviet Union were made plain in a speech by Beck on 1 February 1935.[3] Speculation as to the real nature of Polish-German relationships was intensified by Goering's 'hunting excursion' which kept him in Poland from 21 January to 10 February.[4]

The German reply to the communiqué containing the new Franco-British proposals, was made known on 14 February. Its main object appeared to be to separate one part of the proposals, that for a 'western air pact', from the part relating to security arrangements in Eastern and Central Europe.[5]

The Soviet reply, communicated on 20 February, was clearly intended to make plain its objections to any attempt by the British and French Governments to fall in with the German plan and come to an agreement on Western Europe alone.

'The Soviet Government had long since come to the conclusion that the impossibility of realising complete disarmament and the difficulty of controlling and limiting armaments having been manifested, the only means of counteracting the approaching real danger of a fresh armed conflict of the nations is a system of regional pacts providing for mutual assistance on the part of those States which are sincerely striving to ward off that danger. . . .

'In the establishment of a unified scheme embracing various parts of Europe, the Soviet government is inclined to see a recognition of mutual dependence in the preservation of peace in all these parts, a recognition ensuing from the impossibility under present circumstances of localising a war started at any point in Europe.

'The Soviet Government therefore considers that . . . "the organisation of security in Europe" can only be attained by the realisation of all the regional pacts and agreements mentioned in the London communiqué, and, on the contrary, the disregarding of this or that of these agreements, far from "strengthening the pros-

---

[1] *Documents for 1934*, p. 408.

[2] *Survey for 1935*, vol. i, I (vi). The Franco-British proposals were formulated in a communiqué issued in London on 3 February 1935. Cmd. 5143, pp. 15–17.

[3] Harley, *Colonel Beck*, pp. 132–9.

[4] According to Count Szembek, a former Polish Under-Secretary for Foreign Affairs, Goering offered Pilsudski command of the joint German-Polish forces in the event of his agreeing to an attack on the Soviet Union. Mackiewicz, op. cit., pp. 25–6.

[5] Cmd. 5143, pp. 17–19.

pects of peace", could be rather considered as an open encouragement of a breach of peace in the region concerned.

'The Soviet Government trusts that such is the conception of the official communiqué, and that regional agreements discussed among some States prior to the London (Anglo-French) Conference not only will not be impaired but will receive in the London agreement fresh support.'[1]

The month of March 1935 was notable for the announcement of measures of rearmament by Great Britain and France, and of the reintroduction of conscription in Germany. These events put off for some weeks the further discussion of the various security projects. On 26 March, however, in the course of a visit by Sir John Simon and Mr. Eden to Berlin, they were handed German counter-proposals to the Anglo-French scheme of 3 February 1935. These turned out to involve no more than a new multilateral non-aggression pact, shorn of all provisions for mutual assistance.[2]

'Asked as to his view, if some of the other parties to such a pact entered into an agreement of mutual assistance as amongst themselves, Herr Hitler stated that he considered this idea was dangerous and objectionable, as in his opinion it would tend to create especial interests in a group within the wider system.'[3]

From Berlin, Mr. Eden proceeded to Moscow, and, to judge from the Soviet Press, the cordiality of the conversations which took place moderated Soviet suspicions about Britain's lukewarm adherence to the eastern pact scheme.[4]

Since there appeared little hope of any general scheme being adopted, the Soviet Union seems again to have urged upon France the conclusion of some bilateral arrangement. It was made known on 9 April 1935, that a mutual assistance pact between the Soviet Union and France would shortly be signed.

This announcement thus directly preceded the Stresa Conference, between France, Great Britain, and Italy, which had been called to consider the German reintroduction of conscription. The British Government decided to enquire how far the German offer of 26 March would be affected by a Franco-Soviet agreement on the lines forecast. In consequence, on 12 April, Sir John Simon was able to inform the Stresa Conference of the gist of the German reply. This was that in spite of German objections to mutual assistance pacts, the German offer would

[1] *Documents for 1935*, I, pp. 36–8.   [2] Cmd. 5143, pp. 19–20.
[3] Sir John Simon, *House of Commons Debates*, 9 April 1935.
[4] For Mr. Eden's visit to Moscow, see *Survey for 1935*, vol. 1, pp. 149–51. The joint communiqué of 31 March is printed in *Documents for 1935*, vol. 1, pp. 75–6.

hold good provided the proposed pacts were kept entirely separate from any agreement to which Germany was expected to adhere.

'M. Laval said that this cleared up the position. France now had latitude to make with Russia a bilateral arrangement of mutual assistance without hindering the negotiation and conclusion of a multilateral pact of non-aggression.

'This was all the more agreeable as the French Government had, as a result of negotiations which had been going on for some time, undertaken to conclude a pact of mutual assistance with the Soviet Government. He would give the British and Italian Governments the main lines of this agreement, though the precise terms had not yet been fixed.

'Sir John Simon hoped that whatever arrangement was under negotiation would be carried through in such a way as to make it plain that it was not outside Geneva and the League of Nations but within the framework of the Covenant.

'M. Laval said that Sir John Simon could be completely re-assured on this point.'[1]

Negotiations as to the precise form of the projected pact were begun at Geneva, between Litvinov and Laval. It would seem that France wanted to make certain that she would not be involved in a possible Soviet war against Japan, and that her Locarno and League obligations would be allowed for. On 18 April agreement was sufficiently near for Benes to announce that Czechoslovakia would also conclude a pact with Soviet Russia. Nevertheless Litvinov found it necessary to return to Moscow for consultations. The negotiations were continued in Paris by the Soviet Ambassador, Potemkin. Full agreement was reached on 29 April and the pact was signed by Potemkin and Laval on 2 May.

Meanwhile the British Government had shown some uneasiness lest France 'should be induced to subscribe to any agreement which might oblige her to go to war in circumstances not permitted by Article 2 of the Treaty of Locarno'.[2]

The published text of the pact revealed that these apprehensions were ill-founded. In the event of a threat of aggression by a European State on either the U.S.S.R. or France, the two countries undertook, by Article 1, to consult together concerning the enforcement of Article 10 of the Covenant (i.e. presumably to ensure rapid action by the Council of the League). If Article 16 of the Covenant (the Sanctions Article) was

[1] Cmd. 5143, pp. 21–5.
[2] Sir John Simon to the British Ambassador in Paris, 26 April 1935. Assurances from France were received on the following day. ibid., pp. 25–6.

brought into force against a European aggressor against either of the two Powers (or Article 17 in the case of a non-member of the League), the other party would afford all aid and assistance in the application of that Article (Article 3 of the Pact).

The core of the Pact and of the legal controversies which grew up around it later (as also around the Soviet-Czech Pact) was Article 2:

'In the event of France or the U.S.S.R., in the circumstances specified in Article 15, paragraph 7, of the League of Nations Covenant, being the object, in spite of the genuinely peaceful intentions of both countries, of an unprovoked attack on the part of a European State, the U.S.S.R. and, reciprocally, France, shall immediately give each other aid and assistance.'[1]

This meant that in the event of the Council failing to reach a unanimous decision, the right of the 'Members of the League . . . to take such action as they shall consider necessary for the maintenance of right and justice' was to be interpreted in favour of giving the maximum help to whichever of the two parties to the Pact was the victim of aggression. There could be little genuine objection to this.[2] The only question was how the word 'immediately' was to be interpreted. In other words, how long would France and the U.S.S.R. allow the deliberations of the League to proceed before taking action? It seems probable that the Russians were in favour of fixing a definite time-limit. But the French negotiators (possibly mindful of British susceptibilities) successfully resisted this. A less definite interpretation was registered in a simultaneous protocol of signature:

'It is agreed that the effect of Article 3 is to compel each contracting party immediately to give assistance to the other by complying forthwith with the recommendations of the Council of the League of Nations as soon as they have been made in accordance with Article 16 of the Covenant. It is further agreed that the two contracting parties will take joint action to ensure that the Council issue their recommendations with all the speed required by the circumstances of the case, and that, should the Council nevertheless, for some reason, make no recommendation or fail to reach a unanimous decision, effect shall nevertheless be given to the obligation to render assistance. It is also agreed that the provisions for mutual

[1] ibid., pp. 26–9.
[2] In the Locarno Treaty, the undertaking not to resort to war was not to be binding in the case of 'Action as the result of a decision taken by the Assembly or by the Council of the League of Nations, provided that in this last event the action is directed against a State which was the first to attack.' (Art. 2, Par. 3.)

assistance embodied in this treaty refer only to the case of an attack on either of the contracting parties' own territory.'[1]

This was unplausibly interpreted by some critics of the Pact as meaning that the Soviet Union or France could act, even if the Council decided that no aggression had been committed. It was also argued in Germany, that the Pact could not be described as 'regional' and so did not fall within the category of treaties permitted by Article 21 of the Covenant.[2]

Paragraph 2 of the protocol of signature further safeguarded France's obligations under Locarno by insisting that an act of aggression by Germany which brought the Pact into operation must be one recognised as such by the Locarno guarantors, i.e. Great Britain and Italy:

'The joint purpose of both Governments being in no way to nvalidate by the present treaty the obligations previously undertaken by France and the U.S.S.R. towards third countries, in published treaties, it is agreed that effect shall not be given to provisions of the aforesaid treaty in any way which, being inconsistent with the treaty obligations assumed by one of the contracting parties, would expose the latter to sanctions of an international character.'

The other two paragraphs of the protocol of signature referred to the genesis of the Pact as part of a wider security system for Eastern Europe—still put forward as the ultimate objective—and made it clear that, in consequence of this, the Franco-Soviet Pact would only apply in the case of aggression by the third partner proposed for the Pact, namely Germany.[3] In the case of aggression upon France or Russia by another Power or Powers, the provisions of the Non-Aggression Pact of 29 November 1932, would come into force, that is to say that no assistance would be given by either to the aggressor.

Meanwhile, the German offer of a multilateral non-aggression pact had still been exercising the minds of British statesmen:

'The proposal put forward by Herr Hitler ought not to be allowed to drop,' declared Ramsay MacDonald in the House of Commons on 2 May 1935, 'and we trust that Germany herself will take immediate steps to promote in more concrete shape the idea which her Chancellor has formulated. There is no reason why such a non-aggression pact should not harmonise with the mutual

---

[1] Cmd. 5143, pp. 28–9.

[2] See A. von Freytagh-Loringhoven: 'Les Ententes Régionales', Sections 7 and 8, in Académie de Droit International, *Recueil des Cours*, 1936, II. Another hostile German analysis is in W. Hartlieb, *Das Politische Vertragssystem der Sowjetunion*, chap. 4.

[3] Cf. the report of M. Torrès, *Documents for 1935*, vol. 1, p. 129.

guarantee pact which France and the Soviet Government are now negotiating.'

On the same day Sir John Simon stated that Britain's responsibilities would not be increased by the Franco-Soviet Pact, if, as was anticipated, the Pact was subordinate to the Locarno Treaty. On 3 May Sir John Simon called the German Ambassador's attention to the Prime Minister's declaration.[1]

But in replying to this overture on 10 May, the German Ambassador declared that since the protocol of signature of the Franco-Soviet Pact showed it to be directed solely against Germany, its generalised phraseology was 'hypocritical':

'Herr von Hoesch went on to say that the German Government were now closely studying the Locarno Treaty to see whether it and the new Franco-Russian agreement were really consistent with one another. His personal view was that they were not; there was a great effort made to fit the Franco-Russian agreement into the language of the Covenant; but all this in his view was artificial and unreal and concealed the real character of the arrangement. I said that I could not agree with this view: while I realised that Germany did not like the Franco-Russian arrangement, it seemed to me to have no effect at all upon the provisions of the Locarno Treaty.'[2]

On the same day the *Daily Telegraph* published an interview given by Hitler to the *Literary Digest*:

'We are ready and always have been to sign any document whose full requirements can be foreseen, and whose clear aim is peace. We will sign non-aggression pacts with all the world, but we will not sign a multilateral pact of mutual assistance in the East.

'In no circumstances would Germany fight for the Bolsheviks. Rather than sign such a pact I would hang myself.'[3]

While the German attitude was hardening, the friendly relations between Soviet Russia and Czechoslovakia were reaching their expected climax.[4] On 16 May, a mutual assistance pact was signed at Prague by Benes and the Soviet Minister, Alexandrovsky. Its provisions were identical with those of the Franco-Soviet Pact, but its protocol of signature stipulated that the provisions for mutual assistance should come into force, only if France gave assistance to the country attacked.[5] It was

---

[1] Cmd. 5143, p. 30.   [2] Simon to Phipps, 10 May 1935. ibid., p. 31.
[3] *Hitler's Speeches*, p. 1214.
[4] Vondracek, *The Foreign Policy of Czechoslovakia*, pp. 404–5. Various agreements of a commercial nature had been concluded in March. An air-convention for a Moscow—Prague service was also agreed upon in May; Polish objections prevented the direct route via Warsaw from being used.
[5] *Documents for 1935*, vol. 1, pp. 138–9.

thus made dependent upon the (still unratified) Franco-Soviet Pact or upon the Franco-Czechoslovak Treaty of 18 October 1925.[1]

It is not clear whether this proviso was introduced by Benes in order to prevent internal and external enemies of his Government from branding it as a tool of the Russians, or whether Litvinov insisted on it in order that the Soviet Union should not be committed to a war with Germany from which France might hold aloof.[2] The Germans had already begun to make the most of the opportunity to discredit Czechoslovakia as a focus of the Bolshevist virus.

Von Bülow of the German Foreign Office had done his best to recommend this version to Ambassador Dodd, even before the Pact was signed:

'He said Hitler could never join an Eastern Locarno Pact for the maintenance of the existing boundaries, though he did not use direct statements from Hitler. He was certain Hitler meant to maintain peace, but Soviet Russia, he said, had a treaty with Czechoslovakia whereby a vast number of Soviet planes could land at their air-fields. This means a close alliance with France and aggression against Germany.'[3]

From the Soviet viewpoint the importance of both pacts was limited by the practical measures which were required before they could act as an effective deterrent upon Germany. Laval visited Moscow on 13–15 May 1935. The communiqué published at the conclusion of the visit contained two points of importance; first, a statement that the conclusion of their own agreement had not lessened the determination of the two Powers to work for an Eastern regional pact 'of non-aggression, consultation and non-assistance to the aggressor'; second, a statement that the interests of peace demanded that neither country relax their own defensive preparations: 'In this respect M. Stalin understands and fully approves the policy of national defence followed by France, in order to maintain her armed forces at the level required by her security.[4] The general interpretation of this as an instruction to the French Communist Party to call off its previous line of 'revolutionary defeatism' made this declaration of great importance. In fact the Communist campaign against the lengthening of the period of military service to two years ceased immediately.

[1] Keith, *Speeches and Documents on International Affairs*, vol. 1, pp. 125–6.
[2] 'Pertinax' says that Litvinov had the clause inserted. *Les Fossoyeurs*, vol. ii, pp. 102 ff.
[3] Dodd, op. cit., 16 April, p. 242.
[4] *Documents for 1935*, vol. 1, pp. 137–8.

On the most vital matter of all, the completion of the Pact by definite military agreements, Laval, no doubt intentionally, left the position vague. He apparently did talk to Stalin of a possible agreement between the General Staffs, and some military conversations took place. France, Czechoslovakia, and the Soviet Union sent military missions to each other's army manœuvres, which were held, significantly enough, in Champagne, on the Czech-German frontier, and in the Ukraine, in July, August, and September respectively. The French military mission headed by General Loiseau appears to have been impressed by what it saw in the Soviet Union, but the opinions of the French High Command were less definite. By mid-August 1935 Gamelin's confidence in the wisdom of the Pact seems to have been shaken, and he is said to have expressed anxiety about Communist propaganda in the army. The military talks seem to have been suspended for a time. There were further talks in 1936 when a military mission under General Schweisguth visited Moscow and again reported favourably on the Red Army, but no positive military agreement was ever concluded.[1]

On the political side, Soviet suspicions were aroused by Laval's frequent contacts with Poles and Germans. Early in June 1935, Benes also visited Moscow. On the 9th, ratifications of the Soviet-Czechoslovak Commercial Treaty and the Mutual Assistance Pact were exchanged.[2] A statement by Benes to *Tass* on 8 June, as well as a joint communiqué on the 10th, emphasised the mutual interests of the Soviet Union and Czechoslovakia and their desire to extend their field of collaboration. Benes, however, was careful to distinguish between friendly feelings of this kind and the old 'romantic' pan-Slavism.[3]

The hostility of Poland to any suggestion that Soviet aid to Czechoslovakia might pass through her territory gave special importance to the position of Roumania, which, together with Yugoslavia, had signified approval of the Soviet-Czechoslovak Pact. But there was great opposition inside Roumania to closer relations with the U.S.S.R., and on 27 September 1935 the

---

[1] 'Pertinax', *Les Fossoyeurs*, vol. i, pp. 15–16; vol. ii, p. 93; Schuman, *Europe on the Eve*, p. 140; Vondracek, op. cit., pp. 414–15.

[2] The Commercial Treaty did not powerfully affect the somewhat stagnant commercial relations between the two countries. In 1929–1930, Czechoslovakia supplied 2·4 per cent of the Soviet Union's imports and took 2·2 per cent of its exports. In 1934 it supplied only 0·8 per cent of the Soviet Union's imports and took a mere 0·2 per cent of her exports. In 1935 the figures were 2·4 per cent and 0·3 per cent; in 1936, 3·2 per cent and 1·8 per cent, and in 1937, 1 per cent and 1 per cent.

[3] *Documents for 1935*, vol. i, pp. 139–40.

Little Entente denied that a pact had been signed, opening
Roumanian territory to Soviet troops in the event of the Soviet-
Czechoslovak Pact coming into operation.[1] On 16 October
the Roumanian Foreign Office denied that a mutual assistance
pact with the Soviet Union had been or was being negotiated.[2]

The Soviet press warmly welcomed the defence of his policy
made by Benes in a speech on 5 November 1935. Of particular
interest, in view of the Ruthenian question, was his repeated
reference to the friendship felt for his people by their close
kinsmen the Russians *and* the Ukrainians.[3]

The German campaign against the Eastern Pact idea continued unabated. In a speech of 21 May 1935, Hitler once
again rehearsed the difficulties in the way of an impartial
determination of an aggressor and expressed the fear that
arrangements for mutual assistance would have as their sole
result an extension of the area of conflict. After a characteristic
diatribe against Bolshevism he declared Germany's willingness
to conclude non-aggression pacts with all its neighbours except
Lithuania. The most sinister passage was that in which he
regretted what he called the military alliance between France
and Russia for having brought 'an element of legal insecurity'
into the Locarno Pact, 'the most definite and most really
valuable treaty of mutual assurance in Europe'.[4] It proved to
be the prelude to a German memorandum to France of
25 May, in which the Franco-Soviet Pact was declared incompatible with the Locarno Treaty on the ground that France
claimed for herself 'the right in the event of a German-Soviet
conflict to decide unilaterally and at her own discretion', who
was the aggressor, and, 'in virtue of her decision to take military
action against Germany'.[5]

On 3 June, Laval declared his Government's willingness to
negotiate with Germany for a multilateral Eastern Pact of
Non-Aggression on the lines of the German proposals of
12 April. On 25 June, France replied to the German memorandum of 25 May with a denial that there was any incompatibility between France's obligations under the Pact with Russia,
and those under Locarno. On 5 July, Sir Samuel Hoare, who
had become British Foreign Secretary, made a similar reply,
as did the Italian Government on the 15th, and the Belgian
Government on the 19th.[6]

[1] Vondracek, op. cit., pp. 405–16.   [2] *Survey for 1935*, vol. 1, pp. 82 ff.
[3] *Documents for 1935*, vol. 1, pp. 203–14; Vondracek, op. cit., p. 418.
[4] *Hitler's Speeches*, p. 1237.
[5] Cmd. 5143, pp. 37–9; it is here dated the 29th, the day when it was
communicated to the British Government.
[6] ibid., pp. 41–2, 45–7.

A more definite expression of the British attitude was voiced in a speech by Sir Samuel Hoare on 11 July. He then said that the British Government hoped that the proposed Eastern and Danubian Pacts would be concluded, since this would make possible the Western Air Pact which Hitler was on record as favouring.[1] Like the French overtures, this British move met with no response from the German side.

A British memorandum to the German Government, dated 5 August 1935, noted with regret that Germany now seemed to confine the offer of non-aggression pacts to Poland and Czechoslovakia, with Lithuania to be added if the Memel question were first settled. Esthonia, Latvia, and the Soviet Union did not now come into the German definition of neighbouring States. The British Government urged Germany to return to her wider proposals.

On 16 September, after the Comintern and Nazi Party Congresses, Neurath told Sir Eric Phipps that Germany did not propose to reply to British inquiries about an Eastern Pact until 'quieter times' came along.[2]

There was thus an appreciable effort made by Great Britain in the late summer of 1935, to bring the Eastern Pact scheme to fruition; but the attitude of France itself was more and more dubious from the Soviet point of view. The most ominous sign of the ambiguity of Laval's policy was provided by his decision not to ask the French President to ratify the Pact with Russia by decree according to the normal procedure, but in the first place to submit it for approval by the Chambers.[3] From the beginning of July a concerted attack was made upon the Pact by a large section of the French Press. The arguments used ranged from the possible effects of the Pact upon French party politics to fears that France would be drawn into Russia's Asiatic quarrels. On 19 November, however, the French Ambassador in Berlin informed his British colleague that Laval would be obliged to submit the Pact for ratification at an early date. At the end of the month, it was in fact approved by the Foreign Affairs Commission of the Chamber, although consideration by the Chamber itself was postponed.

The British Government for its part made another attempt to re-open the question of the Air Pact, but Hitler told the British Ambassador on 13 December 1935, that the Franco-

---

[1] *Documents for 1935*, vol. 1, pp. 189–98.   [2] Cmd. 5143, pp. 48–57.
[3] This was unnecessary according to Article 8 of the Constitutional Law of 16 July 1875. E. Cameron, *Prologue to Appeasement*, pp. 122 ff. The Chambers separated on 1 July. The new session did not begin till 29 November.

Soviet military alliance had rendered such a Pact impossible by completely upsetting the European balance of power.

Finally, on 17 January 1936, Neurath told the British Ambassador that the strained relations which had arisen between Great Britain and Italy over the Abyssinian War rendered further discussion of the subject inopportune.[1]

It is perhaps of importance to note that there does not appear to have been any interchange of views between the Western Powers and the Soviet Government while these various proposals were being put forward and discussed with the Germans.

On 29 November 1935, *Izvestia* quoted from the previous day's *Frankfurter Zeitung* a report to the effect that Laval had only signed the Pact with Russia to keep Germany and Russia apart, and that he was willing to negotiate a settlement with Germany.

On 11 January 1936, Molotov made a speech to the Central Executive Committee of the Soviet Union.[2]

He mentioned the Franco-Soviet Pact in connexion with the Soviet Government's desire to strengthen the structure of European security but did not refer directly to the delay in ratification.

The German attack upon the Pact was revived in the middle of January by the news that it would shortly be submitted to the French Chambers. On 27 January Neurath told Mr. Eden that ratification would make the conclusion of a Western Air Pact or Air Limitation scheme more difficult.[3]

At the same time it was generally rumoured that ratification would be the signal for Germany to raise the question of the zone demilitarised under the Locarno Treaty.

On 11 February, the Franco-Soviet Pact finally came before the French Chamber of Deputies, and on the 27th, it was approved by 353 votes to 164.

The debate revealed the seriousness of French Right-Wing opposition to the Franco-Soviet Pact, in spite of its original sponsorship by the conservative Barthou. And even the speeches of its supporters were not always very enthusiastic. The Foreign Minister, Flandin, seemed chiefly concerned to prove that France had not surrendered her freedom of action, and to deny that the Treaty was incompatible with her existing engagements. He even offered, if Germany persisted in her objections, to put this question before the Permanent Court of International Justice.[4]

---

[1] Cmd. 5143, pp. 59–64.   [2] *Documents for 1935*, vol. 1, pp. 222–30.
[3] Cmd. 5143, pp. 64–5.
[4] A. Werth, *The Destiny of France*, pp. 212–17; *Documents for 1936*, pp. 15–35. On 20 February, the German official news agency formally denied the assertion made by M. Herriot in the course of his speech, that Germany had previously agreed, although with reservations, that the Franco-Soviet Pact was not incompatible with the Treaty of Locarno.

Hints thrown out by Hitler, in an interview with a French journalist on 21 February, that he would welcome a new approach from France, led to the French Ambassador's being instructed on the 29th, to see Hitler and to find out whether the German Government had any concrete proposals in mind. But Hitler

'took the line that his interview to *Paris-Midi* took place ten days *before* ratification by Chamber of Franco-Soviet Pact (it was only published the day *after* ratification) and that *fait accompli* had changed the whole situation. It was only in response to urgent pressure of French Ambassador, who pointed out the deplorable impression that would be created by failure to implement offers of friendship made in Press interview, that Hitler consented to make proposals, presumably in writing. M. François-Poncet said France would consider carefully any proposals that did not entail abandonment of her friends or of her League of Nations policy.'[1]

Before such proposals had been produced, German troops had reoccupied the Rhineland. Five days later, on 12 March, the French Senate approved the Pact by 231 votes to 52.

Although the Mutual Assistance Pact had thus been formally accepted, and although English official opinion had shown some hardening against Germany, the extent to which Soviet diplomacy had been successful was far from clear. In Eastern Europe there was but limited success to record. On the credit side there was the pact with Czechoslovakia. On the other hand, Poland was as opposed as ever to the Soviet projects, and Beck's statement of policy on 15 January had not suggested that this attitude was likely to be modified.[2]

Speaking in Moscow on the same day, Tukhachevsky repeated Molotov's hint that a secret understanding now linked Poland with Germany.[3] Roumania, thanks to the efforts of Titulescu, was more friendly, but no decisive step towards an agreement had been taken.

In the Baltic area, Finland had proved unreceptive to the idea of an Eastern Pact, and Tukhachevsky noted the development there 'of a system of aerodromes . . . in excess of the

---

[1] Phipps to Eden, 4 March 1936 (telegram), Cmd. 5143, pp. 71–2.
[2] *Documents for 1935*, vol. 1, pp. 230–4.
[3] *Slavonic Review*, XIV, p. 695. On 4 March, Stalin said in his interview with the American, Roy Howard, in response to the latter's remark on Soviet suspicions of Germany and Poland: 'History shows that when some State is intent on making war against another State, even though it be not adjacent, it begins to seek frontiers across which it could reach the frontiers of the State it desires to attack. . . . I do not know what specific frontiers Germany could use for her purposes, but I think those willing to "lend" can be found.' *Documents for 1936*, p. 465.

requirements of the Finnish air force'.[1] In April 1935, it had become known that the Soviet Union had offered to conclude pacts of mutual assistance with the three Baltic States. On 8 May, a second meeting of the Baltic Conference had ended, and a communiqué had reaffirmed the three Governments' adhesion to the principle of regional security pacts. But it had soon become obvious that they would not enter into such an agreement unless Germany were a participant.[2]

The development of Soviet policy between 1933 and 1936 had shown that there were considerable obstacles in the way of inducing other Powers to accept the Soviet thesis that security could best be assured by automatic commitments to mutual assistance, combined with a formal definition of aggression. Without minimising the importance to her neighbours of avoiding action provocative to Germany, it remains true that a vital factor in their attitude was the fear that close association with the Soviet Union would be bound to have repercussions on the internal situation in the country concerned. It was one thing to exchange with the Soviet Union assurances of peaceful intentions, and promises not to support an aggressor. It was quite another to enter into pacts which, if they were to mean anything, meant close collaboration of the defence forces of a non-Communist State with the Red Army. In addition nearly all the States involved in the negotiations had once been wholly or partially within the Russian Empire, and this gave further weight to their objections to opening their frontiers for the passage of Soviet troops. Instead, they preferred to continue the increasingly perilous attempt to balance between the Soviet Union and Germany.

---

[1] *Slavonic Review*, XIV, p. 696.
[2] *Survey for 1935*, vol. 1, pp. 78–9.

Chapter Thirteen

RUSSIA AND THE FAR EAST, 1933–1936

THE year 1932 had ended with the resumption of diplomatic relations between the U.S.S.R. and the Government of the Chinese Republic, and with the refusal by the Japanese Government of the Russian offer of a pact of non-aggression.

For Soviet commentators, the greatest of the diplomatic successes of the year had been the refusal to allow either the verbal provocation of the Japanese militarists or the various 'incidents' to provoke the Russo-Japanese war for which they were apparently convinced their enemies were working, in order to forestall the triumphant completion of the Five-Year Plans and the consequent strengthening of Russia's defences.[1]

There was an atmosphere of considerable confidence in January 1933, and it was reflected in Stalin's speech on the 7th, to the joint plenum of the Central Committee and the Central Control Commission.

'The Soviet Union has been converted from a weak country, unprepared for defence, into a country mighty in defence, a country prepared for every contingency, a country capable of producing on a mass scale all modern weapons of defence and of equipping its army with them in the event of an attack from without.'[2]

This confidence in the quality and equipment of the Red Army is generally in evidence in Soviet declarations at this time.

Further expressions of Japanese hostility and apprehension brought M. Molotov, when he addressed the Central Executive Committee on 23 January, to deal once again with the Japanese refusal of the suggested pact and to make it plain that Soviet restraint was not to be attributed to fear:

'It is hardly necessary for me to contradict these anti-Soviet fabrications; they contradict themselves. As for the resumption of diplomatic relations with China, the Soviet Union decides such questions for itself irrespective of whether it pleases someone else or not. In such cases the Soviet Union proceeds according to the interest of the general peace and on the basis of its own peace policy.

'M. Ushida, the Japanese Foreign Minister, declares that nothing

[1] D. Bukhartsev: 'Uspekhi Mirnoy Politiki Sovietskovo Soyuza' (Successes of the Peace Policy of the Soviet Union), *Mirovoe Khozaistvo i Mirovaya Politika*, April 1933.

[2] J. Stalin, *Leninism* (London, Allen & Unwin, 1940), pp. 401–40.

untoward has occurred in the relations between Japan and the Soviet Union since the beginning of the Manchurian conflict, and that the Soviet Union has taken up "a prudent attitude". May I say that this policy is not only prudent but also well weighed. Here, too, the Soviet Union has been guided above all by the wish to promote the general peace and strengthen friendly relations with all other countries. This policy, the policy of peace, will be consistently and uninterruptedly pursued by the Soviet Union in its relations with other States, irrespective of the way in which it is regarded by other Governments.'[1]

Sino-Soviet relations did not in fact undergo any very striking change as a result of the arrival in China, as the new Ambassador, of M. Bogomolov. The renewal of diplomatic contact with Soviet Russia did not prevent the Chinese Government from undertaking the further vigorous campaigning against the Chinese Communists which marked the year 1933. The process of re-establishing anything like full co-operation was a very slow one. The events of 1927 were possibly responsible for the comparative restraint and self-effacement of the Russians.

Meanwhile Chiang's most prominent military advisers continued to be the Germans. The German plans for a transcontinental Germany-Russia-China air service (via Sinkiang) through the Eurasia Company set up in 1930 (of which the shareholders were the Chinese Government and the Deutsche Lufthansa A.G.) failed, and the Eurasia Company confined its activities to China proper, although in 1931 mails from Shanghai were delivered by plane to Manchouli to connect with the Trans-Siberian. The route over Mongolia was abandoned after the capture, ill-treatment and imprisonment of a crew which had made a forced landing there in 1931.[2]

German participation in Chinese railway building went ahead very rapidly; China to some extent supplanted Russia from 1933 onwards as a market for German capital goods.[3]

It had been expected that the resumption of diplomatic relations between the U.S.S.R. and China might improve their mutual commercial relations, and some Chinese writers went as far as to envisage close economic collaboration between the two countries. These hopes were disposed of by the renewed friction which developed over the Russian proposal to sell the Chinese Eastern Railway to Manchukuo. Russian exports to China actually showed a decline between 1932 and 1935, and

---

[1] Quoted from *Osteuropa*, VIII, p. 357.

[2] K. Bloch, *Germany's Interests and Policies in the Far East* (I.P.R., 1940), p. 21.

[3] Bloch, op. cit., pp. 22–30. Cf. 'Asiaticus': 'The New Era in Chinese Railway Construction', *Pacific Affairs*, September 1937, pp. 284–5.

an improvement only began in the following year. Russian imports from China dropped in 1933 but thereafter showed some improvement.[1]

In Asia, however, as in Europe, the part played by commercial questions in Soviet foreign policy became less important in 1933 and the following years, and diplomacy in this field can, as has been indicated, best be studied with reference to the Soviet Government's general preoccupation with the problem of security. How far the Japanese threat in these years was a real one may be questioned in view of subsequent developments; but the Russians could not fail to be aware that the stock theme of a series of publications sponsored by the Japanese navy was the need for greater armaments directed against the Soviet Union, and that the Soviet Union normally occupied the first place on the list of Japan's prospective antagonists.[2] The developing *rapprochement* between Japan and Germany was openly regarded by the Japanese as holding out the hope that a German attack on European Russia might coincide with the outbreak of hostilities in the Far East. On the other hand, it was not clear to what extent anti-Communism was a genuine motive in the foreign policy of Japan.[3]

[1] Conolly, *Soviet Trade from the Pacific to the Levant*, pp. 60–1. The reference is of course to China proper, that is to say excluding Manchuria, Outer Mongolia, and Sinkiang. The figures are as follows:

	Soviet Exports to China		Soviet Imports from China	
	Millions of roubles	Percentage of Soviet Exports	Millions of roubles	Percentage of Soviet Imports
1932	8·1	1·41	5·8	0·82
1933	7·1	1·45	2·6	0·76
1934	6·8	1·6	9·4	4·0
1935	6·6	1·8	8·1	3·3
1936	36·7	2·7	38·5	2·8
1937	35·4	2·0	40·7	3·0

(From 1936, the figures are in 'new' roubles and should be divided by 4·38 for purposes of comparison with the preceding years.)

[2] H. Byas, *Government by Assassination* (Allen & Unwin, 1943), p. 156. 'The Japanese Army's operations are really aimed at Russia—not at present, but some time in the future. Japan is afraid of Bolshevism and feels that it must drive Bolshevism out of Asia.' Note made by American Ambassador to Japan of a conversation with a Japanese friend, October 1932. J. C. Grew, *Ten Years in Japan* (New York, Simon & Schuster, 1944), pp. 67–8.

[3] These ambiguities were reflected in the division of opinion among the members of the Russian emigration in Manchuria. Many of these had welcomed the Japanese in 1931, as saviours of Manchuria from Communism, and as possible future deliverers of China and Russia. As it turned out, however, one result of the Japanese occupation was the reduction of the Russian community to a position of complete dependence upon

M

The Japanese invasion of Manchuria and the ensuing events hit both Russia's direct trade with that country—previously an important market for Russian oil and textiles—and the transit trade to Vladivostok. Trade with Japan itself also dropped sharply after 1931 but improved to some extent after the conclusion of the C.E.R. agreement in the spring of 1935. But the fisheries question still gave rise to friction.[1]

Once the Japanese had mastered Manchuria, an extension of their hold into Jehol was to be expected, in view of its importance for the defence of Manchuria and of the long-standing Japanese claim to special interests in Mongolia.[2] From the Russian point of view the occupation of this province, which took place in February 1933, meant the opening up of a corridor into Inner and Outer Mongolia and so onwards into the heart of Asia, right along the Asiatic territories of the U.S.S.R. Furthermore, it was a step 'towards the creation of a Mongolian block comprising the Mongols of Western Manchuria, of Jehol, and of the rest of Inner Mongolia'. The Japanese moves were followed later in the year by the development of a strong 'autonomy' movement among the Mongols

---

the Japanese, and its numbers would appear to have declined from some 100,000 in 1930 to about 54,000 a decade later. This process further emphasised the national and diminished the ideological significance of Japan's actions and policies. S. Vostrotin: 'A Russian View of Manchuria', *Slavonic Review*, January 1932: 'Russia's Crisis in the Far East', ibid., July 1935; G. C. Guins: 'The Russians in Manchuria', *Russian Review*, (New York), Spring, 1943.

[1] The fisheries question is treated in Conolly, op. cit., pp. 36–47. The figures of Russo-Japanese trade are as follows:

	Soviet Exports to Japan		Soviet Imports from Japan	
	Millions of roubles	Percentage of Soviet Exports	Millions of roubles	Percentage of Soviet Imports
1930	16·0	1·5	16·8	1·6
1931	19·0	2·5	12·7	1·1
1932	10·1	1·7	4·8	0·7
1933	9·1	1·8	7·3	2·1
1934	5·8	1·4	6·9	3·0
1935	5·5	1·5	10·9	4·5
1936	27·7	2·0	62·0	4·6
1937	11·7	0·7	54·4	4·1

(From 1936, the figures should be divided by 4·38 for purposes of comparison.)

[2] The remainder of this section is based largely on *Survey for 1933*, IV (iii) and (iv); *Survey for 1934*, IV (iv), (v), (vi); *Survey for 1935*, vol. 1; *Survey for 1936*, VII (v) and (vi). I have also made use of H. Moore, *Soviet Far Eastern Policy, 1931–1945* (I.P.R. Princeton University Press, 1945).

themselves, which was the more dangerous because of trouble in Russia's own satellite, Outer Mongolia, through the application in the period 1929-1932 of over-hasty measures of socialisation.

The conclusion on 31 May of the Tangku truce, the suggestions made that its public provisions concealed far-reaching agreements for co-operation between the Chinese and Japanese authorities, and the establishment at Peiping of a local régime of marked Japanese affiliations, were all of them ominous developments.

Meanwhile the position of the Chinese Eastern Railway had become anomalous, now that the line under the joint control of the Manchurian and Soviet authorities formed an artery of Japan's new Empire. From the commercial point of view the railway was rapidly becoming a wasting asset, traffic being frequently interrupted by 'bandit' raids, made feasible, so the Russians alleged, by the connivance of the Japanese and Manchurian forces. In addition, the Japanese were themselves rapidly pushing forward the building of new lines which cut across the C.E.R. strategically and commercially.[1] Further disputes arose over the alleged retention of rolling-stock on either side of the frontier. Finally, on 8 April 1933, the Manchukuo authorities intervened at Manchouli to stop all through traffic to the Trans-Baikal line.

This brought matters to a head, and after a Soviet protest had been followed by further discussions, it was made known in Moscow on 11 May, that the Russians had offered a radical solution by proposing (on 2 May) to sell their interest in the line to the Japanese.[2]

The Russian readiness to conciliate Japan may be gauged from the fact that before the scheduled conference began in Tokyo in June, they had already made one considerable concession, by agreeing to deal with Manchukuo instead of Japan as the other principal party to the transaction. The proceedings of the conference were slow on account of the very large disparity in the monetary value placed upon the property by the two sides. On 21 September 1933 came the intimation of more serious trouble with a Soviet protest about an alleged Manchukuo-Japanese plot to take control of the line by force, and on 24 September a number of high Russian officials of the line

---

[1] A map of the railways in existence and building in Manchuria at this time will be found at the end of *Survey for 1933*.

[2] The negotiations are dealt with in detail in Conolly, op. cit., chap. 4. On the Russo-Japanese situation in the summer of 1933, see Grew's note of 18 July, op. cit., pp. 95-6.

were in fact arrested. Further trouble in the running of the line, and another Soviet protest, preceded the publication, on 11 October, of alleged Japanese official documents which were claimed to prove the Russian case. The authenticity of the documents was denied by the Japanese and further arrests followed; Japanese official sources put out alarming reports of Russian military concentrations and the negotiations over the sale of the Railway came to a full stop. Foreign observers noticed in this perceptible signs of a hardening in Russia's attitude, attributable to the strengthening of her industrial and military position and to the improvement in her diplomatic position generally.[1]

A new and far-reaching attempt had actually been made by the League of Nations to win Soviet co-operation in its handling of the Far Eastern crisis.[2] After discussions which had gone on since September 1932, the Report of the Committee of Nineteen was adopted by the League Assembly on 24 February 1933. This included a recommendation to invite the co-operation of the Governments of the United States and the U.S.S.R., with a new Consultative Committee. The former accepted the invitation, but the reply of the latter was distinctly unfavourable. Its text was published by *Tass* on 7 March. This noted that whereas the Soviet Government was a party to the Kellogg-Briand Pact, one of the instruments invoked, it was not a signatory of either the League Covenant or the Washington Nine-Power Treaty. The fundamental principles of Soviet foreign policy were restated in familiar language, and it was pointed out that the Soviet disarmament proposals had been more far-reaching than the obligations under the Kellogg-Briand Pact.

'The Consultative Committee created by the decision of the League Assembly, constitutes an organ of the League the one aim of which is to assist the Assembly to fulfil its obligations. It must make recommendations to the Assembly, but on the decisions of the latter, the Soviet Union, being a non-member of the League of Nations, will be unable to exert any influence. . . .

'The majority of the States which are members or prospective members of the consultative committee, namely 13 out of 22, maintain no relations with the Soviet Union and consequently are hostile

[1] In a note on the Russo-Japanese tension, written on 7 September 1933, Grew mentions that the Soviet Ambassador, Yurenev, had recently made, at a dinner to foreign correspondents, a very outspoken speech. This was probably intended to act as an unofficial warning to the Japanese against further provocation, op. cit., pp. 98–9. K. Yurenev took up his post on 20 March 1933, succeeding A. Troyanovsky.

[2] *China Year Book*, 1933, chap. 23.

towards her. It would therefore seem that such a committee scarcely would be in a position to fulfil the task of co-ordinating actions with the Soviet Union, the latter being unable to enter into negotiations with the majority of the represented States or even separately with those whose interests may coincide mostly with her own. . . .

'The Soviet Government, desirous from the very beginning of the Sino-Japanese conflict to prevent the further extension of armed warfare and the possibility of it becoming the source of a fresh world conflagration, adopted a course of strict neutrality. In pursuit of this course and in conformity with its peaceful policy the Soviet Government will always be in solidarity with such actions and recommendations of international organisations and separate Governments as are directed towards a just and speedy solution of the conflict and the securing of peace in the Far East.'

On 18 March 1933, nine days before Japan gave notice of withdrawing from the League, the refusal of the Soviet Union was regretfully taken note of by the Advisory Committee.

The implied reference to the United States in the Soviet reply to the League invitation underlined the importance which the Russians attached to the establishment of relations with the United States.

Negotiations to this end were successfully concluded on 16 November 1933. On 2 December, the report of the United States Secretary of the Navy, recommending a larger building programme, provided a further warning to Japan of possible complications ahead. Japan had indeed shown a rather more accommodating spirit towards the Soviet Union from as early as the end of October, although the proposal on 10 November that clauses of the Russo-Japanese Treaty of Portsmouth of 1905, concerning the demilitarisation of the Korean and Sakhalin frontiers, should now be applied to Manchukuo, can hardly have been meant seriously.[1]

The whole subject of Russo-Japanese relations was dealt with by M. Litvinov in his speech on 29 December 1933.[2] Beginning with a sarcastic reference to the growing friendship between Japan and Germany, 'which have even recognized that they are of common race', he later dealt with the C.E.R. dispute, emphasising Soviet patience in the face of continued provocation.

'Not only is a violent seizure of the line threatened by Japan, but there is a direct threat to our frontiers. In such a state of affairs there was nothing left for our Government to do except to start strengthening our frontiers, transferring thereto the necessary forces and taking other military measures.'

[1] Yurenev was pessimistic on the future of Russo-Japanese relations in a talk with Grew on 20 November. Grew, op. cit., p. 107.

[2] Extracts in *Documents for 1933*, pp. 425–42.

There was, however, 'no lack of sensible people in Japan, who perceive all the dangers for Japan of a war against a giant so full of power and energy as the Soviet Union'. Nor could Japan expect outside sympathy. Like Germany she began

'with the idea that it would be sufficient for her to declare that these moves were directed against the Soviet Government in order to win the whole capitalist world to her side and to obtain its blessing. Here Japan miscalculated. . . . Our policy (he concluded) is clear. We do not aspire to make use of a favourable situation, we do not aspire to wage war under any circumstances. We say to Japan: "We do not threaten you, we do not want your land or other territories lying on your side of the frontiers, we want to live at peace with you as we have done up to the present, respecting your rights and interests and asking only that you adopt the same attitude towards our rights and interests. Your first step to prove your peaceful disposition should be the cessation of repressive police measures on the Chinese Eastern Railway, the restoration of our violated rights, and then a calm continuation of the negotiations for a fair commercial price for the railroad."

'The second step in demonstrating Japan's desire for peace should be the signing of the Pact of Non-Aggression which we proposed two years ago. We should like to entertain the hope that Japan will act in accordance with the counsel of her level-headed patriots and not with that of her militarist adventurers.'

At the Communist Party Congress in January 1934, MM Stalin, Litvinov, and Molotov charged the Japanese with deliberate sabotage of the Railway and with being engaged in military preparations against the U.S.S.R. The Japanese, asserted Litvinov, did not want to buy the Railway but to get it for nothing, built though it was 'with the blood and money of the peoples of the Union, thus constituting their inalienable property'. In February, however, after the release of the Soviet officials arrested in the previous autumn, negotiations were renewed.[1]

As might have been expected, the Russian offer to sell the Railway had provoked violent expressions of disapproval from China. The Chinese Government presented a note at Moscow on 16 May 1933, protesting against 'an unlawful transaction with an unlawful regime', and pointed to the fact that by Article 9 of the Sino-Soviet Treaty of 31 May 1924, the future of the C.E.R. could not be determined except by agreement between 'the Republic of China and the U.S.S.R., to the exclusion of any third party or parties'. In reply, M. Litvinov argued that the agreements of 1924 no longer governed the situation,

[1] Conolly, op. cit., p. 78.

since the Chinese had become physically incapable of carrying out their side of them, owing to the Japanese occupation of Manchuria.[1]

The renewal of the negotiations over the Railway in February had been preceded by a conciliatory speech on the part of the Japanese Foreign Minister, M. Hirota.[2] Nevertheless progress was not rapid. The main difference arose over the price to be paid, and in August, the Manchukuo delegation, having failed to get its last offer accepted, left for home.

Meanwhile, the perennial fisheries problem was again causing trouble between the Soviet Union and Japan. Existing arrangements for the Japanese to fish in Soviet waters were based on the agreement of 1928 and on the supplementary (unpublished) agreement of 1932.[3] The 1928 agreement was due to expire in May 1936, but would automatically be renewed for a further twelve years, unless a year's notice to the contrary had been given by either party. The Japanese now possessed the lease of certain of the fishing grounds and the right to bid at an annual auction for the lease of others. These rights were of great importance to Japan. But the Soviet fishing industry had recently been making rapid progress and had become independent of the Japanese for its equipment. Soviet competition in a disguised form at the auctions was also increasingly in evidence. In February 1934, the Soviet Government further announced that the yen-rouble exchange rate for the purposes of the auctions would be altered in the current year from that prevailing since 1931. The dispute which followed was settled by May, when the auctions were held, and a further provisional settlement was agreed upon in August. But the fundamental issue of the future Japanese participation in the fishing-grounds was still undetermined, and the increase of naval activities in Far Eastern waters made it probable that the Soviet objection to the practice would harden.

The main source of mutual suspicion and recrimination in 1934, remained the military preparations on either side of the Soviet-Manchurian frontier, although actual 'incidents' were

---

[1] Documents in *China Year Book*, 1934, pp. 732–3; the Treaty and the separate Railway Agreement of the same date are printed as Appendices VII and VIII (E), in Conolly, op. cit.

[2] Address before the Diet on 23 January 1934, *Documents for 1933*, pp. 493–8. In a long analysis of Russo-Japanese relations, dated 8 February 1934, Grew concluded that the chances of war had recently diminished, op. cit., pp. 117–21. But a conversation with Yurenev on 9 March found the latter still pessimistic about the chances of peace, ibid., pp. 121–25.

[3] The Fisheries Convention of 1928 is printed as Appendix VI in Conolly, op. cit.

less frequent than they had been. The Japanese were still unwilling to consider the Soviet proposal of a non-aggression pact, while on their side the Russians showed considerable resentment at an informal proposal put forward at the beginning of September, that both sides should withdraw troops from the frontier and dismantle their fortifications. Since the chances of a Soviet invasion of Manchuria were negligible, and since the Manchurian communications were so much better than those of the Soviet Far East, the proposal was an obviously one-sided one.

These diplomatic contacts can only be fully understood against the rapidly shifting background of world events. In the early part of 1934, there was some Soviet anxiety at what looked like a Japanese attempt to achieve a reconciliation with the Western Powers, which might free her hands for some anti-Soviet move. This particular fear was dispelled by the Japanese statement of policy on 18 April—the 'Amau statement' with its far-reaching demand for a monopolistic position for the Japanese in China.[1] On the other hand, the unfavourable reaction of the Western Powers was followed by more friendly contacts between Japan and Germany. At the same time the Soviet Union found itself on an improved footing with the United States and with the leading Powers in the League of Nations.[2] With China, too, relations seemed to be slowly though steadily improving, and this despite the abuse hurled at the Chinese Government from Communist quarters. The final campaign against the Communists in Kiangsi led to the beginning of their retreat to the North-West in October. The Chinese speech of welcome upon the Soviet Union's entry into the League in September was noticeably friendly. Thus a new world political grouping seemed to be shaping in the autumn of 1934 with the U.S.S.R., China, and the Western democracies, aligned against Germany and Japan.[3]

[1] *Documents for 1934*, pp. 472-3. On 25 April, the Japanese Foreign Minister, Hirota, referred to the statement in an interview with the American Ambassador. The former stated that he was doing his best to bring to a successful conclusion the C.E.R. negotiations which should improve Japan's relations with Russia 'and in turn tend to induce better relations between China and Japan'. Joseph C. Grew to Secretary of State, 25 April 1934. *Peace and War*, pp. 214-16.

[2] Nevertheless, in the conversation with Grew already referred to, Yurenev said that according to his information England was showing 'a distinct pro-Japanese tendency,' op. cit., p. 125. Writing in May, Grew seemed to regard the danger of an imminent Russo-Japanese conflict as much diminished. Letter to Prentice B. Gilbert, 17 May 1934, op. cit., pp. 135-9.

[3] Sino-Soviet relations did not alter conspicuously in the following months; they were not ruffled by the attention paid to China by the Comintern Congress in August 1935.

Once again, however, when it came to the point, neither the Soviet Union nor Japan had any desire to go to extremes. Early in September, M. Hirota made a direct approach to the Soviet Ambassador, M. Yurenev, to get the talks re-started.[1] Within a few days a sufficient measure of agreement over the price of the Railway had been reached for formal negotiations to be re-opened. These began on the 21st and the main point was rapidly disposed of. The price of 140,000,000 yen was to be paid for the Railway, with an additional 30,000,000 or 35,000,000 yen to cover pensions for the Soviet officials who would lose their posts. Thus a total of 170,000,000 to 175,000,000 yen was accepted in lieu of the original Russian demand of 650,000,000 yen or 250,000,000 gold roubles. Two-thirds of the agreed price was to be paid in goods and half the remainder over a four-years' period. A Soviet demand that the latter payments should be guaranteed by the Japanese Government held up negotiations once more, but by mid-December the Japanese had given way. The actual agreement between the U.S.S.R. and Manchukuo was initialled on 11 March 1935, and signed on 23 March.[2]

The Chinese Government duly repeated its protest and on 18 March it circulated a memorandum to the signatories of the Nine-Power Treaty of 1922.[3] But the Chinese had obviously nothing to gain by pressing a purely formal issue to the detriment of their relations with the Soviet Union. *Izvestia* pointed out on the 24th that the Chinese would have gained nothing if the Soviet Union had gone to war over the question of the Railway, and that the solution of returning it to the Chinese people which the Russians would have welcomed, was rendered out of the question by the existing position in Manchuria.

The Chinese reluctance to antagonise the Soviet Government arose from the beginning of a new period of crisis in Sino-Japanese relations. Once again the Japanese army appeared unwilling to allow its Foreign Office to attempt to gain Japanese ends by conciliation, and a new forward move began in January 1935 with a Japanese advance into Chahar. Although a local agreement resulted in a new demarcation of the Manchukuo frontier, the chances of this proving a permanent bar to Japanese aggression seemed poor.

---

[1] Yurenev was more optimistic than previously in a talk with Grew on 7 September. Grew, op. cit., pp. 140–2.

[2] Text in Conolly, op. cit., Appendix VIII, (I).

[3] Documents in *China Year Book*, 1935, pp. 138–9. The Nine-Power Treaty of Washington of 6 February 1922, is printed as Appendix II to *China and Japan* (R.I.I.A.).

The sale of the Chinese Eastern Railway was naturally the subject of much discussion abroad. Some observers took it as a major setback for the Soviet Union and as evidence of that Power's weakness; for it was pointed out that the purchase price represented only one-eighth of the cost of the Railway's construction. Further retreat on the part of the Russians was thought probable. It was suggested that the sale of North Sakhalin, Kamchatka, and even of the Maritime Territory itself, might follow.[1] In the following years occasional rumours to this effect found currency in the world's press.

But those who took this view overlooked the immense material and moral investment that was implied in the Soviet development of the Far Eastern provinces.[2] Every announcement of new achievements in that field made the loss of prestige involved in its cession harder to face, and most of the development programme could only be justified by the assumption that a serious attempt would be made to defend the area.

In time of war, the Chinese Eastern Railway would be useless; in time of peace, it had become a wasting asset. The Soviet leaders had always shown that they knew when to cut their losses.

Apart from the settlement of the Railway question, Soviet-Japanese tension did not abate very much in 1935. At the end of January, there was a sharp public exchange between Hirota and Molotov over the question of alleged Soviet designs in Sinkiang. In the same month a frontier skirmish took place on the border between Manchukuo and Outer Mongolia, the area in dispute being finally occupied by Japanese troops. Negotiations over this incident led to a Japanese demand for what amounted to a virtual opening-up of Outer Mongolia to Japanese penetration after a decade and more during which it had been almost completely cut off from the outer world, with the exception of the Soviet Union.

In a press statement on 14 March, after the conclusion of the negotiations over the C.E.R. had been announced, M. Litvinov made a conciliatory gesture towards Japan by indicating that the time might be ripe for some consideration of

---

[1] S. Vostrotin: 'Russia's Crisis in the Far East', *Slavonic Review*, July 1935.

[2] Foreign observers were impressed by these preparations to meet a possible attack. 'The Soviet Ambassador recently told me that a prominent Japanese had said to him that the most important factor in avoiding a Japanese attack on the Maritime Province was the intensive Soviet military preparations in Siberia and Vladivostok. I believe this to be true, and yet again I urge that our own country be adequately prepared to meet all eventualities in the Far East.' Ambassador Joseph Grew writing from Tokio to Secretary Hull, 27 December 1934. *Peace and War*, 1934, p. 244.

proposals for a mutual withdrawal of troops along the Soviet-Manchurian border, while maintaining his objection to the use of the term 'demilitarisation' as inappropriate to a freely negotiated agreement. He pointed out that it was desirable to dissipate the suspicions which Japan had aroused by its rejection of the idea of a non-aggression pact.[1] Perhaps because of this last point, no Japanese response to the overture seems to have been forthcoming.[2]

In April 1935, the Japanese raised the question of revision of the fisheries agreement. The Soviet Government refused to consider major changes until the Japanese had agreed to the prolongation of the agreement as a whole. And in May, the Japanese informed the Russians that they would insist on a fundamental revision. Negotiations accordingly opened in the knowledge that, failing agreement, the whole arrangement would lapse in May 1936.

In May and June 1935, further Japanese advances into Inner Mongolia (Chahar) were made and the threat to Outer Mongolia appeared more acute. Agreement on the Manchukuo-Soviet frontier seemed remote.[3] The Japanese advance, combined with severe diplomatic pressure on the Chinese Government, led to the establishment in December of an 'autonomous' council to administer the provinces of Hopei and Chahar. This meant a definite consolidation of the Japanese position along a vital section of the Outer Mongolian frontier. There was also a renewal of the series of incidents along the Soviet and Outer Mongolian frontiers with Manchukuo.

The closing days of 1935 were marked by reports of troop movements on both sides and by talk of the imminence of hostilities between the Soviet Union and Japan.

[1] *China Year Book*, 1935, p. 139.

[2] In a note on 2 April 1935, Grew discussed the advantages to Japan from the effects of Germany's announcement of her rearmament. 'Amau [the Japanese Foreign Office spokesman] denied yesterday that any steps had been taken for a Soviet-Japanese non-aggression pact. Indeed, under present circumstances, Japan has no need for one. Developments are playing directly into Japanese hands. Amau says that Japan has no alliance or ententes except the more or less defunct sort of informal understanding that exists with Poland, and we have information that there is an intimate exchange of views and information going on between Japan and Germany. But all this is nebulous and the main fact is that Japan can now "sit pretty" and carry on more or less as she wishes with the assurance that the European Powers are much too busy at home to bother much about the Far East.' Grew, op. cit., p. 155.

[3] In a talk with Grew on 17 July, Yurenev expressed confidence about the future of Russo-Japanese relations and tried to convince Grew that the difficulties between the United States and Japan would prove more intractable. Grew, op. cit., pp. 158–9.

These reports were not unconnected with events in Europe, and there was a suggestion in the Soviet press that the incidents had been provoked by Japan, at Germany's request, in order to frighten France out of ratifying the Franco-Soviet Pact, which was under fire from the French Right as likely to drag France into the Soviet Union's Far Eastern troubles.

Early in February 1936, the Soviet Government suggested that recent incidents on their frontier with Manchukuo might be investigated by a commission which should include a representative of a neutral third Power.[1] The Japanese rejected this proposal and stated that the real need was for a proper demarcation of the frontier. The Soviet suggestion for a neutral representative was thereupon dropped in favour of a demand that the Russians should have as many members on the Commission as the Japanese and Manchurians together. They also denied that the frontier required 'demarcation',[2] saying that only 'redemarcation' of a fully recognised line was necessary.

With regard to Outer Mongolia, the Soviet Union's position was defined in an unusually dramatic form. Stalin gave one of his rare interviews to a foreigner (the American press magnate, Roy Howard) on 4 March. The relevant passages ran as follows:

HOWARD: 'What would be the attitude of the Soviet Union if Japan should embark on a serious military drive against the Mongolian People's Republic?'

STALIN: 'If Japan ventures to attack the Mongolian People's Republic seeking to destroy its independence, we will have to assist the Mongolian People's Republic. Litvinov's assistant, Stomoniakov, has already informed the Japanese Ambassador in Moscow of the fact. . . . We will assist the Mongolian People's Republic in the same way as in 1921.'

HOWARD: 'Would a Japanese attempt to seize Ulan Bator necessitate positive action by the U.S.S.R.?'

STALIN: 'Yes, it would.'

HOWARD: 'Have there recently been any new Japanese activities in this region which are construed by the Soviet Government as of an aggressive nature?'

[1] This appears to have been the first occasion upon which the Soviet Government contemplated the admission of a neutral third party into a commission of inquiry with which it was concerned. Hitherto the attitude to such matters had been that there could be no impartial arbiters in a matter concerning the rival worlds of capitalism and socialism. Taracouzio, *The Soviet Union and International Law*, pp. 295–7.

[2] This had been put forward in the summer of 1935 as the Soviet answer to the claim that both Japan and Manchukuo should be represented on the frontier commission. Grew, loc. cit.

STALIN: 'The Japanese seem to be continuing to concentrate troops near the frontier of the Mongolian People's Republic, but so far no new attempts at frontier clashes have been observed.'[1]

Meanwhile the situation had been further obscured by the changes in the Japanese Government consequent upon the rising of the 'young officers' in Tokyo on 26–29 February.[2] M. Hirota, who undertook the task of forming a new ministry, found many of his proposed appointments vetoed by the army, and his Cabinet was not actually completed until two days after Hitler's Rhineland *coup*.

[1] *Documents for 1936*, pp. 464–5.
[2] Grew, op. cit., pp. 169–78.

Chapter Fourteen

SOVIET NATIONALISM AND THE RED ARMY

THE years after 1929 witnessed psychological and moral changes in the U.S.S.R. which were of importance in her international relations; a full examination of them would involve an inquiry into the very nature of the Soviet system.

What is relevant here is the development of the earlier internationalism of the Revolution and its leaders into something which can best be described as Soviet patriotism or even as Soviet nationalism.[1]

Once the Soviet Government realised in the early nineteen-twenties that an immediate spread of the Revolution to other countries was improbable, and that the period of 'socialism in one country' would be more or less prolonged, it was necessary to harness to the prosaic task of economic and social reconstruction the dynamic spirit of devotion and sacrifice which had been excited in the earlier generation of Communist leaders by the prospect of the approaching emancipation of mankind as a whole.

In Stalin, the régime had a leader whose experience and outlook was less cosmopolitan than some of his early rivals for power; and the younger generation of Soviet leaders who were coming to the fore in the early nineteen-thirties were even more emphatically Russian in their outlook. It was thus possible for the ideologues of the régime to make the transition from an emphasis only upon the new socialist elements of the system to one which also pointed out, however discreetly at first, its specifically native heritage. In so doing, the Soviet leaders only renewed an earlier tradition among Russian revolutionaries of different schools, who had seen something unique in the contribution which their country might make to the wider movement of mankind.

The introduction of a patriotic or nationalistic theme was even more apposite when the prospect of foreign war came

[1] The distinction is emphasised, perhaps over-emphasised, by H. Kohn, *Revolutions and Dictatorships* (Harvard University Press, 1939), chap. 5. 'Soviet patriotism is certainly not modern nationalism . . . it is not a Russian patriotism, not the nationalistic love of the Russian fatherland or of the country of another political nation.' op. cit., p. 174. The subject is the theme of chap. 5 (by S. O. Yakobson) of the R.I.I.A. study, *Nationalism* (O.U.P., 1935). Cf. W. Kolarz, *Stalin and Eternal Russia* (Lindsay Drummond, 1944).

closer—particularly as it became clear that the Soviet Union would probably have to fight the war, not as the spearhead of an international revolutionary proletariat, but with the weapons of a State among other States—even if it were a State with an additional weapon in the shape of the Communist International.

A certain ambiguity was involved in the adoption of a truly national appeal because the Soviet Union was itself a multi-national state, although one in which the Great Russians were numerically overwhelmingly preponderant. The liberation of the 'subject nationalities' of the old Russian Empire had been one of the earliest objectives of the Communist Revolution, and the elaboration of a solution of the 'nationalities' problem had been one of its most widely publicised achievements. Nevertheless this had not been achieved without setbacks, both because of the unwillingness of certain national groups to accept the severe limitations upon the expression of their national purposes in other than the cultural field, and because of the unextinguished chauvinism of the Great Russians themselves.[1]

The problem was particularly acute in relation to efforts to strengthen the national spirit of the country by paying greater attention to the positive values of its pre-revolutionary past; for the national histories of some of the subject peoples were largely concerned with their struggles against the rule of Moscow. Nevertheless it was decided that the risk would have to be run. A decree dated 16 May 1934 denounced the historical teaching which had been in vogue since the Revolution under the inspiration of the Marxist historian M. N. Pokrovsky:

'The text-books and oral instruction are of an abstract schematic character. Instead of the teaching of civic history in an animated and entertaining form, with an exposition of the most important events and facts in their chronological sequence, and with sketches of historical personages, the pupils are given abstract definitions of social and economic formations which replace the consecutive exposition of civic history by abstract sociological schemes.'[2]

[1] *Nationalism*, p. 74. The most recent summary of the Soviet 'nationalities' problem is in F. Hertz, *Nationality in History and Politics* (Kegan Paul, 1944), pp. 191–6. Cf. A. Cobban, *National Self-Determination* (R.I.I.A., Oxford University Press, 1945).

[2] Quoted from the translation in *Slavonic Review*, XIII, pp. 204–5. The practical steps taken were the re-opening of history faculties at the Universities of Moscow and Leningrad and the writing of new text-books. In a competition for providing the latter, no first prize was awarded; the history by Professor A. V. Shestakov, which was awarded the second prize, was published in 1937. 'Shestakov's merit lies in the fact that he contrived to produce a common denominator for the history of all the different nationalities in the Soviet Union and that, despite its patriotic Russian tendencies, his book is not a Russian history book in the old, restricted sense of the

The revision of historical teaching was perhaps the most striking of the portents of change in the years with which we are dealing, but the same tendency to re-establish broken links with the past of the Russian State was obvious in a wider field. And the Russian Communist Party found that its rôle had changed accordingly.

The importance of this was recognised by some contemporary commentators:

'The paramount mission of the Union Communist Party is now no longer the achievement of a World-Revolution but the maintenance of a "new nationalism". This Stalinian nationalism has, it is true, a wider basis than the Great Russian linguistic and racial nationalism of the former Tsardom in its last phase. Based, as it is, upon no external or material criterion, but upon the common spiritual possession of the Stalino-Lenino-Marxian ideas and institutions and the common personal and social experience of the extraordinary events of which the Soviet domain has been the theatre since 1917, the new Soviet national consciousness embraces, without any invidious distinctions, the whole medley of peoples that dwell within the Soviet frontiers; and . . . this population in its multitude and its variety is a fair sample of contemporary Mankind. Yet, vast and variegated though it is, this Soviet Union national state is now a parochial affair, and has ceased to be the World-state in embryo that it was originally designed to be.'[1]

The new turn in Soviet policy not unnaturally involved changes in the size, composition, and character of the Red Army, far-reaching in their implications, both for the Soviet Union and for its neighbours.[2] The fundamental organisation of the Red Army dated back to the Revolution and Civil War, and in part to the period of reconstruction which followed the post-Civil War demobilisation of a very large proportion of the victorious Soviet forces. The second period began under Trotsky and continued under the latter's successor, Frunze. It was marked by serious clashes of doctrine in both the operational

---

term. Shestakov gives practically every one of the larger nationalities in the U.S.S.R. its national heroes; in other words, he gives the mark of official approval to the heroes already cherished in the traditions of the respective peoples, and incorporates them into the historical totality of Russia.' Kolarz, op. cit., p. 84. On Soviet historiography, cf. B. H. Sumner, 'Soviet History', *Slavonic Review*, XVI–XVII; A. G. Mazour, *An Outline of Modern Russian Historiography* (University of California Press, 1939).

[1] *Survey for 1934*, p. 371.
[2] The following paragraphs are based largely on the book by D. Fedotoff White, *The Growth of the Red Army* (Princeton University Press, 1944), which draws extensively upon Soviet sources and is decidedly more serious in purpose and execution than the majority of books upon this subject.

and organisational spheres—themselves the product of the dual character of the Red Army, as a spearhead of world revolution and as the defensive arm of the Soviet State.

Those responsible for the Army's development had many difficulties to surmount; the ravages of the Civil War, the low level of industrialisation, the cultural backwardness of the country, and the scarcity of technically trained personnel. They depended for commanding personnel to a considerable extent upon officers of the old Army whose loyalty to the régime was suspect; and the peasantry from whom the bulk of the recruits had to be drawn was disaffected to an appreciable degree. The doctrinal conflict showed itself in sharp disagreements between those who wished for a strong regular Army, for professional reasons or as the nucleus of offensive revolutionary action, and those who wished the Soviet military system to be based on the idea of a popular militia—the people in arms to defend the home of socialism.

In the upshot an uneasy and shifting compromise came into being, with doubtful points usually decided according to the criterion of political advantage to the régime at home, rather than by the test of military efficiency. For this reason the Political Administration of the Army (P.U.R.), through its Commissars and political assistants, occupied a position of unique importance among contemporary armies. From 1924 onwards the principle of unity of command was generally introduced, and the dualism of Commander and Commissar ceased to be as prominent as it had been in the Civil War period, when the Commissar's primary function had been to keep a check on suspect officers drawn from the old Army. Indeed, from 1925, the institution of military Commissars in the old sense ceased to exist throughout most of the military structure. But this did not of course make less important the work of the P.U.R.; and additional safeguards existed in the exclusion of the disfranchised elements of the population from active service units and in repeated efforts to permeate all units, and especially the key ones, with a generous proportion of 'proletarians' and Party members.

From 1932 to 1934, the size of the Red Army (including the Navy and Air Force) remained at 562,000 men. There were also some 150,000 troops of the political police (O.G.P.U.) and about 100,000 frontier guards. The Red Army proper consisted of $71\frac{1}{2}$ infantry and $16\frac{1}{2}$ cavalry divisions, but of the total 88 divisions, 43 were part of the territorial militia whose periods of training were too short for it to be considered a very serious force. The basic period of service with the Regular Army was

N

two years, but Air Force and Coastal Defence Force personnel served for three years and Naval personnel for four years.

The primary problem remained one of cadres. The commanding personnel—for the term officer was still avoided—consisted of an uneasy amalgam of former officers of the Imperial Army, of Civil War personalities (largely N.C.O.s of the old Army), and of the products of the new military schools of the U.S.S.R. The position of the corps was regularised and to some extent professionalised by the basic Statute of 1928.[1]

In spite of an increasing emphasis upon discipline and conventional military training, the Red Army was still meant to remain a political instrument trained to full awareness of its political rôle. The Field Service regulations of 1929 demand that political work in the Army should emphasise the leading rôle of the proletariat in the Soviet system, the class aims of war, and the international interests of the working class. The programme of political studies for the troops, published in the same year, described how class antagonisms rendered irreconcilable the hostility between the U.S.S.R. and the capitalist world. The outside world was depicted as busily engaged in preparing for a new war of intervention. Britain was described as the imperialist state most inimical to Russia, while relations with Germany were singled out as being more normal than those with any other capitalist country because of Germany's sufferings in the imperialist war.

The industrial achievements of the First Five-Year Plan, although not very considerable on the purely military side, paved the way for a large-scale overhaul of the Army's equipment and for its rapid mechanisation in the succeeding years.

From 1933 onwards, the Red Army underwent a rapid process of expansion and modernisation, the scale of which impressed many foreign observers. Attention was paid in particular to the efforts made to decrease the dependence of the Far Eastern region on its long communications with European Russia. But there were other changes of almost equal significance.

The territorial militia element was gradually eliminated and the Army became a single-patterned organisation. It was more and more supplemented as an instrument of training by the various pre-military and subsidiary organisations grouped in the *Osoaviakhim*. The positions of command were to a great extent filled by elements nurtured in the Soviet system, and the position of the commanders was increasingly approximated to that of the officer corps of other European countries. The ethos of the Army was progressively remoulded, like that of

1 This is analysed in White, op. cit., pp. 300–5.

the country at large, on national and patriotic lines. The basis for recruitment was widened to include the country as a whole. Its military doctrine was overwhelmingly dominated by the notion of national defence.

The foundations for these changes, which did not reach their culminating development until after the outbreak of war in 1941, were laid in the years 1934–1936. In his speech to the Seventeenth Party Congress on 30 January 1934, Marshal Voroshilov claimed that since the Sixteenth Congress in 1930, the Army had been completely reborn, becoming in fact 'a fundamentally different Army in regard to quantity and quality of arms, organisational structure and the fighting preparedness of its cadres'. He followed this by giving some detailed information upon the Army's structure and composition, and dwelt upon progress in mechanisation, in the construction of frontier defences, and in naval building. A large portion of the speech was devoted to describing the special steps taken to strengthen the defences of the Far East.[1]

In spite of conventional references to the high level of the political education of the Army and to the importance in this connexion of the soldiers who were Party members, the tone of the speech suggested that the prime concern of the Army was national defence. The speech can indeed be linked directly with Stalin's analysis of the international position given to the Congress four days before.[2] Although Stalin had then declared that any bourgeois Government attacking the U.S.S.R. would be faced with revolution at home, he made it clear that the main obstacle to their success would nevertheless come from the Red Army, and justified Soviet foreign policy as seeking by all means to avoid war.

On 25 March 1934, important changes were introduced into the organisation of the Red Army. In conformity with the general trend towards the abolition of the collegiate system in Soviet administration, the Revolutionary Military Council, the supreme military authority since September 1918, was abolished.[3] The Commissariat for the Army and Navy was

---

[1] The speech is translated in *Socialism Victorious*, pp. 247–93. The preparedness of the Soviet Far East was further emphasised in a speech by General Bluecher, pp. 629–31 of the stenographic report of the Congress: *XVII Sezd Vsesoyuznoy Kommunistichiskoy Partii*.

[2] *Socialism Victorious*, pp. 1–93.

[3] For the organisation of the Commissariats on the collegiate principle, see Batsell, *Soviet Rule in Russia*, pp. 546–7. In 1934, the Collegium of the Commissariat of Foreign Affairs was also abolished and authority concentrated in the Commissar. See Appendix V by A. F. Neymann to S. N. Harper (ed.), *The Soviet Union and World Problems* (Chicago University Press, 1936).

renamed the Commissariat for Defence, and its head, the People's Commissar for Defence, became the sole responsible chief of the Commissariat and of the Land Forces of the Soviet Union. The same concentration of authority in the hands of individuals was effected throughout the administration. This was followed by an increase in the peace-time strength of the Army from 562,000 to 940,000 men.[1] In 1935, further expansion took place which, by 1936, brought the strength of the Army to 1,300,000 men. (This total included the Naval and Air contingents, but not the special troops of the N.K.V.D. nor the seven motorised divisions of frontier guards.)[2]

In a speech before the Central Executive Committee on 15 January 1936, Tukhachevsky justified the increased defence appropriations by reference to the military policies of other Powers and in particular to those of Germany and Japan. He also announced that instead of the 74 per cent territorial and 26 per cent regular troops which had existed prior to 1935, the ratio had been altered, and for the infantry now stood at 77 per cent regulars to 23 per cent territorials.[3]

A further step had also been taken by the Decree of 22 September 1935, in the direction of professionalising the Army. Personal ranks, long eschewed as symbols of the old régime, were reintroduced—those from Lieutenant to Colonel for the Army and the corresponding ones for the Navy. The titles of General and Admiral were still avoided.[4] In addition, however, a new rank (for Russia), that of Marshal, was created, and in November 1935, conferred upon Voroshilov, Egorov, Budenny, and Bluecher. These formal changes were accompanied by greater attention to the material well-being and cultural level of the Soviet officer corps. In 1936, new Field Service regulations were issued, with a commentary by Tukhachevsky which

---

[1] On 30 January 1935, Tukhachevsky announced that this figure had been achieved and gave some facts on the development of mechanisation. Speech before the Seventh All-Union Soviet Congress; extracts in *Documents for 1934*, pp. 415–18.

[2] On 31 December 1937, a separate Commissariat for the Navy was created. The O.G.P.U. was absorbed in the new N.K.V.D., the Commissariat of the Interior, by a Decree of 10 July 1934. Text in *Slavonic Review*, XIII, pp. 436–8.

[3] *Slavonic Review*, XIV, pp. 694–701. At the same session of the Central Executive Committee an estimate of 14,800,000,000 roubles was put forward for defence expenditure. The previous two years' expenditure had been:

1934: 5,000,000,000 (against an estimate of 1,655,000,000) roubles.
1935: 8,200,000,000 (against an estimate of 6,500,000,000) roubles.

Documents for 1934, p. 417; *Survey for 1936*, pp. 124–5.

[4] They were introduced in May 1940.

specifically discarded the doctrine that the morale of the Soviet workers and collective farmers alone sufficed to give the Red Army superior manoeuvrability.[1]

This development must be remembered when one comes to consider the Army crisis of 1936–1937—a crisis of immense importance on the international scene, and one which seemed momentarily to reverse the prevailing tendencies in the direction of autonomy for the military chiefs of the Union, within their own particular sphere.[2]

[1] M. Berchin and E. Ben Horin, *The Red Army* (Allen & Unwin, 1943), chap. 5.

[2] For naval development, see R. J. Kerner, 'Russian Naval Aims', *Foreign Affairs*, January 1946.

Chapter Fifteen

THE SEVENTH CONGRESS OF THE COMINTERN

THE entry into the League of Nations of the Soviet Union, and the growing approximation of its international conduct to that of an ordinary State, might have seemed to call in question the credentials of an institution which owed its existence to the original view of the Soviet Union as being primarily the headquarters of world revolution. On the other hand, the Communist International still enjoyed an enormous prestige in Soviet ideology; and the existence in nearly every foreign country of a Communist Party accustomed by now to complete subservience to the dictates of the All-Union Communist Party, was an asset with which the Soviet leaders were unwilling to dispense. In these circumstances it was not difficult to find for the Comintern a rôle which it could apparently fulfil in the new conditions, and which would keep it in being should the turn of events require it once more to resume its revolutionary activity.

Of the fidelity of the Comintern and its constituent parties to the view which identified the interests of world revolution with the specific interests of the Soviet Union there could be little doubt, if only because the number of countries where Communism was rooted in any large section of the population was minimal. For many of the foreign parties, their link with Moscow, and the prestige which this gave them, was their only real asset. The Communist International strove therefore, at a respectful distance, to keep in step with the evolution of the Russian Party, and accepted its views as to the tactics necessitated by the changing needs of the defence of the Soviet fatherland.

When the Thirteenth Plenum of the Executive Committee met in December 1933, it still adhered to its analysis of the existing international situation as one in which the period of capitalist stabilisation had ended, giving way to a new era of revolutions and wars. It maintained its left extremism and devoted itself to attacks upon the social-democratic leaders and the 'right opportunists' and to renewed advocacy of the slogan: 'the united front from below'.[1]

The same outlook was revealed in the long report made by Manuilsky to the Seventeenth Russian Party Congress on

[1] *Theses and Decisions of the Thirteenth Plenum of the E.C.C.I.* (Modern Books, 1934).

2 February 1934.[1] World reaction, leading up to a counter-revolutionary war against the Soviet Union, was headed by England, which had replaced France in that rôle. Germany and Japan were the spearheads of the attack. On the other hand, the revolutionary upsurge was growing in strength in Central Europe, in Britain and in the colonial and dependent countries. The coming into power of an openly Fascist dictatorship in Germany meant a contraction of the base of bourgeois power in that country and in consequence its weakening. Before the menace of its aggressive designs, France and Poland had been forced to seek support from the U.S.S.R.: 'To-day not one proletarian in the world will move a finger in the event of war to support Fascist Germany in the struggle against Versailles.' The violent tactics of the German Fascists had also helped to undeceive the German workers and to turn them away from Social Democracy and towards Communism. Certain as the victory of the proletarian revolution remained, the interlude of the Fascist dictatorship could have been avoided, but for the treachery of the leaders of the German Social Democratic Party and of their comrades in other countries. It was therefore necessary to intensify the struggle to win over the masses from the delusions of Social Democracy. Manuilsky's phrases were echoed by delegates from the non-Russian Communist Parties, in particular by the German, Heckert. The German bourgeoisie, he declared, had been weakened, not strengthened, by its recourse to open terror, and the German masses would actively intervene to frustrate the aggression which the Nazis were preparing against the Soviet Union.[2]

Since the object of Soviet policy was to gain allies, the subsequent period of the Comintern's history—the era of the 'popular fronts'—is primarily concerned not with countries where the Communist Party was illegal, but with those, such as France and Spain, where it could still influence Government policy by an open appeal to the masses.[3]

Since 1928 the French Communist Party had followed the same intransigent line as the Communist Parties of other countries, and had directed the full force of its venom against the French Socialists (S.F.I.O.) and their leader, Léon Blum. In the Chamber of 1932, the former had only 12 seats against the 129 of the latter. On the other hand, the Communists had a remarkable concentration of strength in Paris and its suburbs,

---

[1] *Socialism Victorious*, pp. 295–359.

[2] *XVII Sezd Vsesoyuznoy Kommunistichiskoy Partii* (17th Party Congress stenographic report), pp. 331–3.

[3] F. Borkenau, *The Communist International*, chaps. 22–3.

where their total vote was reckoned at 244,000 to the 157,000 of the Socialists.

In France, the economic and political situation had by 1934 produced a fertile soil for the growth of extremism whether of the Right or the Left. It was the former that made the running in the spring of 1934, and which was mainly responsible for the riots of 6 February, against the newly formed left-centre Government of Daladier.[1] The rôle of the Communists at this time bore a marked resemblance to that of the German Communists towards the end of 1932—a fact which was not surprising since, as we have seen, the *mots d'ordre* were unchanged. Some Communists certainly took part in the rioting, and both on the streets and in the Chamber the Communists did their best to add to Daladier's embarrassments.

The severity of the riots of 6 February brought home to the Paris working-class the imminence of the Fascist danger, and there would seem to have been a definite sentiment in favour of unity between its two main political parties and their respective trade-union organisations, the Socialist C.G.T. and the Communist C.G.T.U. But after a joint strike and demonstration on 12 February the Communist Party returned to its normal attitude of complete hostility towards the Socialists. On 13 April 1934, the Communist leader, Thorez, writing in *Imprecorr*, denounced those who advocated a *bloc* with the Socialists as a substitute for the 'united front from below'. At this point, the change of attitude in Moscow apparently began to be felt, and by June, when the Party Congress met, it was ready for united action. A formal pact between the parties was signed on 27 July. The new alliance was confined to the defence of democratic liberties, opposition to war preparations, and the combatting of German and Austrian Fascism. Henceforth, Communist propaganda became increasingly national in tone, and they made energetic efforts to extend their influence in all quarters, and among all classes. They even abandoned the hostility to the Catholic Church which had hitherto been a staple of all Left-wing parties in France.[2]

---

[1] On the origins and growth of the French Popular Front, see D. W. Brogan, *The Development of Modern France* (Hamilton, 1940), pp. 651–701; A. Werth, *France in Ferment*, chaps. 7, 8 and 13; *The Destiny of France* (Hamilton, 1937), chap. 10. A Trotskyist angle is given in C. L. R. James, *World Revolution*, pp. 379–85.

[2] Yves Simon, *La Grande Crise de la République Française* (Montreal, 1941), pp. 145 ff. The Comintern made an effort during the period which began in 1934 to find a common ground with the more democratic Catholic groups in other countries—most noticeably in the case of the Saar plebiscite —but, for intelligible reasons, the effort was not destined to be successful. Borkenau, op. cit., p. 398.

Their progress in this direction was rapid—so rapid indeed that the Left elements among the orthodox Socialists found it difficult to follow them. It was not long before the Communists were looking for allies even further to the Right than Léon Blum. They took advantage of the fact that the idea of an agreement to embrace all anti-Fascist parties was very much in the air at the time. As far as the Socialists were concerned, some encouragement was found in the fact that the Spanish Communists supported their Socialist comrades in the Asturias rising in October 1934. Common demonstrations in favour of the insurgents were staged by the two French parties.[1]

The decisive period for the new policy of the Comintern in France was the spring of 1935. On 2 May, the Franco-Soviet Pact was signed; and on 15 May, during Laval's visit to Moscow, a joint communiqué affirmed Stalin's sympathy for the French measures of rearmament.[2] The Communist abandonment of 'revolutionary defeatism' and of Alsatian autonomism were clearly necessary for any wider collaboration.[3] It proved difficult, however, to undo the effect upon Left-wing elements of years of outright anti-military propaganda.[4] In May there was informal and successful co-operation in the municipal elections in Paris between the Communist, Socialist, and Radical Parties.

It was the Socialists who prevented this going further, until the ominous increase in the activities of the Fascist leagues during the latter part of Laval's premiership forced them to jettison their suspicions of Communist sincerity.

At a meeting on 28 June, to celebrate the Paris electoral success, Thorez, Daladier, and Blum spoke from the same platform—the last in his personal capacity. On 14 July 1935, the three Parties took part in a single massive demonstration which outclassed in numbers, if not in discipline, the simultaneous display by the 'Fascist' cohorts of de la Roque. Thus

[1] A direct approach by the Comintern to the Second International on this issue was rebuffed. Borkenau, op. cit., p. 390.

[2] *Documents for 1935*, vol. 1, pp. 137–8.

[3] See Blum's evidence at the 'Riom trial', *Léon Blum before his Judges* (Routledge, 1943), pp. 148 ff. A 'dissident' Communist Party now became the principal focus of Alsatian autonomism, with a decidedly anti-Soviet and pro-German slant. Werth, *The Destiny of France*, pp. 261–3.

[4] According to James (op. cit.), instructions to the French Communist Party to abandon revolutionary defeatism were given earlier in the year, although the reasons for the change of front were not then explained. Early in April two special delegates from Moscow to the French Communist youth organisation made it clear that resistance to the Government's measures of military preparedness was no longer permissible, since France would be fighting as an ally of the U.S.S.R.

in July 1935, when the Comintern Congress at last met, the omens for the new policy in France, at least, seemed reasonably good.

The Seventh Congress of the Comintern sat from 25 July to 25 August and was attended by 510 delegates representing the sixty-five affiliated parties. Although Manuilsky still took a leading rôle, the Congress was unquestionably dominated by the figure of the Bulgar, Dimitrov. The latter was formally elected General Secretary by the Congress, after having been the *de facto* leader of the Comintern for some months. Since this was the first Congress at which a complete display of unanimity was achieved its debates are not very revealing, but they enable one to see how the new Comintern angle was interpreted in theoretical terms, and also to judge to some extent what element of novelty it really embodied.[1]

The opening report by Pieck on the work of the E.C.C.I. discussed the not altogether encouraging seven years of activity since the Congress of 1928, with particular reference to Germany. The Social-Democratic leaders came in for their usual share of abuse for passivity, fatalism, and worse; and it was pointed out that even where Social-Democratic workers had fought, as in Austria in February 1934, and in Spain in October, the leadership of their own Party had proved its incapacity. On the other hand, the Communist Parties did not receive the praise which the German Communist Party had got from the Plenum as late as December 1933. They were now blamed for not having broadened their approach sufficiently and for having shown a culpable sectarianism. Owing to a 'mechanical' interpretation of the resolutions of the 1928 Congress, they had discerned Fascism where it did not exist and failed to recognise it when it was actually upon them. The idea that all bourgeois parties were Fascist was denounced as a total misconception. So far from being encouraged to bring about the collapse of bourgeois parliamentarism for the sake of hastening on a revolutionary situation, the working class was exhorted to cherish every scrap of bourgeois democracy until it could be replaced by proletarian democracy.

'Until these sectarian views are eradicated, it is impossible to establish either a united front with the Social-Democratic workers or a broad people's front with those labouring masses who are still

[1] Borkenau, op. cit., pp. 384–5. The citations in the following paragraphs are from the abridged stenographic report published in Moscow in 1939: *VII Congress of the Communist International*. A full report was published in 1936: *Report of the Seventh World Congress of the Communist International* (London: Modern Books).

far from the Communists, but who, nevertheless, can join us in the struggle against Fascism and war, against the offensive of capitalism, for their partial demands and for the defence of the remnants of bourgeois democracy.'

The errors of the past having thus been jettisoned, the Congress proceeded, under the guidance of Dimitrov, to consider the new tactics, those of the 'People's Front'. Once again, however, it was made clear that, although combinations with Reformist Socialist and even with non-Socialist parties were permissible, and that a situation might even arise in which such a grouping could take over the responsibilities of government, the ultimate object was still to ensure that Communist leadership prevailed.

Considerable attention was reserved at the Congress for the French Communist Party, the only one which had achieved success to any marked degree along the new lines; and French experience was recounted in detail by Cachin and Thorez. In other democratic countries, particularly in Great Britain, the United States, Czechoslovakia, and Scandinavia, the Socialists had been wooed without success. Only in Czechoslovakia, where the Communists had mustered 850,000 votes at the recent elections, could they be regarded as a mass party. The Comintern's version of its recent relations with the Second International itself was given by Pieck:

'We have repeatedly proposed to the Executive Committee of the Second International the establishment of a united front for the purpose of combating the capitalist offensive, Fascism and war. Striving not for mere declarations but for a genuine struggle, we proposed in 1933 that negotiations should be undertaken between individual parties. But the Second International rejected our proposal and declared that negotiations could be conducted only between the two Internationals. In 1934 we proposed to the Executive Committee of the Second International that direct negotiations be started in regard to concrete common action. Again our proposals were rejected. In 1935, before May Day, we once more proposed to the Executive Committee of the Second International to establish a united front. This time it declared that negotiations should take place between the parties, and not between the Internationals.'

Nevertheless, the final resolutions directed that both avenues of co-operation should again be explored.

If the Communist parties were to seek to lead combinations of largely non-proletarian elements, some wider appeal would have to be devised than that of class sectarianism. Some attempt was manifest to try to combine the national with the class appeal, and the German Communists were blamed for having allowed Hitler to capitalise the grievances arising from the Versailles Treaty. The new line can be indicated from two characteristic declarations. The first is that of Thorez:

'In the name of the working-class we claim the intellectual and revolutionary heritage of the Encyclopaedists of the eighteenth century who paved the way for the Great Revolution of 1789 with their works. . . . We glorify the memory of the Commune of 1793 and of the Paris Commune of 1871. . . . We proclaim our love of our homeland, of our people . . . we the great-grandsons of the sansculottes of 1792, of the soldiers of Valmy, deny the aristocrats—the descendants of the emigrés of Coblenz, who returned to France in the train of the foreign counter-revolution. . . . We do not intend to let Fascism usurp the flag of the Great Revolution nor the *Marseillaise*, that hymn of the soldiers of the Convention.'

Earl Browder, the American Communist leader, proclaimed in similar style:

'We have appropriated the traditions of 1776 and 1861, and we have come forward as the bearers and pioneers of that revolutionary tradition out of which the United States was born.'

Dimitrov declared his right to be proud that he was a son of the heroic Bulgarian working class, and went on to point out that national sentiments of this character were not out of harmony with the international mission of the proletariat:

'Comrades, proletarian internationalism must, so to speak, "acclimatise itself" in each country in order to sink deep roots in its native land. *National forms* of the proletarian class struggle and of the labour movement are in no contradiction to proletarian internationalism; on the contrary, it is precisely in these forms that the *international interests* of the proletariat can be successfully defended.'

In a sense, this new emphasis on nationalism may be considered a reflection of the new attitude of the Russian Communist Party itself. But whereas in the case of the Soviet Union no conflict of allegiances could arise, since its interests and that of the international proletariat were by definition identical, it should have been clear that the success of this line in other countries would largely depend on their relation to the international situation in general, and to the Soviet Union in particular. It is when the Congress is considered from this angle, that it becomes apparent to what extent the position in France coloured the general approach to problems of policy, and to what extent the Franco-Soviet Pact was itself at the root of the preoccupation with French affairs.

The Congress's resolutions on the international situation were developed in a speech by the Italian Ercoli (Togliatti) : Japanese imperialism had begun a new world war. The chief instigators of war were the German Fascists who had found allies in Polish Fascism and among dominant sections of the British bourgeoisie. The main antagonism (contradiction) among the imperialist Powers was still declared to be that between the United States and Great Britain. The United States, France, and certain smaller States were considered as forming the *status quo* and hence peace-seeking *bloc*.

A distinction was drawn between the different ways in which the United States and Britain had reacted against the Japanese menace to their positions. The United States was playing for time in order to strengthen its own position and had no immediate aim of conquest. But it was a mistake to think that Britain, just because it already had colonies, was concerned to preserve peace. The very size of the Empire made it unavoidable that Britain should be drawn into conflicts and that contradictions should arise within her policy. In addition, the 'British bourgeoisie (were) the prime instigators in suppressing the liberation movements of the colonial peoples, just as the German Fascists (were) the prime instigators in establishing the dictatorship of the bourgeoisie over the working class'.

For this reason, Britain was endeavouring to canalise German and Japanese aggression against the Soviet Union, the land of Socialism. Hence Britain's support of German rearmament and the annulment of the naval clauses of the Versailles Treaty, which had allowed Germany to create in the Baltic, at the gates of the Soviet Union, a new instrument of aggression.

While reactionary elements of the French bourgeoisie cherished similar hopes, the majority were still sane enough to remember that in the gospel of Hitlerism, France was depicted as the traditional enemy of German imperialism in Europe. Thus the French bourgeoisie knew that every step towards German hegemony in Europe was a direct menace to its own safety, and was concerned to defend the *status quo* on the principle of the indivisibility of peace. They were kept to this line by the pressure of the masses of the people, who were opposed to an anti-Soviet agreement with Hitler. 'That is why the United Front and the People's Front policy of our French Communist Party is a guarantee of peace not only for France but for the working people of the whole world.'

In consequence of the development of the defensive power of the Soviet Union as a result of the victory there of Socialism, the resolutions of the Congress asserted that relations between the Soviet Union and the capitalist countries had entered upon a new phase. The Soviet Union had become the centre of attraction not only for class-conscious workers but for all working people abroad who desired peace.

'The peace policy of the U.S.S.R. has not only upset the plans of the imperialists to isolate the Soviet Union, but has laid the basis for its co-operation in the cause of the preservation of peace *with the small States* to whom war represents a special danger, by placing their independence in jeopardy, as well as with those Governments which at the *present moment* are interested in the preservation of peace.'

This part of the resolution was amplified in Ercoli's speech:

'The proposal for the conclusion of an Eastern Pact was made after the definition of the aggressor had been established. Based on the recognition of the indivisibility of peace and the impossibility of separating the danger of war menacing the East of Europe from the threat of war in the West, this proposal aimed at driving the instigators of war into a corner and rallying all friends of peace, no matter who they might be.

'As is well known, the proposal for the conclusion of an Eastern Pact was rejected by the warmongers, and this was bound to be followed by the establishment of especially close connexions between the Soviet Union and the States interested in active resistance to the present aggressors—which has led to the conclusion of pacts of mutual aid between the Soviet Union and France and with Czechoslovakia.

'. . . The mutual aid pacts concluded by the Soviet Union are serious acts of positive policy which aim at uniting all possible forces for an active defence of peace. On this account we are surprised that anyone could find it strange that the conclusion of the mutual aid pact with France was accompanied by a declaration of Comrade Stalin, in which he expressed "complete understanding and approval of the policy of national defence pursued by France for maintaining her armed forces at the level corresponding to the needs of her security." Rather, I am of the opinion that it would have been strange if a declaration of this kind had not followed, for the absence of such a precise definition of the position would have deprived the mutual aid pact of all its efficacy as an instrument of positive peace policy.'

On the other hand, it was not made clear at the Congress to what extent the Communists of France or of any other country with which the Soviet Union might thus find itself temporarily aligned, were bound to support the military policies of that country. In the resolution on the rôle of the Communist International and its constituent parties in the struggle for peace, all the capitalist countries were lumped together. The Communist Parties were to intensify the struggle against war and to try to identify it with the struggle against Fascism. They were to work together with Socialist, reformist, and pacifist groups, while at the same time doing their best to show up the false tactics or treacherous leaders of the latter.

The resolution concerning the struggle against militarism and armaments was on traditional lines:

'The Communist Parties of all capitalist countries must fight: against military expenditures (war budgets), for the recall of military forces from the colonies and mandated territories; against militarisation measures taken by capitalist Governments, especially the militarisation of the youth, women, and the unemployed; against emergency decrees restricting bourgeois-democratic liberties with the aim of preparing for war; against restricting the rights of workers employed in war industry plants; against subsidising the war industry and against trading in or transporting arms. . . .'

On the other hand it was declared that if a small country were attacked by one or more big Powers, its struggle could be regarded as a war of national liberation and would be entitled to support from its proletariat and Communists, whose duty would be to prevent that country's bourgeoisie from striking a bargain with the attackers.

Since France and Czechoslovakia were clearly among the capitalist countries, Stalin's declaration to Laval would not prevent the Communist Parties there from voting against war budgets and from struggling against the Governments of those countries. Ercoli displayed much dialectical skill in explaining the inner consistency of this attitude, which arose from the fact that the Governments of these countries had signed pacts with the Soviet Union but not with their own working class. The latter had therefore no guarantee that the army would not be utilised as a class army against the home proletariat and the oppressed colonial peoples. Nor had they any guarantee that at the decisive moment such Governments would observe their pacts.

These Governments were thus left to take what comfort they might from the fact that Communists were sternly forbidden to use in their struggle against war what were called anarcho-syndicalist methods, such as refusing to appear for military service, boycotting mobilisation, or sabotaging war plants; but here again the question was one of general tactics and not specifically applicable to countries enjoying mutual assistance pacts with the Soviet Union.

Thus while the Seventh Congress put forward the formation

of a wide People's anti-Fascist Front based upon a proletarian United Front—a single trade union movement and a single mass proletarian party—as the goal of Communist endeavour in all capitalist countries, it had not been able to avoid attracting attention once more to its own equivocal relationship with the Soviet Union. Could an organisation of this kind, even if post-poning revolution to an unspecified to-morrow, be permitted to exist in a State which claimed to be a loyal and co-operative member of the family of nations?

The sharp negative which the United States returned to this question has already been pointed out. A British protest was also made.[1] But the full implications of the equivocal attitude which the various Communist Parties now adopted were not made clear at once, and the immediate effect of the 'popular front' policy was to increase the popularity of the Soviet Union in democratic and moderate Left circles abroad—a circum-stance essentially favourable to the Soviet Union's pursuit of its proclaimed goal of 'collective security'.[2]

[1] The British delegate, Mr. Pollitt, had made the following pronounce-ment *inter alia*: 'The Communist Party does not believe that Socialism can be attained through Parliament, and will always state this standpoint in its agitation and propaganda and will always maintain its international connexions with working-class parties in other countries which maintain the revolutionary point of view.'

[2] Since the above chapter was written, relations between the Second and Third Internationals have been treated from the point of view of the former in John Price, *The International Labour Movement* (R.I.I.A., O.U.P., 1945).

Appendix A

THE U.S.S.R. AND INTERNATIONAL ORGANISATION

THE Council of the League of Nations decided on 10 September 1934 that the Soviet Union should be given a permanent seat on the Council as soon as it joined the League. In order to avoid the necessity of a formal inquiry into the Soviet Union's qualifications, which the lack of unanimity in the Assembly for its admission appeared to make inevitable under existing precedents, a special procedure was devised.[1] When the admission of the Soviet Union finally came before the Assembly on the 18th, 39 states-members voted in favour of it; Switzerland, the Netherlands, and Portugal voted against; Argentina, Belgium, Cuba, Luxemburg, Panama, Peru, and Venezuela abstained.

On the same day, the Soviet delegation took their seats. M. Litvinov in his speech emphasised that it was the potentialities of the League for the organisation of peace, however limited its opportunities and means, which had determined the Soviet Union to enter upon the path of full collaboration with it.[2]

Election to the League carried with it membership of the International Labour Organisation, and in July 1935, the Russians were represented at its Nineteenth Conference. The Russian delegation was composed, however, of Government representatives only, and thus did not rank as complete.[3] In June 1936 the Conference was attended by a Russian workers' delegate and advisers.[4] At the 23rd Session in June 1937, an 'employers'' delegate also attended. The Russian workers' delegate's credentials were unsuccessfully challenged on this occasion. The Employers' group also challenged the credentials of the Russian 'employers'' delegate on the ground that he was in fact merely an additional Government delegate. On the Soviet side, it was pointed out that the delegate in question, N. Andreyev, director of the Trekhgornaya Manufaktura textile factory in Moscow, occupied under the Soviet Constitution a parallel position with regard to labour questions to that of an employer in a capitalist State. The Credentials Committee referred the dispute to the Governing Body of the I.L.O. in order that it might 'examine thoroughly the problem raised by the creation of a new economic system which the authors of the Constitution (of the I.L.O.) could not foresee' and 'adopt any measures . . . necessary or appropriate

---

[1] *Survey for 1934*, pp. 392–402.
[2] Cf. the citations from *Izvestia* and *Pravda* of 20 September in W. P. and Z. K. Coates, *World Affairs and the U.S.S.R.* (Lawrence & Wishart, 1939), pp. 31–2.
[3] *International Labour Review* (I.L.O., Allen & Unwin), XXXII, p. 291.
[4] ibid., XXXIV, p. 291.

for the settlement of this problem'. There apparently the matter rested.[1]

If the I.L.O. had not foreseen the necessity of providing for the collaboration of Socialist States, it is likewise true that the Soviet Union's decision to participate in I.L.O. activities was almost as big a theoretical departure as membership of the League itself.[2]

In contradistinction to its work in the League, however, Soviet participation in the I.L.O.'s activities was minimal and there seems no evidence that the Soviet Union at any time contemplated making their membership of the I.L.O. an avenue towards greater co-operation with the Western democracies, as was hoped by some British Labour circles.[3] And it does not appear to have ratified a single convention.[4]

For the Soviet Union then, the League remained first and foremost an additional method of mobilising resistance to aggression. The fact that the U.S.S.R. brought to the notice of the Council its breach with Uruguay must be attributed partly to a desire to show the genuineness of the Soviet adherence to League principles and partly to the desire for an opportunity of denouncing States which guided their policies towards the Soviet Union by allegations concerning its support for revolution abroad.

Most of the remaining events in League history with which the Soviet Union was perforce connected need not be recounted at length. In September 1934, the Soviet Union was one of the Powers which agreed to prohibit the export of arms to Bolivia and Paraguay. In March 1935, it informed the League that it had, as recommended,

---

[1] ibid., XXXVI, pp. 295–6.

[2] In 1926, Professor E. A. Korovin, the leading Soviet authority on international law, had described the I.L.O. as follows: 'An organisation believing in an illusory possibility of peaceful co-operation between classes (the exploited and the exploiting) and in the possibility of solving social problems of a capitalistic economic order by an evolutionary process, is nothing but a bridge between the bourgeoisie and the "heads" of the bureaucratic professional unions, and a means to overshadow the class consciousness of the toiling masses.' Cited from Taracouzio, *The Soviet Union and International Law*, p. 278.

[3] See the speech of Mr. H. H. Elvin, Chairman of the British T.U.C., at a celebration dinner in honour of the twentieth anniversary of the U.S.S.R. [sic], on 24 November 1937. Printed in the Anglo-Russian Parliamentary Committee pamphlet, *The U.S.S.R. and World Peace*.

[4] See the tables of ratifications appended to the *I.L.O. Year Book*, 1937–1938; 1938–1939. The expulsion of the Soviet Union from the League of Nations on 14 December 1939, was held to have terminated its automatic membership of the I.L.O., according to a decision of the governing body of the latter in February, 1940. *I.L.O. Year Book*, 1939–1940, p. 1. 'It would have been possible for the Soviet Union, if it had so desired, to retain its membership of the I.L.O. after leaving the League, as other States have done, but in fact it took no active part in the work of the I.L.O. two years before it ceased to be a member of the League.' Clifton Robbins, Director, London Office, I.L.O., in a letter to the *Economist*, 11 August 1945.

lifted the embargo against Bolivia and strengthened it against Paraguay.[1]

At the League Council meeting on the 7–10 December 1934, Litvinov supported the Yugoslav demands on Hungary, arising out of the murder of King Alexander, and took the opportunity to utter a strong denunciation of political terrorism as a danger to peace.[2]

On 15 January 1935, Litvinov intimated his Government's desire to see a peaceful solution of the frontier dispute between Iraq and Iran in the region of the Persian Gulf.

The question of the Saar plebiscite differed from all these comparatively minor issues in being directly relevant to the problem of Germany. The local Communists were the firmest adherents of the *status quo* section of the Saar electorate—the instinct of self-preservation was a good enough reason. But the attitude of the Soviet Government on the League Council appears to have been conciliatory throughout.[3] At the meeting on 4 December 1934, Litvinov supported Laval's suggestion that the task of maintaining order in the Saar should be entrusted to an international force, but declared that he would have to consult his Government before promising a Soviet contribution to the contingent. On the 6th, however, the German Government let it be known that they had received assurances from Great Britain and Italy that the troops of certain countries such as Russia and Czechoslovakia would not be employed and made their acceptance of the scheme dependent upon this.[4] At the meeting on 17 January to consider the details of the transfer of the territory, Litvinov acclaimed the peaceable solution of the problem as a contribution to world peace.[5]

More complicated issues were raised by the Italo-Abyssinian dispute. It was true that among the major League Powers, the U.S.S.R. was the only one which had no direct interest in African affairs and only secondary interests in the Mediterranean zone of crisis. But there were other factors to take into account besides the general Soviet desire to strengthen the League. It was necessary to take a line which could be justified on the grounds of anti-imperial-

---

[1] Taracouzio, *War and Peace in Soviet Diplomacy*, pp. 196–7.

[2] The Soviet Government was one of the eleven governments invited to nominate a member to an expert commission appointed to draw up an international convention for the suppression of terrorism. *Survey for 1934*, III, (D), (ii); *Documents for 1934*, pp. 114–16. It does not appear that the Soviet Government raised any objection to the way in which the full investigation of the plot against King Alexander was frustrated in order not to embarrass Franco-Italian relations. On this, see 'Pertinax', *Les Fossoyeurs*, vol. ii, p. 90.

[3] *Survey for 1934*, III (E).

[4] ibid., pp. 612–13. Litvinov also argued that in the event of a *status quo* majority, the League Council would be able to delegate its sovereignty; and that the Saarlanders could not be deprived of the right of self-determination at some later date (i.e. in the event of Germany ceasing to be Nazi). ibid., p. 617.

[5] Taracouzio, op. cit., pp. 196 ff.

ism, an attitude from which the Soviet Union could not openly depart. On the other hand, the U.S.S.R. was linked to Italy by the non-aggression pact of 2 September 1933.[1] Like France, it had no wish to see Italian hesitation over foreign policy transform itself into final adhesion to the German revisionist bloc.

The U.S.S.R. was, in addition, not in a position to overlook altogether the economic aspect of Soviet-Italian relations. In 1934, Russia took from Italy goods to the value of 11·8 million roubles— 5·1 per cent of its total imports—and exported to Italy goods worth 19 million roubles—4·6 per cent of its total exports.[2] From the Italian point of view, the important fact was that in 1934, Italy's imports from Russia of oil products made up 22 per cent of her total imports under that head, Russia standing second only to Roumania among her suppliers. In the late summer and early autumn of 1935, Italy's purchases apart from oil were said to include cereals, coal, and timber.[3]

The Soviet Government appears to have taken no direct part in the negotiations between Italy, France, and Great Britain in the first part of 1935.[4] The League Council met to discuss the dispute at the beginning of September and was appealed to by Ethiopia under Article XV of the Covenant. This appeal was objected to by Italy which resisted the suggestion that it should be referred to a Council 'Committee of Five'. Litvinov, who was reported to have declined to serve on the proposed Committee, on the ground that it was only a device for enabling the Council to shirk its responsibilities, sharply criticised the Italian attitude as being an invitation to the members of the Council to 'repudiate . . . their international obligations, to disregard the Covenant of the League of Nations, on which in no little degree' depended 'the whole edifice of international peace and the security of nations.'[5]

The scene now shifted to the Assembly which met on 11 September to hear Sir Samuel Hoare's declaration of Britain's adherence to the principles of the League. He was followed on the 14th by Litvinov.[6] Litvinov began by pointing out that it was the first time the Soviet Union had been represented at the annual discussion of the report of the Secretary-General. He took the occasion to discuss directions in which the energies of the League might usefully be directed. The first place was assigned by him to the work on the definition of aggression whose topical relevance he did not fail to underline with some obvious irony at Italy's expense. Secondly, he revived the Soviet proposal for 'converting the dying Disarmament Conference into a Permanent Peace Conference'.

---

[1] Documents for 1933, pp. 233–6.
[2] League of Nations, International Trade Statistics.
[3] Survey for 1935, vol. 2, pp. 221 ff., and p. 431.
[4] The Italo-Abyssinian dispute is dealt with at length in Survey for 1935, vol. 2, and Documents for 1935, vol. 2.
[5] Speech of 5 September; L.N.O.J., 1935, pp. 1141–2. The Committee of Five set up on the 6th did not include a Soviet representative.
[6] L.N.O.J. Spec. Supp. 138, p. 71.

Thirdly, he put forward the admitted paradox, that the failure of efforts at partial disarmament suggested the value of a new and thorough investigation of the possibility of total disarmament. He pointed out, in addition, that the Soviet Government regretted that no progress had been made with the project of bringing the League Covenant into harmony with the Briand-Kellogg Pact of Paris, and that the Commission of Inquiry for European Union had also been permitted to sink into inactivity. The necessity of strengthening the security provisions of the Covenant by regional pacts of mutual assistance was emphasised, while it was pointed out that bilateral agreements merely had the effect of adding to existing uneasiness. Finally, in relation to the Italo-Abyssinian dispute he declared that the Soviet Union, undeterred by abuse and threats, would be guided solely by its resolve to defend the Covenant of the League as 'an instrument of peace' and by the impossibility of permitting a new assault 'which would put it completely out of action'.[1]

At the meeting of the Council on the 26th, the Soviet position with regard to the proposals of the Committee of Five (rejected by Italy) appears to have been that they were all too likely to facilitate an Italian colonisation of Abyssinia under League auspices. The proposal that a Committee of Thirteen be set up (i.e. of the whole Council except Italy) was supported by Litvinov who declared that the time had come to cease talking and begin to act. Such was also the opinion of Mussolini, for on 3 October, the Italian campaign began in earnest. The Council met again on the 5th, and set up a Committee of Six to report on the situation. This Committee, of which the U.S.S.R. was not a member, reported on the 7th that Italy had resorted to war in disregard of Article 12 of the Covenant. This report, and that of the Committee of Thirteen, were unanimously accepted by the Council (except for Italy) and these proceedings automatically involved the obligation upon members of the League to impose sanctions. The question went before the Assembly, where objections to sanctions were voiced only by the representatives of Austria, Hungary, and Albania. Potemkin, representing the Soviet Union on this occasion, declared that the news that action had been taken over this issue would put a check on all future attempts 'to disturb peace by attacks on the world's most crucial spots' from 'whatever quarter' they might come. The reference here was obviously to Germany.[2] The Assembly then set up a Co-ordination

---

[1] The Italian Press had for a time included the U.S.S.R. among a number of countries subjected to calculated campaigns of abuse. See the report of the American Ambassador to Italy, Breckinridge Long, 13 September 1935, *Peace and War*, pp. 278–82.

[2] It was increasingly evident during the winter of 1935–1936 that although Germany was not present at Geneva, it was none the less concern regarding Germany which was the decisive factor in the attitude of all the European members of the League. See the dispatch of the American Minister to Switzerland, Hugh R. Wilson, of 13 November 1935, *Peace and War*, pp. 291–2. Germany did not in fact interfere with the application of sanctions.

Committee for the organisation of sanctions, which held its first meeting on the 11th October. By the 19th its recommendations had been formulated—recommendations which Litvinov was careful to point out were by no means exhaustive, and which could not be taken as a precedent against the use of more far-reaching measures at a later date. Litvinov also pointed out the economic losses which the Soviet Government was prepared to incur as a result of applying sanctions and demanded a firm attitude towards States which claimed exemption from the duty of participation in the agreed measures.[1] The Soviet Government had given notice on the previous day that it had already taken the necessary steps for applying sanctions.[2]

The actual effect of sanctions upon Italian trade with the U.S.S.R. can be seen from the following table (values in thousands of 'old' gold dollars):[3]

SOVIET EXPORTS TO ITALY									
December		January		February		March		April	
1934	1935	1935	1936	1935	1936	1935	1936	1935	1936
814	662	384	288	457	540	487	305	306	569

SOVIET IMPORTS FROM ITALY									
December		January		February		March		April	
1934	1935	1935	1936	1935	1936	1935	1936	1935	1936
253	16	325	254	194	—	178	29	371	1

Heavy exports in February–April 1936 were due to the shipment of increased quantities of oil.[4] Taking a longer period, Soviet exports to Italy fell from 4·6 per cent of total Soviet exports in 1934 to 3·3 per cent in 1935 and 3·1 per cent in 1936. Soviet imports fell from 5·1 per cent in 1934 to 2·4 per cent in 1935 and 0·4 per cent in 1936.

On 11 November, the Italian Government sent a protest to all States participating in sanctions and threatened retaliation. On the part of the Soviet Union, the Italian Government met with an unconcealed rebuff.[5] Meanwhile, the failure of Italy to be intimidated by the very partial sanctions imposed, led to the concentration

[1] The Soviet Government was among those which protested against the insistence of Switzerland and Luxemburg in imposing an arms embargo on Ethiopia as well as on Italy when the Committee of Eighteen—the inner co-ordination committee—met again on 31 October. At the conclusion of this meeting on 6 November, an expert committee was set up to examine the application of the agreed sanctions—the U.S.S.R. being again a member-State.

[2] These measures were embodied in decrees of the Council of People's Commissars, dated 17 October. Texts in L.N.O.J. Spec. Supp. No. 150, pp. 298–300.

[3] Documents for 1935, vol. ii, pp. 244–5.

[4] Survey for 1935, vol. ii, p. 441.

[5] Survey for 1935, vol. ii, pp. 237–9. Further Soviet restrictions on trade with Italy were adopted on 14 November, L.N.O.J. Spec. Supp., loc. cit.

of international interest upon the oil sanction. On 25 November, the Russian and Roumanian Governments informed the League of their readiness to agree to an embargo on the export to Italy of petrol, coal, iron, and steel if all other producing countries agreed. Consideration of this was however postponed in favour of a new attempt at conciliation, culminating in the Hoare-Laval proposals early in December. At the meeting of the League Council on the 19th, these proposals, already killed by Italian hostility and the public outcry in Britain, were strongly condemned by Potemkin as incompatible with the Covenant. It was not to be supposed that the Soviet statesmen would overlook the opportunity provided by the outburst of feeling on this issue to drive home the lesson that Soviet policy was governed by motives fundamentally different from those of other Powers. In a speech on 11 January 1936, Molotov put the position as follows:

'In the Italo-Abyssinian war, only the U.S.S.R. took an attitude different in principle, alien to any notion of imperialism and devoid of any intention of colonial conquest. Only the Soviet Union declared openly that it took for its starting point the principle of equality and independence of Abyssinia, which, *à propos*, is a member of the League of Nations, and that it cannot support any actions of the League or of any individual capitalist country intending to destroy this independence and equality.'[1]

At Geneva, discussion of the oil embargo was renewed but on 2 March, in spite of the support which the proposal received from various delegations including that of the Soviet Union, a further postponement virtually killed it.

Five days later the Rhineland *coup* effectively shifted Ethiopia from the centre of the world stage. In Africa, the Italian armies proceeded to their inevitable victory. On 20 April, the Council met under the shadow of the impending collapse of Ethiopian resistance. Potemkin gave voice to the Soviet Union's disappointment at the League's failure, and stressed the fact that the reason lay in the lack of certainty that its members would make common cause against aggression—action essential not only in the case of aggression actually begun but also in the case of 'aggression clearly in course of preparation'—an obvious reference to the Rhineland crisis.[2] Sanctions were abandoned by the Assembly when it met from 30 June to 4 July. Litvinov in his speech of 1 July empha-

---

[1] Cited Taracouzio, *War and Peace in Soviet Diplomacy*, p. 198. Cf. ibid., pp. 197–204 and 229–30 for a further discussion of the Soviet attitude. 'In practice the Soviets viewed the struggle of Abyssinia as the revolutionary war of a backward, semi-colonial people to achieve national liberation. As such it was of interest to the international proletariat.' (p. 229.) As has been seen a more impelling factor was a desire to create precedents for the use of sanctions in cases of aggression nearer home.

[2] *L.N.O.J.*, 1936, p. 380.

sised the special circumstances which had caused the League effort to fail: 'members of the League of Nations for one reason or another, refrained from bringing Article XVI completely into play. But it does not follow from this that Article XVI itself is a failure.'[1] In September 1936, the Soviet Government made its position in the matter of principle clear by taking the lead in opposing the exclusion of the Ethiopian delegation from the Assembly, in spite of the fact that the conquest of Ethiopia had been virtually completed four months previously.[2]

[1] *L.N.O.J. Spec. Supp. 151*, p. 35.
[2] *Survey for 1935*, vol. ii, p. 523. The question of *de jure* recognition of Italian sovereignty was brought before the League Council in May 1938; on British initiative, the U.S.S.R. led the opposition to the proposal and continued to withhold recognition of the conquest. *L.N.O.J., 1938*, p. 340.

Appendix B

THE DEVELOPMENT OF THE SOVIET FAR EAST

ALTHOUGH the vanguard of Russian penetration had reached the mouth of the Amur in the middle of the seventeenth century, the Amur region had not been held by Russia against China. The Treaty of Nerchinsk in 1689—the first ever concluded between the two countries—had stabilised the frontier behind the Argun river nearly a thousand miles west of the Pacific, and expansion did not begin again until the lands north of the Amur were ceded by China in the Treaty of Aigun in 1858. Territory east of the Ussuri, now the Primorskaya (Maritime Territory), including what was to be the site of Vladivostok, was ceded in a convention signed in November 1860.[1] Fifteen years later, Sakhalin was obtained from Japan in exchange for the Kuriles. The decade 1850–1860 saw the foundation of the towns of Khabarovsk, Nikolaevsk, and Vladivostok, but settlement remained sparse. The Siberian boom only began with the building of the Trans-Siberian Railway and the Chinese Eastern Railway (C.E.R.) in 1891–1903. A railway to join Khabarovsk to the Trans-Siberian which avoided non-Russian territory was built between 1908 and 1916. It was not, however, the Far Eastern Province but territory further inland which saw the greatest development in these years with the coming of foreign capital to exploit the mineral resources of the Lena basin.[2]

The War, the Civil War, and the Intervention meant the cessation of development in these territories.[3] Not until the end of 1922, when the Japanese evacuated Vladivostok and the mainland, was the Far Eastern Province once more under the control of the central Russian Government, and full sovietisation was still further delayed. Eastern Siberia as a whole remained a land of scattered and for the most part backward peoples, greatly outnumbered by the Russian and Ukrainian colonists of the pre-Revolutionary migration. There were also a number of Chinese and Koreans. In spite of an effort at planned settlement, the renewal of migration when it came was only at a slow pace. Only 450,000 people migrated from European

[1] H. B. Morse and H. F. MacNair, *Far Eastern International Relations* (2nd ed., Boston, Houghton Mifflin, 1931), pp. 181–3 and 228–9.

[2] For the pre-Revolutionary expansion of Russia in Asia, see A. Lobanov-Rostovsky, *Russia and Asia* (New York, Macmillan, 1943). Cf. G. F. Hudson, *The Far East in World Politics* (Oxford, Clarendon Press, 1937), chaps. 4 and 5.

[3] The remainder of this chapter is based primarily upon V. Conolly, *Soviet Trade from the Pacific to the Levant*; G. F. Hudson and M. Rajchman, *An Explanatory Atlas of the Far East* (Faber & Faber, 1942); E. Raikhman and B. Vvedensky, 'The Resources and Development of the Soviet Far East' in *Problems of the Pacific, 1936* (I.P.R.). Cf. W. Mandel, *The Soviet Far East and Central Asia* (New York, I.P.R., 1944).

Russia to the whole of Siberia in the years 1925–1929. This was the more ominous in that the population of Manchuria, about 15 millions in 1910, had approximately doubled twenty years later, while another flood of Chinese immigrants was decisively altering both the racial composition and the economy of Inner Mongolia.[1]

In 1926, the Far Eastern Territory, with which we are primarily concerned, had a population of 1,291,000.[2] In 1938 it was subdivided into the Khabarovsk and Maritime (Primorskaya) territories. In 1939, the former had a population numbering 1,430,875; the population of the latter numbered 907,220. The total population of the old Far Eastern Territory was thus 2,338,095. The Yakut Autonomous Republic numbered 327,500 people in 1933 and 400,544 at the time of the 1939 census. The population of the Chita province numbered 410,400 in 1926, and 1,159,500 in 1939. The Buriat Mongol Republic south of Lake Baikal had a population of 491,000 in 1926, of 605,000 (estimated) in 1933, and of 542,170 in 1939.[3]

In the sphere of communications, the aeroplane provided from the mid-1920's a new link between the far-flung centres of population in this vast area. Vladivostok was connected by air with Moscow and by 1937 there was a service from Vellin (440 miles from Okhotsk) to Vladivostok.

Aircraft are, however, of limited capacity. The whole life of these territories still depended at the beginning of the 1930's upon the single-track Trans-Siberian Railway.[4] The railway would thus have been the obvious objective of any Japanese advance. One possible route was through Outer Mongolia towards the southern side of Lake Baikal, another was towards Chita along the line linking the Trans-Siberian proper with the C.E.R.; finally there was the possibility of a direct drive across the Manchurian frontier

[1] O. Lattimore, *The Inner Asian Frontiers of China* (New York, Oxford University Press, 1940), pp. 13–14. It has been said that Manchuria had a net increase of population of 600,000 by immigration alone in each of the years 1927, 1928, and 1929, which were admittedly exceptional years. The peak year for Chinese immigration was 1927; it fell off slightly in 1928 and 1929, and fairly rapidly thereafter, even before the Japanese invasion. Cf. *Pioneer Settlement* (American Geographical Society), pp. 313–59.

[2] Article 'Nasilenia' (Population) in *Sibirskaya Sovietskaya Entsiklopedia*, vol. iii (1932), for details.

[3] The 1933 figures are from I. Baransky, *Ekonomicheskaya Geografia, SSSR (Economic Geography of the U.S.S.R.)*, (1936). The figures for Buriat Mongolia need explaining. It has been suggested that the fall was due to migration from the Buriat Mongol Republic to Outer Mongolia (*China Year Book*, 1935, p. 33). In September 1937, however, certain areas were detached from the Buriat Mongol Republic and added to the Chita and Irkutsk provinces. The loss of territory was about one-sixth of the whole, and the transferred districts had at the time a population of 133,500.

[4] As late as 1939, of the 4½ million people in Russian territory, east and north of Lake Baikal, nearly four millions lived along the railway or between the railway and the Amur.

towards the main bases of Soviet military and naval power in the Far Eastern Province. Between 1931 and 1939 the building of 4,000 miles of new railways in Manchuria multiplied the points along the frontier at which Japanese forces could be concentrated for such an attack. Large-scale road construction was also undertaken by the Japanese.[1]

The natural defences of the long frontier with Manchuria are not altogether satisfactory. The rivers Argun, Amur, and Ussuri, form a useful barrier for half the year but are frozen for the other half. From the western end of the frontier round to the autonomous province of Biro-Bijan (about two-thirds of its total length), it is the Manchurian bank which is the higher. Below the confluence of the rivers Bureia and Amur there is a stretch of mountain on both sides. On the Russian side, along the Ussuri, south of Khabarovsk, there is a sharp rise to the coastal Sikhota-Alin range. But neither this nor the mountains a hundred miles or so to the north of the Amur offer protection because, as already noted, the vast body of the country's population, and nearly all its productive capacity are crammed into the river valleys themselves.[2]

Russia's defensive task was thus dictated for her. The special Red Banner Far Eastern Army was organised in 1929 and later divided into two armies based respectively on Khabarovsk and Voroshilovsk (on the Ussuri, formerly Nikolsk). These forces were believed to number 200,000 men in 1934 and perhaps double five years later. It was necessary then to make them as independent as possible of the long haul across Siberia, for supplies of food and

[1] At the earlier date there was no railway connexion with the Russo-Manchurian frontier from the centre of Manchuria other than the two termini of the C.E.R. at Manchouli and Pogranichnaya. By December 1934, a line running north from Harbin had its terminus at Heiho, opposite Blagoveshchensk, which itself lies on a branch of the Trans-Siberian north of the big eastward bend of the Amur. Another line was built out to Hulin, opposite a point half-way down the railway from Khabarovsk to Vladivostok. A line from Hsinking reached a terminus at Halinarshan near the border of Outer Mongolia. Finally, a line completed in 1933 ran into Korea just south of the short Russo-Korean frontier and reached the sea by two branches to Rashin and Seishin. Apart from the increased threat to Vladivostok, these two ports provide a more rapid sea-route from Japan to Manchuria than the old ones through western Korea and Dairen. *Survey for 1934*, pp. 670-1; Hudson and Rajchman, op. cit., pp. 77, 83, 85; *The Industrialization of Japan and Manchuria*, ed. E. B. Schumpeter (New York, 1940), pp. 385-6. The importance of these developments is stressed by V. Avarin in the article 'Ekonomicheskoe Polozhenie Mandjurii posle Okupatsii' (The Economic position of Manchuria after the Occupation), *Mirovoe Khozaistvo i Mirovaya Politika*, April 1933.

[2] 'The Soviet Government's reluctance to entertain Japanese proposals for a demilitarized zone finds sufficient explanation in the fact that Russian strength along the frontier line was fundamentally static, being in the form of military bases, while Japanese strength lay in her railways and roads as aids to mobility in a region which was devoid of important towns and of military concentrations.' *Survey for 1934*, pp. 671-2.

equipment. The Far Eastern fleet with its bases at Vladivostok, Nikolaevsk, and Petropavlovsk (in Kamchatka) likewise needed its own ship-building and repairing yards.

Secondly, there came questions of improving existing transport facilities, by double-tracking or even triple-tracking the main railway and by building feeder lines to it, both in Russian and in Outer Mongolian territory. A still more ambitious scheme was that for an entirely new railway to be built with the double purpose of opening up the still largely unexplored vastness of north-Eastern Siberia and of providing an alternative route to the Far East in the event of a successful Japanese thrust across the Trans-Siberian. The railway was apparently planned to run from Taishet (north-west of Irkutsk) to Vitim on the Lena and there to branch into two, the northern line running via Yakutsk to a Pacific terminus at Okhotsk. A part has been built, apparently as far as the Lena. The southern line was to reach its maritime terminus at Soviet Harbour via Bodaibo and Komsomolsk, or by a route running north of the former and south of the latter. Besides such railway and road development, the navigation of the Amur and Ussuri (as of the Lena) was to be used to the full. And in addition to coastal shipping along the Pacific coast, an attempt was to be made to provide a direct connexion through Arctic waters between Archangel and the Far Eastern ports.[1] Finally, there was the development of aviation and particularly of a Far Eastern bomber fleet as a deterrent to Japanese plans of aggression.

For the working of the heavy industries which these enterprises demanded, it was necessary to increase the population and to provide it with adequate food supplies and consumers' goods. In addition to compulsory migration, various measures of persuasion were applied in order to promote the renewal of large-scale colonisation, from the granting of taxation exemptions and other economic privileges, to direct ideological and patriotic appeals. These incentives were set out in the Decree for the Far Eastern Territory of 11 December 1933, which was extended to Buriat-Mongolia and the trans-Baikalian region in the following February. This was in part aimed at preventing an actual movement away from the frontier in view of the growing tension of the time.[2]

[1] Until 1932 it took two summers with the intervening winter spent ice-bound to make the trip by sea from Archangel to Petropavlovsk.

[2] E. Wollenberg credits General Bluecher with the initiative in this, op. cit., pp. 257–8. The founding in 1928 of the Autonomous Jewish Province of Biro-Bijan comes into this context. Its area was given as 73,000 square miles and its population (in about 1933) as 50,000. Baransky, op. cit., p. 352. Littlepage mentions the extremely liberal terms offered by Russia to gold prospectors after 1933: 'The Soviet gold-rush scheme was instituted at a time when relations between Russia and Japan were particularly acute and when it was important for Russia to fill up the empty spaces in her Far Eastern region as quickly as possible with a population which was reasonably satisfied with conditions.' J. Littlepage and D. Bess, In Search of Soviet Gold, p. 127.

The almost entirely military organisation of the Far Eastern Territory has made reliable news of its progress hard to obtain.[1]

As we have seen, the results obtained by the population policy were not very spectacular. The tripling of the urban population since 1926 was the most important fact revealed by the census of 1939. Vladivostok had grown from a town of about 100,000 inhabitants to one of over 200,000. Khabarovsk had grown from about 50,000 to almost 200,000 and the self-sacrificing energy of the Young Communist League had in seven years produced Komsomolsk, a city of 70,000 people.[2] On the other hand the growth of the rural population was not much more than that for the country as a whole, new settlers having done no more than take the place of those who had gone into industry.[3]

Industrial development is hard to assess accurately in spite of the publication of some statistical information for the period up to 1938. Oil, coal, steel, cement, and electric power have all been developed from small or negligible beginnings. Secondary industries functioning by 1936 included railway equipment and automobile works as well as shipyards. The new yards at Komsomolsk launched their first ocean-going vessels in September 1939. There is some evidence of a greater and more varied agricultural output, and the fisheries—so pervasive in the diplomatic field—were obviously of the first importance as a local source of food. It is nevertheless fairly clear that severe obstacles, of which the greatest continued to be the lack of suitable and sufficient labour, made impossible the rapid fulfilment of some of the more ambitious schemes.

Questions concerning transport are even harder to answer. The measure of success obtained in the opening of the Arctic sea-route has been substantial and the actual tasks of exploration and development form one of the great Soviet epics. The route was declared a normally operating sea-route as far as the Kara Sea, in 1931. An ice-breaker route was organised for the whole Arctic coastline in 1934, and the route declared a normally operating one in 1935. Fourteen steamers passed through in 1937. In 1939, ten ships did the journey through the Bering Strait to Ugolnaya Bay in the Gulf of Anadyr and back to Murmansk in a single season. In 1940, 100 freighters and 13 ice-breakers were engaged in Arctic naviga-

---

[1] Linton Wells, who saw the Far Eastern Territory in February 1934, stated that it was four years since a journalist had been permitted north and east of the Amur. The Russians, according to him, expected an attack during the year, but the evidence of their preparations impressed him. *Blood on the Moon*, pp. 353 ff.

[2] The most rapid growth in Eastern Siberia was that of Ulan-Ude in Buriat-Mongolia, from 29,000 to 130,000 between 1926 and 1939.

[3] It is difficult to compare accurately the rate of growth with that of Manchuria; the latter was clearly the faster. Its population in 1936 is given by Lattimore (op. cit., p. 10) as 32,700,000 and by Schumpeter as 38 millions by the end of 1937. With such discrepancies, calculation becomes impossible.

tion.[1] In spite of this, however, it can hardly be said that any development of this period compensated Russia for the loss in 1905 (after only seven years) of the ice-free and potentially very valuable Port Arthur.

The double tracking of the Trans-Siberian was said to have been completed by the end of 1937—some of the work had been done a good deal earlier.[2] In 1938 a line was built from Ulan-Ude to Kiakhta on the border of Outer Mongolia.[3] The branch line from Khabarovsk to Komsomolsk was single-tracked by 1936 and double-tracked by 1940. In September 1940, the opening was announced of a branch running along the Bureia River to Tyrma in the mining region of the Maly-Kinghan range.[4]

Tyrma is on the projected route of the new trunk railway already referred to, the B.A.M. (Baikal-Amur-Magistral), but the construction of this line 'under the direct auspices of the N.K.V.D.' has been 'shrouded in mystery since 1934'; it may by 1942 have reached Kirensk on the Lena.[5] Molotov announced at the Eighteenth Congress of the C.P.S.U. that a part of the project would be completed under the Third Five-Year Plan.

[1] 'Russian Communications in the Arctic Regions', *B.I.N.*, 18 October, 1941.

[2] H. S. Quigley and G. H. Blakeslee, *The Far East*, p. 213.

[3] In February 1935, the Russians denied that they were building a line into Outer Mongolia. But the railway was continued from Kiakhta to Ulan Bator and opened to traffic in the spring of 1939. Wollenberg, op. cit., p. 309.

[4] In June 1941, Scott noted that the main line of the Trans-Siberian was double-tracked from the Urals to Khabarovsk and triple-tracked from there to Vladivostok. op. cit., p. 263.

[5] V. Conolly, *Soviet Asia* (Oxford University Press, 1942), p. 13.

Appendix C

RUSSIA AND THE CHINESE REVOLUTION

THE prestige of a successful Revolution and Moscow's active sponsoring of 'anti-imperialists' abroad made Russia a factor of the first importance on the Asiatic scene in the early nineteen-twenties, and this was above all true of China. The history of the Communist wing of the Chinese national movement, as it is probably right to style it, is thus of the first importance for an understanding of Soviet foreign policy. Russian sources for events in China are subject, as has been noted, to all the usual difficulties of interpretation.[1] There are, however, two specific difficulties which affect the present aspect of the subject. There was first of all the long polemic over the responsibility for the catastrophe of 1927 which ended the first and most active phase of Russian intervention in Chinese affairs. The policy of the Soviet Union towards China in the years 1925-1927 was hotly disputed inside Russia, and the dispute has coloured the literature of the later period as well.[2] Secondly, for some of the later period, there was little direct contact between the Comintern and the Chinese Soviets.

The immense and tragic events which took place in China between the Sun Yat-sen—Joffe meeting in January 1923 and the suppression of the Canton Commune in 1927 cannot be recapitulated here.[3] The close co-operation of the nationalist movement and of Russian-inspired Communism was of value to the Russians in relation to their general struggle against Western 'imperialism', while from such Russians as Bluecher (Galen) and Borodin the Kuomintang learned the technique and methods of organisation that had proved successful in Russia. The very intimacy of the collaboration may account for some of the violence which accompanied the final break. The Chinese Communist Party had had a separate existence since 1920, but from 1924 joint membership of the Party and the Kuomintang was permitted. The dual allegiance was not for long practic-

[1] A collection of documents entitled *Sovieti v Kitae* (*The Soviets in China*), covering the years 1927-1932, was published in Moscow by the Communist Academy in 1933 under the editorship of E. Johanson and E. Taube. This contains a lengthy introduction and a chronology of the movement. The only non-Soviet writer to have made extensive use of Soviet sources is V. A. Yakhontoff in his book *The Chinese Soviets* (New York, Coward McCann, 1934), which takes the story up to 1933. For other literature see Grierson, op. cit., pp. 144-8.

[2] A Trotskyist history of the subject is H. Isaacs, *The Tragedy of the Chinese Revolution*. For the controversy, see Borkenau, op. cit., chap. 18; Souvarine, op. cit., chap. 9; A. Rosenberg, *History of Bolshevism* (Oxford University Press, 1934), chaps. 10 and 11.

[3] For these years, see especially A. N. Holcombe, *The Chinese Revolution* (Harvard University Press, 2nd ed., 1931).

able.[1] Accounts of the reasons for the break differ, but it would appear that Chiang Kai-shek and other nationalist leaders were afraid of the rising strength of radical agrarianism, and were concerned lest they should be cut off altogether from access to the capital and commerce of the West, and from the Chinese upper bourgeoisie. While conditions in Japanese-owned enterprises were swelling the tide of anti-Japanese feeling on the part of the Chinese proletariat, the Russians were pressing the Chinese further and further along the path of hostility to European interests in the country.[2] The first overt breach with the Russians was that signalised by Chiang Kai-shek's *coup* at Shanghai in April 1927. At this time he was at odds not only with the Russians, but also with the so-called 'left Kuomintang' Government at Hankow. The latter were, however, themselves soon alienated from the Russians, probably because of their knowledge that instructions had been received from Moscow to urge a more revolutionary policy on their Chinese adherents. The Hankow Government broke with its Russian advisers in June, and this enabled a reunion of the nationalist forces to be effected by the end of the year—a reunion marked by the crushing in December of the Communist rising at Canton, and by the final breach between the Nationalist Government (now at Nanking) and the Soviet Government, which was complete before the end of the month.[3] The entire impetus of the nationalist drive was henceforth directed northwards, that is to say, towards the Japanese sphere of interest; Peking fell in June 1928; the Nanking Government was recognised by the United States in July, and by Great Britain in December.[4]

There can be little doubt that Soviet policy in the following years was coloured by the interpretations which were placed on the events of 1927–1928 by Stalin and his associates. The Joint Plenum of the Central Committee and the Central Control Committee of the All-Union Communist Party began a meeting on 29 July 1927,

[1] For the relationship between the two parties, see Yakhontoff, op. cit., chaps. 5 and 6.

[2] The importance of this point is emphasised by G. F. Hudson in his *Far East in World Politics* (Oxford, 1937), pp. 219–24.

[3] Foreign accounts of these events differ as to the precise rôle of Borodin, Bluecher and other Russians, and as to the circumstances of Borodin's final withdrawal. See *Survey for 1927*, III, (ii); Holcombe, op. cit., chaps. 6 and 7; and Nikolaevsky's articles in *Novy Zhurnal*, Nos. 4 and 6. The story is told from the point of view of Chiang Kai-shek in his official biography by Hollington K. Tong, *Chiang Kai-shek* (Hurst & Blackett, 1938), chaps. 5–12. The raid on the Soviet Embassy premises in Peking in April 1927 produced a number of 'documents' relating to Comintern activities in China. These have been published in Mitarevsky, *World-Wide Soviet Plots* (Tientsin, c. 1928). There is a selection in the *China Year Book*, 1928, which also contains an account of the events of 1927.

[4] The British Memorandum of December 1926, indicating the probability of concessions to the Chinese Nationalists, had been one of the factors leading to the Kuomintang decision to break with its extremist elements and their Russian advisers. Sir John Pratt, *War and Politics in China*, p. 203.

two days after Borodin's final departure from Hankow. The resolutions gave considerable place to the Chinese issue. It was pointed out that three possible lines of policy had existed for the Chinese working-class movement. The first was that of the right wing, which was prepared to sacrifice the interests of the proletarian and agrarian masses for the sake of maintaining the unity of all nationalist forces, including the native bourgeoisie, against the foreign imperialist enemy. This was denounced as leading direct to 'Menshevism', and the Chinese Communist Party was reprimanded for having gone too far in that direction, although it was noted that the deviation was now being corrected. The second policy was that of the 'Trotskyists', who were opposed in all circumstances to co-operation with bourgeois elements. By contrast, the Comintern had followed the correct Leninist line. This recognised the necessity of co-operation with the bourgeoisie of a semi-colonial country like China, but only at specific stages of its national struggle and only upon specific conditions. It was essential that the working-class movement should be prepared to seize the appropriate moment to break away from its allies and to begin to fight for its own objectives. Pending the arrival of this moment, it should do everything to strengthen the specifically proletarian organisations involved in the nationalist movement.

Stalin's speech on 1 August gave a considerable place to the justification of the Comintern's policy with regard to China. Denying the charges of the left opposition, he quoted a Comintern directive, issued one and a half months before Chiang's *coup* at Shanghai, and demanding intensification of the work of the Communist cells in the Chinese Army:

'Our course must be steered towards the arming of the workers and peasants, the transformation of the peasants' committees in the localities into actual organs of power accompanied by armed self-defence, etc.'

The object had been to mobilise the masses around the Kuomintang and the Chinese Communist Party in order to expel the treacherous right wing of the Kuomintang.

The resolutions further pointed out that up to the time of Chiang's *coup* at Shanghai, it had been possible for the Chinese Communists to work for their own objects within the general framework of the struggle against the foreign imperialists and the feudal elements represented by Chang Tso-lin and the Peking Government. Shanghai, however, had signalised the desertion of Chiang to the counter-revolutionary camp, and it had become necessary to carry on a struggle against him with the aid of the left Kuomintang.[1] With the subsequent desertion of the revolutionary cause by most

[1] Stalin explained the aims of the Communists during the Wuhan (Hankow) period: 'What was the aim of the Communists in the second stage of the Revolution in China, when the centre of the revolutionary movement had been patently transferred from Canton to Wuhan, and when in addi-

P

of the left Kuomintang leaders, yet another phase had opened, and there should now be a clear struggle between the Chinese Communist Party and the Hankow Government.

It was admitted that the working-class movement in China had suffered a severe setback. This was primarily due to the existing class-relationships in China, and to the unfavourable international situation, coupled with errors of leadership on the part of the Chinese Communist Party, which had not fully followed out the instructions of the Comintern. But the setback was only temporary. The new grouping of social forces in China demanded a direct struggle for the establishment of a workers' and peasants' dictatorship, which alone could solve both the national and the social problem. If it proved impossible to revolutionise the left Kuomintang by the elimination of its existing leaders, it would be necessary to proceed directly to the establishment of Soviets, for which the ground should now be prepared.[1]

The Fifteenth Congress of the All-Union Communist Party met in December 1927, and by the time it had concluded its proceedings on the 19th, the suppression of the Canton rising had resulted in the execution of many Russians (including the Soviet vice-consul), as well as of many Chinese Communists, and in the closing by the Nanking Government of all Soviet consulates in its territory. The Congress recognised the finality of the breach between the Chinese working-class movement and the Kuomintang, and the abandonment of the hope that the latter might be turned into an effective instrument of social revolution. The task of the Chinese Communist Party was now a direct struggle to win power for Chinese Soviets under the leadership of the Chinese proletariat.[2]

---

tion to the revolutionary centre in Wuhan, a counter-revolutionary centre was set up in Nanking? It was to take full advantage of every opportunity for the open organization of the Party, the proletariat (trade-unions), the peasantry (peasant unions) and the revolution generally. It was to impel the Wuhan Kuomintangists to the Left towards the agrarian revolution. It was to make the Wuhan Kuomintang the centre of the fight against counter-revolution and of the future revolutionary-democratic dictatorship of the proletariat and peasantry.' The instructions given had been to strengthen the agrarian revolution in the provinces, and warnings had been given in May that the Wuhan Kuomintang Government would perish unless it became truly revolutionary.

[1] *Vsesoyuznaya Kommunisticheskaya Partia (B) v Resolutsiakh i Resheniakh Sezdov, Konferentsii i Plenumov TSK. II. 1925–1935.* (*The All-Union Communist Party (Bolsheviks) in the Resolutions and Decisions of Congresses, Conferences and Plenums of the Executive Committee, vol. ii, 1925–1935*) (Moscow, 1936), pp. 181–5. Stalin claimed that the tactics of the Comintern had been justified by the fact that the Chinese Communist Party had grown to a mass membership of 60,000, that three million workers had been organised in trades unions and that tens of millions of peasants had been brought into revolutionary peasant unions. The relevant sections of this speech of Stalin's are given in his *Marxism and the National and Colonial Question* (Martin Lawrence, 1936), pp. 232–52.

[2] *All-Union Communist Party Resolutions, etc.*, vol. 2, pp. 237–8.

This leftward turn was confirmed by the Sixth Congress of the Comintern in the following year. What actually took place, however, was an increasingly vigorous persecution of the Chinese Communists by the Nationalist Government—a persecution amounting in the cities to their virtual extermination. There is no evidence that Soviet citizens reappeared in any capacity to guide the policies of the Chinese Communist Party, and the intervention of the Soviet Union in Chinese affairs seems to have been confined to the passing of resolutions. It is therefore not unlikely that the boldness of the tone in which these were couched concealed a realisation on the part of the Soviet authorities that they had been decidedly over-optimistic in their earlier estimates of the capacity of the Chinese working-class movement to act as an independent revolutionary force.[1]

The Chinese official attitude was also powerfully affected by the events of 1927, which drove Chiang into a position of ineradicable hostility to Communism. Henceforth the Chinese national movement sought support not from the Soviet Union but from Great Britain and the United States. Reliance on the United States was encouraged by the American-trained personnel in Chiang's entourage, although their predominance was to some extent challenged by military figures whose inspiration came from Berlin and Tokyo rather than from Washington. At all events, foreign influence was henceforth conservative rather than revolutionary in its bearing, and there appeared no prospect of the Soviet Union's recovering its position of the mid-twenties.

Although hopes of an early Communist revolution in China were abandoned, the post-1927 Communist movement was not the mixture, normal elsewhere, of dissatisfied intellectuals, unemployed proletarians, and a leavening of skilled workers, linked only tenuously with the working masses except in times of exceptional tension. The intellectuals were there in China and so were the unemployed—for the nuclei of the Red Armies were men for whom soldiering was a trade in default of any other; but there was a third element, the element of genuine revolt against the truly intolerable conditions prevailing over vast sections of China's rural areas.[2] How far this third partner—a rebellious peasantry—was truly a willing one, and how far it could be used as an offensive weapon for the spreading of Communist rule, were debatable points. But

---

[1] The note of optimism apparent in the Sixth Congress of the Comintern on the subject of China had been struck by a speech of Stalin's on 13 July 1928 when he referred to 'the powerful development of the Chinese revolutionary movement, that upsurge of the vast masses of the workers and peasants of China which occurred a year ago and which is again occurring now.' This speech is given in the 1933 English edition of *Leninism* (Allen & Unwin), vol. ii, p. 124.

[2] There is a discussion of China's basic social problems in R. H. Tawney, *Land and Labour in China* (Allen & Unwin, 1932). *Agrarian China* (I.P.R., 1939), which consists of translations from Chinese writings, with an introduction by Professor Tawney, is also of value.

the existence of a discontented rural population did in fact make it possible for the Chinese Communists, first in the lower Yangtze Valley and then in northern Shensi, to control actual territory—the only territory in the world outside the U.S.S.R. to be under 'Soviet' rule. Although the boundaries of the Soviet areas were distinctly flexible, especially in the Yangtze stage, so that figures of territory or population under Soviet rule were almost meaningless, and a genuine Communist 'State' out of the question, the possession of some territory did enable the Red Armies to meet their two main problems, the replenishment of the terrible wastage in man-power, and the production of such essential supplies as were not obtained by capture.[1] This 'organisation of intellectuals led by peasants'[2] might be far removed from the proletarian vanguard of the orthodox Marxist, their Communism 'an exotic faith imposed upon a native jacquerie'[3]—the organisation and the faith existed.

Those who chose to regard Communism as still having a rôle to play or who at least did not regard the existing social structure of China as immutable might well have argued that although capitalism in Russia before the Revolution had advanced beyond that of China in the nineteen-thirties, the conditions in the two were not absolutely dissimilar.[4]

The nucleus of the Chinese Red Army was formed, it would seem, of troops of the Kuomintang Fourth Army, who revolted at Nanchang in August 1927. In November 1928, the first Chinese Soviet was set up at Chelin in south-eastern Hunan. Other local Soviets made their appearance in Kiangsi, and in 1929–1930 the movement spread to Hupeh, Fukien, Kiangsu, and Szechuan. Efforts to link up these Communist centres were made at an early stage, and after the foundation of a 'Soviet Government' at Juichin in Kiangsi in

[1] An extreme view of the strength of the Chinese Soviets at the peak of their power in the Yangtze Valley (1933), estimates the territory in their hands as between one-sixth and one-fifth of the territory of China proper, with a population of sixty to eighty millions. Yakhontoff, op. cit., pp. 145–7. Cf. G. E. Sokolsky, *The Tinder Box of Asia* (Allen & Unwin, 1932), p. 341. These figures were ridiculed by Mao Tse-tung in his talks with Edgar Snow in the summer of 1936. His estimate was nine million (at the beginning of 1934). Snow, *Red Star over China*, p. 82.

[2] Borkenau, op. cit., p. 323.

[3] P. Linebarger, *The China of Chiang Kai-shek* (World Peace Foundation, Boston, 1941), p. 165.

[4] 'There are certain similarities of social relationships between the villages of Czarist Russia and those of present-day China. Formerly in Russia and now in China there are two sets of opposing forces, namely landlords versus peasants and agricultural capitalists versus agricultural proletarians. The first indicates the backward feudal social relationships, while the second indicates the progressive capitalist social relationships . . . it is the first set of opposing forces—landlords versus peasants that form the chief obstacle to agricultural development and constitute the focal point of land reform.' From *The Chinese Land Problem, Trade Capital and Usury Capital*, by the Research Society for Chinese Agrarian Economy, 1937. Cited *Agrarian China*, pp. 57–9.

April 1929, inter-area congresses became more frequent.[1] In May 1930, the first All-China Soviet Conference was held in Shanghai, and the basic land and labour laws of the new régime were discussed. Drafts of a Constitution for the Chinese Soviet Republic, of a Land Law, a Labour Law, a Law on Economic Policy, and plans for the setting up of Soviets in areas to be occupied by the Red Army in the future, and for the occupation of the Red Army itself were worked out by the Central Committee of the Chinese Communist Party, and published in March 1931.[2]

Stalin was able to refer on 26 June 1930 to the fact that the disappearance of the Soviet embassies did not seem to have brought the expected peace to China, and commented on the 'most unbridled and most destructive war of generals financed and trained by the "civilised" states of Europe and America. . . . The Chinese workers and peasants have already replied to them (the imperialists who abuse Bolshevism) by setting up Soviets and a Red Army. It is said [sic] that already a Soviet Government has been formed there. I think, if that is true, it is nothing to be surprised at. There can be no doubt that only the Soviets can save China from final collapse and beggary.'[3]

It appears that this speech of Stalin's was the last of those by the recognised leaders of the Soviet Union in which the Chinese revolution received direct encouragement. Henceforth such expressions of sympathy and support were left to purely Comintern personalities like Manuilsky. This was a natural result of the increasing emphasis which the U.S.S.R. placed upon 'security', and later of its efforts to obtain support from Great Britain, the United States, and France, all of whom had interests threatened by the revolutionary ferment in Asia. Soviet policy in China can only be understood if account is taken of the changing relationships between the Soviet Union and the 'imperialist' Powers themselves.

Chiang Kai-shek, President of the National Government since September 1928, was becoming alarmed at the resurgence of Communism. The removal of Russian influence had lowered the discipline and effectiveness of the national armies, and in November 1928 German military advisers were called in.[4]

---

[1] There is a map of the Soviet areas in *The Soviets in China*.

[2] The land and labour laws are printed in the form in which they were accepted by the First All-China Congress in November 1931, in Yakhontoff, op. cit., pp. 221–35. Cf. *Fundamental Laws of the Chinese Soviet Republic*, with an introduction by Bela Kun (London, 1934). The map of Soviet areas in this publication is almost certainly over-optimistic. On the first Soviets see Yakhontoff, chap. 7, and Snow, *Red Star over China*, pp. 162–74. Note that in the early period it was still reasonable to hold that 'the inland Soviet régimes' operated 'almost entirely on their own responsibility, directed neither by Shanghai nor Moscow'. T. A. Bisson, 'The Communist Movement in China', *Foreign Policy Reports*, 26 April 1933, p. 43.

[3] *Political Report to the Sixteenth Party Congress* (1930), p. 20.

[4] Col. Max Bauer, the first leader of the unofficial German military mission, died in the spring of 1929. He was eventually succeeded by

The Communists seized Changsha by a sudden attack in July 1930, but their failure to retain the city for more than a few days showed that they could now make no impression on the mass of the urban proletariat.

In November 1930, Chiang launched the first of his large-scale 'annihilation' or 'extermination' campaigns, which lasted for a couple of months.[1] This campaign and the second and third which followed in April-May and August-September 1931, showed the unreliability of the Kuomintang troops in a struggle of this kind, though it may well be that Chiang Kai-shek was averse to using his best troops in this task, which the skill of the Communists in the tactics of defensive, mobile, guerilla warfare made distinctly unpleasant for their enemies.

On the other hand, there was no real sign that the Communists would ever be in a position to launch major offensives with any hope of far-reaching success, and the military as well as the political wisdom of trying to capture large towns so as to renew the proletarian basis of the movement became more and more questionable. Changes in Moscow as well as local events caused a split in the Chinese Communist Party, which came to a head in the first All-China Congress of Soviets in November 1931, whose task was to adopt a constitution for the 'Chinese Soviet Republic', and to set up a provisional Central Government.[2] The 'Right-wing' Communists, backed by the Comintern, were successful. Wang-ming, who became China's representative at the Comintern headquarters, Mao Tse-tung and Chou En-lai succeeded to the political direction of the Party, in which Chu-teh was already the outstanding military leader. There was now a steadily growing insistence on the anti-imperialist, nationalist aspect of the movement, and within the Communist territories less emphasis on land-redistribution and other radical social policies. Henceforth it appeared as though, in

---

Lt.-Gen. Wetzel, who was in charge from 1929–1932. General von Seeckt assisted Chiang from the spring of 1934 to the spring of 1935, and was succeeded by his chief aide, von Falkenhayn. The mission was only withdrawn in July 1938, and a year later it was estimated that Chiang still received 60 per cent of his military supplies from the Nazis. Snow, *Scorched Earth* (Gollancz, 1941), p. 174.

[1] There is considerable dispute as to the correct dating and nomenclature of these campaigns. They are described in 'The Red Influence in China', by R. Otsuka, a paper prepared for the Sixth I.P.R. Conference and summarised under the title, 'Recent Developments in the Chinese Communist Movement', on pp. 343-75 of *Problems of the Pacific*, 1936.

[2] The manifesto announcing the formation of the Provisional Central Government pointed out that it was formed on 7 November, the anniversary of the Russian Revolution. The Constitution is printed in Yakhontoff, op. cit., pp. 217-21. The Constitution of the Party remained unchanged from 1928. It is printed in Linebarger, op. cit., pp. 359-70. A poster detailing the privileges of Red Army soldiers was found in Kiangsi after the evacuation in 1934, and is printed in G. E. Taylor, *The Struggle for North China* (I.P.R., 1940), as App. XIII.

China, the indigenous peasant movement had in fact been accepted as the base for the Comintern's activities.[1]

The Communists' attitude to the situation caused by the Japanese aggression was shown by their 'declaration of war' in the spring of 1932.[2] It was also no doubt the uncertainties of the situation which prevented any far-reaching anti-Communist campaigning in this year, on the whole a successful one for the Chinese Soviets. The attitude of the Comintern at this juncture can be seen in the Resolutions of the Twelfth Plenum, which met in September 1932. These coupled Japan with France as the two major organisers of the anti-Soviet *bloc*, and charged the United States with endeavouring to foment war between Russia and Japan in order to strengthen her own Pacific position. The answer to these dangers was to be found in the rôle allotted to the Chinese Communists. The relevant 'theses' ran as follows:

'China: 1. to mobilise the masses under the slogan of the revolutionary struggle against the Japanese and other imperialists, and for the independence and integrity of China; 2. to develop and unite the Soviet territories, to strengthen the Red Army; 3. to fight for the overthrow of the Kuomintang régime; 4. to pursue a resolute policy of converting the Red Trade Unions into mass organisations, to win over the workers belonging to the Kuomintang unions; 5. to develop the guerrilla movement, putting forward in Manchuria slogans calling for the formation of peasant committees, for boycotting taxes and government decrees, the confiscation of the property of the agents of the imperialists, the establishment of an elected people's government; 6. the popularisation of the achievements of the Soviet districts and the slogan of the fraternal alliance of the workers and peasants of China with the U.S.S.R.'[3]

The resumption of relations between Nanking and Moscow in December 1932 had no immediate repercussions on the situation inside China. In January 1933 the Communists offered to form a United Front with any elements in the country who would fight Japan—though coupling the appeal to resist Japan with a denunciation of Chiang Kai-shek. They followed this up with a further manifesto in April.[4] The fourth anti-Communist campaign, from April to October 1933, was again indecisive. In November 1933 the Nineteenth Route Army, the heroes of the Shanghai fighting in January-February 1932, revolted in Fukien. This would seem to have offered a chance to put the United Front into practice, but an

---

[1] Snow pointed out the significance of the fact that Mao Tse-tung was the only Communist leader in the world who had never been to Moscow.

[2] The declaration is printed in Yakhontoff, op. cit., pp. 236–8; it is there dated 26 April. But according to *The Soviets in China* (p. 488) it was made in March.

[3] *Twelfth Plenum of the E.C.C.I. Theses and Resolutions* (London; Modern Books, 1932).

[4] Yakhontoff, op. cit., pp. 238–41.

offer from the revolting troops was turned down by the Communists, apparently on Comintern instructions.[1]

In January 1934, the second All-China Congress of Soviets was held at Juichin. Mao Tse-tung's report emphasises the sharp contrast between 'the worker peasant Soviet power' and the 'Kuomintang power of the landlords and bourgeoisie', and points out that

'the occupation of Manchuria, Mongolia, and North China by Japanese robbers and the intensified control of Tibet, Sinkiang, Yunnan, and the Yangtze valley by British, French, and American imperialists, are all directed by the imperialists to wreck the Chinese Soviet power and to completely enslave the Chinese nation as a preliminary step to war against the U.S.S.R.'

Referring to Chiang Kai-shek as 'chief of all traitors', he demanded that the Communists everywhere take the lead in the struggle for the independence of China.[2] Within a few days of this speech, Manuilsky gave the Russian Communist Party at its Seventeenth Congress, a highly encouraging picture of developments in China.[3] He gave the membership of the Party as 416,000, with 60,000 in the non-Communist districts, a total Red Army strength of 350,000, and 600,000 more in armed guerilla detachments.[4]

[1] Borkenau, op. cit., pp. 329–30; Snow, *Red Star over China*; Isaacs declares that the Communists took practically no part in the Shanghai fighting, op. cit., p. 431.

[2] Yakhontoff, op. cit., pp. 249–83.

[3] 'The Chinese Communist Party has won over (the broadest masses of the toiling population of China) by carrying the agrarian revolution to its completion, confiscating the land and stock of the landlords, gentry and kulaks for the benefit of the people, by doing away with the ulcer of the Chinese countryside, the usurer, by strictly regulating trade and handicrafts without, however, socialising them, by organising state and public aid for the peasants who have no cattle or seed, by developing industrial and credit co-operation, by raising education and health protection to a level unprecedented in China.' *Socialism Victorious* (London, 1935), pp. 340–4.

[4] It is a pity that no precise figures are obtainable as to the social composition of the Red Army at this period; one estimate gives it as 68 per cent peasants, 30 per cent workers, 1 per cent officials, 1 per cent others. O. Lang, 'The Good Iron of the New Chinese Army', *Pacific Affairs*, March 1939. The report of the Comintern's activities, prepared for the Seventh Congress in 1935, gives the figure for December 1933, as 410,000, repeating the total of 60,000 for the Communist strength outside Soviet China. The same document endeavoured to define the nature of the movement in the appropriate terminology: 'The present Chinese Soviet Republic is not a bourgeois State. That is clear if only from the fact that on its territory the landlords and the bourgeoisie are deprived of their economic foundations and political rights. At the same time, before the Chinese Soviet Republic there does not stand and cannot stand the immediate task of annihilating capitalism and constructing socialism. It is not yet a proletarian state in spite of the fact that it is a Soviet State under the hegemony of the proletariat and the political monopoly of the Communist

This optimism inside the Communist ranks was belied by the course of events, since the fifth campaign planned by von Seeckt, with its careful combination of military pressure and economic blockade, at last brought success to the Kuomintang armies. In August 1934, the Kuomintang advance began. In October, the Red Army began its northward march and a year later, much depleted, found a stopping place in northern Shensi, where, as in neighbouring Kansu, there had for some time existed a secondary centre of Soviet strength.[1]

At the Comintern Congress in July-August 1935, the purpose and tactics of the 'United Front' received their definition. 'All the key problems of this movement,' declared Manuilsky in September, 'all its tactical problems, revolve around the central axis—the reinforcement of the U.S.S.R. as the *base of the world proletarian revolution*'.[2] Praise was forthcoming for the Chinese Red Army, in spite of the Kiangsi setback, since the struggle there was 'being led by Communist Bolsheviks in the Red Army'. 'The Communist Party of China is striving to make the Soviet movement *the political core of a United China*: it is striving to take the lead of the masses of the people of the whole of China against Japanese imperialism.'[3] Meanwhile, the United Front policy was already in full swing as far as the Chinese Communists were concerned, their 'new strategy' in this respect being proclaimed in August 1935—union even with Chiang, against Japan.[4] This propaganda received a new impetus at this

---

Party, the only directing Party. This is a new type of State; the difficulties of setting it up under present conditions imply further not only that the success of the Soviet Republic has not yet embraced the whole country but that even the existing Soviet territories do not yet represent a complete whole and do not possess the decisive productive centres.' *Kommunisticheski Internatsional Pered VII Vsemirnym Kongressom* (Moscow, 1935), pp. 462–3 (*The Communist International before the Seventh World Congress*).

[1] The story of the Long March is fully recounted by Snow, *Red Star over China*, pp. 183–208. Madame Chiang Kai-shek referred to the Red Army which had just been driven out of Kiangsi as the 'Communist-Bandit-Hordes', in a preface to C. W. H. Young: *New Life for Kiangsi* (Shanghai, 1935), written in the spring of 1935 and purporting to describe the Communist régime and the efforts of the 'New Life Movement' to regenerate the population which had undergone it. Its merit may be gathered from the following quotation (p. 86): 'Contrary to the beliefs of many there is no rapine [*sic*] under the Conservative [*sic*] Communists, no nationalisation of women, as advocated by most of the radicals.'

[2]. D. Z. Manuilsky: *The Work of the Seventh Congress of the Communist International* (London: Modern Books, 1935), p. 14.

[3] ibid., pp. 58–61. On 28 May 1943, the Chinese Communist Party, commenting on the announcement of the dissolution of the Comintern, declared that in practice the Comintern had not intervened in their affairs since 1935. *New York Times*, 29 May 1943.

[4] 'Declaration of Chinese Soviet Government and of Central Committee of Chinese Communist Party', 31 August 1935, in L. K. Rosinger, *China's Wartime Politics* (I.P.R., Princeton University Press, 1944), pp. 63–9.

time from the intensification of Japanese pressure.[1] Although
Chiang himself took over command of the 'anti-Red' forces in the
North-West, little publicity was given to his efforts, perhaps in view
of the public declarations that Communism had already been finally
crushed.[2]

The new united front tactics were particularly noticeable in the
Communists' relations with the Chinese Moslems in the North-
West.[3] The main task confronting the Communists in Northern
Shensi was to build an economy which would enable them to survive
and to do it in such a way as not to alienate the bulk of the peasant
population. Military equipment had still to be obtained principally
by capture, since the Red Army was cut off by the national troops
from any possible contacts with the U.S.S.R. On the other hand if
Russian help was, and had all along been, negligible, Comintern
influence, according to Snow, was as strong as ever.

The unwillingness of the predominantly Manchu troops under
Chang Hsueh-liang to attack the Red Army in its new anti-Japanese
rôle must have been apparent to Chiang Kai-shek as early as
October, but it was, as far as can be seen, only the anti-Comintern
pact in November 1936, and the incident at Sian in December,
when Chiang was 'kidnapped' by the Manchurian troops of Chang
Hsueh-liang, which finally convinced him that the wiser course was
to accept this newly proffered support from his old enemies, and to
concentrate China's strength on the coming clash of arms with
Japan.[4]

Even after Sian, the progress of the reconciliation negotiations
was not very rapid. The full-scale Japanese invasion of China in
July 1937, and the rapid emergence of a threat to the Inner Mongo-

[1] *Survey for 1935*, pp. 319–20, 330–1.

[2] 'It is the opinion of the writer that the Red Movement in China as a
military factor has collapsed and is doomed. On the whole I believe the
Communists can and will be wiped out by General Chiang Kai-shek within
a few years never to return.' Young. op, cit., p. 103.

[3] O. Lattimore, 'The Kimono and the Turban', *Asia and the Americas*
(New York), May 1938; L. Hoover, 'China's Muslims must Choose',
'China's Muslims are Tough', *Asia*, November-December, 1938; E. F.
Carlson, *The Chinese Army* (I.P.R., 1940), pp. 24–31.

[4] There has been considerable difference of opinion as to the Communists' own share, if any, in the Sian incident. Some authors accept the
Japanese version that the kidnapping affair was preceded by an agreement
between Chang Hsueh-liang and the Communists. The bewilderment of
the Soviet Press at these events gives credence to the official Soviet denial
made on 20 December. Indeed the first reaction was that the whole thing
was a Japanese plot designed to weaken Nanking. Then alarm was
expressed at the possible results of the proposed 'punitive' expedition and
finally the line taken was that the whole affair was a misguided but under-
standable reaction on the part of the Manchurian troops who were being
made to fight the Communists when they only wanted to fight the Japanese.
The incident is described at length in James Bertram, *Crisis in China*
(Macmillan, 1939). Chang Hsueh-liang's declaration of 12 December 1936,
is in Rosinger, op. cit., pp. 94–5.

lian provinces, helped no doubt to speed up decisions.[1] The signing of the Sino-Russian pact of non-aggression on 21 August, was followed by an agreement between Chiang and the Communists which reorganised the Red Army, as part of the national forces, under the title of the Eighth Route Army, and turned the Chinese Soviet Republic into the Frontier Area or Border Region (the Shensi-Kansu-Ninghsia Border Government as the Communists called it), with a wide democratic franchise. The programme of Sovietisation was suspended.[2] Yenan became the Communist 'capital' by agreement with Chang Hsueh-liang's forces.

Meanwhile, the rearguard of the Red Army, who had been left in Kiangsi in 1934, had established contact with Mao Tse-tung in the autumn of 1937, and in January 1938 they were recognised as the New Fourth Army. Some confusion of mind was shown in many quarters as to the significance of the change in the position of the Communists. There was no indication that they themselves considered that anything fundamental had been given up by their acceptance of the idea of united resistance to Japan or of the Three Peoples' Principles as the immediate basis for the realisation of such unity.[3]

The first major test of the strength of the United Front came at the end of 1937. The Italian adhesion to the anti-Comintern Pact and the all-out attack against Nanking were accompanied by a determined drive on the part of Japan's German partner to mediate a peace with Nanking. The 16 December broadcast speech in which Chiang pledged himself to further resistance administered a decisive check to these manœuvres. It was greeted by the Communists with a new manifesto urging that co-operation should be further extended.

'The Chinese Communist Party,' it stated, 'has not merely joined hands with the Kuomintang to save the nation during the war, but

---

[1] *Survey for 1937*, I, pp. 154–60.

[2] The text of the Pact is in M. Litvinov, *Against Aggression*, pp. 168–70. The Communists issued a statement on unity on 22 September 1937. On 23 September Chiang called this 'an outstanding instance of the triumph of national sentiment over every other consideration. . . . The various decisions in the Manifesto', declared Chiang Kai-shek 'such as the abandonment of a policy of violence, the cessation of communist propaganda, the abolition of the Chinese Soviet Covenant, and the disbandment of the Red Army are all essential conditions for mobilising our national strength in order that we may meet the menace from without and guarantee our own national existence.' Rosinger, op. cit., pp. 96–7. See also Snow, op. cit., pp. 434–41; L. Epstein, *The People's War* (Gollancz, 1939), pp. 87–8. The signature of the Chinese-Soviet Non-Aggression Pact was followed by the arrival of Russian aircraft and air force personnel at Nanking and other Chinese centres. Carlson, op. cit., p. 47.

[3] Epstein, op. cit., pp. 88–94. For an interesting analysis of the situation at this time, see R. S. Morton, 'Japan and China, a War of Minds', *Pacific Affairs*, September 1937. The Kuomintang also strove to capitalise popular support by putting forward a new agrarian programme in May 1937, but the possibility of its being put into effect was regarded with some scepticism. *Agrarian China*, pp. 154–6.

is determined to co-operate harmoniously with the Kuomintang to reconstruct the nation after the war has ended in victory.'[1]

Two important practical steps marked the beginning of what a Communist sympathiser has called the 'halcyon year of Chinese unity', 1938.[2] In February, Chou En-lai became Vice-President of the Political Department of the Military Affairs Commission in charge of mass mobilisation.[3] This in effect appeared to mean the acceptance of the hitherto rejected idea of basing the war against Japan on the mass resistance of an armed people. In the previous month the work of the Eighth Route Army and forces inspired by it against the Japanese in Shansi culminated in the recognition of the Hopei-Shansi-Chahar Border Government, a 'United Front' Government under Communist inspiration, and exercising authority well inside what were nominally Japanese-occupied zones.[4]

[1] Epstein, op. cit., chap. 6. In January the Communists had been permitted their own daily newspaper in Hankow but it was not allowed openly to declare itself a Communist organ and was subject to the official censorship.

[2] A. L. Strong: 'Eighth Route Regions in Northern China', *Pacific Affairs*, June 1941.

[3] Linebarger, op. cit., p. 64. Carlson, op. cit., p. 32.

[4] The Border Government and its struggle against the Japanese and against the 'Provisional Government' set up by them at Pekin in January 1937, are described in G. E. Taylor, *The Struggle for North China*. See especially pp. 96–117. The book carries the story on to the spring of 1940. Cf. Epstein, op. cit., chaps. 9 and 10; Snow, *Scorched Earth*, pp. 240–8; Carlson, op. cit., pp. 38–9. In an appendix to the same book there is an account of 'The Organisation of a typical Guerrilla Area in S. Shantung'. The author, Wang Yu-chuan, explains that political activity there is not Communist, but based on the principles of Sun Yat-sen. These are however interpreted, it appears, as permitting a redistribution of the burdens of taxation, wider education and 'democratic' local government. The Communists themselves demanded and did no more. For an account of resistance inside Japanese occupied zones, see Haldore Hanson, 'With the Fighting Reds inside the Japanese lines', *Asia*, August 1938.

Appendix D

IT has already been pointed out that a good deal of attention came to be focused in the years 1934 and 1935 upon Soviet activities in the Chinese province of Sinkiang. This was partly due to the possibility that this activity might have immediate repercussions upon the Soviet Union's relations with other Powers, but partly, also, because it was taken as evidence that the Russian 'forward' policy in Asia had not been abandoned. Sinkiang was pointed to as an example of the new Soviet 'imperialism'.

Like Outer Mongolia, Sinkiang (otherwise known as Chinese or Eastern Turkestan) is a border territory of its nominal sovereign the Chinese Republic and is overwhelmingly non-Chinese in its racial and cultural affiliations. Its history since the Chinese and Russian Revolutions has been only a degree less difficult to follow than that of Outer Mongolia itself. But unlike the latter, it has not been hermetically sealed from the eyes of the non-Soviet world. In addition to the information obtainable from natives of the province who have made their way to India, China or further afield, there have been resident Chinese and British officials and there have been visits by a number of European traders, missionaries, journalists, and scientists.[1] On the other hand the problems of Sinkiang are extremely complex owing to the mixed oasis and nomad economy of the province and to its chequered history, with all its legacy of religious, racial, and cultural differences and antipathies. Since Sinkiang contains, in the string of Oases known as the 'silk road', one of the oldest and most famous trans-continental trade routes, it is natural that its fate has always been profoundly affected by the world outside.[2]

[1] Only the missionaries and the consular staffs have experience over considerable periods, and the information which they acquire cannot for obvious reasons normally be made accessible. The Russians have consulates at Urumchi and Kashgar, of which the former is the more important. The British consulate at Kashgar, maintained by the Indian Government, has functioned since 1890. Three nations have maintained Christian missions in Sinkiang; the Swedes at Kashgar Old and New Cities and at Yangi-Hissar and Yarkand—these functioned until 1938—the Germans (the Catholic Societas Verbi Divini) at Urumchi, and the British (the China Inland Mission) at Urumchi. See *The Challenge of Central Asia* by M. Cable and others (World Dominion Press, 1929). When Sir Eric Teichman visited the province in 1935, the only non-Russian foreigners whom he met were one or two German residents in Urumchi and a few wanderers from Turkey, Persia, and Afghanistan.

[2] On the land routes to the Far East, see chap. 1 of *An Explanatory Atlas of the Far East* by G. F. Hudson and M. Rajchman, and *The Silk Road* by Sven Hedin (Routledge, 1938). For a wide-ranging discussion of the pro-

Sinkiang, which is about twice as big as France, has a population of perhaps three and a half million.[1] These are composed first of the Turkis or Uighurs whom the Chinese call Chan-tou and who make up 60 per cent or more of the whole. Together with the Sarts and Noghais, the Turkis make up the great bulk of the Moslem Turki-speaking oasis dwellers. Other settled peoples are the formidable Chinese Moslems the Tungans, who have also been prominent in trade, some non-Moslem Chinese, Tajiks (in the Pamirs) and in the Kulja (Ili) region, Manchus, settled there in the eighteenth century. Among the nomad peoples are Mongols of the western branch of that race—Kalmucks round Karashar and Torguts further east. The South Altai (Kobdo) region, also Mongol in population, was transferred to Sinkiang from Outer Mongolia in 1907.[2] There are also Turki-speaking nomads, the Kazaks in the north and the Kirghiz in the south. To complicate matters further many of the nomads have in the course of their regular migrations been accustomed to disregard the political frontiers to the North and West.[3] A quarter of a century's residence may per-

---

blems of Sinkiang, see O. Lattimore, *Inner Asian Frontiers of China*, chap. 6. The author's first-hand knowledge of the country was however all obtained before 1928. Some of the picture as the British Consular officials see it, comes out of course in the reports of travellers. But from the British side, the authoritative view must be taken as being that of Sir Eric Teichman in his *Journey to Turkistan* (Methuen, 1938). The bias of the missionaries has not unnaturally been anti-Soviet. Two quotations from the excellent survey of their work already referred to, will make this clear: 'It will be seen from the map how completely the whole region (Central Asia) is dominated by the railway system of Soviet Russia, southern extensions of which have already been carried out, and more are contemplated. From this it can readily be gathered how serious is the Soviet menace. The British policy of keeping these frontier lands as buffer states seems to have thrown them into the power of their northern neighbour. In the long run, the three great Powers, Russia, China and British India, will be involved in deciding the future of Central Asia, and the whole region will then be opened to missionary effort'; and again 'there seems little doubt that Russia has designs on the territories of Mongolia, Manchuria, and Sinkiang which the present weakness of China greatly facilitates'. *The Challenge of Central Asia*, pp. iv, 45. The scientists, among whom Dr. Hedin is our chief witness, naturally try to keep out of politics on their expeditions and to maintain friendly relations with all constituted authority. Dr. Filchner, author of *A Scientist in Tartary* (Faber & Faber, 1939), was the happy recipient of congratulatory messages from his Führer and is very liberal with anti-Bolshevik epithets. Dr. Hedin's Nazi sympathies are of course well known.

[1] Estimates vary from two and a half to eight million; Russian authorities usually accept the figure of four million.

[2] G. M. Friters, *The International Position of Outer Mongolia* (Privately printed, Dijon, 1939), pp. 16, 50

[3] The nomenclature and classification of the races of Turkestan is a matter of considerable difficulty. The word 'Sart', for instance, is applied fairly indiscriminately by the Russians to all oasis-dwellers. In fact, although the

haps have qualified the fifty thousand 'White' Russian refugees for inclusion in the racial mosaic of Sinkiang.

The Turki-speaking races compose about three-quarters of the total population, the Mongols 7 per cent, the Chinese and Manchus together between 8 and 10 per cent and the Tungans about 7 per cent. Over four-fifths of the whole are thus Moslems, in a part of the globe where religion rather than race tends to be the major unifying (and disturbing) factor.

The problems of Sinkiang are further complicated by the physical geography of the province. The Tien-shan mountains form an effective barrier, with but few passes, between northern Sinkiang, Jungaria, and southern Sinkiang, Kashgaria. The latter is less adapted to nomadism and is richer in oases. It is racially more homogeneous but is more exposed to external influences. It has been said that it is 'Kashgaria alone that matters, seeing that the wealth and commerce of the country are concentrated there and that the great majority of the revenue comes from it'.[1] Mineral development in the north is, however, probably modifying this state of affairs.[2]

Sarts are akin to the Uzbeks with whom they are grouped in Soviet statistics, they are a separate people. See W. Jochelson, *Peoples of Asiatic Russia* (American Museum of Natural History, 1928), chap. 4. This standard work is however largely based on pre-Revolutionary Russian statistics. See also M. Cable with F. French, *The Gobi Desert* (Hodder & Stoughton, 1942); F. Kazak, *Osttürkestan zwischen den Grossmächten* (Königsberg, 1937), pp. 8–12; A. K. Wu, *Turkistan Tumult*, chaps. 16 and 17; Hudson and Rajchman, op. cit., chap. 8; Teichman, op. cit., chap. 1, and *China Year Book*, 1935, chap. 2. Since the main races (especially the Turanian) and the main religions of Sinkiang are represented over such large portions of Asia, it is obvious that scope exists for the diffusion of partisan information. More important perhaps in relation to the immediate problem—the nature and extent of Soviet influence—is the very wide difference of opinion which exists as to the merits and demerits of the 'nationalities' policy of the U.S.S.R. Those who are impressed by Soviet efforts to raise the standards of the Asiatic peoples of the Union will clearly have less objection to the extension of Soviet influence outside it. This of course depends in part upon the still more general question of the right (or duty) of Great Powers to spread the benefits of industrialisation and its accompaniments, even at the price of disturbing traditional social organisations and ways of life, and of disregarding the claims of national self-determination. A recent writer makes a strong attack upon Soviet policy inside its own Asiatic frontiers as being dictated 'by the meretricious ideal of so-called progress'. For this writer 'the so-called neglect the Russian (Tsarist) Government is accused of did at least have the great merit of not upsetting the lives of the majority of its colonials. The process of deracination, disintegration, and the conscious attack on the traditional life of the non-Russian inhabitants of Siberia, in the name of development and progress, is a marked feature after 1917'. E. Hill, 'Russia, the U.S.S.R. and Asia', *J.R.C.A.S.*, January 1943.

[1] *J.R.C.A.S.*, 1934, p. 86.
[2] 'China and Soviet Russia in Sinkiang', *B.I.N.*, XVII., 16 November 1940.

Jungaria falls within the Sino-Russian-Mongol sphere. Urumchi, the capital since the eighteen-eighties, is on the caravan route from Lanchow (in Kansu) through Hami. This route to the west from China afterwards branches into two. One road goes by way of Chuguchak (Tacheng) to Ayuguz (Sergiopol) on the Turksib railway. The other reaches the Soviet frontier at Kulja and thence continues to Alma Ata and Tashkent. The two routes which skirt the Taklamakan desert in the centre of Kashgaria meet again at Kashgar. The southern one, which passes through Cherchen, Khotan, and Yarkand, is the original Silk Road. Kashgar is the centre for many currents in Asiatic trade and politics. South of the Silk Road lie the Kunlun mountains which separate Sinkiang from Tibet, the centre of the world of Lamaist Buddhism. To the south-west of Kashgaria, the passes of the Karakoram lead to Kashmir and India. Afghanistan to the west—elongated to touch Sinkiang in 1895, in order to provide a buffer between Britain and Russia—is Sinkiang's link with free Moslem Asia. The Silk Road itself finally crosses into Soviet territory at Irkeshtan, giving communication with what are now the Soviet Kirghiz and Tajik republics. It is not hard to see why Chinese rule in Sinkiang, asserted by successive imperial dynasties and nominally maintained by the Republic, was always in the nature of a *tour de force*. A certain local autonomy was in fact normal. The province raised and spent its own revenues and was never included in the great machinery of the national Customs system. When attempts were made to introduce Chinese settlers, formidable natural and political obstacles were encountered. In the nineteenth century Sinkiang felt the repercussions of the Russian advance into western Turkestan. Russia could henceforward not be indifferent to any movement which might affect the tranquillity of her own Moslem Turanian subjects. British attention grew less strained, for the advance of geographical knowledge dispelled the bogy of an invasion of India through the Pamirs. British Indians were however important as traders, and their enjoyment of extra-territorial rights made 'British interests tend to protrude unduly into the body politic of Chinese Turkestan and suffer the resultant friction.'[1] Sinkiang was also affected by what went on among the Chinese Moslems in Kansu and Ninghsia as well as by events in Mongolia and Tibet.

Direct Chinese rule over Sinkiang in modern times dates from the middle of the eighteenth century when a Kalmuck State in Jungaria was overthrown. The first treaty governing the external relations of the province was the Sino-Russian treaty of Kulja in 1851 by which the Russians gained important commercial advantages. Soon afterwards, however, the internal troubles which had stirred Sinkiang intermittently since 1826 came to a head. From 1863, the overland trade between Russia and China was almost brought to a standstill. In the following year the Turkis revolted under Yakub Bey, and his Emirate of Yarkand came to embrace the

---

[1] Teichman, op. cit., pp. 108 ff.

greater part of Sinkiang. Russian recognition of Yakub Bey was granted in 1872, but this did not represent a permanent policy. The position can in fact only be explained if account is taken of the general rivalry between Russia and Britain at that time.

'The interests of Russia and England in Eastern Turkestan were real, intensive and intimately connected with the broader policies being pursued throughout the continent. As in Afghanistan, their interests collided there and the conflict was resolved only after a long diplomatic duel. It was the possible strategic danger that led to the idea of adding Kashgar to the buffer-States of the Indian Empire and so to the British recognition of Yakub Bey in 1874.'

But 'while the British were placing their faith in the power and endurance of the Kashgar State, Russia backed China to win'. In 1871, the Russians took advantage of the situation to occupy Kulja but they seem to have supported the efforts of the Chinese to re-establish themselves in the remainder of the province. By 1878, Sinkiang was again in Chinese hands and a new Sino-Russian agreement, the Treaty of Livadia of 1879, confirmed the Russians in the possession of Kulja. The terms of this Treaty caused an outburst of nationalist feeling in China but Britain counselled prudence. Negotiations were re-opened and the Treaty of St. Petersburg in 1881 did in fact give back Kulja itself and most of the surrounding territory but the Russians achieved their main objective in the form of special commercial advantages.[1]

'Four years later Russia was again accused of fostering disaffection in Kashgaria; and England, partly to set a watch on Muscovite doings, took occasion to ask facilities for Indian trade there. Russian economic and political penetration of Kashgaria continued up to the Russo-Japanese war.'[2]

Russo-British competition in Sinkiang and particularly in its south-western portion did not end in 1881, but the gradual lessening of the tension between the two Powers made itself felt in this sphere as in others, although Sinkiang was not touched upon in the Anglo-Russian convention of 1907.[3]

Up till the Chinese Revolution, then, Sinkiang was kept as an area of Chinese colonisation and as a destination for political deportees; but the Central Government only maintained its hold through costly subsidies and by relying on the skill of its governors to play off the various local peoples against each other. After the Revolution, the subsidies stopped and the element of diplomacy became all the more important. There was a period of stabilisation

[1] E. V. G. Kiernan, *British Diplomacy in China, 1880–1885* (Cambridge University Press, 1939), pp. 38–72.

[2] ibid., p. 72. Cf. pp. 189, 207, 283–5, 302. The author sometimes uses Kashgaria to denote Sinkiang as a whole.

[3] L. E. Frechtling, 'Anglo-Russian Rivalry in Eastern Turkestan', *J.R.C.A.S.*, 1939.

under Governor Yang Tseng-hsin, from soon after the Revolution until his assassination in 1928.

Russian influence in Sinkiang continued to increase up to the time of the Russian Revolution, and commercial relations had become increasingly important.[1] Some trouble was caused by the flight into Sinkiang of Kirghiz and Kazak tribesmen after the crushing of the rebellion in Russian Central Asia in September 1916.[2] The Revolution and the upheavals in Russian Central Asia were responsible for a new influx of fugitives—many of them Russians. They also put a stop to Russian trade with Sinkiang; and American, German, Japanese, and British merchants began to pay attention to the potentialities of the province. The road through Chuguchak was replaced as the chief outlet for Sinkiang by that running through Kashgar and the Indian passes. A renewal of Russian demands for special treatment would seem to have been excluded by the Russian renunciation of the fruits of Tsarist imperialism in China.[3] Once the authority of the new régime in Russia had been fully established, complete disinterestedness in the affairs of Sinkiang came to an end. According to one account, Yang made a commercial treaty with the Soviets as early as 1920.[4] The Russians were also concerned lest political activities inimical to the Soviets should be carried on across the Sinkiang frontier by the Russian subjects who had sought refuge there. On the Russian side, propaganda vaunting the agrarian reforms of the new régime in Russia is said to have begun in 1922, but the extent of Russian influence in Yang's time is uncertain.[5]

The main attraction for the Soviet Union in Sinkiang (as in Outer Mongolia) lay in the products of its flocks. Later, as has been noted, evidence of considerable mineral wealth began to accumulate.[6] During the 1920's Soviet Consulates were established in

[1] G. Vasel: 'Ost-Türkestan: Sinkiang oder "Jugurstan"?', *Osteuropa*, October 1935.

[2] W. M. Mandel: 'Soviet Central Asia', *Pacific Affairs*, December 1942. The figure of one million fugitives given in this article is obviously an exaggeration.

[3] The Declaration of 25 July 1919, to the Chinese people, and the note to China of 27 October 1920. They are printed in the Appendix to V. A. Yakhontoff, *Russia and the Soviet Union in the Far East*.

[4] S. Hedin, *The Flight of Big Horse* (Macmillan, 1936) pp. 11. Cf. also his *Across the Gobi Desert* (Routledge, 1931). Russo-Sinkiang economic relations in the 1920's are authoritatively treated in Conolly, *Soviet Economic Development in the East*, chap. 5.

[5] E. K. Maillart, *Forbidden Journey* (Heinemann, 1937), p. 211. Miss Maillart was the companion of Peter Fleming in the journey which produced the latter's *News from Tartary* (Cape, 1936). Fleming did more than any other writer in the 1930's to attract attention to the affairs of Sinkiang. The political chapters of his book have a melodramatic flavour which tends to make him appear more biased against the Russians than was perhaps the case.

[6] 'The richest deposits of minerals in the Altais may probably lie on the Chinese side of the border in Sinkiang.' J. Littlepage and D. Bess, *In Search of Soviet Gold*, p. 259.

Sinkiang and Sinkiang representatives on Soviet soil. This was accompanied by a rapid growth in Soviet trade at the expense of Russia's competitors. But the old transit trade with China did not recover, since from about 1925 the caravan route was disrupted by civil war.[1]

Significant of the close relations existing between the Soviet Union and Sinkiang was the fact that Consular and commercial relations were unaffected by the breach between Moscow and Nanking in 1927 or by the C.E.R. dispute in 1929. Russia's geographical advantages as against her commercial competitors were shortly afterwards further enhanced by the completion (in 1930) of the Turksib railway. From Chuguchak to Ayuguz, the nearest railhead, was only 150 miles. The distance from Chuguchak to the nearest Chinese railhead, Sian, is about 2,750 miles. Throughout most of the period the quickest way to Sinkiang from most of China was through Soviet territory. The Nanking official, A. K. Wu, travelled to Urumchi in November-December 1932, via Japan, Vladivostok, the Trans-Siberian and Turksib railways. This of course gave the Soviet Government a measure of control through its right to withhold visas.

The Chinese Government were unreconciled to this position and in the summer of 1933 commissioned Dr. Hedin to make a survey with a view to the construction of two motor-roads to link Sinkiang with the rest of China.[2]

The new time of troubles in Sinkiang was heralded by the murder of Governor Yang on the 7 July 1928.[3] Under his incompetent and unpopular successor, Chin Shu-yen (or Chin Shu-ren or Jen Shu-jen), the delicate balance between Chinese officialdom and the non-Chinese population was upset. The growing hold of the Russian foreign trade monopoly over the commerce of Sinkiang was detrimental to the interests of the local merchants and cotton growers. The decline in the fortunes of the merchants was reflected in a fall

[1] A. Barker and N. D. Hanwell: 'The emergence of China's Far West', *Far Eastern Survey* (I.P.R., New York), 26 April 1929. For events in Sinkiang up to 1933, see also T. A. Bisson: 'The Dismemberment of China', *Foreign Policy Reports*, 25 April 1933.

[2] S. Hedin, *The Silk Road*, Introduction; *The Flight of Big Horse*, p. 191. The strategic rôle of Sinkiang in relation to the communications of Central Asia is dealt with in an article by W. E. Wheeler: 'The control of Land Routes: Russian Railways in Central Asia', *J.R.C.A.S.*, 1934. The most illuminating of the available maps is that in *The Challenge of Central Asia*.

[3] The account given here of the origins and progress of the revolt of 1931–1934 is based on the already cited works by A. K. Wu, Sir Eric Teichman, Miss Cable, Dr. Hedin, Mr. Fleming, Miss Maillart, Dr. Kazak, and G. Vasel, and the article by N. Vakar in the *Slavonic Review*, July 1935. Herr Vasel was working for the Eurasia Air-line at the time and was for a period held prisoner by the rebels at Kulja. Cf. also *Survey for 1934*, pp. 686–9. The various sources are by no means in agreement on the precise chronology of events or on the relations between the various rebel groups. A thorough study of Sinkiang by an expert on Central Asiatic affairs is much to be desired.

in the revenue and additional taxation had to be devised. Currency difficulties added to the growing volume of discontent.[1] A final grievance was provided by clumsy attempts to settle Chinese and Tungan emigrants from Kansu on land held by local owners; and the trouble among the Moslems of Kansu was an additional factor of disturbance.

In 1929, the ban on the export of arms from India was lifted. But if the intention was to enable the Sinkiang administration to deal with possible trouble, the effect was the opposite. Some of the arms almost certainly reached what were to be rebel hands and this was used to justify the charge that Britain was behind the revolt, when it actually broke out.[2]

Ma Chung-yin, the young Moslem military boss of Kansu, and Governor of Lanchow, stopped most of the members of his Tungan forces who attempted to join their co-religionists.[3]

In the summer of 1931, a group of rebels at Hami appealed for help to Ma Chung-yin, who now entered Sinkiang. After initial success, he was wounded in a victorious engagement with Chin's forces and withdrew with his army to Suchow.

It was probably at this juncture that Chin, realising that his troubles were not over, concluded with the Soviet Government the secret treaty of 31 October 1931. This treaty is said to have given the Soviet Union tariff privileges, the right to open trade in all important centres and unrestricted freedom of movement within Sinkiang for Soviet citizens. In return Soviet aid was to be forthcoming for local schemes of electrification and for the improvement of transport and agriculture, such help to include the loan of specialists.[4]

In 1932, the revolt spread to the Tungan territory and into Kashgaria. The Urumchi administration called to its aid a contingent of about 1,500 troops which had been newly raised from among the 'White' Russians. These came to the capital from Kulja under the command of Sheng Shih-tsai. Sheng was a former officer in the Manchurian army.

By February 1933, some of Ma's troops were again besieging Urumchi. During March the Government forces were further reinforced by about 7,000 men of the Manchurian army, who, having been forced across the Siberian border by the Japanese, had been

---

[1] Teichman, op. cit., pp. 87–8, 153.

[2] *China Year Book*, 1935, p. 43; O. Lattimore, *Inner Asian Frontiers of China*, p. 195; Kazak, op. cit., p. 17; Yakhontoff, *Chinese Soviets*, p. 186.

[3] Interesting light on Ma and a first-hand account of what his rule meant to the unfortunate populations who underwent it, is given in Cable and French, op. cit., pp. 222–4, 232–4.

[4] Hedin gives the date as 1 October, and says that its existence was not discovered by Nanking until June 1933, when the Nanking Pacification Commissioner, General Hwang Ma-sung, arrived in Sinkiang, *The Flight of Big Horse*, p. 11. Chin's plenipotentiary was a certain Chen; the Russian signatory was a M. Slavutsky. Cable and French, op. cit., p. 231; *J.R.C.A.S.*, October 1933.

transported to Sinkiang over the Trans-Siberian and Turksib railways. This nucleus of strongly anti-Japanese and apparently strongly pro-Soviet troops was henceforward under the command of Sheng Shih-tsai, and formed the basis of his subsequent rise to power.

At about the same time, the civil war spread to western Kashgaria. Among the tribal levies taken into service by the local Chinese commander were Andijanis from Soviet Turkestan.

In April 1933, events at Urumchi took a new turn. The Russian troops, alleging mishandling by Chin, staged a *coup d'état* against him. Chin retired towards Chuguchak, announcing his intention to return. But on 5 May, Nanking announced that the Government had accepted his 'resignation'. Chin travelled via the Soviet Union to Tientsin. He was later imprisoned by the Chinese Government for having made an agreement with a foreign Power without Nanking's assent, that is, for the treaty of October 1931, with the Soviet Union.[1]

On 13 April, two days after the *coup*, Sheng Shih-tsai returned from the front to the capital and assumed the title of Provisional Border Defence Commissioner. Henceforward, in spite of a succession of Governors, it was Sheng who wielded authority. It was fairly clear that the policy of friendship with the Soviet Union was likely to be strengthened. At a rally on 22 April, in celebration of the new régime, the staff of the Soviet Consulate were much in evidence and the proclamation which, on 4 May, put forward, as a basis for the régime, the ideal of 'equal rights' for all the races of Sinkiang, had a certain Soviet flavour.[2]

The military situation did not allow much by way of internal reform, for Ma Chung-yin again advanced. Sheng ordered his Chief-of-Staff to fly to Nanking to ask for assistance, but the latter returned in June having inexplicably got no further than Moscow. Meanwhile, Sheng had defeated the rebels and the authority of Urumchi in northern Sinkiang seemed to have been re-established.

There was considerable doubt whether Sheng's *de facto* authority would be upheld by the Central Government, but after some discussion the Executive Yuan gave their assent. Sheng's formal appointment was announced on 3 August 1933.

At about the same time, the rebels in Kashgaria proclaimed a

---

[1] In 1940 he was living in retirement at Lanchow. G. Hogg, *I See a New China* (Boston, Little Brown, 1944), p. 149.

[2] Note in this connexion the fourteenth of the aims of the 'Chinese Soviet Republic', as set out in its Constitution of November 1931. The significant passage runs as follows: 'The Soviet Government in China recognises the right of self-determination of the national minorities in China, their right to complete separation from China and to the formation of an independent State for each national minority. All Mongolians, Tibetans, Miao, Yao, Koreans, and others living on the territory of China shall enjoy the full right to self-determination. . . .' It continues with a promise to assist national minorities to liberate themselves 'from the yoke of the imperialists, the Kuomintang militarists, the princes, lamas and others', and to encourage their national cultures. Yakhontoff, *Chinese Soviets*, pp. 220-1.

'Republic' of Eastern Turkestan. Help was sought from Turkish anti-Kemalist exiles, from Afghanistan and even apparently from the U.S.S.R., in spite of the fact that the ideology of the new 'republic' was clearly pan-Islamic and anti-Soviet. At the beginning of February 1934, two envoys from the 'republic' arrived at Delhi to seek British recognition and proposed to go on to Kabul, Teheran, and Ankara.

At Delhi they received an immediate rebuff.[1] This did not prevent the Moscow press from denouncing the entire affair as a product of British imperialist intrigue. As early as 15 August 1933, *Pravda* had asserted that England was considering the creation of a great Tibetan Empire with Sinkiang and Szechwan as dependent portions of it. In the following spring, *Krasnaya Zvezda* and *Pravda* returned to these charges in a variety of forms. According to one account, Britain aimed at absorbing Kashgar, Yarkand, and Khotan by placing them under the rule of an Indian Moslem prince. And there was some discrepancy as to whether Great Britain was acting in conjunction with or against Japan.[2]

These polemics must probably be taken as preparation for the Soviet decision to intervene more actively in Sinkiang. Growing dissension between the Tungan and Turki elements among the rebels involved the very real danger that the province would become increasingly the prey of anarchy.

It was actually in December, 1933, that Sheng seems to have made his own agreement with the Soviet representative Pogodin. It is hard to see that he had any alternative.[3] It involved a purge on

[1] 'So far as Delhi is concerned, the Republicans have gone to the wrong address. Sinkiang is the province of a State with which the British Government are on good terms, and the delegates will get no more than the advice to settle their differences with Sinkiang before worse befalls them.' *The Times*, 8 and 22 February 1934.

[2] *The Times*, 6 April 1934. Rumours of this kind spread outside Soviet circles. A 'well-informed' German in Peking was sure that Lawrence of Arabia had a hand in the plot. Maillart, op. cit., p. 218. Cf. the undated interview with a Turki from Sinkiang, headed 'Central Asia from Within', *J.R.C.A.S.*, 1935. A Chinese writer later defined British policy in this area as follows: 'England has one constant aim in regard to Sinkiang. It is to establish on the South Road round Kashgar an independent government which will form a buffer between them and the Russians.' Chiang Chun-chang, cited by M. R. Norins: 'The New Sinkiang', *Pacific Affairs*, December 1942, p. 464. Comments such as this ignored the changes in the situation which had come about since the 1870s. Britain could not however be indifferent altogether to events in Sinkiang, quite apart from the economic interests of her Indian subjects: 'How much of the brew may bubble over or seep through the physical barrier into British India the next few years will show. It is as well to remember that these huge mountain walls were as penetrable to the forays and excursions of Daulat Beg's fifteenth-century Moghals as they were to the evangelists of the Guatama before him.' *The Times*, 3 April 1934.

[3] Hedin, *The Silk Road*, p. 298, *The Flight of Big Horse*, p. 12; Teichman, op. cit., p. 105.

10 December of some of his Manchu and 'White' Russian officers. But thereafter his position improved. His own troops received Russian supplies and at the end of the month, Soviet troops to the number of perhaps 7,000 and fully equipped with tanks, artillery and aircraft entered Chuguchak and Kulja. These troops were, it seems, not in the uniform of the Red Army and were not officially part of it. Later on the 'White' Russian levies of the Sinkiang administration were incorporated into this force and there is hence a suggestion that the Soviet Government had been privy to the April *coup* as well as to the December purge. Subsequently, however, many of the former 'White' troops were disbanded, presumably as being politically unreliable.

After putting down a revolt in the Kulja area the Russians attacked Ma Chung-yin and forced him to retreat.[1] Soviet influence was believed to have been responsible for the decision of some Turki leaders to come over to the Administration, and to help in putting an end to the eastern Turkestan 'republic'. By the spring of 1934 this had been accomplished.[2]

Meanwhile in the areas which they had helped reconquer, the influence of the Soviet forces was obviously on the increase. With their support the authority of Urumchi and so nominally of the Chinese Government was gradually restored, although Sheng's own relations with Nanking remained ambiguous and even worsened in 1934. The Turkis had all been reduced to submission by July. Ma Chung-yin and his Tungans had retired to Kashgar in April.

On 5 July, however, Ma himself evacuated Kashgar, and two days later, with a number of personal followers, crossed into Soviet territory at Irkeshtan in company with Konstantinov, the Secretary of the Soviet Consulate at Kashgar. This surprising event caused a great deal of surmise, and many rumours as to his fate were current in the following years. As far as can be ascertained he was well treated by the Soviet authorities and groomed for possible future use in the vicissitudes of Central Asian politics.

After Ma's abandonment of Kashgar, the Tungans remained for some time in possession of a string of oases in the south, with new headquarters at Khotan. From there they protested their allegiance

---

[1] Teichman, op. cit., pp. 186-7. Miss Maillart puts the number of Soviet troops engaged in the decisive battle with Ma at no more than a thousand, and regards their victory as having been due to their possession of bombing aircraft and of five tanks. Fleming's assertion that the Soviet troops used gas is unconfirmed by any other source.

[2] It was at this stage that the British Consulate at Kashgar was involved in the fighting, probably accidentally. Teichman, op. cit., p. 148. General Kung Cheng-hang arrived at Kashgar in August with a number of Government troops in the capacity of pacification commissioner and expressed regret for the incident, involving the Consulate as well as the administration's gratitude for the proper attitude taken by the Consulate throughout the troubles. This was taken as dissociating the Sinkiang administration. from Soviet accusations of British partisanship for the rebels. *The Times*, 23 August 1934.

to Nanking and demanded assistance in order to combat Soviet influence in the province.[1]

The intervention of the Soviet Union was thus undoubtedly the major factor in the suppression of the Sinkiang revolt. The motives for intervention would appear to have been two in number: Sinkiang was still important enough from the economic point of view for the Soviet Union to wish it to remain peaceful; and, second, there was always the danger that revolt among the Moslems might spread to Soviet Turkestan. The Chinese administration, backed by the Russians, seemed the most likely factor of stability, if the Russians were to avoid the trouble and odium of annexing the province themselves. The Russians thus intervened 'for the sake of maintaining order', the classic imperialist excuse.[2]

One reason for the confusion at the time as to the Soviet objective, was the contradictory accounts of the events in Sinkiang put out by Soviet or near-Soviet sources. To the Japanese accusation that the Tungans were agents of the Comintern directed via Outer Mongolia, Soviet newspapers retorted that the whole thing was part of a Japanese plot for a Manchu-Mongol Empire or of the well-known Pan-Islamic intrigues of Japan.[3] On the other hand, the Tashkent Communist paper applauded Ma Chung-yin as a leader of oppressed peasants in revolt against militaristic feudalism.[4] This line was also that taken by the Chinese Communists, who seem to have considered it in order to denounce the Chinese administration of Sinkiang, at precisely the moment when their Russian comrades were engaged in re-imposing its authority by force. Mao Tse-tung in his report to the Second National Soviet Congress in January 1934, said that in Tibet, Sinkiang, and Inner Mongolia the ruling classes had 'directly surrendered to imperialism and accelerated the colonisation of their country'.[5]

Many observers regarded what had happened as much more than a reimposition of Chinese authority coupled with increased Soviet influence. 'In a few years, Outer Mongolia became what it is now, a Bolshevik possession, a docile appanage of Moscow. Nothing can save Sinkiang from a similar fate.'[6] In the earlier part of Sheng's rule, Soviet influence appears in fact to have been confined almost wholly to the economic sphere. The Soviet authorities may have

[1] Filchner, *A Scientist in Tartary*, p. 279.

[2] *China Year Book*, 1935, p. 44.

[3] On 9 March 1934, Yurenev told the American Ambassador at Tokyo that General Hayashi, who had become Japanese war minister in January, 'had constantly worked against Soviet Russia, particularly in Sinkiang'. Grew, *Ten Years in Japan*, pp. 123–5.

[4] Maillart, op. cit., p. 217. A further search of the Soviet Press might throw a little more light on all this. According to Vakar, Ma's forces were equipped with Soviet arms which had been given to General Feng Yu-hsiang and had later been passed on by Feng to Ma.

[5] Yakhontoff, *The Chinese Soviets*, p. 277.

[6] *J.R.C.A.S.*, 1935, p. 104. Cf. the remarks of W. J. Oudendyk, ibid., p. 392.

been concerned about the future attitude of the Russians in Sinkiang. In 1936 the Archbishop of Pekin consecrated a Bishop from Harbin to the See of Urumchi, but after fruitless efforts to gain admission to Sinkiang he was forced to return to Manchukuo.[1]

Henceforward, the Japanese aspect of the situation receives increasing emphasis and it is arguable that an independent Moslem Sinkiang would have provided a useful field for Japanese intrigue on a Pan-Turanian or Pan-Islamic basis.[2] It has been suggested that Ma actually had Japanese advisers with him. There may have been Japanese observers with his troops at some point, but nothing in his career suggests him as a likely Japanese puppet. Any serious foreign influences in his entourage were probably Turkish.[3] In the spring of 1934, there were Soviet press reports that Abdul Karim Effendi, a descendant of the Sultan Abdul Hamid, had been in touch with the Japanese in Shanghai with a view to their putting him forward as a candidate for the throne of Sinkiang.[4]

Whatever Japan's own plans, if any, for Sinkiang may have been, the prominent position held by the Russians there was an obvious propaganda point. On 22 January 1935, the Japanese Foreign Minister Hirota referred to Japanese concern at 'reports of the Sovietisation of Sinkiang'.[5] Six days later, Molotov replied to this in his speech to the Seventh All-Union Congress of Soviets:

'It remains for me to say a couple of words on the slanderous rumours about the Sovietisation of Sinkiang. One is struck by the

---

[1] S. Bolshakoff, *The Foreign Missions of the Russian Orthodox Church* (S.P.C.K., 1943), pp. 68–9.

[2] An article in the *Moslem World* (abstracted in *J.R.C.A.S.*, 1935, under the heading 'Chinese Turkestan') is based upon the report of a former Chinese official of the Urumchi administration. It gives some indication of Japanese and Turkish interest in Sinkiang, and treats Pan-Turanianism as a movement genuinely feared by the Soviet Union. The article points out that Pan-Islamism could only succeed on a Pan-Turanian basis and that Sinkiang under Turki rule would complete a Turanian chain from the Caspian to the border of Mongolia. Another curious document is a resolution of the 'League of Oriental Workers' passed in Paris on 6 August 1933, and published in *Filastin* on the 17th. (Translated in *Oriente Moderno*.) This applauded 'the brothers in Turkestan who were struggling for independence' and protested 'against any sort of interference by foreign imperialist States, even if it assumed the indirect form of assistance to the Chinese'. The nature of this League has not been ascertainable. It claimed to have had the collaboration, in examining the Sinkiang problem, of 'some workmen and revolutionary youths from Turkestan who were living in certain European countries'. It is to be regretted that no study of the Pan-Turanian movement seems to have been made by any English authority on Central Asia.

[3] Kemal Kaya Effendi, a Turk, had been Ma's military adviser in Kansu. Hedin, *The Flight of Big Horse*, p. 59.

[4] *The Times*, 6 April 1934. Cf. Yakhontoff, op. cit., p. 187.

[5] *Documents for 1934*, p. 484. According to one story, Japan had had hopes that Sheng himself might fall in with their plans. 'Central Asia from Within', *J.R.C.A.S.*, 1935.

fact that special efforts to spread this slander against the U.S.S.R. are being made in Japan whose policy in relation to China is known to everybody and cannot possibly be covered up by the spreading of inventions. I consider it necessary to emphasise the real Soviet policy towards China: the Soviet Union considers as incompatible with its policy the seizure of foreign territories, and is an absolute adherent of the independence, integrity, and sovereignty of China over all her parts including Sinkiang.'[1]

In the same month, Sheng found it advisable to telegraph to Nanking fresh assurances of his loyalty and to explain that although there were some foreign technicians in the provinces, they did not hold any Government posts. He also reported that the Soviet Government had offered credits to be repaid in commodities. Ho Ying-cheng replied assuring Sheng that he had no need to be worried about Japanese inspired rumours. On 26 September, *Tass* put out a denial that a Soviet republic had been set up in Sinkiang and Sheng once more telegraphed assurances of his loyalty.[2]

What is certain is that the new economic development of the province went on almost entirely under Soviet guidance.[3] In spite of Sir Eric Teichman's journey from Pekin to Urumchi and Kashgar in the autumn and winter of 1935, the elimination of British trade went on apace. Sir Eric himself pointed out on his return to England that the economic connexion of Sinkiang with Russia is a natural one which will always exist unless artificial obstacles get in the way.[4] On the other hand, 'artificial' obstacles were henceforth increasingly put in the way of the no less 'natural' trade across the Karakoram.

[1] *Documents for 1934*, p. 410.
[2] Kazak, op. cit., p. 79.
[3] The article 'Sinkiang: China's Back Door', by C. W. Meng (*Amerasia*, New York, November 1941) deals at some length with Sheng's economic and cultural achievements but makes no mention of Soviet participation in them.
[4] Sir Eric Teichman: 'Chinese Turkestan', *J.R.C.A.S.*, 1936.

Appendix E

THE re-assertion of Russian influence in Outer Mongolia was an important event in the history of Russo-Chinese and Russo-Japanese relations.[1]

Russia entered into negotiations with China on the question of Mongolia's frontiers as early as the eighteenth century.[2] The real

[1] The Buriat Mongols, whose homeland lies within the U.S.S.R. itself, are not touched upon here except in so far as they have been used as an instrument of Russian penetration among the other branches of the Mongol race. Tannu Tuva (formerly known as Uriankhai) is Turki rather than Mongol and does not seem to demand prolonged consideration here. It was not included in the autonomous Outer Mongolia, set up in 1911–1912, and the Russians then tried to detach it from China altogether. Claimed by China in 1919, it was again under Russian control by 1921, when it was made into a separate Republic. Thereafter the miniature Republic, with a population estimated in 1935 as consisting of 70,000 natives and 16,000 Russian colonists, was carefully steered away from its Mongol orbit, shut off from the outside world and completely dominated by Soviet Russia, with whom its relations were defined in a treaty of August 1926, very similar to the Russo-Mongol agreement of 1921. According to a later account Russian colonization continued to such effect that the immigrants outnumbered the natives. F. S. Mansvetov, 'Russia and China in Outer Mongolia', *Foreign Affairs*, October 1945. There was also a Tuva-Mongolian Treaty in this year, whereby the two Republics recognised each other and established diplomatic representation. The Russians monopolised its trade and directed its economic life towards a settled agriculture and away from nomadism. From 1931 onwards, the property of the 'feudal' lords and of the lamas was confiscated, but complete collectivisation was not introduced. Efforts were made to encourage the growth of an independent native non-Mongol culture, and in 1930–1931, the Tuvinian language was provided with an alphabet. A Soviet author describing Tannu Tuva in 1939 wrote of it as 'a country of the people's revolutionary, anti-imperialist, anti-feudal bourgeois democratic republic of a new type, gradually progressing along the path of non-capitalistic development.' Its constitution of November, 1924, was similar to that adopted by Outer Mongolia at almost exactly the same time, and it gave effective control to the Tannu Tuva People's Revolutionary Party, numbering in 1939, 5,000 members. In fact 'in politics and economics it is as closely bound to the U.S.S.R. as Nevada is to the U.S.A.' W. Ballis, 'Soviet Russia's Asiatic Frontier Technique: Tannu Tuva', *Pacific Affairs*, March 1941. Cf. *China Year Book*, 1935, p. 32: V. Conolly, *Soviet Economic Policy in the East*, pp. 112–14: O. Mänchen-Helfen: *Reise ins asiatische Tuwa* (Berlin, 1931). Tannu-Tuva has since been absorbed into the U.S.S.R. as the Tuva province of the R.S.F.S.R., *The Times*, 2 January 1945.

[2] The population of Outer Mongolia is between three-quarters of a million and one million. There are about two and a half million Mongols

awakening of Russian interest in the economic possibilities of Mongolia dates from about 1860. Russian-made goods could not however in the long run compete with the British and American wares of the Chinese traders, and Russian mercantile interests began to demand a 'forward' policy. Outer Mongolia was accepted as part of the Russian sphere of influence by Japan in the secret agreement which followed the Russo-Japanese war. Scope for Russian pressure and intrigue was provided by the resentment of the Mongols against Chinese commercial penetration and their own increasing indebtedness resulting therefrom. In 1911, the Mongols, not without Russian assistance, declared themselves independent of China and set up the Urga Living Buddha as their secular ruler (the Bogdo Khan). In November 1912, an agreement between Outer Mongolia and Russia was signed, but the Russians were nervous of possible international complications and the position was made more difficult by Mongol claims in Sinkiang and Inner Mongolia. There was in fact a considerable movement for union with the Outer (Khalkha) Mongols, in Inner Mongolia and among the Barguts of North-west Manchuria. In the case of Inner Mongolia, the predominating factor was the encroachments of the growing

---

in Inner Mongolia, including Jehol. *China Year Book*, 1935, pp. 25–35. It is not intended to deal here at any great length with the problem of Mongolia. A detailed study of the subject, which will undoubtedly become a standard work, has been made by Dr. G. M. Friters. Unfortunately the only portion of his researches so far available to the general public is that contained in the two articles: 'The Prelude to Outer Mongolian Independence' and the 'Development of Outer Mongolian Independence', *Pacific Affairs*, 1937. Dr. Friters has however kindly permitted the use of a part of his Ph.D. thesis entitled *The International Position of Outer Mongolia* (which was privately printed in 1939). Except where other specific references are given this section is based upon Dr. Friters's work. The only other recent full scale study available is that entitled *The Outer Mongolian People's Republic* by Yasuo Misshima and Tomio Goto (Tokyo, 1939). Use has been made of this valuable (though far from impartial) book through the summarised translation made for the I.P.R. in 1942 (mimeographed), by A. J. Grajdanzev, under the title: 'A Japanese View of Outer Mongolia'. A recent suggestive study of the question is to be found in chap. 4 of *Inner Asian Frontiers of China*, by O. Lattimore, the author of many previous books and articles on the Mongols. Geographical information will be found in G. F. Hudson and M. Rajchman, *An Explanatory Atlas of the Far East* (see especially pp. 92–6). On the Soviet side there are in particular the valuable articles entitled 'Mongolskaya Narodnaya Respublika' (Mongol People's Republic) in vol. iii of the *Sovietskaya Sibirskaya Entsiklopedia* (*Soviet Siberian Encyclopedia*), (1932), and in vol. xl of the *Bolshaya Sovietskaya Entsiklopedia* (*Great Soviet Encyclopedia*), (1938). Both have useful maps. There are important bibliographies in the books by Friters and Lattimore. Cf. W. Korostovetz: *Vom Cinggis Khan zur Sowjet-republik* (Berlin, 1926). It will be appreciated that there is very little first-hand information available outside Soviet sources, since the country has been pretty well sealed to foreigners since about 1928. There have been no missionaries there since the Swedish mission was expelled from Urga in 1924.

number of Chinese agricultural colonists upon their grazing grounds.[1]

The Russians did not apparently want to incur the permanent hostility which the formal separation of Outer Mongolia from China with their assistance would involve. (Outer Mongolia was never considered a part of China proper and claimed to have had no connexion except with the Manchu dynasty, which ended on the latter's fall in 1911.) In her negotiations with China, Russia confined herself to a demand for a recognition of special rights in an autonomous Outer Mongolia in which China should be recognised as the legal suzerain. This object was finally attained in the Kiakhta agreement of June 1915.[2] The leading authority on this sums up the result of Russian diplomacy at this time as follows: 'By manœuvring in such a way as to prevent coalition between Chinese and Mongols, Russia was able to rule Mongolia by pretending that the Mongols were free, and also to keep the rest of the world from interfering with its monopoly, by allowing it to be inferred that the Mongols were not free.'[3]

The first step after the collapse of Russian authority in 1917 was the Mongolian expedition of the Chinese general Hsiu Chou-chen in 1919. It has been suggested that the main object of the Chinese Government was to get rid of the general and his army, out of whom it was hoped to make colonists,[4] but in view of the fact that Hsiu belonged to the pro-Japanese Anfu clique there is reason 'to regard the Chinese intervention as being at the same time a Japanese manœuvre to replace Russian control of Outer Mongolia with an indirect Japanese control under Chinese agents'.[5] Hsiu arrived in Urga in October 1919, and in November, the Mongols under pressure requested the abrogation of their autonomy. The general did not remain in Urga long but the Chinese troops stayed until the city was captured in February 1921, by Baron von Ungern-Sternberg and his mixed force of Mongols and 'White' Russians. The Baron was in touch with the Japanese-supported Ataman Semenov, and his establishment in Urga may have been connected with further Japanese projects relating to the future of Mongolia and Eastern Siberia.[6] Soviet Russia could obviously not remain

---

[1] There is a map of Chinese agricultural penetration into Eastern Inner Mongolia in *The Challenge of Central Asia* by M. Cable and others, 1929. On the Barguts see E. J. Lindgren, 'North-western Manchuria and the Reindeer Tungus', *Geographical Journal* (Royal Geographical Society, London), June 1930. Cf. *Pioneer Settlement*, pp. 273-312.

[2] The agreements of this period will be found in *Treaties and Agreements concerning Outer Mongolia, 1881-1916* (Washington, Carnegie Endowment, 1921) and in vol. ii of J. V. A. Macmurray: *Treaties and Agreements with and concerning China, 1894-1919* (New York, Carnegie Endowment, 1921).

[3] G. M. Friters, 'The Prelude to Outer Mongolian Independence' *Pacific Affairs*, 1937.

[4] R. Verbrugge, *La Mongolie Un Instant Autonome* (Antwerp, 1936), pp.30-1.

[5] G. M. Friters, loc. cit.

[6] L. Fischer, *The Soviets in World Affairs*, pp. 531-8.

indifferent to his presence, in spite of the fact that an address to the
Mongol people had specifically renounced Russia's special rights in
Outer Mongolia as being the fruit of Tsarist imperialism. Ungern-
Sternberg's reign of terror helped to turn the Mongols once more
towards Russia. In March 1921, Mongol partisan forces, meeting
near the Russian frontier, formed a provisional government with
the object of driving out the Chinese and other foreigners with the
assistance of the Soviet power. In the course of a campaign against
them, Ungern-Sternberg entered Soviet territory, where in June
1921, he was captured and shot. By July, Urga (shortly to be
renamed Ulan Bator or Red Warrior) was in the hands of the Mongol
People's Party, as the revolutionaries called themselves, and by the
end of the year, they and their Soviet allies controlled the whole
country. Chinese plans for reconquering the country were dashed
by China's own internal difficulties, and the future of the country
seemed once more to depend wholly on Russia. On 5 November
1921, an agreement was reached between the People's Republic of
Outer Mongolia and Soviet Russia, and the two sides for the first
time signed as equal partners. It contained the usual reciprocal
provisions concerning the suppression in each country of organisations hostile to the other's Government.[1] The opposition of the
leaders of the autonomy movement initiated in 1912, coming chiefly
from the hereditary aristocracy and the Church, was henceforth
insufficient to prevent the increase of Soviet influence. China was
also in no position to intervene. It was however on the grounds of
having conducted 'treasonable' negotiations with China that the
Prime Minister, Bodo, and fifteen other officials were shot in April
1922; and there were further disturbances at the end of the year
and in 1923.

Some continuity between Tsarist and Soviet policy was suggested
by the renewal of Russian economic penetration. In July 1922, a
Soviet writer put the matter quite bluntly: 'Here our commercial
transactions are the obvious basis for our potential political influence
... trade representatives will be our best diplomatists.'[2] In addition
to economic pressure which told on Chinese interests, Soviet influence was naturally hostile to that of the Lamaist Church and
especially to its politically and economically powerful upper
hierarchy. (The number of lamas in the male population of
Mongolia at the time has been put at between 40 and 60 per cent.)[3]
In the anti-clerical campaign the leaders were largely Buriat
Mongols from Russia. The Russians indeed tried to use Buriats to
a great extent for furthering their influence in Mongolia. There
had been many westernised and well-educated Buriats in Russia
proper even before the Revolution. In 1923 the Buriat Mongol
Autonomous Republic was set up within the U.S.S.R.

The establishment in 1924 of the Mongol Industrial and Com-

---

[1] *Treaties and Agreements with and concerning China*, pp. 53-6.
[2] Quoted by Conolly, op. cit., p. 98.
[3] *China Year Book*, 1935, p. 27.

mercial Bank, under Russian control, marked the beginning of a period of rapid growth in Soviet-Mongol trade. 'From 1926, Soviet commercial transactions became more and more intertwined with the Mongol State economic machinery.' Foreign firms found themselves increasingly handicapped. All American and other foreign firms had closed down by the summer of 1928, although some German commercial agents continued to visit the country for some time afterwards. By 1928 the Russians had a virtual monopoly of the wool trade. At the same time there was a steady rise in Soviet exports, particularly of grain and oil, and the Russian trade balance became very favourable, in striking contrast to the 1913–1915 situation.[1] On the political side the extent of Soviet control was shown by the fact that, from 1924 on, visas for Outer Mongolia could be obtained only at Ulan Bator or Moscow.[2]

But the Russians were still unwilling to allow the question of Outer Mongolia to interfere with the establishment of normal relations with China. After the Shanghai talks between Sun Yat-sen and Joffe in 1923, the latter stated that it was not the purpose of the Soviet Government to pursue any imperialistic policy in Outer Mongolia or to induce the Mongolian Republic to secede from China. Sun declared that he had no objection to the temporary occupation of Outer Mongolia by Soviet Forces.[3] The treaty of Pekin of 31 May 1924, recognised the sovereignty of China in Outer Mongolia (in contrast to the more vague position of 'suzerain' to which China submitted in 1915) and promised the withdrawal of Soviet troops.[4] Soviet troops, apart from some military advisers, were withdrawn in 1925.

In July 1924, the Living Buddha died and the Mongolian People's Republic was proclaimed. In August there took place the Third Party Congress of the Mongolian People's Party. Of this, only one account seems to be available, and its reliability is uncertain. We there find that Vassiliev, the Soviet representative, who had arrived in January, made it clear in his speech that the Russians would not countenance the Mongol desire to regain Tannu Tuva. He also stressed the importance of the Comintern's rôle in the development of the country. (The application by the Mongol People's Party for affiliation to the Comintern was apparently of recent date.) On the other hand, Mongol speakers freely criticised

---

[1] Conolly, op. cit., pp. 98–112. The development of Mongol industries and transport and of the much needed health services for man and beast, all provided scope for Soviet infiltration. A difficulty confronting plans for such expansion in industry and mining as the country's limited resources allowed was the lack of suitable labour. The Mongols were unsuitable and the Soviet authorities were willing neither to permit workers to come from the U.S.S.R. nor to allow the immigration of Chinese. See F. Weiske, 'Die wirtschaftlichen Verhältnisse der Ausseren Mongolei', *Osteuropa*, December 1928.

[2] A. N. Holcombe, *The Chinese Revolution*, p. 12.

[3] ibid., p. 160.

[4] *Treaties and Agreements with and concerning China, 1919–1929*, pp. 133–40.

economic and political conditions and the state of the army. Some
even talked of trying to establish commercial connexions with other
foreign countries. This manifestation of an independent attitude
towards the U.S.S.R. was followed on 30 August by a *coup d'état*.
The Buriat Ricino, leader of the Left wing, had Danzan (Vice-
Premier and Commander-in-Chief), and another high official,
arrested and shot. This move was greeted by Vassiliev as a contribution to Soviet-Mongol unity.[1] The close connexion between the
new régime and the ideology of the Soviet Union was manifest in
the new constitution reinaugurated on 21 November 1924.[2]

By clause 1 'Mongolia is proclaimed as an independent People's
Republic in which the whole Government belongs to the labouring
people. The people exercise their power through the Great
Assembly (Khuruldan) of all the people and the Government
elected by the latter.'[3] In clause 2 we learn that 'the primary
object of the Mongolian Republic consists in the destruction of the
remnants of the feudal theocratic régime and the consolidation of
the principles of the new republican order on the basis of complete
democratisation of the State administration'. The land and natural
resources are to be nationalised and a State monopoly of foreign
trade is to be introduced gradually as circumstances permit.

Clause 3 gives the clue to the country's foreign policy:

'In view of the fact that the toilers of the whole world are aspiring
after the radical abolition of capitalism and the attainment of
socialism (communism) the People's Republic of the toilers must
conduct its foreign policy in conformity with the interests and fundamental tasks of small oppressed nations and of the revolutionary
toilers of the entire world.'

A policy of friendly relations with foreign Powers was not however
precluded.

The assertion of Soviet influence was followed by the exclusion of

[1] *Mongolia, Yesterday and To-day.* (This obscure pamphlet was printed at
Tientsin, apparently in 1924 or 1925.) Cf. H. Haslund, *Tents in Mongolia*
(Kegan Paul, 1924), chap. 10, an account of the changes in Mongolia by
an eye-witness in the mid-twenties. The author had very little sympathy
for the new régime. It is interesting to find that in 1928, Ricino himself was
attacked by a Government spokesman for his 'nationalist' opinions, he
having by then apparently become converted to the cause of Mongol
unity. There was however support from Urga for a new revolt by the
Barguts in North-west Manchuria in 1928. The Barguts succeeded in
getting the Chinese to limit their area of settlement. The direct Russian
incursion into the Barga province at the time of the C.E.R. dispute was a
military demonstration and had no permanent territorial results, although
achieving its purpose so far as the railway dispute was concerned.

[2] The constitution is printed in full (but misdated, 1921) in *British and
Foreign State Papers*, vol. cxxxiv, 1931, pp. 1224–32.

[3] In this State, the franchise was to include all workers and soldiers but
not exploiters of others' labour, merchants, usurers, former princes,
Hutuktus ('living Buddhas') and religious persons residing in monasteries,

representatives of other countries. The Russians desired to reduce Outer Mongolia's foreign contacts to the minimum compatible with what they regarded as necessary for the country's economic development, viewed largely in relation to the demands of Soviet economy. The fiction of Chinese sovereignty made it possible to deny to foreign States the right to official representation in Outer Mongolia. In the period 1925–1930, some foreign technicians were employed—Germans, Swedes, Swiss, and one Hungarian. These foreigners built two power stations, a brick factory and other installations in Urga. A Mongol trade delegation was sent to Berlin in 1925, but was withdrawn in 1928, after a suggestion that the Mongols might follow it up with a Consulate.[1] Between 1928 and 1930, the foreigners were got rid of, as their contracts expired.

In the years following 1928, Outer Mongolia was the scene of a drive for collectivisation. This move had serious consequences for the country's economy, since much livestock was destroyed by its opponents. It also alienated from the régime many Mongols of whom large numbers attempted to cross over into Inner Mongolia, many of them being shot by frontier guards while making the attempt. Some fifteen to twenty thousand are said to have run the gauntlet successfully.[2] There was also a fairly serious rebellion in the western part of the country which was only suppressed after severe fighting.

The full collectivisation policy was abandoned after the revolt in 1932 and a new policy was confirmed at the time of the Prime Minister Gendun's Moscow visit at the end of 1934. One feature of this period was the partial restoration of the trade route to China via Kalgan which was carried on by a company called the Wostwag, registered as German. This did not involve any serious breach in the country's seclusion, since freights were reloaded at the frontier. The route continued in use till 1936.[3] Nor did it involve much of an obstacle to the virtual monopolisation of Mongolian trade by Soviet Russia which in 1934 was responsible for 91 per cent of the foreign·trade of the Republic. The only important non-Russian item in the country's imports was tea from China, normally imported via Vladivostok, an enormous detour compared with the ancient caravan route. Soviet-Mongol trade continued meanwhile to expand and, with it, the favourable balance for the U.S.S.R. expanded also.[4]

[1] Since then the Mongols have had no representative abroad except for the one in Moscow.

[2] *China Year Book*, 1935, p. 35.

[3] K. Barnes: 'Outer Mongolia on the World Stage', *Far Eastern Survey*, 30 August 1939; a useful account of economic development in the 1930s.

[4] The following figures (in thousands of roubles) illustrate the position: 'A Japanese View of Outer Mongolia,' p. 44:

Year	U.S.S.R. Imports to Mongolia	Mongolian Exports to U.S.S.R.	Mongol Balance
1913	2,689	8,403	+ 5,714
1933	28,562	17,269	− 11,293
1938	50,433	32,120	− 18,313

At the same time road and water transport were improved with Russian aid, and there were repeated rumours of railway construction, although the only lines known to have been built were the one from Kiakhta to Ulan Bator and a narrow gauge one for bringing coal from the mines to the capital. A general improvement seems to have taken place in these years in the economic condition of the country as a whole. The theoretical aspect of the new phase was stated by Gendun in his speech to the Seventh Great Khuruldan when he castigated the errors of the preceding period:

'Our Republic is a bourgeois democratic Republic of the new type, anti-feudalistic and anti-imperialistic, gradually advancing on the road of non-capitalistic development. But our national-democratic and anti-feudalistic revolution did not reach the socialistic stage. In order to build a strong foundation for the Mongolian national economy we should develop private (though not unrestricted) economics. . . . Of course we should aim for the gradual limitation of exploiting elements while doing everything in order to improve the private economy and the material well-being of the poor and middle arats.'[1]

Another aspect of the new phase was the abandonment of the all-out attack upon the lamas and an effort instead to drive a wedge between the upper hierarchy and the poorer lamas.

'We must make a distinction on the one hand between the high lamas who used to exploit both the low-ranking lamas and arats and, on the other hand, the low lamas. The low-ranking monks and lamas should be treated differently from the high dignitaries of the church. They should receive education (and in this case be exempted from special taxes) and if they take part in work they should be allowed to vote. The Government should try to separate them from the hierarchy who exploit them. The Government should apply compulsory education to all illiterate officials and by all means try to advance the culture and national economy of Outer Mongolia, emulating the example of the Soviet Union.'[2]

The changes in Outer Mongolia were of importance because of new political developments in the Far East. The danger did not come now from China, although a memorandum putting forward the Chinese claim to full sovereignty there was among those presented to the Lytton Commission on behalf of the Chinese Govern-

[1] 'A Japanese View of Outer Mongolia,' pp. 13–14.
[2] ibid., p. 14. The following figures are given for the number of lamas: 1917, 117 thousands; 1928, 95 thousand; 1932, 82 thousand; 1938, 80 thousand. The same source quotes with scepticism the remarks attributed in April 1939 to the then Prime Minister of Mongolia, by *Bezbozhnik* (*The Atheist*) to the effect that there were no more lamas in Outer Mongolia. ibid., p. 48.

ment.[1] It was Japan from its new acquisitions, Manchuria and Jehol, that was in a position to try to use Mongol nationalism for its own benefit, and to profit where China had failed, by its religious links with the Mongols (they belong to two widely divergent branches of the Buddhist faith). The Japanese, remembering that the Manchu Empire had been a Mongol-Manchu overlordship of China, thought that the re-establishment of a Manchu Emperor would win over the Mongols. The setting up of Manchukuo (the Manchu Kingdom), afterwards for a short time called Manchutikuo (the Manchu Empire), did not have the hoped-for effect. The confirmation of semi-autonomy within Manchukuo for the Mongol province of Hsingan was another attempt at winning Mongol sympathies. But the Japanese, feeling that Mongol allegiance was not to be won in this way, developed a more threatening attitude. The Russians showed their awareness of the danger by concluding with Outer Mongolia the 'gentleman's agreement' of 27 November 1934; this preceded by only a short while the return to Outer Mongolia of Soviet troops.

Tension was heightened from 1935 by incidents on the Manchukuo—Outer Mongolian frontier. The Japanese proposed a joint frontier commission early in 1935; this was clearly a first step in a programme of breaking down Outer Mongolia's seclusion, and permanently opening it to Japanese and Manchukuo representatives.[2]

On 1 March 1936, Stalin announced Russia's intention of defending Outer Mongolia. Eleven days later an agreement amounting to a full defensive alliance was signed.[3]

Both Japan and the U.S.S.R. showed by their actions that they recognised the reality and persistence of Mongol nationalism, based on the ancient military tradition of the Mongol people, but were unwilling to support modern Pan-Mongol aims.[4] Whereas it does not seem unlikely that the Mongols of Manchuria at first welcomed the Japanese as protection against Chinese and possibly Russian designs, they were rapidly disillusioned by the Japanese version of autonomy. In April 1936, four leading officials of the Hsingan province were shot for having conspired with the Outer Mongolian delegation to the frontier conference.[5]

Meanwhile Japanese influence was reaching out into the remainder of Inner Mongolia and there receiving assistance from a group of young Mongol Princes headed by Teh Wang. It has been alleged that Teh Wang believed that if his followers were supplied

[1] Wellington Koo, *Memoranda presented to the Lytton Commission* (New York, 1932), p. 664.

[2] *Survey for 1935*, vol. 1, II, v: *Survey for 1936*, VII, vi, (c).

[3] *Documents for 1936*, pp. 464–74.

[4] Cf. O. Lattimore, *Mongol Journeys* (Cape, 1941).

[5] Cf. Mansvetov, loc. cit., pp. 151–2. The latter remarks that no Russian immigration into Outer Mongolia was allowed but that Pan-Mongolism was suppressed in both Outer Mongolia and Buriat Mongolia. He also asserts that Outer Mongolia was not used as a channel for supplying the Chinese Communists.

with arms, they could take advantage of the persistent discontent with Soviet domination to fuse the two Mongolias into a single State analogous to Manchukuo.[1] Not only Russo-Japanese relations, but Russo-Chinese relations also, were affected by these events. China protested against the Soviet-Mongol pact as an infringement of her sovereignty—a protest which the U.S.S.R. rejected.[2] And China was still more intimately concerned with the growing threat that Inner Mongolia might be shortly absorbed into the Japanese mainland empire. Opinions as to the views of the Mongols themselves at this time varied.[3] Some people believed that China might have come out better had it not been for her previous failure to give the Mongols reasonable autonomy. One English expert, discussing the likelihood of a Japanese victory in the event of a clash with Russia wrote: 'As for the Outer Mongols, they dislike the Russians more strongly than the Chinese in Manchuria dislike the Japanese.'[4]

The border negotiations between Outer Mongolia and Manchukuo broke down in June 1937 and later in October the advance of the Japanese army made the Inner Mongolian question a more burning one than ever. In October a Mongolian Autonomous Republic was created by the Japanese.[5] It is not unreasonable to assume that the purges and disturbances of 1937–1939 in Outer Mongolia were linked with these events, although the Japanese speak of the Russian talk of external danger as a blind and connect the purges with a new Leftward and anti-religious drive in internal affairs.[6]

The Japanese handling of the Mongols was not apparently very successful, and by April 1938, the Pekin correspondent of *The Times* was reporting that the upper-class elements supporting the Japanese did not apparently amount to more than 5 per cent of the population and that 80 per cent would prefer union with Outer Mongolia to Japanese rule.[7] The centre of Russo-Japanese tension in 1937–1938 was, however, further to the east.

Although the ultimate objective of all sections of the Mongols may well have been total independence, it seemed in 1938 that nothing short of the breakdown of the whole Soviet position in the Far East was likely to weaken the ties between the U.S.S.R. and Outer Mongolia.

[1] *China Year Book*, 1936, pp. 165-6.   [2] ibid., pp. 20-3.
[3] See 'The Mongol Dilemma', *J.R.C.A.S.*, 1935, pp. 464-7; cf. *Problems of the Pacific*, 1936, pp. 124-5, 134 ff.
[4] Sir Charles Bell, 'The Struggle for Mongolia', *J.R.C.A.S.*, 1937, pp. 66-7. (The author had recently been in Inner Mongolia.)
[5] *Survey for 1937*, pp. 249-50.
[6] 'A Japanese View of Outer Mongolia', pp. 21-3.
[7] *The Times*, 4 April 1938. Cf. E. F. Carlson, 'The Chinese-Mongol Front in Suiyan', *Pacific Affairs*, September 1939.

LIST OF ABBREVIATIONS

I.P.R. Institute of Pacific Relations.
L.N.T.S. League of Nations Publications: *Treaty Series.*
L.N.O.J. *League of Nations: Official Journal.*
L.N.O.J. Spec. Supp. *League of Nations: Official Journal: Special Supplement.*
C.P.S.U. Communist Party of the Soviet Union.
R.I.I.A. Royal Institute of International Affairs.
Survey for . . . A. J. Toynbee: *Survey of International Affairs.* (R.I.I.A., O.U.P., 1920–1938.)
Documents for . . . *Documents on International Affairs* (ed. J. Wheeler-Bennett, and others. R.I.I.A., O.U.P., 1928—in progress).
J.R.C.A.S. *Journal of the Royal Central Asian Society.*
Int. Conc. *International Conciliation.* (Documents: Carnegie Endowment for International Peace.)
B.I.N. *Bulletin of International News.* (R.I.I.A.)

INDEX

REPRINTED LITHOGRAPHICALLY
IN GREAT BRITAIN
BY JARROLD AND SONS LIMITED,
NORWICH